Education
and
Education-Related Serials

Education
and
Education-Related Serials

A Directory

Wayne J. Krepel
Charles R. DuVall

1977

Libraries Unlimited, Inc.
Littleton, Colo.

LIBRARIES UNLIMITED, INC.
P.O. Box 263
Littleton, Colorado 80160

Library of Congress Cataloging in Publication Data

Krepel, Wayne J   1933–
    Education and education-related serials.

    Includes index.
        1.   Education—Periodicals—Bibliography.
I.   DuVall, Charles R., 1929–   joint author.
II.   Title.
Z5813.K74   [LB5]   016.37   76-47040
ISBN 0-87287-131-2

PREFACE

Scholars in education and education-related fields continue to explore and investigate within their areas of academic expertise. This last quarter of the twentieth century promises to be a most exciting period of time for educators. New and innovative developments are constantly emerging and need to be disseminated in current periodical literature. Ample opportunity for the sharing of ideas exists for scholars who wish to make the professional effort necessary to put their thoughts into article form. This directory is designed to help writers choose the journal most appropriate to the topic presented, thus giving the idea, research effort, or investigation the widest possible exposure.

The authors are grateful to the more than 500 editors who provided data for our consideration. Their cooperation was essential for the successful completion of this directory. Thanks also are due to our typists, Ann Rospopo and Betty Rusk, for their diligent efforts. A special thank you goes to our wives, Katie and Willie, for their patience and understanding during these past months.

W.J.K.
C.R.D.

TABLE OF CONTENTS

INTRODUCTION

Institutions of higher learning have traditionally been the repositories of knowledge. One of their chief functions has been the transmission of the cultural heritage, which usually takes the form of the printed word. This distinct function of colleges and universities has caused faculty members to seek publishing outlets for their research findings, ideas, and unique contributions. This directory has been prepared in order to acquaint members of education and education-related professions with a number of journals and newsletters that accept manuscripts from outside contributors.

Education and Education-Related Serials presents descriptions of 501 journals and newsletters, all related in some way to the field of education. The data presented were collected from editors of serial publications in the United States and Canada.

Detailed descriptions are given for those journals that have a policy of accepting manuscripts from non-staff members. Journals that do not accept unsolicited manuscripts for consideration but whose editors will answer letters of inquiry are also included here.

Although most professionals are able to recognize and identify an education or education-related serial publication, it is obvious that each person would choose somewhat different works to include in a compendium of this type. A key concern of the authors during the selection process was to choose journals whose contents deal with teaching and learning. The journal articles may be directed toward teachers (professors), school and university administrators, parents, or other educational specialists who are interested in, and/or involved with, some phase of teaching and learning, regardless of grade or instructional level.

Newsletters and the journals of state organizations are included. Many of these publications accept unsolicited manuscripts, and they are often quality publications that serve an important audience.

Serial publications whose audience consists primarily of persons in a particular selected discipline, even though this discipline may be related to the education process, have been excluded. For example, library journals such as *American Libraries* and *College and Research Libraries* are excluded, whereas *Journal of Education for Librarianship* is retained. Psychology publications intended primarily for the psychology professor or researcher, or for the practicing psychologist or psychiatrist, are avoided but those journals related to education, such as *Educational Psychologist* and *Journal of Educational Psychology* are included. A number of journals serve a diverse audience in several related disciplines.

The serial publications included in this compendium have circulations ranging from 100 to over 1,000,000 copies per issue. Many of the journals are quite catholic in their content, serving a wide range of reader interests, while others have limited or controlled circulations and serve a more specialized readership.

Data for this publication were obtained using a normative survey instrument specifically designed for that purpose. Editors and publishers were surveyed and data presented were obtained from an analysis of the replies received and an examination of the publications themselves. Draft copies of all entries were sent to the editors (or publishers) late in 1975 to insure that the data were current and accurate. All entries in this book have been verified in this manner.

In order to establish uniformity, several editorial decisions concerning the style of presentation in this book were made. The following data, when provided, were included in the description:

Title. The journal's current title introduces each entry. If a title change has occurred (and was identified) during the journal's publication history, the title under which it previously was published is given.

Publisher or sponsoring agency. The name and address of the publisher or sponsoring agency are given when available.

Circulation. These figures were taken from the responses given on the questionnaire. No attempt was made to verify these data. All circulation figures were rounded upward to the nearest hundred.

Frequency. The frequency is expressed in the number of issues published per year. In cases of unusual frequency patterns, a brief explanation is provided.

Subscription. The subscription price is presented as cost per year to persons living in the country of publication. Special variations in price are not included. If a portion of the organization membership dues is applied toward the subscription price, the phrase "Included with association membership" is used. Whenever given, or found through examination of the journal itself, the non-member, library, and/or institution rate is provided. Because of inflationary forces the reader is cautioned that the subscription prices are subject to change.

Annual index. If the contents of the serial publication are indexed annually, or the tables of contents are published annually in combined form, then the issue in which that compendium appears is given. In cases where journals are indexed in other than annual form and/or in separate publications, this fact is indicated.

Year of first issue. The year in which the journal was first published is given. If the publication has changed title, the year of first issue for each title is given, when known, in abbreviated form.

Editor. The editor's name (or the names of co-editors) is indicated. If the editorship of a journal changes on an annual or other regular basis, or if no name was provided, then the term "Editor" is used.

Editor's address or manuscript to. If manuscripts are to be sent to an address different from that of the sponsoring agency, then the editor's address is given. In the event that a contributor's manuscript should be sent to a person other than the editor, this name is provided and the address (if different from that of the sponsor) is given.

Book reviews to. The names and addresses of book review editors are provided. When the editor also serves in the capacity of book review editor, the entry "Editor" is indicated. The citation "No book reviews" is used when the journal normally does not carry book reviews. If the journal publishes book reviews but does not accept unsolicited reviews or reviews from outside sources, an appropriate notation is made.

Indexed in. This entry is a listing of the agencies or publications that index (or abstract) a particular journal. These data were compiled from three sources: 1) the title page(s) of the journal itself; 2) the replies received from the respondents to the questionnaire; and, 3) the responses received from indexing and abstracting agencies.

Approximately 200 indexing and abstracting agencies throughout the world were contacted. The authors scanned the lists of publications provided by these agencies, identifying all journals that might be included in this book. These entries then were placed in a computer data bank, and the entries in this data bank were matched with the journals listed in *Education and Education-Related Serials.*

Some indexing (abstracting) agencies publish several indexes based on a common list of serials. In all of these cases such possible multiple indexing has been indicated by an asterisk (*). The authors also have attempted to clarify and correct terminology whenever possible. The indexing and abstracting agencies whose lists of journals were scanned by the authors and placed in the data bank are presented in the appendix.

Journal description. A narrative description, comprised of several selected factors, is presented for each serial publication. This information was derived primarily from the data provided by the respondents, but also from an examination of several selected issues. An effort was made to indicate the purpose of the journal, the intended audience, and other pertinent general information. In some cases examples of recent articles, themes, or regular features are presented to help the reader determine editorial interest.

A second narrative paragraph contains items of special interest to prospective authors, as described below:

Solicited or unsolicited manuscripts. The editor's preference for obtaining manuscripts is given. A notation also is made when letters of inquiry are encouraged or required.

Length of manuscript. Manuscript length is presented in an approximate number of words. A rate of 250 words per typewritten page was used in estimating manuscript length.

Preferred style. Editors were queried regarding their preference, if any, for style requirements. Journal editors usually prefer one of three style manuals. They are:

American Psychological Association. *Publication Manual.* Revised edition. Washington: American Psychological Association, 1974.

Modern Language Association of America. *MLA Style Sheet.* 2nd edition. New York: Modern Language Association of America, 1970.

The University of Chicago Press. *A Manual of Style.* 12th edition, revised. Chicago: The University of Chicago Press, 1969.

These style manuals are referred to respectively as "APA," "MLA," and "Chicago." If an editor indicated another style, it is presented in the terms used by the respondent. When publishers and/or editors have style sheets and make these available to prospective authors, this fact is indicated.

Time for editorial decision. The time required for an editorial decision is given in terms of weeks after receipt by the editor. The times listed are those reported in the questionnaire by the respondents.

Number of copies. This number is reported only if more than one copy is required by the editor. Usually the original must be sent. In most cases, if multiple copies are required, copying machine duplication is acceptable.

Time from acceptance to publication. This time is reported in months and is based on the information given by the respondent. Factors such as holidays, the academic rather than the calendar year, and other variables may affect this time factor.

Simultaneous submission. When simultaneous submission is permitted, this fact is indicated. If the editor discourages or does not permit this practice, no notation is made.

Payment. Most academic journals do not pay for manuscripts—indeed, in some cases a payment by the author, upon acceptance, is required prior to publication. Only in cases where payment is made or charged is this fact noted.

Theme issues. If the editor indicated that one or more issues of a journal are dedicated to central themes, this fact is mentioned. The manner suggested for learning of these themes is included when applicable.

Copyright. Copyright information, when provided, is included in the summary. This notation is not intended for legal advice, but rather as an indication for the guidance of prospective authors.

MANUSCRIPT PREPARATION

Introduction. For many persons the idea of writing for publication may be one of "publish or perish"; the best reason for writing, however, is that an individual has something to say. It may be a new or unique idea, a report of research, or a "how to do it" or "how I did it" piece. Another reason for writing is to express a reaction to something that has been read or heard. Most editors do not want exhortation unsupported by fact. They appreciate well-written articles dealing with significant research, opinion pieces reflecting cogent reasoning supported by sound logic and clear thinking, and interesting reports of current practice. Editors are searching for the best possible material for their journals. Authors should be sure that their contributions are worthy of being shared with others.

Organization. Preliminary organization of the material will help the author prepare the first draft of the manuscript. An outline, prepared on file cards for ease of reorganization, is one way to begin to write, though there are, of course, other methods of outlining or setting down thoughts.

Authors should write the first draft of their manuscript using a style that is familiar to them. The outline and this first draft copy serve the purpose of getting thoughts into written form in an organized manner.

Journal search. Upon the completion of the first, or rough draft, copy it is advisable to begin the search for an appropriate journal to publish the work. The aim of *Education and Education-Related Serials* is to assist authors in this task. Authors are urged to consult the subject index provided in this book and then to read the descriptions of the relevant journals. One or more journals should be chosen.

Letter of inquiry. If a letter of inquiry is suggested, a briefly written letter outlining the proposed article should be prepared and sent. A self-addressed postage-paid envelope for a reply should be enclosed with the letter.

Unsolicited manuscript. An author may decide to submit a manuscript without a letter of inquiry—that is, unsolicited. In this case the final manuscript must be prepared to conform with the requirements specified by the editor of the journal chosen. Although some editors permit, and even encourage, simultaneous submission of manuscripts to other journals, a majority of them do not permit it, or at least discourage the practice. It is recommended that authors adhere to the wishes of the editor in regard to this matter.

Final manuscript preparation. The rough draft should be reworked to satisfy the editorial requirements of the journal chosen. Style sheets available from editors, as well as the style manuals cited in this book, may be helpful to the prospective author. Final copy should be typed on bond paper, double-spaced, with margins of at least one inch on all sides; pages should be numbered. The appropriate number of copies should be prepared.

Manuscript submission. The manuscript should be submitted to the editor or other designated person. All manuscripts should be accompanied by a cover letter and a self-addressed, postage-paid envelope for the return of unaccepted manuscripts. The author should always retain copies of both the manuscript and the cover letter. In the event a response is not received from the editor within the time limit specified in this book, the author should query the editor regarding the disposition of the manuscript.

Manuscript rejection. In the event the manuscript is rejected the author should not become unduly discouraged. Most journals receive many more manuscripts than they can possibly publish. If the manuscript is returned, the author should select a new publisher. The article content should be compared with the editorial specifications of the newly chosen journal and appropriate revisions made. If an editor has critically analyzed the manuscript prior to rejection, the author may wish to rewrite the article and incorporate suggested changes.

1. **AAHPER UPDATE.** 1970– . American Alliance for Health, Physical Education, and Recreation, 1201 Sixteenth Street, N.W., Washington, DC 20036. Circ.: 40,000. 9 issues/yr. Subscription included with alliance membership; non-member rate, $15.00/yr. No annual index. Editor: Marjorie Blaufarb. No book reviews.

The *Update* counts members of physical education faculties at both the college and public school level, coaches, athletic directors, health, dance, safety and recreation teachers among its readership. Its purpose is to inform the membership about the organization's activities, as well as legislation and government activities. The format is a 12 to 16 page tabloid.

While most of the material is staff written the editor encourages the submission of short articles (500 words) dealing with curriculum innovations and teaching methods. The MLA style is utilized. Material is not copyrighted. One week is required for an editorial decision with publication following in approximately one month.

2. **AAUP BULLETIN.** 1915– . American Association of University Professors, Suite 500, One Dupont Circle, Washington, DC 20036. Circ.: 83,000. 4 issues/yr. $10.00/yr. Annual index: winter issue. Editor: Robert K. Webb. Book reviews to: editor.

Indexed in: America: History and Life*; College Student Personnel Abstracts; Current Contents: Social & Behavioral Sciences; Current Index to Journals in Education; Education Index; Educational Administration Abstracts; Index to Periodical Articles Related to Law; Public Affairs Information Service Bulletin; Women Studies Abstracts.

This journal, sent to all members of the AAUP, deals with a wide range of issues in higher education. Association news and current developments in higher education are as a rule dealt with in the companion newsletter, *Academe*, but the *Bulletin* is the vehicle for formal statements of policy and reports on Association business, among which are annual reports on the economic status of the profession and reports on investigations of cases involving violation of AAUP standards of academic freedom and tenure. In addition, the *Bulletin* functions as a journal of opinion and controversy on subjects in the field of higher education.

All book reviews and some articles, particularly in issues exploring a single major topic, are commissioned, but unsolicited articles are considered. Length is not specified. A minimum of six weeks is required for an editorial decision; the length of time between acceptance and publication may vary from six months to a year, depending on availability of space and the balance of subjects. Authors should follow the Chicago style requirements. Copyright for published material is held by the publisher. Two copies of all manuscripts should be submitted, and no manuscripts will be returned unless accompanied by a self-addressed stamped envelope.

3. **AAUW JOURNAL.** 1882– . American Association of University Women, 2401 Virginia Avenue, N.W., Washington, DC 20037. Circ.: 200,000. 7 issues/yr. Subscription included with association membership; non-member rate, $4.00/yr. No annual index. Editor: Jean Fox. No book reviews.

Indexed in: Public Affairs Information Service Bulletin; Women Studies Abstracts.

The *AAUW Journal* is intended primarily for women who are college and university graduates. The purpose of this magazine/tabloid is to further the educational development of women, to lend support to education (especially women's and continuing education), and to provide a program for women with degrees for greater self-development and impact on their communities.

The editor solicits some material directly from various persons, but also will consider unsolicited articles and letters of inquiry. No specific style is required and length is open. Copyright is held by the publisher who pays authors at a rate that varies. Issues are dedicated to central themes and prospective contributors should query the editor for future topics. Simultaneous submission to other journals is permitted, but the editor requests immediate verification of acceptance by other publications. Times are not given for editorial decisions and publication because of the infrequency of this journal's publication in the magazine format.

4. **AEDS JOURNAL.** 1967— . Association for Educational Data Systems, 1201 Sixteenth Street, N.W., Washington, DC 20036. Circ.: 1,800. 4 issues/yr. Subscription included with association membership; non-member rate, $15.00/yr. Annual index: summer issue. Editor: Bruce K. Alcorn. Manuscript to: current editor as noted in recent issue or association address as given above. Book reviews to: editor.

   Indexed in: Computer and Control Abstracts*; Computing Review; Current Contents: Social & Behavioral Sciences; Current Index to Journals in Education; Data Processing Digest.

This journal is intended for managers, administrators, teachers, members of consulting firms and government officials interested in data processing. Its purpose is to disseminate indepth information regarding studies, projects and research related to the field of educational information systems.

Unsolicited articles are accepted for consideration. Authors are given no particular style requirements. An editorial decision is made within eight weeks with publication following within three months. The copyright is held by the publisher. Inquiry letters concerning article ideas are encouraged. This journal uses approximately two book reviews per issue, each of approximately 500 words. The maximum article length is 5,000 words. Three copies of the manuscript should be submitted.

5. **AEN BULLETIN.** 1970— . Association of Educational Negotiators, Suite 908, 1835 K Street, N.W., Washington, DC 20006. Circ.: 500. 10 issues/yr. Subscription included with association membership. No annual index. Editor: Richard G. Neal. No book reviews.

The *AEN Bulletin* is intended for public school management personnel and school board members who are chief negotiators or for negotiations team members. It is intended to provide a clearinghouse of news, information, ideas and advice on collective bargaining with school employees. The editor prefers hard-hitting "how-to-do-it" pieces, and practical advice on combating teacher militancy at the bargaining table. The annual membership list is published in the *Bulletin*.

Unsolicited articles as well as letters of inquiry are encouraged. The editor also solicits some materials. Articles should be between 1,000 and 1,500 words in length, with single copies of the manuscript submitted. The copyright is held by the publisher. Editorial decisions are made within two weeks with publication following within one month. Authors should follow the MLA style requirements.

6. **AHEA NEWSLETTER.** 1967– . Alberta Home Economics Association, P.O. Box 1052, Calgary, Alberta, Canada. Circ.: 600. 4 issues/yr. $4.00/yr. No annual index. Editor: Mrs. R.P. Mullen. Editor's address: 20 Marlboro Road, Edmonton, Alberta, Canada T6J 2C6. Book reviews to: editor.

The *AHEA Newsletter* acts as a primary communication media for the association. It is a vehicle for reporting the results of studies and research from the School of Household Economics, University of Alberta and from others. It is intended to aid home economists in keeping up-to-date with their subject matter. Articles included in this newsletter are those of interest and use to home economists in any area, such as nutrition and dietetics, clothing and textiles, housing, communications, family relations, child care, child and youth development, education and related topics.

The editor solicits articles directly from professionals in the field of home economics, but also welcomes unsolicited manuscripts. A letter of inquiry prior to submission is recommended. Preferred length of articles is 1,000 to 1,500 words and simultaneous submission to other journals is permitted. Copyright is held by the author. Contributors may expect an editorial decision in two weeks and publication follows in two to three months. Two to four book reviews are contained in each issue and these are approximately 300 words long.

7. **AMS NEWS.** 1970– (several forerunners existed). American Montessori Society, 175 Fifth Avenue, New York, NY 10010. Circ.: 4,500. 4 issues/yr. Subscription included with society membership. No annual index. Editor: Judith Delman. Book reviews to: editor.

The *AMS News* is intended for those interested in early childhood education, particularly people working in Montessori Schools, parents whose children attend these schools, and other parents wishing to bring the Montessori approach into their homes. Its purpose is to provide news of current developments in the field of Montessori education. Short articles deal with items of current interest. Regular features include Around the Schools, In the Home, Book Reviews and a calendar of events.

Authors are urged to submit "concise, bright and factual" pieces. Two copies of the manuscript should be submitted. All articles must be Montessori related. While many of the pieces are written by the editor, unsolicited manuscripts are encouraged. Approximately eight to ten weeks is required for an editorial decision with publication following within three to six months after acceptance. Book reviews are used on a varying basis, usually one to four per issue.

8. **ASBSD BULLETIN.** 1947– . Associated School Boards of South Dakota, P.O. Box 143, Huron, SD 57350. Circ.: 2,200. 24 issues/yr. $5.00/yr. No annual index. Editor: Gordon Nelson, ASBSD Executive Secretary. Book reviews to: editor.

The intended audience of this publication includes school board members and administrators. Its purpose is to coordinate the policy-making role of school boards in South Dakota. Articles on finance, organization and evaluation are preferred for inclusion in the *ASBSD Bulletin*.

The editor solicits some material from selected professionals, but also welcomes unsolicited manuscripts. A letter of inquiry prior to submission is encouraged. Articles should be about 500 words in length and submitted in duplicate. No special style is required and copyright is held by the author. Simultaneous submission to other journals is permitted. An editorial decision is given in four weeks and publication of accepted pieces follows in one month. Six book reviews are included in this publication each year. Requirements for reviews are the same as for articles.

9. **ASHA.** 1959– . American Speech and Hearing Association, 9030 Old Georgetown Road, Washington, DC 20014. Circ.: 25,000. 12 issues/yr. $28.00/yr. Annual index: December issue. Editor: Kenneth O. Johnson. Book reviews are assigned.
   Indexed in: dsh Abstracts; Educational Administration Abstracts; Exceptional Child Education Abstracts; Index Medicus; Speed.

   Speech pathologists and audiologists are among the intended audience of this journal. Its purpose is to keep members of the organization informed of current trends, research, innovations and activities. Articles are considered appropriate when they are of professional and general interest. Various types may include those containing information about the profession, philosophical in nature, conceptual in nature, historical in nature and those presenting a synthesis of ideas. This journal also includes a variety of special reports.

   Manuscripts should follow the Chicago style requirements. The editor does not specify a preferred length. Two copies of the article are to be submitted. Copyright is held by the author and the author pays the publisher at the rate of $50.00 per page. Unsolicited manuscripts are accepted for consideration. An editorial decision as to acceptance can be expected within eight weeks. Publication will follow in six months.

10. **ATA MAGAZINE.** 1920– . The Alberta Teachers' Association, Barnett House, 11010 142nd Street, Edmonton, Alberta, Canada T5N 2R1. Circ.: 27,300. 5 issues/yr. Subscription included with association membership; nonmember rate, $6.00/yr. No annual index. Editor: T. W. McConaghy. Book reviewer chosen by editor.
    Indexed in: Canadian Education Index.

    The journal is intended to inform educators and others of current school issues. Articles may deal with educational philosophy, controversial issues, or be of an informative nature concerned with education. Among the regular features are book reviews, letters, a president's column, a secretary's column and an editorial. The audience of this journal includes classroom teachers and principals, teachers in training, government officials and school boards.

    Manuscripts of less than 2,000 words are accepted by the editor for consideration. Articles sometimes are solicited directly from persons in education and related fields. An editorial decision is given in six weeks with publication following in twelve months. The one or two book reviews in each issue are done by a book review editor. Style is not specified.

11. **ATE NEWSLETTER.** 1967– (in present format). Association of Teacher Educators, 1701 K Street, N.W., Suite 1201, Washington, DC 20006. Circ.: 3,000. 6 issues/yr. Subscription included with association membership. No annual index. Editor: Melvin C. Buller. No book reviews.

This newsletter is intended for teacher educators and those interested in teacher education. Its purpose is to bring the membership current information on issues in teacher education, ideas and opinions expressed by writers, and the current happenings of the sponsoring association. Articles considered appropriate for inclusion are those related to clinical field experiences and teacher education, including such topical areas as humanizing teacher education and affective teaching.

Unsolicited articles are accepted for consideration, with priority given to contributions from membership. A letter of inquiry prior to submission is encouraged. It is preferred that articles not exceed 750 words in length. The editor requests that two copies of the manuscript be submitted. This newsletter is not copyrighted. Copyrighted articles are not to be submitted unless clearance accompanies the material. Estimated time for an editorial decision concerning acceptability of an article for publication varies from four to six weeks. Time from acceptance to publication is four months.

12. **AV COMMUNICATION REVIEW.** 1953— . Association for Educational Communication and Technology, 1201 Sixteenth Street, N.W., Washington, DC 20036. Circ.: 8,000. 4 issues/yr. $7.50/yr. with association membership; non-member rate, $19.50/yr. Annual index: winter issue. Editor: Robert Heinich. Editor's address: Audio Visual Center, Indiana University, Bloomington, IN 47401. Book reviews to: John B. Haney, Director of Instructional Development, Queens College - CUNY, 65 - 30 Kissena Boulevard, Flushing, NY 11367.

    Indexed in: Current Contents: Social & Behavioral Sciences; Current Index to Journals in Education; Education Index; Information Science Abstracts; Psychological Abstracts; Social Sciences Citation Index.

The purpose of the *AV Communication Review* is to disseminate research findings and encourage innovative work in educational technology. It is intended to reach researchers, educators and students interested in technology related to instruction and learning. The editor prefers reports of research and papers synthesizing a body of research in instructional technology or learning. The journal regularly features book reviews and research abstracts.

Three copies of all manuscripts are required, and the editor encourages the submission of unsolicited manuscripts. Only occasional issues are dedicated to a central theme, and the editor usually solicits manuscripts for these issues. Manuscript length may vary between 2,000 and 7,500 words. Twenty-six weeks is required to consider a manuscript, with publication of accepted work following within six to twelve months. The copyright is held by the publisher. Approximately four to eight books are reviewed in each issue. Persons interested in reviewing books should contact the book review editor for assignment. Authors should follow APA style requirements.

13. **AV GUIDE NEWSLETTER.** 1922— . Educational Screen, Inc., 434 South Wabash Avenue, Chicago, IL 60605. Circ.: 8,500. 12 issues/yr. $6.00/yr. No annual index. Editor: George L. Littlefield, Jr. Editor does not accept outside book reviews except in special cases.

    This newsletter is intended for the audience of teachers, librarians and
AV people. Its purpose is to keep subscribers informed of new, challenging

and/or different products and ideas. All materials are presented in a concise and factual manner and are audio-visual oriented.

This newsletter depends upon unsolicited manuscripts, between 200 to 600 words in length. The editor states that "articles and product descriptions should be concise. If they are not concise when they arrive, rest assured they will be when they see print." One copy of the manuscript is required with six weeks being the normal time for an editorial decision. Accepted manuscripts usually are published within one month. The copyright is held by the publisher.

14. **ACADEMIC THERAPY.** 1965– . Academic Therapy Publications, Inc., 1539 Fourth Street, San Rafael, CA 94909. Circ.: 8,500. 6 issues/yr. $6.00/yr. Annual index: summer issue. Editor: John Arena. Book reviews to: editor.

>Indexed in: Current Contents: Social & Behavioral Sciences; Current Index to Journals in Education; dsh Abstracts; Education Index; Exceptional Child Education Abstracts; Language and Language Behavior Abstracts; Psychological Abstracts; Rehabilitation Literature; Social Sciences Citation Index.

Academic Therapy's intended audience includes remedial diagnosticians, special class teachers and others working with learning-disabled children. Its purpose is to describe improved methods of diagnosis, identification and remediation. Articles usually deal with specific techniques of remediation. Its regular features include International Scene, Learning from Living, and a guest editorial.

Unsolicited articles, two copies, are accepted for consideration and should follow MLA style requirements. These should be from 2,000 to 2,500 words in length. The copyright is held by the publisher. Some issues are dedicated to central themes and these announcements are made in preceding issues. Three weeks is required for an editorial decision with publication usually following within nine months to one year later. Book reviews are used periodically, up to 30 appearing at one time. These are short, usually being approximately 100 words in length. Letters of inquiry are encouraged.

15. **THE ADMINISTRATIVE SCENE.** 1971– . Saskatchewan Teacher's Federation, Council on Educational Administration, 2317 Arlington Avenue, Saskatoon, Saskatchewan, Canada. Circ.: 400. 3 issues/yr. Subscription included with council membership. No annual index. Editor: Kevin Wilson. No book reviews.

The intended audience of this publication is comprised primarily of administrators in the Saskatchewan area. Its purpose is to convey the activities of the ten regional groups of the Saskatchewan Council on Educational Administration. *The Administrative Scene* is a newsletter primarily of local interest.

Unsolicited articles are received for consideration and some editorials and articles are solicited directly from persons in the administrative field. The estimated time for an editorial decision is three weeks with publication of accepted material following in one month. Preferred length and style are not specified. Copyright is held by the publisher.

16. **THE ADMINISTRATOR.** 1970– . The Buckeye Association of School Administrators, 750 Brooksedge Boulevard, Westerville, OH 43081. Circ.: 1,200. 4 issues/yr. $8.00/yr. No annual index. Editor: Paul C. Hayes. Editor's address: College of Education, The University of Akron, Akron, OH 44325. No book reviews.

The Administrator is the official organ of The Buckeye Association of School Administrators and is intended for superintendents, principals and central office workers. Each issue is devoted to a central theme dealing with current problems of educational organizations. Sample topics from recent issues were: External Pressure Groups; The Superintendent and the Specialists; The Volunteer; and New Financial Phenomena.

Writers are solicited for specific articles and only requested manuscripts are accepted. The author should follow APA style requirements and the preferred length of articles is 2,500 words. Two copies of the work should be submitted. Copyright is held by the publisher. The estimated time for an editorial decision is two weeks with publication to follow in four months. Although unsolicited manuscripts are not accepted, letters of inquiry are welcomed by the editor.

17. **ADMINISTRATOR'S NOTEBOOK.** 1952– . Midwest Administration Center, The University of Chicago, 5835 Kimbark Avenue, Chicago, IL 60637. Circ.: 2,000. 9 issues/yr. $5.00/yr. No annual index. Editor: Barry W. Furze. No book reviews.

Indexed in: Current Index to Journals in Education; Educational Administration Abstracts.

This journal is intended for professors of educational administration, practicing school administrators and students. Its purpose is to disseminate research findings and other materials of interest to the people in the field of educational administration. Articles preferred for inclusion are reports and evaluations of empirical studies, essay reviews and analyses of topical problems. Each issue contains one article.

Although the editor solicits articles from various persons, unsolicited articles are welcome also. A letter of inquiry prior to submission is encouraged. Simultaneous submission to other journals is permitted. Manuscript should be approximately 2,500 to 3,000 words. Copyright is held by the publisher. An editorial decision is made in three weeks and the estimated time from acceptance to publication varies from two to three months. Two copies of all work should be submitted.

18. **ADOLESCENCE.** 1966– . Libra Publishers, Incorporated, P.O. Box 165, 391 Willets Road, Roslyn Heights, NY 11577. Circ.: 3,000. 4 issues/yr. $10.00/yr. Annual index: winter issue. Editor: William Kroll. Book reviews written by staff.

Indexed in: Abstracts in Anthropology; Abstracts of Sociology; Abstracts on Police Science*; College Student Personnel Abstracts; Current Contents: Social & Behavioral Sciences; Current Index to Journals in Education; dsh Abstracts; Data Processing Digest; Education Index; Exceptional Child Education Abstracts; Excerpta Medica; Index Medicus; Pierian Press; Psychological Abstracts; Rehabilitation Literature; Social Sciences Citation Index; Social Sciences Index; Sociological Abstracts; Speed; Women Studies Abstracts.

ADOLESCENCE (cont'd)

This international quarterly is devoted to the physiological, psychological, psychiatric, sociological and educational aspects of the second decade of human life. The journal is the result of a conviction that society's all too numerous failures in coping with the problems of adolescents stem from lack of coordination among the various disciplines just listed. The main objective, therefore, is the achievement of such coordination rather than the presentation of a specific point of view.

Authors should write a letter of inquiry accompanied by a short abstract prior to submission of the article. Simultaneous submission to other journals is permitted. Preferred length of articles is 3,000 words and the copyright is held by the publisher. Contributors should submit two copies of their manuscript. An editorial decision will be given in three weeks with estimated publication time of 18 months. It is recommended that writers consult the journal for detailed manuscript information.

19. **ADULT EDUCATION.** 1951– . Adult Education Association of the United States, 810 18th Street, N.W., Washington, DC 20006. Circ.: 5,000. 4 issues/yr. Subscription included with association membership; non-member rate $11.00/yr. Annual index: summer issue (biennial). Editor: Gordon Darkenwald. Editor's address: Center for Adult Education, Teachers College, Columbia University, New York, NY 10027. Book reviews to: editor.

   Indexed in: Book Review Index; Current Contents: Social & Behavioral Sciences; Current Index to Journals in Education; Education Index; Educational Administration Abstracts; Psychological Abstracts; Public Affairs Information Service Bulletin; Sociology of Education Abstracts; Speed; Technical Education Abstracts.

Adult Education is devoted to research and theory in the field of adult education. The journal seeks articles pertaining to empirical research, formal philosophy of adult education, history of adult education, theoretical formulations, studies of comparative education and interpretative reviews of the literature. Regular features include book reviews and adult education reports.

Unsolicited articles are accepted for consideration. Two copies of the manuscript and a 100 to 125 word abstract should be submitted. Estimated time for an editorial decision is eight to ten weeks and publication will follow in three to six months. Three to five book reviews appear in each issue. The editor suggests that persons interested in submitting a manuscript should write for the set of guidelines which are available. Copyright is held by the publisher.

20. **ADULT EDUCATION NEWS.** 1967– . Office of Special Projects, Division of University Extension, University of Wyoming, Laramie, WY 82070. Circ.: 1,000. 4 issues/yr. Single copies free. No annual index. Editor: Brad Pietens. Editor's address: Box 3274 University Station, Laramie, WY 82070. No book reviews.

This newsletter is designed to serve those interested in adult education. Its purpose is to share news items, research results and opinions about adult education activities in Wyoming and the Rocky Mountain region. The editor seeks articles based upon research or theories and opinions pertinent to adult education. It also contains news of conferences, institutes, seminars and related activities at the University of Wyoming and Wyoming's seven community colleges.

Authors are urged to submit articles, using the APA style, of no set length. Simultaneous submission to other journals is permitted. An editorial decision usually is made within two to three weeks with publication following within three months. Copyright is held by the author. Letters of inquiry are encouraged.

21. **ADULT LEADERSHIP.** 1952– . Adult Education Association of the U.S.A., 810 18th Street, N.W., Washington, DC 20006. Circ.: 7,000. 10 issues/yr. Subscription included with association membership; non-member rate, $13.00/yr. Annual index: April issue. Editor: Nicholas P. Mitchell. Editor's address: University of South Carolina, Columbia, SC 29208. Book reviews to: (United States publishers) H. Mason Atwood, Ball State University, Muncie, IN; (international publishers) Jindra Kulich, University of British Columbia, Vancouver, Canada.

   Indexed in: Book Review Index; Current Index to Journals in Education; Education Index; Hospital Literature Index; Sociological Abstracts.

The intended audience of this journal includes all persons who regard themselves as adult educators, either as professionals or volunteers. Its purpose is to serve as the major professional magazine of the Adult Education Association. Articles preferred are the "how to" types rather than philosophical content, with few, if any, footnotes. Several features appear regularly, including Accent on Social Philosophy, Open for Discussion and The Trading Post.

Unsolicited articles are accepted for consideration. Manuscripts following APA style requirements, about 2,500 words in length, are to be submitted in duplicate. Copyright is held by the publisher. Four of the ten issues are devoted to central themes. A guest editor usually solicits material for these issues. An editorial decision concerning acceptability is given in eight weeks. Estimated time from acceptance to publication varies from three to six months. Three to six book reviews are included in this journal. Reviews may be 250 to 400 words and should be submitted to the appropriate review editor as cited above.

22. **ALABAMA ASSOCIATION OF SECONDARY SCHOOL PRINCIPAL'S BULLETIN.** 1964– . Alabama Association of Secondary School Principals. Circ.: 1,100. 3 issues/yr. Subscription included with association membership; non-member rate, $3.00/yr. No annual index. Editor: Ed Richardson. Editor's address: Andalusia High School, Andalusia, AL 36420. Book reviews to: editor.

This journal is intended for high school principals, particularly those who are members of the AASSP. Its purpose is to improve the administration of secondary schools. The editor is interested in articles which address this purpose.

Unsolicited articles as well as letters of inquiry are welcomed by the editor. Articles should be between 750 and 1,500 words in length. Style is not specified. Simultaneous submission to other journals is permitted. One week is required for an editorial decision with two months elapsing before publication. A maximum of three book reviews are published in each issue of this journal and these should be no longer than 500 words.

23. **THE ALBERTA JOURNAL OF EDUCATIONAL RESEARCH.** 1955– . Faculty of Education, The University of Alberta, Edmonton, Alberta, Canada

40203

T6G 2G5, Circ.: 750. 4 issues/yr. $6.00/yr. Annual index: December issue.
Editor: Thomas E. Kieren. Book reviews to: editor.

Indexed in: Canadian Education Index; Current Contents: Social &
Behavioral Sciences; Current Index to Journals in Education;
Educational Administration Abstracts; Psychological Abstracts;
Social Sciences Citation Index; Sociological Abstracts; Sociology
of Education Abstracts.

The *AJER* is intended for governmental, institutional, school and university
personnel interested in educational research. The editor is interested in articles
dealing with empirical research, criticism or theory. Articles should elaborate on
various aspects of the research including theoretical and practical implications,
rather than simply reporting data. Manuscripts may deal with any area of education or associated fields.

Contributors should follow the APA format and submit two copies of articles
between 2,500 and 5,000 words in length. The copyright is held by the publisher.
Occasional issues of this journal are dedicated to specific topics with announcement
being made well in advance in the journal. Simultaneous submission of manuscripts
to other journals is permitted. An editorial decision, based upon the decision of at
least two referees, is usually made within a six to eight week period with publication
following within three to six months. This journal regularly carries one to five book
reviews which should be between 500 to 700 words in length. Detailed manuscript
information is contained on the inside back cover of each issue.

24. **THE ALBERTA SCHOOL TRUSTEE.** 1933– . The Alberta School Trustees'
Association, 311 Royal Alex Place, Edmonton, Alberta, Canada T5G 0B4.
Circ.: 2,500. 4 issues/yr. $3.00/yr. No annual index. Editor: Hal Martin.
Book reviews to: editor.

Indexed in: Canadian Education Index.

The Alberta School Trustee is published by the oldest educational organization
in Alberta—The Alberta School Trustees' Association, founded in 1907. This journal
is intended for distribution to school trustees and those interested in general education topics. It is mailed to all members of the ASTA and is distributed to all members
of the Legislative Assembly, Alberta Members of Parliament, and other education
officials. The editor is interested in articles related to all aspects of education and
school system administration.

Authors are encouraged to submit one copy of their manuscripts which should
be approximately 1,200 words long. The editor does solicit manuscripts, will read
unsolicited manuscripts and encourages letters of inquiry prior to submission of
materials. An editorial decision usually is made within two weeks and publication
follows within three months. This journal includes four book reviews in each issue.
Book reviews should be approximately 200 words in length. Copyright is held by
the publisher.

25. **ALBERTA SCIENCE EDUCATION.** (formerly **S.C.A.T.**). 1973– (ASE);
1962– (S.C.A.T.). Science Council of the Alberta Teachers' Association,
11010 142nd Street, Edmonton, Alberta, Canada T5N 2R1. Circ.: 800.
2-4 issues/yr. (depends upon volume of acceptable material). $8.00/yr. with

ALBERTA SCIENCE EDUCATION (cont'd)

membership; institutional rate $15.00/yr. No annual index. Editor: John Wilkes. Editor's address: 4923 Claret Street, N.W., Calgary, Alberta, Canada T2L 1C2. No book reviews.

Indexed in: Canadian Education Index.

This journal is designed to appeal to teachers grades K–12 as well as those teaching in higher education. Its purpose is to make available knowledge of new ideas and programs available to science teachers. All types of articles are solicited, especially those dealing with science teaching in the elementary schools.

Contributors are urged to submit manuscripts of a minimum of 1,000 words. An editorial decision will be made within two weeks with publication of accepted manuscripts following within three to five months. No particular style is recommended. Simultaneous submission to other journals is permitted.

26. **AMERICAN ANNALS OF THE DEAF.** 1847– . Conference of Executives of American Schools for the Deaf, 5034 Wisconsin Avenue, N.W., Washington, DC 20016. Circ.: 5,500. 6 issues/yr. $13.50/yr. Annual index: issue number six. Editor: McCay Vernon. Editor's address: Department of Psychology, Western Maryland College, Westminister, MD 21157. Book reviews to: editor.

Indexed in: Child Development Abstracts and Bibliography; Current Contents: Social & Behavioral Sciences; Current Index to Journals in Education; dsh Abstracts; Education Index; Educational Administration Abstracts; Exceptional Child Education Abstracts; Excerpta Medica; Index Medicus; Psychological Abstracts; Public Affairs Information Service Bulletin; Rehabilitation Literature; Social Sciences Citation Index; Sociological Abstracts.

American Annals of the Deaf is the official organ for the Conference of Executives of American Schools for the Deaf (founded 1868) and The Convention of American Instructors of the Deaf (founded 1850), two professional associations concerned with education of the deaf. Its audience includes teachers and parents of deaf children and other professionals and laity interested in the problem. Articles concerning behavioral aspects of deafness are preferred. The journal also contains book reviews, editorials and comments.

Authors interested in submitting manuscripts should follow the style set forth by the American Medical Association. Unsolicited manuscripts are encouraged, with one copy being submitted. The copyright is held by the publisher. Twelve weeks is required for an editorial decision with publication following acceptance in eight months. Between eight and twenty book reviews are published in each issue. The required length for these is 250 words.

27. **AMERICAN BEHAVIORAL SCIENTIST.** (formerly **PROD**). 1960– (ABS); 1957– (P). Sage Publications, Inc., 275 South Beverly Drive, Beverly Hills, CA 90212. Circ.: not given. 6 issues/yr. $14.40/yr. for professionals; institutional rate, $24.00/yr. Annual index: issue number six. Editor: guest editor for each issue. No book reviews.

Indexed in: ABC: Political Science and Government; Abstracts on Criminology and Penology; Abstracts on Police Science*; Book Review Index to Social Science Annuals; Current Contents: Social & Behavioral Sciences; Current Index to Journals in Education; Educational

Administration Abstracts; Human Resources Abstracts; Index to Periodical Articles Related to Law; Information Science Abstracts; Psychological Abstracts; Public Affairs Information Service Bulletin; Sage Public Administration Abstracts; Sage Urban Studies Abstracts; Science Citation Index; Social Science Annals; Social Sciences Citation Index; Social Sciences Index; Sociological Abstracts; Urban Affairs Abstracts; Women Studies Abstracts.

The *American Behavioral Scientist* is intended for all social scientists. It deals with the cross-disciplinary interests of its audience and also publishes articles concerned with research findings and discussion of problems in the social sciences. Each issue is organized around a particular theme and is edited by a guest editor, an expert in that area.

Prospective authors interested in future theme titles and the names of guest editors may correspond with the publisher to obtain these data. A style sheet will be provided also, or inspection of the latest issues of this journal will answer many questions concerning format. Article selection and length are matters determined by the guest editor within the publication considerations imposed by the publisher. Copyright on accepted materials is held by the publisher. Times for an editorial decision and publication are not indicated.

28. **AMERICAN CHORAL REVIEW.** 1958– . The American Choral Foundation, Inc., Association of Choral Conductors, 130 West 56th Street, New York, NY 10019. Circ.: 1,800. 4 issues/yr. Subscription included with association membership. No annual index. Editor: Alfred Mann. Manuscript to: Alfreda Hays, Assistant Editor, 215 Kent Place Boulevard, Summit, NJ 07901. Book reviews to: editor.

Indexed in: Music Article Guide; The Music Index; RILM Abstracts of Music Literature.

The *American Choral Review* is a journal for composers, conductors, musicologists and students of choral music. It contains articles dealing with choral music. It has regular features dealing with the conductor, school music, liturgy, and international performances of merit, also reviews of books, records and scores. Occasionally one issue is devoted to a central theme.

Unsolicited articles are encouraged, as are letters of inquiry. Authors are to submit all manuscripts in duplicate. No suggested length for manuscript is specified. The copyright is held by the publisher and an honorarium is paid authors of accepted manuscripts. One or two book reviews are used in each issue with no length requirements. Editorial decisions are made within four weeks with publication following in twelve months. Authors should follow the MLA style requirements.

29. **AMERICAN EDUCATION.** (formerly **HIGHER EDUCATION** and **SCHOOL LIFE**). 1965– (AE). U. S. Department of Health, Education and Welfare, Office of Education, Washington, DC 20202. Circ.: not given. 10 issues/yr. $13.50/yr. Annual index: December issue. Editor: William A. Horn. Editor's address: Office of Education, 400 Maryland Avenue, S.W., Room 2089-B, Washington, DC 20202. No book reviews.

AMERICAN EDUCATION (cont'd)

Indexed in: America: History and Life*; Current Contents: Social & Behavioral Sciences; Current Index to Journals in Education; dsh Abstracts; Education Index; Exceptional Child Education Abstracts; Hospital Literature Index; Human Resources Abstracts; Index to U.S. Government Periodicals; Language and Language Behavior Abstracts; Readers Guide to Periodical Literature; Rehabilitation Literature.

American Education is produced by the U.S. Office of Education and is written to reflect the Federal interest in education at all levels. Its audience includes educators throughout the country, as well as other persons directly interested and involved in education. Among its regular features are Federal Funds, Research Developments, Recent Publications and Statistic of the Month.

The editor solicits articles from educators and others across the country, but also welcomes unsolicited manuscripts. A letter of inquiry prior to submission is advised. Articles should be written in a popular as opposed to a scholarly style and may vary in length from 700 to 3,500 words, with 2,500 words the norm for a regular feature presentation. Payment is based upon length and quality and ranges from $150.00 to $500.00 the average being approximately $350.00. The journal is not copyrighted. An editorial decision concerning acceptability is usually given in two weeks. Publication will follow four to six months later.

30. **AMERICAN JOURNAL OF ART THERAPY.** 1961– . Published by Elinor Ulman in affiliation with the American Art Therapy Association, 6010 Broad Branch Road, N.W., Washington, DC 20015. Circ.: 2,500. 4 issues/yr. $10.00/yr. Annual index: issue number four. Editor: Elinor Ulman. Editor's address: P.O. Box 4918, Washington, DC 20008. Book reviews to: Claire A. Levy, Book Editor.

Indexed in: Current Contents: Social & Behavioral Sciences; Excerpta Medica; Hospital Literature Index; Index Medicus; Psychological Abstracts; Rehabilitation Literature; Social Sciences Citation Index; Speed.

The journal is written for those working with art as it contributes to human understanding and mental health. It provides a forum for art therapists, psychotherapists, psychologists, teachers, psychiatrists, and others interested in art and in rehabilitation to share ideas and discuss problems. The journal contains reports of research, new theoretical formulations, descriptions of actual programs, reviews, and bibliographical information.

Articles of unlimited length will be considered for publication. Contributors should consult a recent journal for basic format and style requirements. Copyright is held by the publisher. The time for an editorial decision is not specified, and the estimated time from acceptance to publication is three months. Book reviews vary in length but must focus upon the relevance of the work under discussion to art therapy. Two copies of all work, double spaced, should be submitted.

31. **AMERICAN JOURNAL OF MENTAL DEFICIENCY.** (formerly **PROCEEDINGS OF THE AMERICAN ASSOCIATION ON MENTAL DEFICIENCY, PROCEEDINGS OF THE AMERICAN ASSOCIATION FOR THE STUDY OF THE FEEBLE-MINDED, JOURNAL OF PSYCHO-ASTHENICS,** and

AMERICAN JOURNAL OF MENTAL DEFICIENCY (cont'd)

PROCEEDINGS OF THE ASSOCIATION OF MEDICAL OFFICERS OF
AMERICAN INSTITUTIONS FOR IDIOTIC AND FEEBLE-MINDED
PERSONS). 1940— (AJMD); 1933— (PAAMD); 1918— (PAASF-M);
1896— (JP-A); 1876— (PAMOAIIF-MP). American Association on Mental
Deficiency, 5201 Connecticut Avenue, N.W., Washington, DC 20015.
Circ.: not given. 6 issues/yr. $20.00/yr.; library rate, $40.00/yr. Annual
index: May issue. Editor: H. Carl Haywood. Editor's address: Box 503,
Peabody College, Nashville, TN 37203. Book reviewers chosen by book
review editor.

Indexed in: Bulletin Signaletique, Section 390: Psychologie-Psychopathologie-
Psychiatrie; Child Development Abstracts and Bibliography; Computer and
Information Systems Abstracts; Current Contents: Life Sciences; Current
Contents: Social & Behavioral Sciences; Current Index to Journals in
Education; dsh Abstracts; Education Index; Excerpta Medica; Index
Medicus; Information Retrieval Limited*; Mental Retardation Abstracts;
Nuclear Science Abstracts; Psychological Abstracts; Rehabilitation
Literature; Social Sciences Citation Index; Sociological Abstracts;
Sociology of Education Abstracts; Speed; Women Studies Abstracts.

The intended audience of this journal includes members of the several disciplines
concerned with mental retardation who are interested in professional and scientific
information in the field. Articles should deal with material in the behavioral and
biological sciences, and should extend knowledge of mental retardation and characteristics of mentally retarded persons. Types of articles preferred are original
research, theoretical articles, and comprehensive, critical, systematic reviews of
special areas relating to mental retardation.

Unsolicited articles of up to 5,000 words conforming to the APA style are
preferred. Contributors are to send three copies of their work. Copyright is held by
the publisher. The estimated time for an editorial decision concerning acceptability
is sixteen weeks. Publication will follow within six months.

32. **AMERICAN JOURNAL OF PHARMACEUTICAL EDUCATION.** 1937— .
American Association of Colleges of Pharmacy, 4630 Montgomery Avenue,
Suite 201, Bethesda, MD 20014. Circ.: 2,000. 5 issues/yr. Subscription
included with association membership; non-member rate $25.00/yr. Annual
index: issue number four for first four issues; issue number five is indexed
separately. Editor: Marvin H. Malone. Editor's address: University of the
Pacific, School of Pharmacy, Stockton, CA 95211. Book reviews to: editor.

Indexed in: Biological Abstracts; Chemical Abstracts; Chemical Titles;
Current Contents: Life Sciences; Current Contents: Social & Behavioral
Sciences; Excerpta Medica; Hospital Literature Index; Information
Retrieval Limited*; International Pharmaceutical Abstracts; Nuclear
Science Abstracts; Speed.

This journal is intended for collegiate educators involved with undergraduate
and graduate pharmaceutical education. Its purpose is to document and advance
the quality of pharmaceutical education. Articles deal with information and data
that will appeal to a national and international audience. The annual proceedings

AMERICAN JOURNAL OF PHARMACEUTICAL EDUCATION (cont'd)

of the AACP meeting are published. Issue number five constitutes the proceedings of the annual AACP Teachers' Seminar.

Articles submitted for editorial consideration should be between 2,000 and 10,000 words in length. Three copies are required. The copyright is held by the publisher but will be yielded to the author upon request. Unsolicited manuscripts are considered and letters of inquiry are encouraged. An editorial decision will be made from four to eight weeks after receipt of manuscript. Publication usually follows from four to twelve months after acceptance. A minimum of 20 book reviews are presented in each issue; however, a letter of inquiry should always be made before submitting an unsolicited book review in order to prevent duplication of effort. General style requirements are those of the MLA; however, technical decisions should follow the *Council of Biology Editors Style Manual.*

33. **THE AMERICAN MONTESSORI BULLETIN.** 1960– . American Montessori Society, 175 Fifth Avenue, New York, NY 10010. Circ.: 4,000-6,000. 4 issues/yr. Subscription included with society membership. No annual index. Editor: Cleo Monson. No book reviews.

The separate issues of this bulletin are devoted to single topics, all related to some form of Montessori education. Its purpose is to educate, inform and promote greater understanding of Montessori concepts and related ideas. The intended audience includes teachers, administrators and others interested in Montessori schools, including parents and everyone concerned with young children.

Authors are encouraged to submit articles between 7,500 and 10,000 words in length. Each issue of the *Bulletin* publishes only one such paper. The time for an editorial decision is from eight to ten weeks. Publication time of an accepted manuscript is not specified. The copyright is held by the publisher. Simultaneous submission to other journals is permitted.

34. **THE AMERICAN MUSIC TEACHER.** 1951– . Music Teachers National Association, Inc., 408 Carew Tower, Cincinnati, OH 45202. Circ.: 15,000. 6 issues/yr. Subscription included with association membership; non-member rate, $4.00/yr. No annual index. Editor: Homer Ulrich. Editor's address: 3587 South Leisure World Boulevard, Silver Spring, MD 20906. Book reviews to: editor.

Indexed in: Education Index; Music Articles Guide; The Music Index.

This journal is intended for music teachers, both private and institutional, at all levels and in all fields of music. Its purpose is to provide its readers with a balanced overview of topics of interest to teachers. Articles deal with areas of music history and theory, analyses of old or new music, teaching techniques, and subjects of general interest.

Unsolicited manuscripts, written following the Chicago style requirements, may be submitted for possible inclusion in this journal. Preferred length is 1,500 to 2,000 words. Copyright is held by the publisher. Estimated time for an editorial decision concerning acceptability of an article for publication is two weeks. Time from acceptance to publication is four months. Approximately six to eight books and 30 to 40 music items are reviewed each issue. Length of reviews depends upon the item, therefore, writers should consult recent issues for appropriate style and length.

35. **AMERICAN SCHOOL AND UNIVERSITY.** 1928– . Education Division
   of North American Publishing Company, 134 North 13th Street,
   Philadelphia, PA 19107. Circ.: 35,000. 12 issues/yr. $15.00/yr. Annual
   index: published separately. Editor: James R. Russo. Book reviews to:
   editor.
   Indexed in: College Student Personnel Abstracts; Consumers Index;
   Current Index to Journals in Education; Educational Administration
   Abstracts.
   This journal is concerned with educational facilities and administration. It
deals with construction, planning, furnishings, equipment, audio-visual systems,
maintenance, business equipment and techniques. The information is intended for
administrators and others interested in educational facilities. Regular features
include New Products, Future Facilities, Product Applications, Marketplace,
Literature, Classified Ads, Publisher's Corner, Facilities Newsfront, AV/TV
Facilities, Plant Maintenance and an Index to Advertisers.
   A number of the continuing features and articles are written by the editor
and four regular contributing editors. Manuscript information concerning other
articles is not specified. The journal also contains reviews of books dealing with
educational facilities. It is recommended that interested contributors send a letter
of inquiry to the editor.

36. **THE AMERICAN SCHOOL BOARD JOURNAL.** 1891– . National
   School Boards Association, 800 State National Bank Plaza,
   Evanston, IL 60201. Circ.: 50,000. 12 issues/yr. $18.00/yr. Annual
   index: published separately. Editor: James Betchkal. Book reviews
   are assigned.
   Indexed in: Current Index to Journals in Education; Education Index;
   Educational Administration Abstracts; Index to Periodical Articles
   Related to Law; Public Affairs Information Service Bulletin; Women
   Studies Abstracts.
   The journal is intended for school board members, superintendents and other
school administrators. Its purpose is to give editorial coverage to the various issues
in public education. Several regular features are Journal After the Fact, Washington
Report, Books for Boardman and Write Us a Letter.
   The editor solicits articles for publication, but also accepts unsolicited manuscripts for consideration. A letter of inquiry prior to submission is encouraged. The
original copy of about 1,500 words is to be submitted. Copyright is held by the
publisher. Payment is made only for assigned material and the amount is negotiated.
The time for an editorial decision concerning acceptance is eight weeks. Publication
will follow within six months. The December issue is devoted to book reviews which
are assigned.

37. **AMERICAN SECONDARY EDUCATION.** 1970– . Ohio Association of
   Secondary School Principals. Circ.: 2,800. 4 issues/yr. Subscription included
   with association membership; non-member rate, $12.00/yr. Annual index:
   September issue. Editor: Charles L. Wood. Editor's address: College of
   Education, The University of Akron, Akron, OH 44325. Book reviews to:
   editor.

This journal is intended for teachers and principals of secondary schools. Its purpose is to serve as a resource for secondary personnel. Articles are practical and factual, and focus on problems, programs, services and personnel in secondary education.

The editor welcomes writers to submit manuscripts written in the APA style. Articles of 2,500 words should be submitted in five copies. Copyright is held by the publisher. The editor reserves the right to edit the manuscript. Estimated time for a decision concerning acceptability is sixteen weeks. Publication time, after acceptance, is five months. Book reviews, 250 words in length, are a part of the journal periodically.

38. **AMERICAN SPEECH.** 1925– . American Dialect Society, Columbia University Press, 562 West 113th Street, New York, NY 10025. Circ.: not given. 4 issues/yr. Subscription included with society membership; non-member rate $10.00/yr. Annual index: winter issue. Editor: John Algeo. Editor's address: Park Hall, University of Georgia, Athens, GA 30602. Book reviews to: editor.
   Indexed in: Abstracts of Folklore Studies; Analytical Abstracts; dsh Abstracts; Humanities Index; Modern Language Abstracts; Social Science and Humanities Abstracts.

This journal is intended for persons interested in the development and current status of the English language in America, both professional scholars and laity. Its purpose is to record the use of the English language in the western hemisphere, and secondarily the use of English in other parts of the world, the relationship between English and other languages, and general linguistic theory. The editor welcomes articles dealing with current usage, dialectology, and the history and structure of English. Preference is given to articles that are likely to be of current interest to a wide readership.

Unsolicited articles are welcomed for editorial consideration. Articles should be a maximum of 5,000 words in length and submitted in two copies. The copyright is held by the publisher. Approximately twelve weeks is required for an editorial decision, with publication of accepted manuscripts following eighteen months after acceptance. This journal includes about four book reviews in each issue. While unsolicited book reviews are not encouraged, the editor will be happy to receive letters of inquiry regarding reviews. Authors should follow the Chicago style requirements.

39. **AMERICAN STRING TEACHER.** 1951– . American String Teachers Association. Circ.: 4,100. 4 issues/yr. Subscription available only with association membership. No annual index. Editor: John Zurfluh, Sr. Editor's address: 1801 West Scott Street, Sherman, TX 75090. Book reviews to: editor.
   Indexed in: Current Contents: Social & Behavioral Sciences; The Music Index.

The *American String Teacher* is intended for teachers, performers and students of string playing of the violin, viola, cello, string bass, harp and classical guitar. Its purpose is to stimulate and promote study and performance of string playing. Articles give information concerning methods and techniques of teaching and performing as related to the string instruments. Columns with special editors in various instrumental and action areas are a regular feature.

The original copy of a manuscript should be sent to the editor to be considered for possible inclusion in the journal. A letter of inquiry prior to submission is encouraged. Articles are to be 800 to 1,200 words in length. Simultaneous submission to other journals is permitted. Copyright may be held by author or publisher. Journal issues are dedicated to themes. Authors should examine recent issues to determine forthcoming themes. Estimated time for an editorial decision concerning acceptability of an article for publication is six to eight weeks. The time from acceptance to publication varies. Several book reviews appear in each issue. Preferred length of these reviews is 150 words.

40. **AMERICAN TEACHER.** 1916– . American Federation of Teachers, AFL-CIO, 11 Dupont Circle, N.W., Washington, DC 20036. Circ.: 525,000. 10 issues/yr. Subscription included with federation membership; non-member rate, $7.00/yr. No annual index. Editor: David A. Elsila. Book reviews to: editor.
   Indexed in: Current Contents: Social & Behavioral Sciences; Current Index to Journals in Education; Employment Relations Abstracts*; Women Studies Abstracts.

American Teacher is intended for classroom teachers, kindergarten through college level. Its purpose is to inform members of the American Federation of Teachers and other classroom teachers of union activities and programs, and current education and labor events. Articles deal with classroom experiences, academic freedom and teacher unionism.

Writers are encouraged to submit articles for possible inclusion in this publication, but a letter of inquiry prior to submission is advised. Preferred length of articles is 750 to 2,000 words. Authors should examine this tabloid for preferred style and format. The publisher pays the author. The rate varies, but the minimum is $75.00 per contribution. Simultaneous submission to other journals is permitted. An editorial decision is made in six weeks and the estimated time from acceptance to publication is six months. Copyright is held by the author. Two or three book reviews appear in each issue. These reviews are 1,000 words in length.

41. **AMERICAN VOCATIONAL JOURNAL.** 1926– . American Vocational Association, Inc., 1510 H Street, N.W., Washington, DC 20005. Circ.: 60,000. 9 issues/yr. Subscription included with association membership; non-member rate, $8.00/yr. Annual index: published separately. Editor: Lowell A. Burkett. Manuscript to: Harry H. Cutler, Managing Editor. Book reviews to: managing editor.
   Indexed in: Business Education Index; Current Contents: Social & Behavioral Sciences; Current Index to Journals in Education; Education Index; Graphic Arts Abstracts.

This journal is written for vocational education teachers, administrators and guidance counselors. It is intended to keep readers abreast of developments, issues and concerns within the profession. It also provides information to help them in their daily work. Descriptions of teaching aids, new equipment, book previews, and news from Washington are among the several regular features.

Authors who want material considered for publication should submit manuscripts in duplicate, typed double space, between 1,500 and 3,000 words long. Journal editors reserve the right to edit for style. Authors may wish to look at current issues for guidelines. Twelve weeks is required for an editorial decision with three months between acceptance and publication being normal. The copyright is held by the publisher.

42. **ANDOVER NEWTON QUARTERLY.** 1960– . Andover Newton Theological School, 210 Herrick Road, Newton Center, MA 02159. Circ.: 10,000. 4 issues/yr. Subscription: no charge. Annual index: March issue. Editor: Charles E. Carlston. Book reviews to: editor.

Indexed in: Book Reviews of the Month; Elenchus Bibliographicus Biblicus; Index to Religious Periodical Literature; New Testament Abstracts; Religious and Theological Abstracts; Sociological Abstracts; Women Studies Abstracts.

This quarterly is intended for college teachers of religion, ministers and alumni of Andover Newton. Its purpose is to communicate ideas relating to theological questions and concerns of the Church. It also attempts to present reflections of the intellectual and religious life and outlook of the school. It presents popular and semi-technical discussions of theological topics.

Unsolicited manuscripts are accepted for consideration and simultaneous submission to other journals is permitted. MLA style should be followed with articles being between 3,000 and 4,000 words in length. One copy of the manuscript is required. The copyright is held by the publisher. Six to eight weeks is required for an editorial decision with publication following between three and twelve months later. One to three book reviews are published in each issue. These should be between 500 and 1,000 words long.

43. **APPALACHIA.** 1967– . Appalachian Regional Commission, 1666 Connecticut Avenue, N.W., Washington, DC 20235. Circ.: 20,000. 6 issues/yr. Subscription: no charge. Annual index: August-September issue. Editor: Elise Kendrick. Editor does not accept outside book reviews.

Indexed in: Current Index to Journals in Education; Environmental Periodicals Bibliography; Medical Care Review; Public Affairs Information Service Bulletin.

This journal is intended for those interested in the economic development and human resource development in the Appalachian states. Its purpose is to communicate the developing plans, programs, and policies of the Appalachian Regional Commission to the people of the region, as well as to communicate regional development ideas to the public. Non-technical articles dealing with new developments in Appalachia in the fields of health, education, transportation, industrial development and other areas of interest are included in the journals examined.

Unsolicited articles are considered, however, a letter of inquiry is suggested. The editor prefers manuscripts of between 3,000 to 5,000 words, with the MLA style being followed. The estimated time for an editorial decision is six weeks with four months being the normal time for publication following acceptance. The copyright may be held by either the author or the publisher.

44. **THE ARITHMETIC TEACHER.** 1954— . National Council of Teachers of Mathematics, 1906 Association Drive, Reston, VA 22091. Circ.: 44,000. 8 issues/yr. $11.00/yr.; institutional rate, $13.00/yr. Annual index: December issue. Editor: Jane M. Hill, Managing Editor. Book reviews to: editor.

Indexed in: Current Index to Journals in Education; Education Index; Exceptional Child Education Abstracts.

This journal offers a forum for the exchange of ideas, where responsible contributors may evaluate developments, share classroom techniques, or deal with any part of the broad spectrum of mathematics education in the elementary school. It is intended for teachers, prospective teachers, and trainers of teachers interested in the teaching of mathematics to preschool and elementary school children. A number of regular features are contained in this refereed journal.

Unsolicited articles are encouraged, with two copies being required for consideration. Articles should be between 1,500 and 2,500 words. Manuscripts are acknowledged and unpublished materials returned. The copyright is held by the publisher. Twelve weeks is required for an editorial decision with six to twelve months required for publication following acceptance. Five to ten book reviews of 250 to 500 words in length are published with each issue. Authors should follow the Chicago style requirements.

45. **ARIZONA ENGLISH BULLETIN.** 1958— . Arizona English Teachers Association. Circ.: not given. 3 issues/yr. Subscription: in-state, with membership only; out-of-state, $5.50/yr. No annual index. Editor: Ken Donelson. Editor's address: English Department, Arizona State University, Tempe, AZ 85281. No book reviews.

The purpose of the *Bulletin* is to keep all teachers of English informed and up-to-date concerning trends and problems in the field. Articles are intended to be practical and interesting to the classroom English teacher. Each issue is dedicated to a theme. Prospective contributors should write the editor before submitting a manuscript.

Articles are frequently solicited by the editor, but unsolicited works, preceded by a letter of inquiry, are welcome. Articles may vary from 1,000 to 2,000 words in length. An editorial decision concerning acceptability is normally given in two weeks. Time from acceptance to publication varies depending upon the issue. The editor suggests that prospective contributors examine the journal for style.

46. **ARKANSAS DEPARTMENT OF EDUCATION NEWSMAGAZINE.** 1963— . Arkansas Department of Education, State Capitol, Little Rock, AR 72201. Circ.: 25,000. 5 issues/yr. Subscription: no charge. No annual index. Editor: Elbert Edward Hardcastle. No book reviews.

This newsmagazine contains matters related to school events and personalities. In addition to the professional areas concerning public schools, the publication includes material from institutions of higher learning to augment the regular features. A balanced review of education is the goal of the Arkansas Department of Education. Continuing features of future magazines are Great Southern Writers, Observation, Noted Arkansans and essays prepared by the state's educators.

Articles are usually solicited by the editor, but unsolicited manuscripts are accepted for consideration. A letter of inquiry prior to submission is encouraged. Articles of 200 to 250 words are preferred. Simultaneous submission to other journals is permitted. An editorial decision concerning acceptability is given in three weeks. Publication will follow in less than one month.

47. **ART EDUCATION.** 1948– . National Art Education Association, 1916 Association Drive, Reston, VA 22091. Circ.: 10,000. 8 issues/yr. Subscription: included with association membership; non-member rate, $15.00/yr. No annual index. Editor: John J. Mahlmann. Book reviewers are chosen by editor.

Indexed in: Current Index to Journals in Education; Education Index.

The purpose of this journal is to offer scholarly articles on latest developments in art education and sensitive and imaginative essays on needs, problems, and philosophies pertaining to art education. It is intended for elementary and secondary art teachers, college and university art education faculty and students, and art museum educational personnel. The editor prefers well written essays which give an interesting, imaginative and thorough discussion of some specific problem, issue, need, or philosophy relating to teaching the visual arts at any or all levels of education.

Unsolicited articles are accepted for consideration. These works should be 2,000 to 4,000 words in length and are to be submitted in duplicate. The time for an editorial decision concerning acceptance is approximately eight weeks. Publication of the contribution will follow in about twelve months.

48. **ART JOURNAL.** (formerly **COLLEGE ART JOURNAL**). 1941– (CAJ). College Art Association of America, Inc., 16 East 52nd Street, New York, NY 10022. Circ.: 9,000. 4 issues/yr. Subscription included with association membership; non-member rate, $8.00/yr. No annual index. Editor: Diane M. Kelder. Book reviews to: book review editor.

Indexed in: Art Index; Book Review Index; Women Studies Abstracts.

The intended audience of *Art Journal* includes art historians, artists, art educators and people in the museum and library fields. This journal attempts to keep its readers informed about developments within the association and disseminates information about college and public museums. It also contains news of the activities of members who teach in institutions of higher education and covers virtually all important news that might affect professionals in the field of art. Most articles have been slanted historically towards the period after 1800, but the *Art Journal* has no policy regarding period or area.

Unsolicited articles are accepted for consideration, but the editor encourages a letter of inquiry prior to submission. At least twice a year this journal is dedicated to a central theme. Preferred article length is about 3,750 words. The time for an editorial decision concerning acceptance is ten weeks. Publication time, after

ART JOURNAL (cont'd)

acceptance, is twelve months. Approximately six to eight book reviews appear in each issue. Preferred length of these reviews is 750 to 1,500 words.

49. **ARTS AND ACTIVITIES.** 1937– . Publishers' Development Corporation, 8150 North Central Park Avenue, Skokie, IL 60076. Circ.: 35,000. 10 issues/yr. $9.00/yr. Annual index: January and June issues. Editor: Morton Handler. Book reviews to: Ivan E. Johnson.

  Indexed in: Education Index; Media Review Digest; Subject Index to Children's Magazines.

The intended audience of this journal includes art teachers and other interested educators. Its purpose is to provide worthwhile ideas for classroom projects. The editor prefers articles which are the result of experience. Regular features are Shoptalk, Book Reviews, Young Artist and Professionally Speaking.

Writers are encouraged to submit manuscripts to be considered for inclusion in this journal. Preferred length of articles is 500 to 1,000 words. Copyright is held by the publisher, who pays the author for published material. An editorial decision is given in two weeks. Publication will follow within three to ten months.

50. **THE ATHLETIC DIRECTOR.** 1969– . National Council of Secondary School Athletic Directors, 1201 Sixteenth Street, N.W., Washington, DC 20036. Circ.: 3,000. 6 issues/yr. Subscription included with council membership. No annual index. Editor: Gordon Jeppson. No book reviews.

This newsletter is intended for athletic directors in high schools throughout the United States. Its purpose is to keep athletic directors and administrators acquainted with, and informed of, current trends and issues in athletic administration. The editor always welcomes articles concerning current issues in secondary school athletics.

Both unsolicited and solicited manuscripts are used in this newsletter. No length restrictions are given. Multiple copies of each article should be submitted. The copyright is held by the publisher. Simultaneous submission to other publications is permitted. An editorial decision is given in ten weeks. Three months after acceptance the manuscript is published.

51. **ATHLETIC JOURNAL.** 1921– . Athletic Journal Publishing Company, 1719 Howard Street, Evanston, IL 60202. Circ.: 31,000. 10 issues/yr. $5.00/yr. Annual index: June issue. Editor: M. M. Arns. Manuscript to: John L. Griffith, Publisher, see address above. Book reviews are written by staff.

  Indexed in: Book Review Index; Education Index.

The intended audience of this journal is high school and college coaches and athletic directors. Its purpose is to serve as clearing house for technical information on coaching and administration of high school and college athletics. Highly technical articles are preferred. Regular features include book reviews, a news column, new product reviews and a coaches' clinic page. The publisher indicates that all articles must be by men or women actually engaged in administration or coaching of high school or college athletics.

ATHLETIC JOURNAL (cont'd)

A single copy of the article, 1,500 words in length preferred, is to be submitted. The editor solicits some articles but also welcomes unsolicited manuscripts. Copyright is held by the publisher. The publisher pays authors at the rate of $25.00 and up depending upon material. An editorial decision concerning acceptability of an article will be given in two weeks with publication following in twelve months.

52. **AUDIOVISUAL INSTRUCTION.** 1956– . Association for Educational Communications and Technology, 1201 Sixteenth Street, N.W., Washington, DC 20036. Circ.: 20,000. 10 issues/yr. Subscription included with association membership; non-member rate, $18.00/yr. Annual index: December issue. Editor: Howard Hitchens. Book reviews are assigned.

   Indexed in: Computer and Control Abstracts*; Current Contents: Social & Behavioral Sciences; Current Index to Journals in Education; Education Index; Exceptional Child Education Abstracts; Information Science Abstracts; INSPEC Science Abstracts; Media Review Digest; Psychological Abstracts; Research into Higher Education.

This journal is written for teachers, librarians, AV coordinators and directors, and all those involved with instructional media. The intent is to present current trends and technological developments in an effort to keep the media professional current in the field. The journal includes new products and materials information, association news, reviews of literature and various happenings of interest to the media professional.

The APA style is preferred for articles to be considered for possible inclusion in *Audiovisual Instruction*. Two copies of the manuscript, about 1,500 words in length, are to be submitted. Copyright is held by the publisher. Issues are devoted to themes and prospective contributors should consult the "Clips" feature of a recent issue or write the editor for themes to be used in the future. An editorial decision concerning acceptance is made in twelve weeks. Publication time varies. The editor welcomes unsolicited articles for consideration.

53. **THE BC SCIENCE TEACHER.** 1959– . British Columbia Science Teachers Association, Room 105, 2235 Burrard Street, Vancouver, British Columbia, Canada V6J 3H9. Circ.: 900. 6 or 7 issues/yr. $6.00 with association membership; non-member rate $10.00/yr. No annual index. Editor: Gordon R. Gore. Editor's address: 910 Ida Lane, Kamloops, British Columbia, Canada V2B 6V1. No book reviews.

This journal is intended for science teachers in grades Kindergarten through 12. Its purpose is to promote the growth of science education in British Columbia through providing information on new developments and teaching tips. A unique feature of one issue examined was the inclusion of a "master" suitable for use in making a transparency for classroom instruction. Sample article titles are: Ideas About Earthquake Prediction; Science Lab Assistants in Some Secondary Schools; Ideas for Fieldtrips to the Seashore; and Tin Foil Planetarium.

Authors of unsolicited articles are encouraged to submit them. Manuscripts should be between 500 and 1,000 words in length. Details concerning style are given in the journal. Simultaneous submission to other journals is permitted. Approximately one week is required for an editorial decision with publication following within one month. The copyright is held by the author, if desired.

54. **THE BALANCE SHEET.** 1919– . South-Western Publishing Company, 5101 Madison Road, Cincinnati, OH 45227. Circ.: 140,000. 7 issues/yr. Subscription: no charge, controlled circulation. No annual index. Editor: Wayne K. Mayes. No book reviews.

Indexed in: Business Education Index; Current Index to Journals in Education; Media Review Digest.

The intended audience of this journal includes primarily business, distributive and economic educators. *The Balance Sheet* provides a forum for the constructive discussion of problems of interest to the profession. Regular features are Professional News, Worth Reading Reviews, and Audiovisual Aids Reviews.

The editor accepts unsolicited manuscripts for consideration. A letter of inquiry prior to submission is encouraged. Style requirements are not specified. Preferred length is 1,800 to 2,400 words and two copies of the article are to be submitted. An editorial decision concerning acceptability is given in four weeks. Publication time varies.

55. **BEHAVIORAL SCIENCE.** 1956– . University of Louisville, P.O. Box 1055, Louisville, KY 40201. Circ.: not given. 6 issues/yr. $18.00/yr., U.S. and Canada; institution rate $30.00/yr. Annual index: November issue. Editor: James G. Miller. Book reviews to: Howell R. Porter, Systems Science, University of Louisville, Louisville, KY 40208.

Indexed in: ABC: Political Science and Government; Abstracts on Police Science*; Anthropological Index; Computer and Control Abstracts*; Computer and Information Systems Abstracts; Computing Review; Current Contents: Social & Behavioral Sciences; Data Processing Digest; Educational Administration Abstracts; Exceptional Child Education Abstracts; Excerpta Medica; Information Retrieval Limited*; Nuclear Science Abstracts; Operations Research/Management Science Abstracts Services; Psychological Abstracts; Sage Public Administration Abstracts; Science Citation Index; Social Sciences Citation Index; Sociological Abstracts; Women Studies Abstract.

Behavioral Science publishes original articles concerning both living and non-living systems. The editors are especially interested in the submission of manuscripts with broad interdisciplinary approaches which normally would not be found in a journal devoted to a single discipline. Articles are acceptable which concern either basic research or scholarship, or systems applications. Priority will be given to articles which analyze isomorphisms among systems or which generalize across types or levels of systems, particularly if they include precise observations and quantitative data.

Unsolicited manuscripts are considered for publication. These works should be between 5,000 and 7,500 words in length. A style sheet is available from the editor upon request. The copyright is held by the publisher. Between six and twelve weeks is required for an editorial decision with publication following acceptance within four months. Book reviews are contained in each issue. The length is at the discretion of the book review editor. A full citation is required. Three copies of all work should be submitted.

56. **BETHANY GUIDE.** (formerly **THE BETHANY CHURCH SCHOOL GUIDE**). 1951– (BG); 1926– (BCSG). Christian Board of Publication, Christian Church (Disciples of Christ), P.O. Box 179, St. Louis, MO 63166. Circ.: 7,500. 12 issues/yr. $5.20/yr. Annual index: September issue. Editor: Arthur H. Syverson. No book reviews.

The intended audience of this journal includes teachers and administrators of Christian education in local congregations. The scope of concerns dealt with cover all educational settings, both within congregations and away from the local church. Its purpose is to give guidance on planning and implementing the congregation's educational program and to provide help for workers in that program. Approximately one-third of the magazine deals with specific age group concerns.

The editor solicits some articles directly for inclusion in this journal, but also welcomes unsolicited manuscripts and letters of inquiry. The style of the Christian Board of Publication is to be followed. Preferred length is 1,500 words and copyright is held by the publisher. Authors are paid at an average rate of $30.00 per piece. Issues are dedicated to themes which are indicated in the journal, or authors may query the editor for future topics. An editorial decision is given in two weeks and publication of accepted material follows in five months.

57. **THE BLACK PERSPECTIVE IN MUSIC.** 1973– . Foundation for Research in the Afro-American Creative Arts, Inc., P.O. Box 149, Cambria Heights, NY 11411. Circ.: 1,000. 2 issues/yr. $5.00/yr. Annual index: fall issue. Editor: Eileen Southern. Book reviews to: editor.

Indexed in: The Music Index; RILM Abstracts of Music Literature.

This journal is intended for college teachers, graduate and undergraduate students, librarians, and those interested in black history and music. It is intended to serve as a source of current history of Afro-American and African music and to provide information about the historical past of this music. The editor prefers articles that are scholarly in tone, dealing with biographical, historical or analytical topics.

The editor seeks unsolicited manuscripts as well as letters of inquiry. The length of the manuscript is unimportant, but the Chicago style is to be followed. Two copies of all manuscripts should be submitted. The copyright is held by the publisher. Approximately six to eight weeks is required for an editorial decision. Publication of accepted manuscripts will follow within six months to a year. Between four and five book reviews are published in each issue of this journal. These reviews range between 500 and 800 words in length.

58. **THE BLACK SCHOLAR.** 1969– . The Black World Foundation, P.O. Box 908, Sausalito, CA 94965. Circ.: 20,000. 10 issues/yr. $12.00/yr. Annual index: September issue. Editor: Robert Chrisman. Book reviews to: editor.

Indexed in: Alternative Press Index; Current Index to Journals in Education; Human Resources Abstracts; Sage Public Administration Abstracts; Social Sciences Index; Women Studies Abstracts.

THE BLACK SCHOLAR (cont'd)

This journal is intended for black activists, educators, intellectuals and decision makers. Its purpose is to educate and expose various social change ideologies for debate and analysis. The editor is interested in clear, coherent writing of a critical or scholarly nature done with energy and conviction related to the purpose of the journal.

This journal is dedicated to central themes which are published in the journal or may be obtained by writing the editor. Unsolicited manuscripts and letters of inquiry are welcome. Manuscript length should be between 2,000 and 5,000 words. Simultaneous submission to other journals is permitted after consultation with the editor. An editorial decision usually is made within eight weeks. Publication of accepted manuscripts follows within two months of acceptance. The copyright is held by the publisher. Between two and four book reviews are published in each issue and these are between 250 and 500 words in length.

59. **THE BOARDMAN.** 1947– . Louisiana School Boards Association, P.O. Drawer 53217, Baton Rouge, LA 70805. Circ.: 3,200. 10 issues/yr. Subscription included with association membership; non-member rate, $2.00/yr. Annual index: September issue. Editor: James D. Prescott. No book reviews.

The intended audience of this journal includes school board members and all education professional groups. Its purpose is to provide coverage of new ideas, changes in education, research reports and photographs of educational activities. Articles preferred are those reporting successful ideas in education. A calendar of events, editorial and humor page are regular features.

The editor welcomes unsolicited articles for consideration. A narrative style is preferred and the length is to be 1,200 words. Copyright is held by the author. An editorial decision is made in four to six weeks and the estimated time from acceptance to publication is four to six months.

60. **THE BRITISH STUDIES MONITOR.** 1970– . The Anglo-American Associates. Circ.: 800. 3 issues/yr. $2.50/yr. Annual index: issue number three. Editor: Roger Howell, Jr. Editor's address: President's Office, Bowdoin College, Brunswick, ME 04011. Book reviews written by editor.

Scholars interested in any aspect of British studies are among the intended audience of this journal. *The British Studies Monitor* is interdisciplinary in approach and seeks to be a major source of information about mutual activities and concerns of scholars in British studies in the United States, the United Kingdom, Commonwealth and elsewhere. The articles are bibliographic in approach and either report on work in progress or assess current trends in scholarship. No other types are acceptable except as notes to previously published articles.

Unsolicited manuscripts are not accepted for consideration, but letters of inquiry are encouraged. Most articles are solicited directly by the editor. The Chicago style is required and preferred length is 3,750 to 5,000 words. The journal is not copyrighted, but copyright could be taken in the author's name. Simultaneous submission to other journals is permitted. An editorial decision is given in eight weeks and the time from acceptance to publication is eighteen months.

61. **BULLETIN OF THE AMERICAN ASSOCIATION OF TEACHERS OF ESPERANTO.** 1963– . American Association of Teachers of Esperanto. Circ.: 100. 4 issues/yr. Subscription included with association membership, non-member rate, $2.50/yr. No annual index. Editor: Dorothy Holland. Editor's address: 5140 San Lorenzo Drive, Santa Barbara, CA 93111. Book reviews to: editor.

This mimeographed publication is intended for professional teachers who are interested in Esperanto and for non-professionals who have taught, are teaching, or intend to teach Esperanto. It is designed to promote the teaching of Esperanto, to keep educators informed of pedagogical activity in other parts of the country, and to keep a record of where and by whom Esperanto is being taught. Specific suggestions for improving teaching and the curriculum and news of classes being taught are welcomed by the editor.

Unsolicited articles written in either English or Esperanto are accepted for consideration. Approximately 250 words is the maximum length. This publication is not copyrighted. Simultaneous submission to other journals is permitted. An editorial decision is given in two weeks and publication follows acceptance in three months. Book reviews of 100 to 150 words appear occasionally and are usually limited to textbooks or books suitable for student reading.

62. **BULLETIN OF THE COUNCIL FOR RESEARCH IN MUSIC EDUCATION.** 1963– . Council for Research in Music Education, School of Music, University of Illinois, Urbana, IL 61801. Circ.: 1,500. 4 issues/yr. $5.00/yr. Annual index: published every four years. Editor: Richard Colwell. Book reviews to: editor.

Indexed in: The Music Index; RILM Abstracts of Music Literature.

The *Bulletin* is intended for scholars in music education. Its purpose is to critique research for teachers and researchers and to disseminate information on funded research. The three categories of material appearing in this publication are Feature Articles, Articles of Interest, and Critiques.

The editor solicits articles, but also welcomes unsolicited manuscripts and letters of inquiry. Simultaneous submission to other journals is permitted. The MLA style is required, but no preference is given as to length. Copyright is held by the author. The time for an editorial decision concerning acceptance is four weeks. Publication follows in five months. The number of book reviews in each issue varies. Their length is about 1,000 words.

63. **CABE JOURNAL.** (formerly **CONCERNS OF CABE**). 1974– (CJ). Connecticut Association of Boards of Education, Inc., 410 Asylum Street, Hartford, CT 06103. Circ.: 2,100. 26 issues/yr. Subscription included with association membership. Annual index: issue varies. Editor: Steven Mansfield. No book reviews.

This "loose-leaf" journal is intended primarily for Connecticut school board members. It provides in-depth studies and background information on issues pertinent to its audience. Regular features of this publication are: CABE News; Outlook; Legislative News; School Law Reports; Communications Report; Boardmanship Reports; Education Reports; and, Research Reports.

The editor solicits material from various specialists, but also accepts letters of inquiry and unsolicited manuscripts. Simultaneous submission to other journals

CABE JOURNAL (cont'd)

is permitted. Preferred length of articles is 1,500 words and the MLA style requirements are to be followed. Copyright is held by the publisher. An editorial decision is given in four weeks and publication of accepted pieces generally follows in two months.

64. **C.A.U.T. BULLETIN.** 1951– . Canadian Association of University Teachers. Circ.: 18,000. 6 issues/yr. $12.00/yr. No annual index. Editor: Israel Cinman. Editor's address: 66 Lisgar Street, Ottawa, Ontario, Canada K2P 0C1. Book reviews to: editor.

This journal is designed to promote the interests of teachers and researchers in Canadian universities and colleges, to advance the standards of their profession, and to seek to improve the quality of higher education in Canada. General articles on the current state of higher education in Canada or in a particular province are welcomed by the editor. Also desired for publication are articles dealing with specific issues of importance to the profession, such as student evaluation of professors, collective bargaining for university professors, and other similar topics.

Unsolicited manuscripts written in a free journalistic style are accepted for consideration. A letter of inquiry prior to submission is encouraged. The editor also solicits material directly from selected professionals. Articles should be 2,000 to 2,500 words long and are to be submitted in duplicate. Copyright on published material is held by the author. Issues are dedicated to central themes and prospective contributors should query the editor for future topics. Estimated time for an editorial decision is four to five weeks. If accepted, publication follows in one to three months. Two to five book reviews of 500 words each are included in this journal.

65. **CEA ADVISOR.** 1957– . Connecticut Education Association, 21 Oak Street, Hartford, CT 06106. Circ.: 29,000. 10 issues/yr. Subscription included with association membership; non-member rate, $1.50/yr. No annual index. Editor: Harvey H. Olson. Manuscript to: Norman E. Delisle, Director of Public Relations. No book reviews.

The *Advisor* is intended for public school teacher members of the Connecticut Education Association throughout the state. Its purpose is to keep the members informed of major association activities and policies and also to bring to them new ideas and philosophies in the area of public school education. Articles preferred are those relating to teaching techniques, ways of reaching children and making teaching more effective in every respect. Also included in this publication are items of specific interest to teachers as individuals.

Unsolicited articles of about 800 words are accepted for consideration. A letter of inquiry prior to submission is encouraged. Simultaneous submission to other journals is permitted. Contributors should follow the style found in National Education Association publications. Authors may expect an editorial decision concerning acceptance within two weeks. If accepted, publication follows in about three months. Material in this tabloid is not copyrighted.

66. **CEFP JOURNAL.** 1962– (as newsletter). Council for Educational Facility Planners International, 29 West Woodruff Avenue, Columbus, OH 43210. Circ.: 1,800. 6 issues/yr. Subscription included with council membership;

non-member rate, $9.00/yr. Annual index: November-December issue.
Editor: Dwayne E. Gardner. Book reviews to: editor.
　　Indexed in: Current Index to Journals in Education.
　　This journal is intended to reach professionals in education, architecture, planning and industry who deal with school environment. It is intended as a forum for the discussion of topics of interest to the professionals specified above and to identify emerging developments and trends. The editor is interested in materials dealing with research, explanations and descriptions and analyses of investigations.
　　Both unsolicited manuscripts and letters of inquiry are encouraged by the editor. Manuscripts should be between 1,500 and 2,500 words, but may be longer if the material warrants it. The copyright is held by the publisher but no reprints are authorized without the author's consent. Approximately four weeks is required for an editorial decision with two months required for the publication of accepted manuscripts. Book reports are published on a space available basis. No length is specified.

67. **CLA JOURNAL.** 1957– . College Language Association. Circ.: 1,100. 4 issues/yr. Subscription included with association membership; non-member rate $8.50/yr. Annual index: June issue. Editor: Therman B. O'Daniel. Editor's address: Morgan State University, Baltimore, MD 21239. Book reviews to: editor.
　　Indexed in: Current Index to Journals in Education; Humanities Index; Modern Language Abstracts; Women Studies Abstracts.
　　This journal is concerned with research in all aspects of language and literature, American and foreign. Although most articles are written in English, articles in foreign languages are acceptable also. The articles are critical and interpretive and designed mainly for the college and university level, although many may be read with profit by high school students and the non-academic audience with an interest in language and literature. Any article of a scholarly type dealing with language and literature will be considered.
　　Unsolicited manuscripts are accepted for consideration. Two copies of the work are to be submitted. Contributors should follow the MLA style and length may vary from 2,500 to 3,000 words. Some issues are dedicated to central themes and these are announced by the editor. Copyright is held by the publisher. An editorial decision is made in eight weeks and publication follows in twelve months. About five or six book reviews appear in each issue. These reviews are 250 to 500 words in length.

68. **CTA ACTION.** 1962– . California Teachers Association, 1705 Murchison Drive, Burlingame, CA 94010. Circ.: 185,000. 16 issues/yr. Subscription included with association membership. No annual index. Editor: Bill Livingston. Book reviews to: Vivian L. Toewe.
　　This newspaper is intended for members of the California Teachers Association. Its purpose is to keep members informed of association programs and policies and of outstanding performance by California teachers. It presents new ideas on classroom performance and techniques.
　　This paper is staff written. However, outside authors may query the editor if they have ideas. Such articles must have a California basis. An editorial decision is

CTA ACTION (cont'd)

given promptly. Book reviews must be short and give complete data. Preference is given CTA members. These reviews appear in a column which is a regular part of the paper.

69. **CALIFORNIA JOURNAL OF EDUCATIONAL RESEARCH.** 1950– . California Teachers Association, 1705 Murchison Drive, Burlingame, CA 94010. Circ.: 1,500. 4 issues/yr. $10.00/yr. Annual index: November issue. Editor: William P. Osborn. Editor's address: Department of Psychology, San Jose State University, San Jose, CA 95192. Book reviews to: editor.

Indexed in: College Student Personnel Abstracts; Current Contents: Social & Behavioral Sciences; dsh Abstracts; Education Index; Exceptional Child Education Abstracts; Language and Language Behavior Abstracts; Psychological Abstracts; Research into Higher Education; Social Sciences Citation Index.

This journal is intended for professional educators at all levels. Its purpose is to publish reports of educational research which will aid the practitioner. Sample articles from recent issues include: Problems in the Use of Interest Inventories; Self Concept and I.Q.; Disadvantaged Kindergarten Children; and, Teacher Performance. It is published by the California Teachers Association for the California Advisory Council on Educational Research.

Unsolicited manuscripts conforming to APA style requirements are accepted for consideration, although a letter of inquiry prior to submission is encouraged. Preferred length of articles is 1,500 words and two copies are requested. One issue per year is dedicated to a central theme and is announced in other issues of the journal. An editorial decision as to acceptance can be expected in eight weeks. Publication follows in twelve months. Copyright is held by the publisher. A book review of 200 words is included in some issues.

70. **THE CALIFORNIA READER.** 1968– . California Reading Association. Circ.: 14,000. 4 issues/yr. Subscription included with association membership. No annual index. Editor: Becca Wachtmann. Editor's address: 1049 Fair Oaks Avenue, Arroyo Grande, CA 93420. Book reviews to: editor.

This newsletter format journal is intended for teachers, administrators, reading specialists, and anyone with an interest in the teaching of reading. It is designed to be both informational and instructional as well as to provide help with in-service programs. The editor is interested in receiving articles dealing with research reports, new materials, and topics of current interest.

Unsolicited as well as solicited manuscripts are considered by the editor for inclusion in this newsletter-journal. The editor also welcomes letters of inquiry. Manuscripts should be approximately 1,500 words in length. The copyright is held by the publisher, however, simultaneous submission to other journals is permitted. Six weeks is required for an editorial decision with publication of accepted manuscripts following in six to eight months. Two book reviews are published in each issue and these should be 700 words in length.

71. **CALIFORNIA YOUTH AUTHORITY QUARTERLY.** 1948– . Department of the Youth Authority, 714 P Street, Room 1050, Sacramento, CA 95814. Circ.: 4,600. 4 issues/yr. $3.00/yr. Annual index: not given. Editor: Arthur L. German. No book reviews.

   Indexed in: Abstracts on Police Science*; Index to Periodical Articles Related to Law.

This journal is intended for those who are interested in the problems of youth. The contents of the journal deal with youth correction. Articles may be research-oriented or descriptions of programs in operation. Sample article titles are: National Study of Women's Correctional Programs; Help Wanted—But How About the Ex-Offender?; Clerical Development Program; and, A Snag in Inmate Rights.

Unsolicited manuscripts as well as letters of inquiry are welcomed. Manuscripts should be between 1,000 and 4,000 words in length. Three weeks is required for an editorial decision with publication following within three months for accepted articles. Occasional issues of the journal are dedicated to central themes and these may be determined in advance by writing to the editor. Simultaneous submission to other journals is permitted.

72. **THE CALIPER.** 1946– . The Canadian Paraplegic Association, 520 Sutherland Drive, Toronto, Ontario, Canada M4G 3V9. Circ.: 5,500. 4 issues/yr. $2.00/yr. No annual index. Editor: Paul C. O'Neill. Book reviews to: editor.

   Indexed in: Rehabilitation Literature.

This journal contains achievements and problems of paraplegics and other news of special interest to its readers. Its purpose is to help educate paraplegics, their relatives and associates, and teachers in an effort to solve problems of the paraplegic. Articles on hobbies, descriptions of how to overcome handicaps, or any topic that will help the paraplegic are welcome.

Most articles are written by the editorial staff, but sometimes the editor solicits material for inclusion in this journal. Authors with ideas that will be of help or encouragement to the paraplegic should send a letter of inquiry to the editor. Maximum length of articles should be 1,500 words and the publisher pays authors at the rate of three cents per word. Copyright is held by the author. Most material should have a Canadian slant or be outside a specific country context. Style requirements are not specified. An editorial decision is made in six weeks. Publication time varies. One or two book reviews on books that deal with the paraplegic appear in each issue. Reviews should be about 500 words long.

73. **THE CANADIAN ADMINISTRATOR.** 1961– . Department of Educational Administration, The University of Alberta, Edmonton, Alberta, Canada T6G 2E1. Circ.: 1,200. 8 issues/yr. $3.00/yr. No annual index. Editor: J. H. Balderson. No book reviews.

   Indexed in: Canadian Education Index; Educational Administration Abstracts.

This newsletter is intended for educational administrators and professors of educational administration. It reports research findings and conceptualizations pertinent to the field. The editor is interested in articles which attempt to translate research for consumption by practitioners.

THE CANADIAN ADMINISTRATOR (cont'd)

The submission of unsolicited manuscripts is encouraged. One article is used in each issue and the copyright is held by the publisher. The preferred manuscript length is approximately 3,000 words, and the APA style should be followed. Three weeks is required for an editorial decision with three months required for publication following acceptance of the manuscript.

74. **CANADIAN AND INTERNATIONAL EDUCATION.** 1972– . The Comparative and International Education Society of Canada, Faculty of Education, Althouse College, University of Western Ontario, London, Ontario, Canada N6G 1G7. Circ.: 600. 2 issues/yr. Subscription included with society membership; non-member rate, $6.00/yr. Annual index: issue number two. Editor: David Radcliffe. Book reviews to: editor.

Indexed in: Canadian Education Index.

The journal is intended for those interested in comparative and international education, particularly scholars, students and researchers. It is intended to provide a medium for the expression of Canadian scholarship in the field, as well as other scholars of international repute. All studies falling within the field of comparative education will be considered.

Authors are encouraged to submit two copies of manuscripts, between 3,000 and 20,000 words in length, together with a brief (100-200 word) abstract. Abstracts are printed with the article in the alternate official language (French or English). An editorial decision can be expected within four to eight weeks, with publication of accepted manuscripts following in three to nine months. The APA style requirements should be followed. Copyright is held by the publisher. Unsolicited book reviews are accepted. The number published varies greatly from issue to issue. These reviews should be between 250 and 350 words in length. Simultaneous submission to other journals is permitted, provided the editor is notified.

75. **CANADIAN COUNCIL OF TEACHERS OF ENGLISH NEWSLETTER.** Canadian Council of Teachers of English, 806 Avenue X North, Saskatoon, Saskatchewan, Canada. Circ.: 1,000. 4-6 issues/yr. Subscription included with council membership. No annual index. Editor: Lionel Wilson. Book reviews to: editor.

This newsletter is written for teachers of English, primarily members and prospective members of CCTE. Its purpose is to maintain inter-provincial communication and to stimulate mutually beneficial exchanges. Notices and brief opinions are preferred for this publication. Longer articles appear in *English Quarterly*, journal of CCTE.

Unsolicited articles of no more than 500 words are accepted for consideration. Simultaneous submission to other journals is permitted. Time estimates for an editorial decision and publication are not specified. No particular style is requested, but all material should be well-written. Annotations of books also are included in this newsletter.

76. **CANADIAN HOME ECONOMICS JOURNAL.** 1950– . Canadian Home Economics Association, 151 Slater Street, Ottawa, Ontario, Canada K1P 5H3. Circ.: 1,600. 4 issues/yr. $8.00/yr. No annual index: Editor: Jane C.

Hope. Editor's address: Home Service Department, Consumers' Gas Company, 19 Toronto Street, Toronto, Ontario, Canada M5C 2E8. Book reviewers chosen by editor.

The *Journal* is intended for home economists in business, teachers at all levels, home economics consultants, dietitians and consumer consultants. Its aim is to keep members of the home economics profession up-to-date in the various areas of interest and it acts as a communication link for the membership. Articles are concerned with topics such as family living, consumer studies, metric system, textiles and nutrition.

The editor accepts unsolicited articles for consideration, although a letter of inquiry prior to submission is encouraged. The length of articles in a recent issue of this journal ranged from approximately 1,000 to 3,000 words. Copyright of published material is held by the author. Style is not specified. Contributors may expect an editorial decision concerning acceptance in eight weeks. If accepted, publication will follow in three to six months. Seven to eight book reviews of about 400 words each appear in each issue.

77. **CANADIAN JOURNAL OF HISTORY OF SPORT AND PHYSICAL EDUCATION.** 1970– . Canadian Association for Health, Physical Education and Recreation, 333 River Road, Vanier City, Ontario, Canada K1L 8B9. Circ.: 600. 2 issues/yr. $4.00/yr. Annual index: every three years. Editor: Michael A. Salter. Editor's address: Faculty of Human Kinetics, University of Windsor, Windsor, Ontario, Canada N9B 3P4. Book reviews to: editor.
   Indexed in: America: History and Life*.

The intended audience of this journal includes university professors and researchers. Research articles related to sport history are preferred. Regular features are Forthcoming Events and Book Reviews.

The editor of this refereed journal accepts unsolicited manuscripts for possible inclusion. No limit is set on the length of articles. Two copies are to be submitted. The time for an editorial decision concerning acceptance is four to six weeks. Publication will follow within six months. Copyright is held by the publisher. Three book reviews appear in each issue. These reviews are 750 to 1,000 words in length.

78. **THE CANADIAN JOURNAL OF LINGUISTICS/LA REVUE CANADIENNE DE LINGUISTIQUE.** 1954– . Canadian Linguistic Association. Circ.: 900. 2 issues/yr. Subscription included with association membership. Annual index: published every three years. Editor: Professor E. N. Burstynsky. Editor's address: Department of Linguistic Studies, University of Toronto, Toronto, Ontario, Canada M5S 1A1. Book reviews to: editor.
   Indexed in: Abstracts in Anthropology; Modern Language Abstracts; Social Sciences Citation Index.

Scholarly articles dealing with linguistic theory and/or specific language problems are included in this journal. It is intended for linguists and those persons who deal with languages. Sample article titles from recent issues are: Indeterminacy in Syntax; Onology, Simplification, and the History of French; and, The Intonation of *wh*-questions in Franco-Ontarian.

Manuscripts written in English or French may be submitted for consideration. A letter of inquiry before submission is encouraged and a style sheet should be obtained from the editor prior to final typing of the article. Preferred length of work is 2,500 to 5,000 words and two copies should be sent. Copyright is held by the publisher. The time for an editorial decision concerning acceptance is eight weeks. Publication will follow in eight months. The six to ten book reviews that appear in each issue vary in length from 500 to 2,000 words.

79. **THE CANADIAN MUSIC EDUCATOR.** 1959– . Canadian Music Educators' Association, 34 Cameron Road, St. Catharines, Ontario, Canada. Circ.: not given. 4 issues/yr. $10.00/yr. No annual index. Editor: Duane A. Bates, Editor's address: Department of Music, Queen's University, Kingston, Ontario, Canada K7L 3N6. Book reviews to: Professor Clifford Crawley, see editor's address.
    Indexed in: Canadian Education Index.

This journal is intended for music educators of Canada. In addition to presenting a wide scope of music articles, the journal is intended to improve dialogue among the music educators of Canada. On occasion, musical compositions appear in this publication.

The editor accepts unsolicited manuscripts for possible inclusion in *The Canadian Music Educator.* A letter of inquiry prior to submission is encouraged. Articles should follow MLA style requirements and are to be submitted in duplicate. Copyright of accepted material is held by the publisher. An editorial decision concerning acceptability of articles usually is given in six weeks. Publication time is not specified. Several book reviews of varying length appear in the journal.

80. **CANADIAN SOCIETY FOR EDUCATION THROUGH ART NEWSLETTER.** 1955– . Canadian Society for Education Through Art, 112 Oakdale Avenue, St. Catharines, Ontario, Canada L2P 3J9. Circ.: 500. 4 issues/yr. Subscription included with society membership. No annual index. Editor: Arnel W. Pattemore. Book reviews to: editor.

The intended audience of this newsletter includes primarily those persons in art education. It serves as a voice of the Canadian Society for Education through Art. Types of articles preferred are news, practical ideas and research reports.

Articles are solicited by the editor and authors are encouraged to submit unsolicited articles as well. Simultaneous submission to other journals is permitted. Some editions are devoted to central themes and prospective contributors should consult the editor for information. Style and estimated time for an editorial decision are not specified. From two to ten book reviews appear in each issue.

81. **CANADIAN VOCATIONAL JOURNAL.** 1965– . Canadian Vocational Association, Suite 608, 251 Bank Street, Ottawa, Ontario, Canada K2P 1X3. Circ.: 3,000. 4 issues/yr. $4.00/yr. No annual index. Editor: Peter Findlay. Book reviews to: editor.
    Indexed in: CIRF Abstracts; Canadian Education Index; Current Index to Journals in Education; International Labour Documentation (Geneva).

CANADIAN VOCATIONAL JOURNAL (cont'd)

This journal's purpose is the development of Canada's human resources at the technical, vocational and industrial levels. It presents a variety of articles on vocational and technical education and training programs in industry. Its readers compose a cross-section of the field, including those engaged in vocational training, teaching, industrial training, personnel management, counseling, research and administration.

The editor accepts unsolicited articles for consideration, however, the issues of this journal usually are dedicated to central themes. These themes may be ascertained by writing the editor. Articles are about 2,000 words in length, with two copies of the manuscript being required. Simultaneous submission to other journals is permitted. The copyright is held by the publisher. Two weeks time usually is needed for an editorial decision with two to three months being required for publication after acceptance. Book reviews are approximately 200 words in length with four or fewer used in each issue.

82. **CASE CURRENTS.** (formerly **TECHNIQUES**). 1975– (CC); 1966– (T). Council for Advancement and Support of Education, One Dupont Circle, Suite 600, Washington, DC 20036. Circ.: 7,000. 11 issues/yr. Subscription included with council membership; non-member rate, $15.00/yr. Annual index: December issue. Editor: Virginia L. Carter. Book reviews to: William McNamara.

This journal is intended for organization member representatives who work in alumni affairs, fund raising, publications and public relations, and governmental relations in colleges, universities and independent schools. It serves as a medium for success stories in job oriented matters, so that others can benefit from them. Practical, "how to do it" articles on functions represented among member representatives are preferred; a few general features are used. Regular features of this publication are a summary of the month's literature on higher education, a Washington report, and news from the campuses.

Unsolicited manuscripts are accepted for consideration. A letter of inquiry prior to submission is encouraged. The Chicago style should be followed and the length is to be 1,000 to 1,500 words. Copyright is held by the publisher. An editorial decision is given in five weeks. If accepted, publication follows in two months.

83. **CATECHIST.** 1967– . Pflaum/Standard, 2285 Arbor Boulevard, Dayton, OH 45439. Circ.: 22,000. 8 issues/yr. $6.00/yr. Annual index: May issue. Editor: Rod Brownsfield. Book reviewers chosen by editor.
   Indexed in: Media Review Digest.

Catechist is intended for religion teachers, especially primary through senior high and chiefly for a Catholic audience. Regular features include Insight, Help/Books, DRE (Director of Religious Education) Newsletter and Help/AV (reviews of media materials).

Articles are solicited by the editor. Unsolicited manuscripts also are accepted for consideration, but a letter of inquiry prior to submission is encouraged. Preferred length is 1,500 to 1,800 words and the publisher pays authors at the rate of $60.00 to $80.00 for each article accepted. Copyright is held by the publisher. Style is not specified and prospective contributors should examine recent issues of the journal.

An editorial decision is made in three weeks. Publication will follow within four months and often occurs immediately following acceptance.

84. **CENTRAL STATES SPEECH JOURNAL.** 1949– . Central States Speech Association, Department of Communications, Purdue University, West Lafayette, IN 47907. Circ.: 2,500. 4 issues/yr. $10.00/yr. with association membership; institution rate, $35.00/yr.; library rate, $15.00/yr. Annual index: winter issue. Editor: Donovan J. Ochs. Editor's address: Rhetoric Program, University of Iowa, Iowa City, IA 52242. No book reviews.

    Indexed in: Abstracts in Anthropology; Current Index to Journals in Education; dsh Abstracts; Education Index; Social Sciences Citation Index.

    This journal attempts to reach teachers and scholars of speech communication. It makes available the research findings of scholars in the history of criticism and application of the general areas of speech. The editor is interested in work which extends knowledge of the speech processes.

    Unsolicited articles are accepted for publication consideration. Manuscripts should be submitted in two copies and be less than 4,000 words in length. The copyright is jointly held by the author and publisher. Between four and six weeks is required for an editorial decision with three to six months being required for publication after acceptance. This is a refereed journal in that the editor submits all manuscripts to readers within the area of expertise of the subject matter. The MLA style format should be followed.

85. **CHALLENGE IN EDUCATIONAL ADMINISTRATION.** (formerly **CSA BULLETIN**). 1970– (CEA); 1962– (CSAB). Council on School Administration of the Alberta Teachers' Association, 11010 142nd Street, Edmonton, Alberta, Canada T5N 2R1. Circ.: 800. 4 issues/yr. Subscription included with association membership; non-member rate, $10.00/yr. Editors: Bob Bryce and Ken Ward. Manuscript to R. Bryce, Department of Educational Administration, Faculty of Education, University of Alberta, Edmonton, Alberta, Canada. No book reviews.

    Indexed in: Canadian Education Index.

    This journal is intended to analyze administrative problems in education, consider the social content of educational administration, and continue the study of major social and educational administrators in the Province of Alberta. The editors are interested in the type of articles that challenge, are inspirational, and provide information to the readership.

    Two copies of all manuscripts should be submitted. Letters of inquiry as well as unsolicited manuscripts are welcomed. Simultaneous submission to other journals is permitted. Three weeks is required for an editorial decision with two months required from acceptance to publication. Articles should be about 2,500 words in length.

86. **CHANGE.** 1969– . Educational Change, Inc., NBW Tower, New Rochelle, NY 10801. Circ.: 30,000. 10 issues/yr. $14.00/yr. Annual index: published separately. Editor: George W. Bonham, Editor-in-Chief. Manuscript to: Articles Editor. Book reviews are assigned.

Indexed in: America: History and Life*; College Student Personnel
Abstracts; Current Contents: Social & Behavioral Sciences; Current
Index to Journals in Education; Educational Administration Abstracts;
Exceptional Child Education Abstracts; Human Resources Abstracts;
Index to Periodical Articles Related to Law; Women Studies Abstracts.

This opinion magazine is designed to provide a forum for discussion of issues
in higher education. Articles preferred are concerned with research, first person
accounts, reports or innovations in higher education, and general philosophical
essays. Among the regular features are Viewpoint, Science Policy, Community
Colleges, Practically Speaking, Washington and Reviews.

Articles are solicited by the editor and unsolicited manuscripts also are
accepted for consideration. Unsolicited manuscripts should be accompanied by
a self-addressed stamped envelope. A letter of inquiry prior to submission is
encouraged. A journalistic style of writing is preferred. Length of articles is
2,000 to 5,000 words. Copyright is held by the publisher who pays the author
at a rate that varies from $100.00 to $350.00. An editorial decision is given in
six weeks and publication follows in two to six months. The three to five book
reviews, all assigned, that appear in each issue are 500 to 1,000 words long.

87. **CHILD STUDY JOURNAL.** 1970– . Faculty of Professional Studies, State
University College at Buffalo, 1300 Elmwood Avenue, Buffalo, NY 14222.
Circ.: 500. 4 issues/yr. $6.00/yr.; library rate, $12.00/yr. Annual index:
biennial index, issue number four of even numbered years. Editor: Donald
E. Carter. Book reviews to: Henry D. Olsen, Division of Teacher
Education, Medgar Evers College, City University of New York, 1500
Carroll Street, Brooklyn, NY 11225.

Indexed in: Current Contents: Social & Behavioral Sciences; Current Index
to Journals in Education; Education Index; Exceptional Child Education
Abstracts; Psychological Abstracts; The Psychological Readers Guide;
Social Sciences Citation Index; Sociological Abstracts.

This journal is intended for educators, psychologists, child development specialists and counselors. It is intended as a medium for the sharing of ideas for theory
and dissemination of results of research on child and adolescent behavior. The editor
prefers articles devoted to the educational and psychological aspects of human
development.

Authors are urged to submit manuscripts of between 1,000 and 2,500 words
to the editor for consideration. The APA style should be followed. Copyright is
held by the publisher. Approximately ten weeks is required for an editorial decision
with twelve months elapsing between acceptance of manuscripts and their publication. Book reviews should be approximately 250 to 500 words in length. Approximately six reviews are used in each issue. Books reviewed should be recently published, that is, within the last twelve months.

88. **CHILD WELFARE.** 1920– . Child Welfare League of America, Inc., 67
Irving Place, New York, NY 10003. Circ.: 10,000. 10 issues/yr. $8.00/yr.
Annual index: December issue. Editor: Carl Schoenberg. Book reviews to:
editor.

CHILD WELFARE (cont'd)

Indexed in: Abstracts for Social Workers; Abstracts on Police Science*; Child Development Abstracts and Bibliography; Current Contents: Social & Behavioral Sciences; Current Index to Journals in Education; Education Index; Exceptional Child Education Abstracts; Excerpta Medica; Human Resources Abstracts; Index to Periodical Articles Related to Law; Public Affairs Information Service Bulletin; Rehabilitation Literature; Selected References on the Abused and Battered Child; Selected Sources of Inexpensive Mental Health Materials; Social Sciences Citation Index; Women Studies Abstracts; World Agricultural Economics and Rural Sociology Abstracts (WAERSA).

This journal is intended for all levels of personnel active in child welfare education and services. Its purpose is to improve the quality of training and programs of those persons working with children and their families. Materials published deal with many aspects of child welfare such as administration, supervision, casework, groupwork, community organization, teaching, research and interpretation. Articles on interdisciplinary approaches to this field and on social policy concerning children's welfare also are included.

Authors are encouraged to submit manuscripts of 3,000 to 4,000 words following MLA style requirements. All material should be double-spaced. Complete style guidelines are available from the editor. Two copies of the article are to be submitted for consideration. The time for an editorial decision concerning acceptability is three to four weeks. Publication follows in six to nine months. Copyright is held by the publisher. Approximately two book reviews appear in each issue and these are 500 words in length.

89. **CHILDHOOD EDUCATION.** 1924– . Association for Childhood Education International, 3615 Wisconsin Avenue, N.W., Washington, DC 20016. Circ.: 27,000. 6 issues/yr. Subscription included with association membership. Annual index: April-May issue. Editor: Monroe D. Cohen. Book reviews are prepared by review committees.

Indexed in: Alesco Periodical Guide; Book Review Index; Current Index to Journals in Education; Edpress Directory; Education Index; Exceptional Child Education Abstracts; Kenlines; Porter-Sargent Handbook.

This journal is the voice of ACEI and is a professional medium for those concerned with the education of children from birth to age 14. It seeks to stimulate thinking rather than advocate fixed practices. The editor prefers manuscripts that explore emerging ideas, probe various points of view, or present conflicting opinions, supported wherever possible with research findings.

Authors are urged to submit inquiry letters but unsolicited manuscripts are considered for publication. In some cases the editor will solicit manuscripts. One issue of the journal is a non-theme issue. The other issues are dedicated to central themes whose topics are announced in the spring issue preceding the publication year. Three copies of manuscripts are preferred. The copyright is held by the publisher. Twelve weeks is required for an editorial decision with publication of accepted manuscripts following at any time within the publication year. Authors should follow Chicago style requirements. Manuscript length may vary from 1,000 to 3,000 words.

90. **CHILDREN TODAY.** (formerly **CHILDREN** and **THE CHILD**). 1972– (CT); 1954– (C); 1936– (TC). Children's Bureau, Office of Child Development, Office of Human Development, Department of Health, Education and Welfare, Washington, DC 20201. Circ.: 29,000. 6 issues/yr. $6.10/yr. Annual index: published separately. Editor: Judith Reed. Editor's address: Office of Child Development, Children's Bureau, P.O. Box 1182, Washington, DC 20013. Book reviews to: editor.

Indexed in: Abstracts for Social Workers; Book Review Index; Cumulative Index to Nursing Literature; Current Index to Journals in Education; dsh Abstracts; Education Index; Exceptional Child Education Abstracts; Excerpta Medica; Hospital Literature Index; Index Medicus; Medical Care Review; Nursing Research; Rehabilitation Literature; Women Studies Abstracts.

Children Today is an interdisciplinary journal written by and for those whose daily jobs and interests are focused on children, youth and families. Authors include teachers, social workers, doctors, nurses, psychologists, parents and public and civic leaders. The publication seeks to provide a means of communication among readers on the needs of children and youth, on methods of meeting these needs, on successes and failures in the application of programs and techniques of care, and on current issues and trends. Preferred articles are those describing programs and projects to improve the health, education and welfare of children from infancy through high school years, reports of findings from recent research studies and discussion of current issues in child health and welfare.

Articles are solicited by the editor, but unsolicited articles are accepted for consideration also. A letter of inquiry prior to submission is encouraged. Manuscripts of 2,500 to 3,000 words are preferred. Magazine article format should be followed. Published material is not copyrighted. Estimated time for an editorial decision concerning acceptability of work varies from six to sixteen weeks. Publication follows in two to eight months. The three to four book reviews in each issue are 750 to 1,000 words long.

91. **CHILDREN'S HOUSE MAGAZINE.** 1966– . Children's House, Inc., P.O. Box 111, Caldwell, NJ 07006. Circ.: 50,000. 6 issues/yr. $5.50/yr. No annual index. Editor: Kenneth Edelson. Book reviews to: editor.

Indexed in: dsh Abstracts; Ebsco Librarian Handbook; Exceptional Child Education Abstracts; Rehabilitation Literature.

This journal, basically a voice for the Montessori educator, contains articles which deal with all facets of child development and training, not only that of the Montessori school. It is intended for teachers, psychologists, clinicians, therapists, opthalmologists and parents. Most of the contents of this journal deal with new methods of education, both in the home and at school.

The editor appreciates receiving unsolicited manuscripts as well as letters of inquiry. Articles should follow the APA style and be between 800 and 2,500 words in length. Some issues are dedicated to central themes and these can be determined by writing the publisher. The copyright is held by the publisher. Simultaneous submission to other journals is permitted. Between six and ten weeks is required for an editorial decision and publication usually follows between three and six months after acceptance. Between twenty and forty book reviews are printed in each issue. These reviews should be between 200 and 500 words in length.

92. **CHRISTIAN HOME AND SCHOOL.** 1922— . National Union of Christian
Schools, 865 Twenty-eighth Street, S.E., Grand Rapids, MI 49508. Circ.:
15,000. 10 issues/yr. $3.25/yr. No annual index. Editor: John A. Vander
Ark. Book reviews to: editor.

This journal is the official organ of the National Union of Christian Schools.
It is intended for parents, teachers, and patrons of Christian elementary and secondary
schools. The purpose of *Christian Home and School* is to bring before the Christian
community the compelling claims of Christian day school education, to challenge
Christian parents to take up their responsibilities in the nurture of their children in
the home and school, and to inform the North American Christian school communities of the development of Christian education.

The editor rarely accepts unsolicited manuscripts, therefore, authors who
believe their material may meet the needs of this journal should submit a letter of
inquiry. The style used is basically Chicago. The publisher pays authors at the rate
of $10.00 per page of approximately 750 words. Articles are approximately 1,200
words in length. Four weeks is required for an editorial decision with a two to six
months time lag before publication. Each issue carries three book reviews for adults
and three for children between 8 and 12 years of age. These should be 200 words in
length and compatible with the purpose of the magazine. Copyright on all material
is held by the publisher.

93. **CHRISTIAN TEACHER.** 1963— . National Association of Christian Schools,
P.O. Box 550, Wheaton, IL 60187. Circ.: 4,000. 5 issues/yr. $5.00/yr. No
annual index. Editor: Phil Landrum. Editor's address: 1308 Santa Rosa,
Wheaton, IL 60187. Book reviews to: editor.

Indexed in: Christian Periodical Index.

The intended audience of this journal includes administrators, teachers and
board members of Christian schools. Its purpose is to inspire and encourage its readership concerning Christian schools and give them an occasional "how to." The
journal features five main articles plus the columns: Focus (news); Weathervane
(trends); Worth It (book reviews); Parents; Board Forum; RX (health); In the
Classroom (how to); and, Perspective (editorial).

The majority of the articles in *Christian Teacher* are solicited directly by the
editor. Only rarely are unsolicited articles accepted. A letter of inquiry prior to submission is recommended. Simultaneous submission to other journals is permitted.
Copyright is held by the publisher. Preferred length of manuscript is 500 to 1,500
words and contributors should examine journal for style. An editorial decision is
given in about twenty weeks and publication follows in nine months. Reviews of
books that would aid administrators and teachers of Christian schools are included.
The number ranges from one to five reviews and each has 200 to 1,000 words.

94. **THE CHRONICLE OF HIGHER EDUCATION.** 1966— . Editorial Projects
for Education, Inc., 1717 Massachusetts Avenue, N.W., Washington, DC
20036. Circ.: 43,000. 42 issues/yr. $21.00/yr. Annual index: semi-annual,
last issue of each volume. Editor: Corbin Gwaltney. Manuscript to: Edward
R. Weidlein, Senior Editor. Most book reviews are assigned by editor.

Indexed in: College Student Personnel Abstracts; Women Studies Abstracts.

The *Chronicle* is intended for administrators and faculty members in higher
education. It includes news on campus developments and opinion type articles

dealing with current issues as related to higher education. Among the regular features are Bulletin Board (positions available), Campus News in Brief, Fact-File, Calendar of Coming Events, Washington News, Grants and Deadlines.

Articles for publication are often solicited by the editor, but unsolicited articles also are accepted for consideration. Simultaneous submission to other journals is permitted. Manuscript length is to be about 1,500 words and the publisher pays the author. Copyright is held by the publisher. Maximum time required for an editorial decision is three weeks and publication follows within several weeks except in summer. Persons interested in writing book reviews should inquire prior to submission since most are assigned. Authors should follow Chicago style requirements.

95. CITIZEN ACTION IN EDUCATION. 1973– . Institute for Responsive Education, 704 Commonwealth Avenue, Boston, MA 02215. Circ.: 10,000. 4 issues/yr. Contribution schedule sent upon request. No annual index. Editor: Barbara Prentice. Book reviews to: editor.

The intended audience of this publication includes parents and other citizens interested in education reform. Its purpose is to stimulate citizen action in education. Regular features include a book review and news about parent/citizen activities.

Articles are solicited by the editor and unsolicited articles also are welcomed for consideration. A letter of inquiry prior to submission is encouraged. Two copies of the manuscript are to be submitted. Chicago style requirements should be followed and length may vary from 1,000 to 2,500 words. Simultaneous submission to other journals is permitted. An editorial decision is given in four weeks. The time from acceptance to publication may vary from twelve to sixteen months. One book review appears in each issue. Its length is similar to that of the articles.

96. CLAVIER. 1962 - . Instrumentalist Company, 1418 Lake Street, Evanston, IL 60204. Circ.: 19,000. 9 issues/yr. $8.00/yr. Annual index: December issue. Editor: Dorothy Packard. Book reviews written by staff.

Indexed in: Music Article Guide; The Music Index.

This journal is intended for teachers and advanced performers of keyboard instruments. It contains articles of general interest to this audience, as well as music of interest to the same group. Among the regular features are reviews of new piano and organ music, and Teachers Idea Exchange. Sample article titles in recent issues are: A Funny Thing Happened to Your Music Order; High Speed Piano Playing; Chopin, Mallorca, and Pianos; and Ives Innovations in Piano Music.

The editor is always looking for manuscripts of interest, however, journal issues are dedicated to central themes. The themes of future issues may be obtained by writing the editor. Approximately six weeks is required for an editorial decision with varying periods of time elapsing from acceptance to publication. The editor states that it may be "two weeks to two years." Payment for accepted manuscripts is made at the rate of $18.00 per page, which is slightly more than one cent per word. The Chicago style should be followed, and the copyright is held by the publisher. Length may vary from 1,000 to 4,000 words.

97. **THE CLEARING HOUSE.** 1926– . HELDREF Publications, 4000 Albemarle Street, N.W., Washington, DC 20016. Circ.: 10,000. 9 issues/yr. $6.00/yr.; institution rate, $8.50/yr. Annual index: May issue. Editor: Margaret Disney. No book reviews.

Indexed in: Business Education Index; Current Contents: Social & Behavioral Sciences; Current Index to Journals in Education; Education Index; Exceptional Child Education Abstracts; Index to Periodical Articles Related to Law; Media Review Digest; Readers Guide to Periodical Literature.

This journal is intended to reach faculty members and administrators of junior and senior high schools. Preferred articles are those dealing with accomplishments such as units, courses, teaching methods, administrative procedures, school programs, as well as controversial issues in secondary education. The journal also reports the results of research, written in a popular manner.

Authors are urged to submit articles for consideration. These works should be between 600 and 2,500 words in length. The copyright is held by the publisher. Between eight and twenty weeks is required for an editorial decision with publication of manuscripts following within two to four months of acceptance. Authors should follow Chicago style requirements.

98. **COGNITIVE PSYCHOLOGY.** 1970– . Academic Press, Inc., 111 Fifth Avenue, New York, NY 10003. Circ.: not given. 4 issues/yr. $16.50/yr. for personal use or membership; institution rate, $39.50/yr. Annual index: issue number four. Editor: Earl Hunt. Editor's address: Department of Psychology, University of Washington, Seattle, WA 98195. No book reviews.

Indexed in: Bulletin Signaletique, Section 390: Psychologie-Psychopathologie-Psychiatrie; Child Development Abstracts and Bibliography; Computer and Control Abstracts*; Current Contents: Social & Behavioral Sciences; Current Index to Journals in Education; Psychological Abstracts; The Psychological Readers Guide; Social Sciences Citation Index.

The intended audience of *Cognitive Psychology* includes linguists, computer scientists, cognitive and developmental psychologists, educators or anyone interested in the psychology of language, thought, memory and information processing. The editor states that the journal's purpose is "to publish original, empirical, theoretical, tutorial, methodological, critical review papers dealing with memory, language processing, perception, problem solving and thinking. Emphasis is on the organization of human information processing." Innovative, theoretical papers of high intellectual quality are sought.

Unsolicited articles are accepted for consideration. The editor indicates that, as a rule, papers judged to be more appropriate for other journals are not published. Over 85 per cent of the papers received are rejected. Manuscript is to be submitted in triplicate and should follow APA style requirements. No length restrictions are imposed upon the writer. Further information for authors may be found in each issue of this journal. Copyright is held by the publisher. Estimated time for an editorial decision concerning acceptability is eight to twelve weeks. Publication follows in eleven months.

99. **COLLEGE AND UNIVERSITY.** (formerly **AMERICAN ASSOCIATION OF COLLEGIATE REGISTRARS JOURNAL, AMERICAN ASSOCIATION OF COLLEGIATE REGISTRARS BULLETIN,** and **AMERICAN ASSOCIATION**

OF COLLEGIATE REGISTRARS PROCEEDINGS). 1974– (CU); 1937–
(AACRF); 1925– (AACRB); 1910– (AACRP). American Association of
Collegiate Registrars and Admission Officers, One Dupont Circle, N.W.,
Washington, DC 20036. Circ.: 6,300. 4 issues/yr. Subscription included with
association membership; non-member rate, $14.00/yr. Annual index: summer
issue. Editor: Robert E. Mahn. Editor's address: Office of the Secretary of
the University, Cutler Hall, Ohio University, Athens, OH 45701. Book
reviews to: editor.

> Indexed in: Book Review Index; Clearinghouse on Higher Education;
> College Student Personnel Abstracts; Current Contents: Social &
> Behavioral Sciences; Current Index to Journals in Education; Education
> Index; Index to Periodical Articles Related to Law; Social Sciences
> Citation Index; Sociological Abstracts.

The intended audience of this journal includes members of the AACRAO and
others interested in those matters dealt with by this association. The purpose of the
journal is to promote the advancement of education, particularly higher education.
Contributions are welcomed and those relating to higher education in the United
States and abroad and to the purposes of the association will have preference.

Unsolicited manuscripts are accepted for consideration. The Chicago style
should be followed, with articles being approximately 2,000 words in length. This
journal is not copyrighted, however, the editor expects that accepted manuscripts
will not be submitted to other journals. Six weeks is required for an editorial
decision with publication of accepted manuscripts following within six months.
Between eight and twelve book reviews are published in each issue. These reviews
should be between 250 and 500 words in length.

100. **THE COLLEGE BOARD REVIEW.** 1947– . The College Entrance Examination
Board, 888 Seventh Avenue, New York, NY 10019. Circ.: 15,000. 4 issues/yr.
$5.00/yr. Annual index: biennial index, fall issue of even numbered years.
Editor: David Coleman. No book reviews.

> Indexed in: College Student Personnel Abstracts; Current Index to Journals
> in Education; Social Sciences Index.

This journal is designed to reach school and college administrators, admissions
officers, financial aids officers and guidance counselors. It is intended as a forum for
the exchange of ideas in education, secondary as well as post-secondary, with special
attention to the transitional period between high school and college. The editor is
interested in consumer style "think" pieces. No formal research papers are considered.
They must be well written and have practical application in the work of education.

Unsolicited manuscripts as well as letters of inquiry are considered. The editor
also solicits and assigns topics to writers. Manuscripts vary in length from 2,500 to
4,000 words. Payment is made at the rate of $100.00 per piece, with the copyright
being held by the publisher. Between six and eight weeks is required for an editorial
decision with four months elapsing between acceptance and publication of manuscripts. Two copies of all manuscripts are required. Authors should follow Chicago
style requirements.

101. **COLLEGE COMPOSITION AND COMMUNICATION.** 1950– . National Council of Teachers of English, 1111 Kenyon Road, Urbana, IL 61801. Circ.: 5,000. 4 issues/yr. $5.00/yr. with association membership. Annual index: every three years, December issue. Editor: Edward P. J. Corbett. Editor's address: Department of English, Ohio State University, Columbus, OH 43210. Book reviews are commissioned by editor.

Indexed in: Education Index; Language and Language Behavior Abstracts; Modern Language Abstracts.

The intended audience includes directors and teachers of college level writing courses and more generally all teachers of undergraduate English courses. Its purpose is to keep members informed of the latest theories and practices in the teaching of English courses at that level. The editor invites manuscripts pertaining to: the theory, practice, and teaching of composition or communication at all college levels; reports of research on usage, grammar, rhetoric, and the logic of composition; studies in linguistics of interest to the generalist; and, analyses of nonfiction prose commonly studied in composition courses.

Unsolicited manuscripts conforming to MLA style and of approximately 2,500 words are accepted for possible inclusion in this journal. Copyright is held by the publisher. The estimated time for an editorial decision concerning acceptability is four to six weeks. Publication follows in six to nine months. The number of book reviews varies. The February issue contains up to 25 book reviews. Length of each review is a maximum of 2,500 words. Only occasionally are reviews published in the three other issues.

102. **COLLEGE ENGLISH.** 1939– . National Council of Teachers of English, 1111 Kenyon Road, Urbana, IL 61801. Circ.: 12,000. 8 issues/yr. $15.00/yr. Annual index: April or May issue. Editor: Richard Ohmann. Editor's address: Wesleyan University, Middletown, CT 06457. Book reviews are assigned.

Indexed in: Current Contents: Social & Behavioral Sciences; Current Index to Journals in Education; dsh Abstracts; Education Index; Modern Language Abstracts; Women Studies Abstracts.

The journal is intended to be a forum for departments of English in colleges and universities. *College English* will publish articles which are calculated to have an impact on critical theory, curricular thinking, pedagogy, and related areas. Articles dealing with the working concepts of criticism (e.g., structure, genre, influence, period, myth, and rhetoric) are invited. In addition, the editor welcomes manuscripts having useful applications and implications for the profession.

Unsolicited articles of no more than 10,000 words, conforming to MLA style, are accepted for consideration. A letter of inquiry prior to submission is encouraged. An editorial decision concerning acceptability of material is given in twelve weeks, with publication of accepted manuscripts following in three months. Copyright is held by the publisher.

103. **COLLEGE STUDENT JOURNAL.** (formerly **COLLEGE STUDENT SURVEY**). 1971– (CSJ); 1967– (CSS). Project Innovation, 1362 Santa Cruz Court, Chula Vista, CA 92010. Circ.: 1,000. 4 issues/yr. $7.50/yr.; institution rate, $10.00/yr. Subscription rates include *College Student Journal Monographs*. Annual index: issue number four. Editor: Russell N. Cassel. Editor's address: P.O. Box 566, Chula Vista, CA 92010. Book reviews to: managing editor.

COLLEGE STUDENT JOURNAL (cont'd)

Indexed in: College Student Personnel Abstracts; Current Contents: Social & Behavioral Sciences; Current Index to Journals in Education; Language and Language Behavior Abstracts; Psychological Abstracts; Sociological Abstracts; Speed; Women Studies Abstracts.

This journal is intended for college students, educators, psychologists and all persons interested in college students. Included in the *Journal* are original investigations and theoretical papers as related to college students. Articles may deal with student values, attitudes, opinions and learning.

Unsolicited manuscripts, submitted in duplicate, are accepted for consideration. The APA style is to be followed and length should be about 2,000 words. A publication charge is sometimes made for accepted papers. Copyright is held by the publisher. An editorial decision is given in four weeks and the estimated time from acceptance to publication is ten to twelve months. Book reviews of 50 to 100 words appear in each issue.

104. **COLLEGE STUDENT JOURNAL MONOGRAPH.** 1971– . Project Innovation, 1362 Santa Cruz Court, Chula Vista, CA 92010. Circ.: 1,000. Number of issues varies. Subscription included with *College Student Journal.* Annual index: issue number four of *College Student Journal.* Editor: Russel N. Cassel. Editor's address: P.O. Box 566, Chula Vista, CA 92010. No book reviews.

Indexed in: College Student Personnel Abstracts; Current Contents: Social & Behavioral Sciences; Language and Language Behavior Abstracts; Psychological Abstracts; Sociological Abstracts; Speed.

The purpose of the *College Student Journal Monograph* is to provide an opportunity for publication of longer than usual articles. These materials also may be given broader dissemination because of possible use as a class text. The intended audience includes college students, professors, personnel workers and others concerned with college students.

Authors may submit manuscripts for consideration. An editorial decision concerning acceptability of the work is given in six weeks. The estimated time from acceptance to publication is ten to twelve months. Articles should conform to APA style requirements and length is not to exceed 25,000 words (100 pages). Copyright is held by the publisher and a publication charge is made for accepted papers.

105. **COLORADO JOURNAL OF EDUCATIONAL RESEARCH.** (formerly **JOURNAL OF RESEARCH SERVICES**). 1962– . Bureau of Research and the University of Northern Colorado, Chapter of Phi Delta Kappa, University of Northern Colorado, Greeley, CO 80631. Circ.: not given. 4 issues/yr. $6.00/yr. No annual index. Editor: Donald W. Chaloupka. No book reviews.

Indexed in: Current Index to Journals in Education; Exceptional Child Education Abstracts.

This journal is directed toward all members of the education profession who are interested in applied research. Its purpose is to disseminate the findings of research related to public education at all levels. Sample article titles from recent issues include: You Don't Have to Get a Degree to Learn, But; Competency

COLORADO JOURNAL OF EDUCATIONAL RESEARCH (cont'd)

Based Teacher Evaluation; Remediation of Language Skills of Navajo Children; and, Collective Bargaining Alternatives.

The editor accepts unsolicited articles for publication consideration, preferably from Colorado. Length and style requirements are not specified. Two copies of manuscripts should be submitted. Approximately two weeks is required for an editorial decision with three to six months time elapsing between acceptance and publication of a manuscript. Simultaneous submission to other journals is permitted.

106. COMMUNICATION EDUCATION. (formerly **THE SPEECH TEACHER**). 1976– (CE); 1952– (ST). Speech Communication Association, 5205 Leesburg Pike, Falls Church, VA 20041. Circ.: 5,500. 4 issues/yr. Subscription included with association membership. Annual index: November issue. Editor: Kenneth L. Brown. Editor's address: Department of Communication Studies, University of Massachusetts, Amherst, MA 01002. Book reviews to: Sharon Ratliffe, Department of Communication Arts and Sciences, Western Michigan University, Kalamazoo, MI 49001.

Indexed in: Current Contents: Social & Behavioral Sciences; Current Index to Journals in Education; dsh Abstracts; Education Index; Exceptional Child Education Abstracts; Media Review Digest; Social Sciences Citation Index.

This journal is intended for classroom teachers of speech communication in elementary, secondary, and higher education levels. Its purpose is to provide speech communication teachers with practical, well-conceived ideas and resources for developing speech communication competencies in their students. It serves as an aid to classroom teachers in applying communications theory and research to teaching and learning in all fields of study. Articles relating to all aspects of teaching speech communication are welcomed. Topics considered appropriate include interpersonal communication, small group communication, public speaking, mass communication, oral interpretation, theatre, and language development. Also included are brief descriptions of teaching practices and research articles that apply theory to classroom teaching.

Unsolicited manuscripts are accepted for consideration. Authors should follow the MLA style and length of articles may vary from 3,750 to 5,000 words. Copyright is held by the publisher. Estimated time for an editorial decision concerning acceptability is six to eight weeks. Publication follows in six months. About twelve book reviews of 500 words each appear in this journal.

107. COMMUNICATION QUARTERLY. (formerly **TODAY'S SPEECH**). 1976– (CQ); 1953– (TS). Eastern Communication Assocation, Executive Secretary, Department of Speech, University of Rhode Island, Kingston, RI 02881. Circ.: 2,700. 4 issues/yr. $15.00/yr. Annual index: fall issue. Editor: Thomas W. Benson. Editor's address: Department of Speech Communication, Pennsylvania State University, University Park, PA 16802. Book reviews to: editor.

Indexed in: Current Index to Journals in Education; dsh Abstracts; Education Index; Humanities Index.

COMMUNICATION QUARTERLY (cont'd)

This journal is intended for teachers of communication at all educational levels. Emphasis is on mass media, television, film, public speaking, forensics and theater. Its purpose is to present discussions of practical and theoretical probes of communication activities. Critical, empirical and applied studies are preferred for publication.

Unsolicited manuscripts are welcomed for consideration. The MLA style is to be followed and length may vary from 3,000 to 5,000 words. Two copies of the article are required. Simultaneous submission to other journals is permitted. Copyright is held by the publisher. Some issues are dedicated to central themes and these are announced in the journal. Estimated time for an editorial decision is four to six weeks. If accepted, publication follows in six months. Five to ten book reviews are included in each issue. These reviews are 300 to 500 words in length.

108. **COMMUNICATION RESEARCH.** 1974– . Sage Publications, Inc., 275 South Beverly Drive, Beverly Hills, CA 90212. Circ.: not given. 4 issues/yr. $12.00/yr. for professionals; institutional rate, $20.00/yr. Annual index: issue number four. Editor: F. Gerald Kline. Editor's address: Department of Journalism, Room 2040, LS & A Building, University of Michigan, Ann Arbor, MI 48104. Book reviews to: James Carey, Book Review Editor, Institute of Communication Research, University of Illinois, Urbana, IL 61801.

    Indexed in: Current Contents: Social & Behavioral Sciences; Human Resources Abstracts; Psychological Abstracts; Sage Public Administration Abstracts; Social Sciences Citation Index; Theatre and Speech Index.

The intended audience of this journal includes all persons, regardless of academic discipline, interested in communication. One of the expressed aims of *Communication Research* is the cross-discipline unification of the communication arts based upon common interests. This publication is intended to facilitate the publication of research and assist in theory building in the expanding field of communication as broadly related to other disciplines such as psychology, marketing, economics, political science, and sociology. Papers should provide theoretical contributions derived from supporting data that meet specific standards.

Unsolicited manuscripts should be submitted in triplicate. An abstract of less than 200 words must accompany each manuscript copy. A copy of the style sheet may be obtained from the editor or publisher. No length limitations are specified. *Communication Research* is a refereed journal. The copyright is held by the publisher. Potential contributors of book reviews and review essays are advised to correspond with the book review editor before submission of manuscripts. Times for an editorial decision and publication are not indicated.

109. **THE COMMUNICATOR.** (formerly **WVSBA QUARTERLY REVIEW**). 1971– (C); 1952– (WQR). West Virginia School Boards Association, P.O. Box 1008, Charleston, WV 25324. Circ.: 3,000. 4 issues/yr. Subscription included with association membership. No charge to others, controlled circulation. No annual index. Editor: John F. Scott. Book reviews to: editor.

    Indexed in: Current Index to Journals in Education; Rehabilitation Literature.

THE COMMUNICATOR (cont'd)

This journal is intended to provide information about current trends in public education. School board members, administrators, educators, legislators and interested citizens are among its readers. Regular features are messages from the president and executive secretary.

Although the editor solicits articles directly from experts in the field, authors are encouraged to submit unsolicited articles for consideration. A letter of inquiry prior to submission is recommended. Manuscript of about 750 words is desired. The editor prefers that authors use the Associated Press-United Press International style. Simultaneous submission to other journals is permitted. An editorial decision is made in one week and the estimated time from acceptance to publication is four months at the most. Book reviews are to be about 500 words long. Copyright on all materials is held by the author.

110. **COMMUNITY AND JUNIOR COLLEGE JOURNAL.** (formerly **THE JUNIOR COLLEGE JOURNAL**). 1972– (CJCJ); 1930– (JCJ). American Association of Community and Junior Colleges, One Dupont Circle, N.W., Washington, DC 20036. Circ.: 40,000. 9 issues/yr. $7.00/yr. Annual index: June/July issue. Editor: William A. Harper. No book reviews.

    Indexed in: College Student Personnel Abstracts; Current Index to Journals in Education; Education Index; Educational Administration Abstracts; Nursing Research.

This journal is intended for administrators, faculty, trustees and other interested persons of community and junior colleges. Its purpose is to stimulate educational improvement at this level of education. Articles dealing with research, new ideas and successful "how we did it" reports are preferred.

Unsolicited manuscripts are accepted for consideration. The editor states, however, that more manuscripts are received than can be used and preference is given to articles written by community and junior college personnel. A letter of inquiry is urged prior to submission. Style of contributions should follow that of the National Education Association publications. Length is to be approximately 1,500 words. An editorial decision is made in eight weeks and the estimated time from acceptance to publication may vary from five to twelve months. Copyright is held by the publisher.

111. **COMPACT.** 1966– . Education Commission of the States, 1806 Lincoln Street, Denver, CO 80203. Circ.: 13,300. 6 issues/yr. $6.00/yr. Annual index: December issue. Editor: Robert L. Jacobson. Book reviews to: editor.

    Indexed in: Current Index to Journals in Education; Education Index; Exceptional Child Education Abstracts.

The purpose of this journal is to present a variety of views on important issues in education, with special attention to state-related activities. The intended audience for this publication includes state legislators and political leaders, state education officials, and others in the fields of education and politics.

This journal does not accept unsolicited manuscripts. Query letters are welcome. The editor prefers manuscripts that range between 1,500 and 2,000 words. Payment is made upon publication with the copyright being held by the publisher. Between two

COMPACT (cont'd)

and four weeks is required for an editorial decision. Approximately three book reviews are published in each issue.

112. **COMPARATIVE EDUCATION REVIEW.** 1957– . Comparative and International Education Society, Thomas J. La Belle, Business Manager, Graduate School of Education, University of California, 405 Hilgard Avenue, Los Angeles, CA 90024. Circ.: 3,000. 3 issues/yr. $15.00/yr. Annual index: October issue. Editor: Andreas M. Kazamias. Editor's address: Education Building, Box 71, University of Wisconsin, Madison, WI 53706. Book reviews to: editor.

Indexed in: CIRF Abstracts; Current Contents: Social & Behavioral Sciences; Current Index to Journals in Education; Education Index; Public Affairs Information Service Bulletin; Social Science Citation Index; Sociology of Education Abstracts.

This journal is the official publication of the Comparative and International Education Society. The intended audience includes those individuals who are interested in international education, particularly in the relationship between school and society. It provides a forum for scholarly articles devoted to the interpretation of educational processes or problems and policies from a variety of comparative perspectives such as sociological, anthropological, political, economic or pedagogical.

Authors are encouraged to submit articles for possible inclusion in this journal. The Chicago style should be followed and the manuscript submitted in triplicate. A maximum of 7,500 words is the preferred length. Estimated time for an editorial decision concerning acceptability of an article is twelve to sixteen weeks. Time from acceptance to publication varies from six to nine months. Copyright is held by the publisher. The number of book reviews in each issue varies. Their length is 600 to 800 words. Additional information for contributors is summarized on the inside back cover of each journal.

113. **CONTEMPORARY EDUCATION.** 1929– . School of Education, Indiana State University, Terre Haute, IN 47809. Circ.: 3,700. 4 issues/yr. $7.00/yr. Annual index: summer issue. Editor: M. Dale Baughman. Editor's address: Room 201/204, Reeve Hall, Indiana State University, Terre Haute, IN 47809. Book reviews to: editor.

Indexed in: America: History and Life*; Current Contents: Social & Behavioral Sciences; Current Index to Journals in Education; Education Index; Language and Language Behavior Abstracts; Social Sciences Citation Index.

The intended audience is prospective and in-service teachers and administrators in public schools, and also university staff members and advanced degree students. Keeps educators abreast of current educational ideas, trends and issues. Prefers articles that succinctly examine dimensions of major issues, that clearly describe successful practices, and that report research findings effectively.

Half the articles are solicited by the editor; the others are unsolicited. Prior letter of inquiry is preferred. Two copies of articles, following APA style requirements, are to be submitted. Length should be 1,500 to 3,000 words. An editorial decision is given in eight weeks and publication follows in six to twelve months.

CONTEMPORARY EDUCATION (cont'd)

Copyright is held by the publisher. Sometimes an issue is dedicated to a central theme; this is noted in the journal. Two book reviews (300-600 words) appear in each issue.

114. **THE CORE TEACHER.** 1951– . National Association for Core Curriculum, Inc., 404-F Education Building, Kent State University, Kent, OH 44242. Circ.: 300. 4 issues/yr. Subscription included with association membership; non-member rate, $5.00/yr. No annual index. Editor: Gordon F. Vars. Book reviews to: editor.

Presents articles, bibliographies and research abstracts about core and related programs. Intended for teachers, administrators, curriculum directors and professors of education. Promotes the development of core, block-time, humanities, and similar interdisciplinary programs. Considers articles about interdisciplinary education.

Unsolicited manuscripts, of no specified length, are encouraged; no particular style is followed. Simultaneous submission to other journals is permitted; copyright is held by the author. An editorial decision takes about three weeks and publication is within three months. Book reviews are published on an irregular (space available) basis.

115. **COUNSELING AND VALUES.** 1956– . National Catholic Guidance Conference, a Division of American Personnel and Guidance Association, 1607 New Hampshire Avenue, N.W., Washington, DC 20009. Circ.: 800. 4 issues/yr. Subscription included with conference membership; non-member rate, $10.00/yr. Annual index: issue number four. Editor: Donald A. Biggs. Editor's address: 332 Walter Library, University of Minnesota, Minneapolis, MN 55455. Book reviews to: editor.

Indexed in: The Catholic Periodical and Literature Index; College Student Personnel Abstracts; Current Index to Journals in Education; Psychological Abstracts.

Counseling and Values is the official journal of the National Catholic Guidance Conference. Its purpose is to present theory, research, and informed opinion about problems and issues in guidance, counseling, student personnel administration, and supporting psychological services in educational institutions and school-related agencies. The editor welcomes articles inclined theoretically, philosophically, empirically or methodologically to the statement of purpose presented above.

Unsolicited articles and letters of inquiry are welcomed by the editor. Articles should be between 2,000 and 3,000 words in length and three copies of the manuscript are to be submitted. The APA style should be followed. The copyright is held by the publisher. Journal issues are dedicated to central themes and these may be obtained from the editor. Approximately twelve weeks is required for an editorial decision with six months elapsing after acceptance before publication. Book reviews are included occasionally.

116. **THE COUNSELING PSYCHOLOGIST.** 1969– . Division of Counseling Psychology, American Psychological Association. Circ.: 5,000. 4 issues/yr. Subscription included with membership in Division 17 of APA; non-member rate, $10.00/yr. No annual index. Editor: John M. Whiteley. Editor's address: Office of the Dean of Students, University of California, Irvine, Irvine, CA 92664. No book reviews.

THE COUNSELING PSYCHOLOGIST (cont'd)

Indexed in: Abstracts on Police Science*; College Student Personnel Abstracts; Current Index to Journals in Education; The Psychological Readers Guide; Social Sciences Citation Index; Social Sciences Index.

This journal is intended for counseling psychologists and other professional persons interested in the application of counseling and other behavioral science methods to the improvement of the human condition. Each issue focuses on a different topic and is created to advance the knowledge of the helping professions in a particular area. Several topics of past issues are Vocational Development Theory, Client Centered Therapy, Student Unrest, Behavioral Counseling, Black Students in Higher Education, Encounter Groups, Career Counseling and Gestalt Therapy.

The editor solicits articles and also welcomes unsolicited pieces from authors for possible inclusion in this journal. Manuscripts following APA style requirements are to be submitted in duplicate. Length of articles is negotiated with the editor. Issues are dedicated to central themes and authors should read the editor's introductory column to determine themes of future issues. An editorial decision is made in six weeks and the estimated time from acceptance to publication is four months. Copyright is held by the publisher.

117. **COUNSELOR EDUCATION AND SUPERVISION.** 1961– . Association for Counselor Education and Supervision, American Personnel and Guidance Association, 1607 New Hampshire Avenue, N.W., Washington, DC 20009. Circ.: not given. 4 issues/yr. Subscription included with ACES membership; $4.50/yr. with APGA membership; non-member rate, $6.00/yr. Editor: C. D. Kehas. Editor's address: P.O. Box 545, Manchester, NH 03105. Book review section is under consideration.

Indexed in: College Student Personnel Abstracts; Current Index to Journals in Education; Education Index; Psychological Abstracts; Social Sciences Citation Index; Women Studies Abstracts.

This journal is directed toward the publication of manuscripts concerned with research, theory development, and program applications pertinent to counselor education and supervision. It is the official publication of the Association for Counselor Education and Supervision and its contents are directed primarily toward the association membership and those interested in this field.

The editor encourages unsolicited articles for publication consideration; some contributions are invited. The APA style is specified and manuscripts may be up to 3,000 words in length. Three copies of all manuscripts are to be submitted. The copyright is held by the publisher. Journal issues are periodically dedicated to central themes. Approximately twelve weeks is required for an editorial decision with twelve months elapsing before publication of accepted manuscripts.

118. **CRIMINAL JUSTICE AND BEHAVIOR.** 1974– . Sage Publications, Inc., 275 South Beverly Drive, Beverly Hills, CA 90212. Circ.: not given. 4 issues/yr. $12.00/yr. for professionals; institutional rate, $20.00/yr. Annual index: issue number four. Editor: Stanley L. Brodsky. Editor's address: Department of Psychology, University of Alabama, Box 2968, University, AL 35486. Book reviews to: Asher Pacht, Bureau of Clinical Services, Dept. of Corrections, Box 669, Madison, WI 53706.

CRIMINAL JUSTICE AND BEHAVIOR (cont'd)

Indexed in: Abstracts in Criminology; Abstracts on Police Science*; Crime & Delinquency Literature; Current Contents: Social & Behavioral Sciences; Human Resources Abstracts; Psychological Abstracts; The Psychological Readers Guide; Public Affairs Information Service Bulletin; Sage Urban Studies Abstracts; Social Sciences Citation Index; Sociological Abstracts.

This journal, the official publication of the American Association of Correctional Psychologists, seeks to examine the behavioral, psychological, and interactional foundations of clientele and employees in the criminal justice system. It strives to present information on processes of law violation, deterrence, behavior change and functioning of systems, groups and individuals. Articles are desired which describe original research in these areas, theoretical aspects, and developments of innovative programs and practices.

Unsolicited manuscripts should be submitted in three copies to the editor. Copies of the style sheet may be obtained upon request. An abstract of no more than 100 words should accompany the manuscript. Simultaneous submission to other journals should be clearly acknowledged. The copyright is held by the American Association of Correctional Psychologists. Potential contributors to the book review section are invited to correspond with the book review editor prior to submission of manuscripts. Times for editorial decision and publication are not indicated.

119. **CURRICULUM THEORY NETWORK.** 1968— . Ontario Institute for Studies in Education, 252 Bloor Street West, Toronto, Ontario, Canada M5S 1V6. Circ.: 1,500. 4 issues/yr. $8.00/yr.; institution rate, $10.00/yr. Annual index: issue number four. Editor: Joel Weiss. Book reviewers chosen by editor.

Indexed in: Canadian Education Index; Current Contents: Social & Behavioral Sciences; Current Index to Journals in Education; Social Sciences Citation Index.

This journal is intended for teachers, principals, scholars, educational planners, administrators and curriculum developers. Its purpose is to connect ideas on curriculum theory, practice and research. The editor prefers scholarly pieces or notes on research.

The submission of unsolicited manuscripts is encouraged. Length is not specified, however, four copies must be submitted. The copyright is held by the publisher. Eight weeks is usually required for an editorial decision with publication of accepted material following approximately six months later. Authors should follow Chicago style requirements.

120. **DELTA PI EPSILON JOURNAL.** 1957— . Delta Pi Epsilon National Office, Gustavus Adolphus College, St. Peter, MN 56082. Circ.: 1,300. 4 issues/yr. $4.00/yr. No annual index. Editor: Doris and Floyd Crank. Editor's address: Department of Business Education, Northern Illinois University, DeKalb, IL 60115. No book reviews.

Indexed in: Business Education Index; Current Index to Journals in Education.

The purpose of this journal is to expand research knowledge in business education. *Delta Pi Epsilon Journal* is intended for business educators and other persons interested in research and teaching in business education. The editors prefer articles based on research, including some of the actual data obtained.

Unsolicited manuscripts are accepted and welcomed from business educators (members of the fraternity or non-members), from persons in business, and from educators in disciplines related to business education. A letter of inquiry prior to submission is encouraged. The APA style should be followed and length may vary from 2,000 to 8,000 words. Two copies of the article are required. Estimated time for an editorial decision concerning acceptability is four to six weeks. Time from acceptance to publication varies from six to twelve months. Copyright is held by the fraternity.

121. **DEVELOPMENTAL PSYCHOLOGY**. 1969– . American Psychological Association, Inc., 1200 Seventeenth Street, N.W., Washington, DC 20036. Circ.: not given. 6 issues/yr. $10.00/yr. with APA membership; non-member rate, $30.00/yr. Annual index: November issue. Editor: Richard D. Odom. Editor's address: Department of Psychology, 134 Wesley Hall, Vanderbilt University, Nashville, TN 37240. No book reviews.

Indexed in: Child Development Abstracts and Bibliography; College Student Personnel Abstracts; Current Contents: Social & Behavioral Sciences; Current Index to Journals in Education; dsh Abstracts; Excerpta Medica; Information Retrieval Limited; Psychological Abstracts; The Psychological Readers Guide; Social Sciences Index; Women Studies Abstracts.

This journal is intended to reach those persons interested in the psychological and physical development of humans and other animals. Its purpose is to publish articles that significantly advance knowledge about growth and development. The editor is interested in empirical research in which the developmental implications are clear.

Unsolicited articles are welcomed for editorial consideration. These works should be between 3,750 and 5,000 words in length and follow the APA style format. Articles are to be submitted in triplicate. The copyright is held by the publisher. Six weeks is required for an editorial decision with at least eight and one-half months elapsing after acceptance before publication.

122. **THE DIAPASON**. 1909– . The Diapason Office of Publication, 434 South Wabash Avenue, Chicago, IL 60605. Circ.: 8,000. 12 issues/yr. $7.50/yr. Annual index: January issue. Editor: Robert Schuneman. Book reviews are assigned.

Indexed in: The Music Index.

The Diapason is intended for professional players, teachers, designers and builders of pipe organs and harpsichords, church musicians, pipe organ enthusiasts of serious music, and composers of music for these instruments. Its purpose is to provide articles on music, instruments and related matters to the intended audience. The publication also provides monthly news in the profession, including news of appointments, deaths, retirements, professional activities, and a calendar of national scope. Articles conform to magazine format and deal with historical, interpretative or theoretical music.

THE DIAPASON (cont'd)

About one-half of the articles in this publication are solicited by the editor and the remainder are selected from unsolicited manuscripts. The Chicago style is to be followed and copyright may be held by either the author or publisher. No restrictions are placed on length of material, except that manuscripts which must be serialized beyond three issues are not accepted. Contributors can expect an editorial decision in eight weeks. Publication follows in eight to twelve months. The number of book and performance reviews varies. Unsolicited reviews are never accepted.

123. **DISSEMINATION SERVICES ON THE MIDDLE GRADES.** 1970– .
Educational Leadership Institute, Inc., P.O. Box 863, Springfield, MA 01101.
Circ.: 700. 9 issues/yr. $6.00/yr. No annual index. Editor: Philip Pumerantz and James Beane. No book reviews.

This publication is intended for educators and others concerned with the education of the emerging adolescent learner. It deals with modern practices in the middle grades and offers ideas for implementing change. The editors prefer practical and useful articles relative to the middle school movement.

Articles are solicited directly by the editors, however, unsolicited manuscripts and letters of inquiry are welcomed. The style is open and length should be 2,000 words. Two copies of the work are required. Copyright is held by the publisher. An editorial decision is made in ten weeks and the estimated time from acceptance to publication is two months. Issues are dedicated to central themes and authors may obtain future themes by writing the editor.

124. **DRAMATICS.** (formerly **THE HIGH SCHOOL THESPIAN**). 1929– (HST).
The International Thespian Society, Publisher, College Hill Station, Box E, Cincinnati, OH 45224. Circ.: 55,000. 5 issues/yr. $3.00/yr. with society membership; non-member rate, $5.00/yr. Annual index: May-June issue. Editor: Thomas A. Barker. Book reviews are staff written.
Indexed in: Current Contents: Social & Behavioral Sciences.

This journal is the official magazine of The International Thespian Society, a non-secret, non-social honorary society devoted to the advancement and improvement of theatre arts in secondary schools around the world and to raising the consciousness of all to fine theatre. The editor indicates that 40,000 of its readers are student members of the society. Even though *Dramatics* is published by, and serves the membership of, The Thespian Society, it is not considered a "house organ."

The editor solicits articles directly from persons in this field of study, but also welcomes unsolicited manuscripts for consideration. The MLA style is to be followed and the preferred length is 2,000 words. Copyright is held by the publisher, who pays authors an honorarium that varies from $15.00 to $40.00 per contribution. The maximum time required for an editorial decision regarding acceptability is twelve weeks, occasionally slightly longer. Publication of accepted articles follows in about two months. A detailed sheet of guidelines for authors is available from the editor.

125. DRUGS IN HEALTH CARE. 1974– . American Society of Hospital Pharmacists Research and Education Foundation, Inc., 4630 Montgomery Avenue, Washington, DC 20014. Circ.: 1,000. 4 issues/yr. $15.00/yr. Annual index: fall issue. Editor: George P. Provost. Book reviews to: editor.

Indexed in: International Pharmaceutical Abstracts.

This journal serves as a vehicle for articles on drug-related health services research. It is intended for health practitioners, administrators, researchers, teachers, sociologists and economists. Research reports of the social, administrative and economic aspects of drug use process are included in this journal. Articles also desired for inclusion are those dealing with conceptual problems regarding the provision of drugs and drug-related services and those related to public policy considerations in legitimate drug use.

The editor welcomes unsolicited manuscripts for consideration. A letter of inquiry prior to submission is encouraged. Length of articles may range from 3,000 to 5,000 words and two copies of the work are required. Style is not specified and copyright is held by the publisher. Estimated time for an editorial decision is four to six weeks and publication of accepted articles follows in three to six months. The four to six book reviews in this publication are from 300 to 500 words long. Complete information for authors is printed in each issue of *Drugs in Health Care.*

126. THE DUKE DIVINITY SCHOOL REVIEW. (formerly **DUKE DIVINITY SCHOOL BULLETIN**). 1936– (DDSB). Divinity School, Duke University, Durham, NC 27706. Circ.: 3,000. 3 issues/yr. No charge, controlled circulation. No annual index. Editor: Creighton Lacy. Book reviews to: editor.

Indexed in: Index to Religious Periodical Literature.

This journal is intended for alumni, campus chaplains, seminaries, departments of religious education and church leaders throughout the nation. It provides examples of lectures and research being presented at the school, and articles which deal with specific themes of theological education and disciplines. The editor is interested in material which is of intellectual or practical stimulation to ministers.

Outside articles from non-faculty are solicited only for planned themes, but unsolicited manuscripts are considered by the editorial committee. Manuscripts should be between 3,000 and 5,000 words in length. Simultaneous submission to other journals is permitted and the copyright is held by the publisher. Three weeks is required for an editorial decision with three months being required for publication following acceptance. Between ten and twelve book reviews are published in each issue. These reviews should have relevance to the ministry or theological education and be approximately 500 words in length. All work should be written following the Chicago style.

127. ERIC/HIGHER EDUCATION RESEARCH REPORTS. 1972– . ERIC/Higher Education, The George Washington University and the American Association for Higher Education. Circ.: 2,500. 10 issues/yr. $15.00/yr. with AAHE membership; non-member rate, $25.00/yr. No annual index. Editor: William V. Mayville. Manuscript to: Jonathan D. Fife, Associate Director, ERIC/Higher Education, The George Washington University, One Dupont Circle, Suite 630, Washington, DC 20036. No book reviews.

The intended audience of this publication includes everyone concerned with higher education. Its purpose is to synthesize and analyze the latest literature that relates to the critical issues in higher education with particular attention to the literature cited in *Resources in Education* and available through the ERIC microfiche library. Topics and authors are selected by a review panel. Each issue contains one report or research study.

Manuscripts are solicited directly by the director and associate director who also welcome proposals and letters of inquiry from authors. The APA style is to be followed and length may range from 12,500 to 18,750 words (50 to 75 pages). Two copies of the work should be submitted. Copyright of material is not allowed. The publisher pays authors at a rate that is negotiated. A guide for preparation of manuscripts is available from the editor. Estimated time for an editorial decision concerning acceptability is four to eight weeks. Publication time is not specified.

128. **EARLY YEARS.** 1971– . Allen Raymond, Inc., 11 Hale Lane, Darien, CT 06820. Circ.: 100,000. 9 issues/yr. $8.00/yr. No annual index. Editor: Allen A. Raymond. Manuscript to: Lorraine Ulrich, Managing Editor. Book reviews are staff written.

 Indexed in: Exceptional Child Education Abstracts; Rehabilitation Literature.

This journal is intended for teachers of preschool through grade three. It strives to be of maximum help to teachers of these primary grades. The emphasis is on usefulness. Practical, current ideas on teaching for the primary grades are preferred for inclusion in *Early Years*. Appearing regularly in this journal are columns entitled: Exceptional Child; Classroom Management; Curriculum; Skill Building (over 100 ideas monthly) Section; and various features dealing with mathematics, reading, open classrooms and related areas.

Unsolicited manuscripts are accepted for consideration, however, a letter of inquiry prior to submission is recommended. The editor has no special style requirements. Length should be about 1,000 words. The publisher pays authors at a rate that varies and copyright is held by the publisher. Contributors may expect an editorial decision in three weeks and publication of accepted material follows in three months.

129. **EDCENTRIC.** 1969– . Center for Educational Reform, Inc., P.O. Box 10085, Eugene, OR 97401. Circ.: 5,000. 6 issues/yr. $6.00/yr.; institutional rate, $10.00/yr. No annual index. Editorial collective. Book reviews to: editorial collective.

 Indexed in: Alternative Press Index; Current Index to Journals in Education; Women Studies Abstracts.

This journal contains primarily non-fiction articles dealing with education and social change and is directed toward both students and teachers. Its purpose is to aid people in making the connection between educational innovation and the larger, over-all movement for social and political change. The editors welcome non-fiction essays on various aspects of the movement for social change, particularly those pieces which tie in educational change with the other aspects of social change.

EDCENTRIC (cont'd)

Unsolicited manuscripts are welcomed by the editors who also solicit articles directly from persons in this field of study. Articles should be between 3,000 and 5,000 words in length with the copyright being held by the publisher. Journal issues usually are dedicated to central themes which are announced in the journal in advance of the publication deadline. Simultaneous submission to other journals is permitted but should be discussed with the editor(s). Between four and seven weeks is required for an editorial decision with one to three months elapsing between acceptance and publication. Book reviews are accepted and may be up to 2,000 words in length. The only limitation cited is that the books be of interest and use to the readership of this journal. No preferred style is specified.

130. EDNEWS. (formerly **SCHOOL NEWS**). 1975– (E); 1962– (SN). Kentucky Department of Education, Capitol Plaza Tower, Frankfort, KY 40601. Circ.: 12,500. 9 issues/yr. No charge, controlled circulation. No annual index. Editor: Nancy Carpenter. Editor's address: 1634 Capitol Plaza Tower, Frankfort, KY 40601. Book reviews to: editor.

This tabloid is intended for teachers, administrators and other educational personnel in Kentucky. Also among its audience are legislators, media personnel and others concerned with Kentucky education. Its purpose is to inform its readers of department news and of the programs available from the Department of Education. Articles on innovative classroom techniques and programs, and background articles on educational issues such as funding and accountability, are preferred.

Since *Ednews* is directed specifically to educators in Kentucky, manuscripts are not generally solicited or accepted. However, consideration will be given to manuscripts on topics which would appeal to, and be of concern to, Kentucky educators. Style requirements of the Associated Press are to be followed. Length is not specified. Some issues are dedicated to central themes and prospective contributors should query the editor for future topics. An editorial decision is given in six weeks and publication time varies. Book reviews are an occasional feature.

131. EDUCATING CHILDREN: EARLY AND MIDDLE YEARS. (formerly **KEEPING UP WITH ELEMENTARY EDUCATION**). 1972– (ECEMY); 1956– (KUEE). American Association of Elementary-Kindergarten-Nursery Educators, 1201 Sixteenth Street, N.W., Washington, DC 20036. Circ.: 3,000. 3 issues/yr. Subscription included with association membership. No annual index. Submit manuscripts to editor. Unsolicited book reviews not accepted.

This journal is intended for all professional personnel involved in the education of preschool through upper elementary children. Through this journal the sponsoring association seeks to promote a humanistic kind of education which is supportive of a child's way of learning, as well as to sustain the professional growth of educators. The editor is seeking manuscripts which reflect this philosophy and emphasize practical classroom implementation.

Unsolicited manuscripts as well as letters of inquiry are welcomed by the editor. The maximum length of articles should be 1,500 words and two copies of the manuscript are to be submitted. The copyright is held by the publisher. Simultaneous submission to other journals is permitted. Eight weeks is required for an

EDUCATING CHILDREN: EARLY AND MIDDLE YEARS (cont'd)

editorial decision with publication of accepted manuscripts following within three to eight months. The editorship changes each year, therefore, manuscripts are sent to the association office.

132. **EDUCATION.** 1880– . Project Innovation, P.O. Box 566, Chula Vista, CA 92010. Circ.: 3,500. 4 issues/yr. $7.50/yr.; institution rate, $12.00/yr. Annual index: issue number four. Editor: Russell N. Cassel. Book reviews to: editor.

Indexed in: Current Contents: Social & Behavioral Sciences; Current Index to Journals in Education; Education Index; Educational Administration Abstracts; Guide to Social Science and Religion in Periodical Literature; Language and Language Behavior Abstracts; Psychological Abstracts; Social Abstracts, Inc.; Sociological Abstracts; Technical Education Abstracts; Women Studies Abstracts.

This journal is intended for educators, psychologists and all other persons interested in education. *Education* includes articles which deal with innovations as related to school practices. Manuscripts may describe proposed or actual innovations in education at all levels and every area of learning.

Articles are solicited for special theme issues. Unsolicited manuscripts are welcomed for other issues. Two copies of the work should be submitted. Length may range from 2,000 to 3,000 words and the APA style requirements are to be followed. Copyright on accepted materials is held by the publisher. Generally, authors pay for publication of their work. Rates and other publication information are included in a guide available from the editor. Contributors may expect an editorial decision in four weeks. Publication of accepted material follows in twelve months. The twelve to fourteen book reviews contained in *Education* are about 150 words each.

133. **EDUCATION AND URBAN SOCIETY.** 1968– . Sage Publications, Inc., 275 South Beverly Drive, Beverly Hills, CA 90212. Circ.: not given. 4 issues/yr. $12.00/yr. for professionals; institutional rate, $20.00/yr. Annual index: issue number four. Editor: guest editor each issue. No book reviews.

Indexed in: America: History and Life*; Current Contents: Social & Behavioral Sciences; Current Index to Journals in Education; Educational Administration Abstracts; Human Resources Abstracts; Index to Periodical Articles Related to Law; Public Affairs Information Service Bulletin; Sage Public Administration Abstracts; Sage Urban Studies Abstracts; Social Sciences Citation Index; Sociological Abstracts; Sociology of Education Abstracts; Urban Affairs Abstracts.

This quarterly is intended for social scientists, particularly those who are interested in research and opinion dealing with urban society and with education as a social institution. The primary thrust of this journal is to present views on the various means of improving the urban educational environment and the administration of urban schools. Articles related to education both as an institution and as an emerging force for social change are preferred.

EDUCATION AND URBAN SOCIETY (cont'd)

Each issue of *Education and Urban Society* is devoted to a special topic under the direction of an invited guest editor. Unsolicited manuscripts are not accepted and will be returned to authors. Further information about the journal's format and editorial policies may be obtained from the publisher. Times for an editorial decision and publication are not indicated. Copyright is held by the publisher.

134. **EDUCATION CANADA.** (formerly **CANADIAN EDUCATION AND RESEARCH DIGEST** and **CANADIAN EDUCATION**). 1969– (EC); 1961– (CERD); 1945– (CE). Canadian Education Association, 252 Bloor Street West, Toronto, Ontario, Canada M5S 1V5. Circ.: 4,500. 4 issues/yr. Subscription included with association membership; institution rate, $5.00/yr. Annual index: winter issue. Editor: Harriett Goldsborough. Book reviews written by staff.

Indexed in: Canadian Education Index; Canadian Periodical Index; Current Contents: Social & Behavioral Sciences; Current Index to Journals in Education; Education Index; Educational Administration Abstracts; Exceptional Child Education Abstracts; Sociology of Education Abstracts; Speed; Women Studies Abstracts.

Education Canada provides a forum for opinions and ideas on Canadian school systems and serves as a vehicle for keeping the association membership and other educators informed about current views on elementary and secondary education. Its intended audience, in addition to association members, includes senior education officials (directors of education and superintendents of schools), school boards, school trustees, administrative officials in provincial departments of education, and heads of teacher training institutions.

Articles are solicited directly by the editor who also welcomes unsolicited manuscripts for consideration. Style is a combination of that of the *Toronto Star* and the Oxford University Press. Length may vary from 2,000 to 5,000 words. Copyright is held by the publisher. An editorial decision is given in seven weeks and publication follows in four to six months. A set of guidelines for prospective contributors may be obtained from the editor.

135. **EDUCATION OF THE VISUALLY HANDICAPPED.** (formerly **INTERNATIONAL JOURNAL FOR THE EDUCATION OF THE BLIND**). 1969– (EVH); 1951– (IJEB). Association for Education of the Visually Handicapped, 919 Walnut Street, 4th Floor, Philadelphia, PA 19107. Circ.: not given. 4 issues/yr. Subscription included with association membership; non-member rate, $6.00/yr. Annual index: December issue. Editor: Don L. Walker. Editor's address: Department of Special Education, 152 Ruffner Hall, University of Virginia, Charlottesville, VA 22903. Book reviews to: editor.

Indexed in: Current Contents: Social & Behavioral Sciences; Current Index to Journals in Education; Education Index; Exceptional Child Education Abstracts; Psychological Abstracts; Rehabilitation Literature.

This journal is designed to disseminate research results and implications, descriptions of programs, and "how to do it" articles. The audience consists primarily of teacher educators and educators of visually impaired children. A president's page and editorial are regular features of *Education of the Visually Handicapped*.

Unsolicited manuscripts and letters of inquiry are welcomed by the editor. The APA style is to be followed and the maximum length desired is 3,500 words. Two copies of the article should be submitted. Copyright is held by the publisher. Contributors may expect an editorial decision in six to eight weeks. If accepted, publication normally follows in three to six months. Book reviews, usually not more than two per issue, are no more than 1,500 words in length.

136. EDUCATION UPDATE. 1966– . Minnesota Department of Education, 760 Capitol Square, St. Paul, MN 55101. Circ.: 65,000. 9 issues/yr. $2.50/yr. No annual index. Editor: James Lee. Book reviews to: editor.

This tabloid is intended for all teachers in the State of Minnesota. Its purpose is to communicate State Department policies and activities as well as significant educational activities of the state school system. The editor prefers feature type articles.

Unsolicited manuscripts as well as letters of inquiry are encouraged. The editor also solicits manuscripts on specific topics. Simultaneous submission to other publications is permitted. This newsletter is not copyrighted. Contributors can expect an editorial decision in two weeks. One to three months usually elapses between acceptance and publication of manuscripts. Book reviews in varying numbers are used as space is available. No length is specified.

137. EDUCATION U.S.A. 1958– . National School Public Relations Association, 1801 North Moore Street, Arlington, VA 22209. Circ.: 14,000. 52 issues/yr. $34.00/yr. Annual index: twice yearly. Editor: Rose Marie Levey, Executive Editor. Book reviews to: executive editor.

The purpose of this publication is to provide the most recent coverage possible of news, trends, legislative developments and federal programs affecting education. Its intended audience includes school superintendents and principals, school board members, state and national legislators and any others concerned with education. This weekly newspaper has as a regular feature a preview page of books, magazines, television programs and reports.

The editor solicits material directly, but also accepts unsolicited articles for consideration. A letter of inquiry prior to submission is encouraged. The APA style requirements are to be followed and the preferred length is 550 words. Copyright is held by the publisher, who pays authors at the rate of $100.00 per page for acceptable material. An editorial decision is given in one week and publication follows in one month or less. One book review of 170 words appears in each issue of *Education U.S.A.*

138. EDUCATIONAL ADMINISTRATION QUARTERLY. 1965– . University Council for Educational Administration, 29 West Woodruff Avenue, Columbus, OH 43210. Circ.: not given. 3 issues/yr. $10.00/yr. Annual index: autumn issue. Editor: F. Don Carver. Editor's address: 325 Education Building, University of Illinois, Urbana, IL 61801. Book reviews to: Donald Anderson,

EDUCATIONAL ADMINISTRATION QUARTERLY (cont'd)

Associate Dean, College of Education, The Ohio State University, Columbus, OH 43210.
Indexed in: Current Index to Journals in Education; Education Index; Educational Administration Abstracts.

This journal is directed toward professors, graduate students, and practitioners in educational administration and related fields. Its purpose is to promote communication among students of educational administration. The editor is interested in manuscripts dealing with conceptualized formulations, reports of empirical research, problem identification and field definition as well as policy analysis in the field.

The editor is interested in receiving unsolicited manuscripts. These works should be between 3,500 and 5,000 words in length and submitted in three copies. Style is not specified but all footnotes should be numbered and placed at the end of the manuscript. The copyright is held by the publisher. The estimated time for an editorial decision is eight weeks and the time for publication of a manuscript after acceptance is between three and twelve months. Approximately two to three book reviews are published in each issue.

139. **EDUCATIONAL & INDUSTRIAL TELEVISION.** 1968– . C. S. Tepfer Publishing Company, Inc., 607 Main Street, Ridgefield, CT 06877. Circ.: 25,000. 12 issues/yr. $12.00/yr. Annual index: January issue. Editor: Mary M. Woolf, Managing Editor. No book reviews.
Indexed in: Current Index to Journals in Education; Media Review Digest.

This journal is intended for professionals who use television for non-commercial applications in schools, business, industry, hospitals and medical centers, public broadcasting stations, and wherever television is used for training, teaching, or information dissemination. Its purpose is to enable these professionals to do their jobs better, quicker and more easily. The journal provides ideas for applications of television to their jobs, solutions to technical and production problems, and helps to keep them abreast of new products, programs, literature, and developments in the television field. Articles preferred are those that are factual and based on concrete experience.

The editor welcomes unsolicited manuscripts and letters of inquiry. The Chicago style is to be followed but with some modifications. It is recommended that prospective contributors examine the one page style guidelines for authors that is available from the editor. Length may vary from 500 to 2,500 words but these are suggested lengths only. Content is more important than length for inclusion in this journal. Copyright is held by the publisher. Some issues are dedicated to central themes and authors should request a list of these from the editor. Estimated time for an editorial decision concerning acceptability of an article is eight to twelve weeks. Publication time ranges from two to twelve months.

140. **EDUCATIONAL AND PSYCHOLOGICAL MEASUREMENT.** 1941– . Educational and Psychological Measurement, Box 6907 College Station, Durham, NC 27708. Circ.: 3,500. 4 issues/yr. $20.00/yr. Annual index: winter issue. Editor: W. Scott Gehman. Book reviews to: Max Engelhart, 2419 Perkins Road, Durham, NC 27705.

Indexed in: College Student Personnel Abstracts; Computer and
Information Systems Abstracts; Current Contents: Social & Behavioral
Sciences; Current Index to Journals in Education; dsh Abstracts;
Education Index; Psychological Abstracts; Science Citation Index;
Sociological Abstracts; Women Studies Abstracts.

This publication is intended for those in the profession and for others interested
in the field of educational and psychological measurement. One purpose of *Educational
and Psychological Measurement* is to provide a forum for the discussion of problems
associated with the measurement field. Research articles dealing with tests and measurement instrument use and development are sought. Another focus of this journal
is the presentation of reports which describe testing programs.

Unsolicited manuscripts are sought by the editor. Authors should follow the
APA style and are to submit two copies of the manuscript. The copyright is held by
the publisher. Length limitations are not given. A page charge is assessed the author
upon acceptance for publication. The estimated time for an editorial decision is
six to eight weeks with publication of accepted manuscripts following in twenty-
four months. Approximately eight to ten book reviews appear in each issue of this
journal.

141. **EDUCATIONAL CONSIDERATIONS.** 1973– . College of Education, Holton
Hall, Kansas State University, Manhattan, KS 66506. Circ.: 1,200. 3 issues/yr.
$4.00/yr. No annual index. Editors: Charles E. Litz and Sandra Williams Ernst.
Manuscript to: Charles E. Litz. Book reviews to: Charles E. Litz.

The intent of this journal is to provide educators with general interest articles
on the educational scene which cross disciplines and levels. The editors prefer articles on innovations, analyses of current practices, case studies, perspectives and
debates.

The editors solicit manuscripts directly from professionals, but also accept
unsolicited articles for consideration. A letter of inquiry prior to submission is encouraged. Occasional issues are dedicated to central themes and these are announced in
the journal. Preferred length of contributions is 1,500 to 2,000 words. The MLA
style requirements should be followed and copyright is held by the author. An
editorial decision concerning acceptability is given in ten weeks. Publication time
varies from three to six months.

142. **THE EDUCATIONAL FORUM.** 1936– . Kappa Delta Pi, P.O. Box A, West
Lafayette, IN 47906. Circ.: 55,000. 4 issues/yr. $7.00/yr. Annual index: May
issue. Editor: Jack R. Frymier. Editor's address: The Ohio State University,
116 Ramseyer Hall, 29 West Woodruff Avenue, Columbus, OH 43210. Book
reviews to: editor.

Indexed in: Current Index to Journals in Education; Education Index;
Educational Administration Abstracts; Sociological Abstracts; Women
Studies Abstracts.

The basic purpose of this journal is to stimulate professional discussion of
contemporary problems in education. The *Forum* is a refereed journal and is
committed to presenting scholarly analyses and interpretations of important

THE EDUCATIONAL FORUM (cont'd)

educational issues. Acceptance of articles for inclusion is based upon the potential interest and usefulness to practicing and prospective educators.

Unsolicited manuscripts are accepted for consideration. The Chicago style is to be followed and two copies should be submitted. Length may range from 1,500 to 7,500 words. Copyright is held by the publisher. An editorial decision is made in twelve weeks and publication of accepted material follows in twelve months. Ten book reviews of 750 to 1,000 words each are included in issues of this journal.

143. EDUCATIONAL FREEDOM. 1962– . The Research Committee, Educational Freedom Foundation, 20 Parkland Avenue, Glendale, MO 63122. Circ.: 1,000. 2 issues/yr. $2.00/yr. No annual index. Editor: Daniel D. McGarry. Editor's address: Department of History, Saint Louis University, Saint Louis, MO 63103. Book reviews to: editor.

Indexed in: Index to Periodical Articles Related to Law.

This publication is intended primarily for parents and teachers. Its purpose is to explore means of pursuing and promoting freedom in education. Articles on various aspects of educational freedom, diversity and progress are preferred for inclusion in *Educational Freedom.*

The editor welcomes unsolicited manuscripts for consideration. Letters of inquiry prior to submission are encouraged. Style is not specified and length may range from 1,250 to 6,250 words. Simultaneous submission to other journals is permitted. Contributors can expect an editorial decision concerning acceptability in two weeks. Publication follows in one to four months. The two to three book reviews in each issue are 250 to 500 words in length. Copyright on all materials is held by the publisher.

144. EDUCATIONAL HORIZONS. (formerly PI LAMBDA THETA JOURNAL). 1933– (EH); 1921– (PLTJ). Pi Lambda Theta, 2000 East 8th Street, Bloomington, IN 47401. Circ.: 20,000. 4 issues/yr. Subscription included with association membership; non-member rate, $5.00/yr. No annual index. Submit manuscripts to editor. Book reviews to: editor.

Indexed in: Current Contents: Social & Behavioral Sciences; Current Index to Journals in Education; Education Index.

Educational Horizons is the official publication of Pi Lambda Theta, a national honor and professional association for women in education. This journal is intended for educators at all levels of the profession. Its purpose is the dissemination of knowledgeable articles in the hope of challenging everyone who is concerned with education to approach today's problems from an objective standpoint, utilizing factual information which is available. In addition it strives to stimulate, conduct, and utilize research, one of the stated purposes of the association.

Three issues each year are dedicated to central themes, for which articles are solicited by the editor. Unsolicited articles are welcomed for editorial consideration for the fourth issue. Two copies of all manuscripts should be submitted. Length may vary from 4,000 to 6,000 words. Authors should follow Chicago style requirements. Simultaneous submission to other journals is permitted. The journal contents are not copyrighted. Eight weeks is required for an editorial decision. Publication of accepted manuscripts usually follows within six months. The journal publishes occasional book reviews. These reviews are 250 to 750 words in length.

145. **EDUCATIONAL LEADERSHIP.** 1943– . Association for Supervision and Curriculum Development, 1701 K Street, N.W., Suite 1100, Washington, DC 20006. Circ.: 22,500. 8 issues/yr. Subscription included with association membership; non-member rate, $10.00/yr. Annual index: May issue. Editor: Robert R. Leeper. Book reviews to: editor.

Indexed in: Book Review Index; Business Education Index; Current Contents: Social & Behavioral Sciences; Current Index to Journals in Education; Education Index; Educational Administration Abstracts; Exceptional Child Education Abstracts; Index to Periodical Articles Related to Law; Readers Guide to Periodical Literature; Women Studies Abstracts.

Educational Leadership is the official journal of the Association for Supervision and Curriculum Development. Its content is directed to ASCD members and other interested educators. Issues are dedicated to central themes and future topics are published in the spring issues. Feature articles by leading educators, news of curriculum development, book reviews, and reports of curriculum research are included.

The editor solicits material directly from professionals in the field, but also accepts unsolicited manuscripts for consideration. Preferred length of articles is 1,500 words and two copies are to be submitted. Style requirements are not specified. Copyright is held by the publisher. An editorial decision concerning acceptability, and publication of accepted work, occur as soon as possible. Five or six book reviews are included in each issue of this journal and each of these is about 400 words long.

146. **EDUCATIONAL PERSPECTIVES.** 1962– . University of Hawaii, Manoa, College of Education, 1776 University Avenue, Honolulu, HI 96822. Circ.: 1,000. 4 issues/yr. $2.00/yr. No annual index. Editor: Alex L. Pickens. No book reviews.

Indexed in: Current Index to Journals in Education.

This journal is designed for professional educators from elementary through university level and for all interested lay persons. It is intended to disseminate current information, ideas, and philosophies of education in Hawaii and the Pacific, as well as the continental United States. The editor prefers articles which deal with themes adopted at least one year in advance of publication.

Unsolicited articles are considered for publication but they must be in keeping with the adopted themes. A letter of inquiry to the editor concerning future themes is recommended. Articles should be between 2,500 and 3,500 words in length. Simultaneous submission to other journals is permitted. The copyright is held by the publisher. Three weeks is required for an editorial decision. No time is given for publication delay. All manuscripts should adhere to the Chicago style.

147. **EDUCATIONAL PSYCHOLOGIST.** 1963– . Division of Educational
Psychology, American Psychological Association, 1200 17th Street, N.W.,
Washington, DC 20036. Circ.: 3,700. 3 issues/yr. Subscription included with
Division 15 membership; non-member rate, $5.00/yr.; institution rate,
$10.00/yr. Annual index: issue number three. Editor: Frank H. Farley.
Editor's address: Educational Sciences Building, Room 878, 1025 West
Johnson Street, Madison, WI 53706. Book reviewers chosen by editor.
    Indexed in: Psychological Abstracts.

The intended audience of this journal includes educational psychologists and
others interested in the application of psychology to education, or the relationship
of psychology and education. It provides discussion and serves as a forum for matters bearing on educational psychology. Activities of the Division of Educational
Psychology and its members are reported also. Articles dealing with theories or
models, in-depth essays, and critiques of relevance to educational psychology are
preferred for this journal.

    Unsolicited manuscripts are welcomed for consideration. The APA style is
to be followed and the original plus three copies of the article are to be submitted.
Authors are given no length restrictions. Copyright is held by the publisher. Times
required for an editorial decision and publication are not indicated.

148. **EDUCATIONAL RECORD.** 1920– . American Council on Education, One
Dupont Circle, Washington, DC 20036. Circ.: 10,000. 4 issues/yr. $14.00/yr.
Annual index: fall issue. Editor: Clifford B. Fair. Book reviews to: editor.
    Indexed in: College Student Personnel Abstracts; Current Contents: Social
& Behavioral Sciences; Current Index to Journals in Education; Education
Index; Educational Administration Abstracts; Index to Periodical Articles
Related to Law; Psychological Abstracts; Public Affairs Information Service
Bulletin; Women Studies Abstracts.

This journal is intended to be read by college and university administrators as
well as faculty and other persons interested in higher education. Its purpose is to
present information which may be of use to those engaged in higher education. The
journal is not designed to advance a special point of view. The editor welcomes
"controversy and variety, constrained only by standards of quality."

    Unsolicited manuscripts are welcomed for editorial consideration. The pre-
ferred length for articles is approximately 4,000 words. The journal has its own
style sheet which is available upon request. The copyright is held by the publisher.
Eight weeks is required for an editorial decision with three months being the usual
delay for publication following acceptance. Between two and four book reviews
are published in each issue. No other specifications are given.

149. **EDUCATIONAL RESEARCHER.** 1972– . American Educational Research
Association, 1126 Sixteenth Street, N.W., Washington, DC 20036. Circ.:
13,000. 11 issues/yr. $10.00/yr.; institution rate, $12.00/yr. Annual index:
issue number eleven. Editor: Richard E. Schutz. Editor's address: Office
of the Editor, 4665 Lampson Avenue, Los Alamitos, CA 90720. Book
reviews to: editor.
    Indexed in: Current Index to Journals in Education; Educational
Administration Abstracts; Exceptional Child Education Abstracts;
Sociology of Education Abstracts.

EDUCATIONAL RESEARCHER (cont'd)

This journal is intended for members of the AERA as well as others interested in research. The editorial board seeks scholarly articles, but prefers those which are written in relatively non-technical language. Manuscripts should emphasize the applicability of the topic to the field of education, particularly to research and development. Sample article titles from recent issues are: Women in Educational Governance—A Statistical Portrait; The Place of Theory in Educational Research; and, Decision Process Paradigms in Education.

Unsolicited manuscripts as well as letters of inquiry are welcomed for editorial consideration. All manuscripts should be 5,000 words or less in length and submitted in duplicate. The copyright is held by the publisher. Two weeks is required for a preliminary editorial decision. Following preliminary acceptance articles are submitted to a panel of referees for final editorial decision. The time necessary for this process is not estimated. Publication following final acceptance occurs within two months. Essay reviews of books and other materials are considered. No other editorial specifications are indicated. A style sheet is available upon request.

150. EDUCATIONAL THEATRE JOURNAL. 1949— . University and College Theatre Association, a division of American Theatre Association, Inc., 1029 Vermont Avenue, N.W., Washington, DC 20005. Circ.: 5,500. 4 issues/yr. Subscription included with association membership; library rate, $15.00/yr. Annual index: December issue. Editor: Virginia Scott. Editor's address: 82 Perham Street, Farmington, ME 04938. Book reviews are usually assigned.

Indexed in: Current Contents: Social & Behavioral Sciences; Current Index to Journals in Education; Education Index; Humanities Index; Modern Language Abstracts; Modern Language Bibliography.

Educational Theatre Journal provides an outlet for scholarship and criticism in the theatre arts. It is intended for members of university theatre departments and especially for all persons interested in theatre criticism and history. Among the regular features are translations of documents or foreign essays, reviews of theatre productions in university and professional theatres around the world, and book reviews.

Unsolicited articles are welcomed for consideration. Manuscripts should conform to the MLA style and are to be no longer than 10,000 words. Copyright is held by the publisher, but permission to reprint always is granted to the author. Some issues are dedicated to central themes and these are announced in advance in the journal. An editorial decision concerning acceptability is given within eight weeks. Publication time varies but usually is nine months. About 12 theatre reviews and 12 book reviews are included in this journal. Most book reviews are solicited directly from selected professionals. About one-half of the theatre reviews are solicited and the remainder are unsolicited. Review editors are listed in each issue.

151. EDUCATIONAL THEORY. 1951— . John Dewey Society and the Philosophy of Education Society, Editorial Office, Education Building, University of Illinois, Urbana, IL 61801. Circ.: 2,500. 4 issues/yr. $7.00/yr. with society membership; non-member rate, $10.00/yr. Annual index: fall issue. Editor:

EDUCATIONAL THEORY (cont'd)

Joe R. Burnett. Manuscript to: editorial assistant. Book reviews to: editorial assistant.

Indexed in: Current Contents: Social & Behavioral Sciences; Current Index to Journals in Education; Education Index; Language and Language Behavior Abstracts; Philosopher's Index; Sociological Abstracts; Sociology of Education Abstracts.

This journal is intended to reach university faculty in Education or Philosophy. Its purpose is to explore the relation of philosophy and education, to deal with movements within education, and to expand communication between theoreticians in education and related fields. The editor prefers manuscripts which are analytic in nature, dealing with a problem that in some way relates to education and other specialized fields related to the journal's stated purpose.

Unsolicited manuscripts of approximately 4,000 words and following the MLA style are accepted for editorial consideration. The copyright is held by the publisher. Themes for the issues are based upon the submitted manuscripts. Between six and eight weeks is required for editorial consideration with publication of manuscripts following between six and twelve months after acceptance. One to two book reviews are published in each issue and these may be the same length as articles. They must be analytic and follow the same requirements as any other manuscript. Four copies of all manuscripts should be submitted. Manuscripts are returned only if a self-addressed stamped envelope is included.

152. EDUCATORS NEGOTIATING SERVICE. 1965– . Educational Service Bureau, Inc., 1835 K Street, N.W., Washington, DC 20006. Circ.: 1,000. 20 issues/yr. $108.00/yr. Annual index: August 1 issue. Editor: Richard G. Neal. Book reviews to: editor.

The intended audience of this publication includes all persons interested in collective bargaining in public education. Its purpose is to provide unbiased, impartial news, reports and complete texts of bills, laws, court decisions, arbitration awards, speeches, testimony and related information on educational negotiations. A regular feature is Views and Reviews.

Only editorials are accepted for publication and these may be biased toward either management or labor. These editorials should follow MLA style requirements and may range from 500 to 1,000 words in length. Copyright is held by the publisher. Simultaneous submission to other journals is permitted. Estimated time for an editorial decision concerning acceptability of material is three weeks. Publication follows in one month. Book reviews must be on collective bargaining in the public sector and may be from 500 to 1,000 words long.

153. EDUCOM BULLETIN. 1966– . Interuniversity Communications Council, Inc., Box 364 Rosedale Road, Princeton, NJ 08540. Circ.: 10,000. 4 issues/yr. Subscription included with council membership; non-member rate, $10.00/yr. Annual index: spring issue. Editor: staff edited. No book reviews.

Indexed in: Excerpta Medica; Quarterly Bibliography of Computers and Data Processing.

This journal is intended for educators and others interested in the application of computers and other technology to problem solving in higher education. Its purpose is to promote resource sharing in the application of technology to solve educational problems. The editor is interested in materials which present applications of technology and resource sharing that will be of use to a variety of educators.

The editor solicits manuscripts directly from professionals in the field of study, however, unsolicited articles and letters of inquiry also are accepted. Manuscripts should be approximately 3,000 words in length and follow the Chicago style. The copyright is held by the publisher. Four weeks is required for an editorial decision with six months usually elapsing between acceptance and publication.

154. ELEMENTARY SCHOOL GUIDANCE AND COUNSELING. 1967— .
American School Counselor Association, a division of the American Personnel and Guidance Association, 1607 New Hampshire Avenue, N.W., Washington, DC 20009. Circ.: 18,000. 4 issues/yr. $6.00/yr. with APGA membership; non-member rate, $8.00/yr. Annual index: issue number four. Editor: Robert D. Myrick. Editor's address: College of Education, University of Florida, Gainesville, FL 32611. Book reviews to: editor.
   Indexed in: Education Index; Psychological Abstracts; Social Worker
   Abstracts.
The intended audience of this journal includes educators and pupil personnel specialists involved in the counseling and guidance of elementary school children. Its purpose is to provide a professional publication for school personnel and to ASCA membership. Among the types of articles in this publication are position statements, personal experiences, descriptive programs, innovative approaches, new theories, and applied theory and research.

Unsolicited articles are accepted for consideration. The APA style is specified, but prospective contributors should examine the guidelines published in the journal. Manuscripts should be 2,500 words in length and be submitted in triplicate. Copyright on accepted material is held by the publisher. Some issues are dedicated to central themes and authors should consult recent ASCA newsletters or journals for the topic titles. An editorial decision is made in eight weeks and the estimated time from acceptance to publication is four to six months or less. Book reviews are included occasionally and these are 250 to 500 words each.

155. THE ELEMENTARY SCHOOL JOURNAL. 1900— . The University of Chicago Press with the Department of Education and the Graduate School of Education of the University of Chicago. Circ.: 17,000. 8 issues/yr. $10.00/yr.; institution rate, $12.00/yr. Annual index: May issue. Editor: Philip W. Jackson. Editor's address: 5835 Kimbark Avenue, Judd Hall, University of Chicago, Chicago, IL 60637. No book reviews.
   Indexed in: Abstracts for Social Workers; Current Contents: Social &
   Behavioral Sciences; Current Index to Journals in Education; dsh Abstracts;
   Education Index; Educational Administration Abstracts; Exceptional
   Child Education Abstracts; Index to Periodical Articles Related to Law;
   Psychological Abstracts; Rehabilitation Literature; Sociological Abstracts;
   Sociology of Education Abstracts; Women Studies Abstracts.
This journal contains research reports and articles on administration, supervision, evaluation, social concerns and teacher preparation. The intended audience

THE ELEMENTARY SCHOOL JOURNAL (cont'd)

includes principals, superintendents, subject matter specialists, professors of education, students of education, librarians, and classroom teachers. *The Journal* serves as a forum for professionals in elementary education.

Unsolicited manuscripts are accepted for consideration. The editor urges prospective contributors to examine recent issues for style. One or two copies of articles, about 2,000 words in length, should be submitted. Copyright on published material is held by the University of Chicago. The time for an editorial decision is four to eight weeks. Publication follows from three to twelve months later. A sheet of instructions for authors is available from the editor.

156. **ENGLISH JOURNAL.**1912– . National Council of Teachers of English, 1111 Kenyon Road, Urbana, IL 61801. Circ.: 55,000. 9 issues/yr. Subscription included with council membership. Annual index: December issue. Editor: Stephen N. Judy. Editor's address: P.O. Box 112, East Lansing, MI 48823. Unsolicited book reviews not accepted.

Indexed in: Book Review Index; Current Contents: Social & Behavioral Sciences; Current Index to Journals in Education; dsh Abstracts; Education Index; Exceptional Child Education Abstracts; Media Review Digest; Readers Guide to Periodical Literature; Women Studies Abstracts.

This journal provides theoretical and applied essays dealing with a wide range of issues, problems, concerns and teaching approaches in English and the language arts. *English Journal* is intended for junior high/middle school and senior high school English and language arts teachers. Prospective contributors are advised to review recent issues to gain a sense of what type articles the readership expects.

Unsolicited manuscripts are accepted for consideration. Issues are dedicated to central themes and these are announced in the journal. A list of projected topics and manuscript deadlines is available from the editor. The Chicago style requirements should be followed and length is to be between 3,000 and 4,000 words. Copyright on accepted material is held by the publisher. Estimated time for an editorial decision is eight to ten weeks. Publication follows in four to six months.

157. **ENVIRONMENT AND BEHAVIOR.** 1969– . Sage Publications, Inc., 275 South Beverly Drive, Beverly Hills, CA 90212. Circ.: not given. 4 issues/yr. $14.40/yr. for professionals; institutional rate, $24.00/yr. Annual index: issue number four. Editor: Gary H. Winkel. Editor's address: Environmental Psychology Program, City University of New York, 33 West 42nd Street, New York, NY 10036. Book reviews to: editor.

Indexed in: Bulletin Signaletique, Section 390: Psychologie-Psychopathologie-Psychiatrie; Computer and Information Systems Abstracts; Current Contents: Social & Behavioral Sciences; Current Index to Journals in Education; Environmental Information Access; Environmental Periodicals Bibliography; Excerpta Medica; Human Resources Abstracts; Index to Periodical Articles Related to Law; Psychological Abstracts; The Psychological Readers Guide; Public Affairs Information Service Bulletin; Sage Public Administration Abstracts; Sage Urban Studies Abstracts; Social Sciences Citation Index; Social Sciences Index; Sociological Abstracts; Urban Affairs Abstracts.

ENVIRONMENT AND BEHAVIOR (cont'd)

This publication is an interdisciplinary journal concerned with the study, design, and control of the physical environment and its interaction with human behavioral systems. Examples of recent article titles illustrate the breadth of its content: Predator Control and Ranchers' Attitudes; Room Size, Group Size, and Density-Behavior Patterns in a Children's Psychiatric Facility; Images of the Retailing Environment—An Example of the Use of the Repertory Grid Methodology.

Unsolicited articles are welcomed for editorial consideration. Matters of style and length may be discussed in a letter of inquiry. The copyright is held by the publisher. A copy of the style sheet may be obtained from the editor or publisher. Times for an editorial decision and publication are not indicated.

158. ETC.: A REVIEW OF GENERAL SEMANTICS. 1943— . International Society for General Semantics, P.O. Box 2469, San Francisco, CA 94126. Circ.: 5,000. 4 issues/yr. $6.00/yr. Annual index: December issue. Editor: Thomas M. Weiss. Editor's address: College of Education, University of Wyoming, Laramie, WY 82070. Book reviews to: Book Editor, P.O. Box 2469, San Francisco, CA 94126.

> Indexed in: Current Contents: Social & Behavioral Sciences; Current Index to Journals in Education; Humanities Index; Index to Periodical Articles Related to Law; Psychological Abstracts; Speed; Women Studies Abstracts.

This journal is the official organ of the International Society for General Semantics. It is designed to encourage scientific research and theoretical inquiry into nonaristotelian systems and general semantics. The editor welcomes general semantics oriented articles that are Korzybskian oriented.

Unsolicited manuscripts are welcomed for editorial consideration. Manuscripts should be submitted in two copies and follow the APA style. Articles should be between 3,000 and 4,500 words in length. The copyright is held by the publisher. Twelve weeks is required for an editorial decision with ten to twelve months elapsing between acceptance and publication. Between five and fifteen book reviews are carried in each issue. These reviews must be related to general semantics and should be between 250 and 500 words in length.

159. EXCEPTIONAL CHILDREN. 1934— . The Council for Exceptional Children, 1920 Association Drive, Reston, VA 22091. Circ.: 67,000. 8 issues/yr. Subscription included with council membership; non-member rate, $12.50/yr. Annual index: May issue (summer issue in some previous years). Editor: M. Angele Thomas. Book reviews to: editor.

> Indexed in: Abstracts for Social Workers; Bulletin Signaletique, Section 390: Psychologie-Psychopathologie-Psychiatrie; Child Development Abstracts and Bibliography; Current Index to Journals in Education; dsh Abstracts; Education Index; Educational Administration Abstracts; Exceptional Child Education Abstracts; Excerpta Medica; Index Medicus; Index to Periodical Articles Related to Law; Media Review Digest; Psychological Abstracts; Rehabilitation Literature; Sociological Abstracts.

This journal is intended for special educators, administrators, teachers, teacher educators, psychologists, counselors, and those in the allied health professions.

EXCEPTIONAL CHILDREN (cont'd)

The purpose of this journal is to benefit all handicapped and gifted children through improving their education in the broadest sense. The editor is interested in manuscripts dealing with practical research, evaluation, methodology, programs, and philosophical views.

Unsolicited manuscripts between 3,500 and 5,000 words in length are welcomed for editorial consideration as well as letters of inquiry. All materials should be submitted in four copies. Dedicated issues, which appear occasionally, are always announced well in advance in the journal. Approximately twelve weeks are required for an editorial decision while publication of accepted manuscripts occurs in nine to twelve months after editorial acceptance. Between two and five book reviews are published in each issue of *Exceptional Children*. These reviews are between 250 and 500 words in length. The copyright is held by the publisher. Authors should follow the APA style for all contributions.

160. **THE EXCEPTIONAL PARENT.** 1971– . Psy-Ed Corporation, 264 Beacon Street, Boston, MA 02116. Circ.: 11,000. 6 issues/yr. $10.00/yr. No annual index. Editor: Stanley D. Klein. Manuscript to: Christine Stilton, Assistant to the Editors. Book reviews to: Christine Stilton.

Indexed in: Current Index to Journals in Education; Exceptional Child Education Abstracts; Rehabilitation Literature.

This magazine's primary purpose is to provide practical guidance for parents and professionals concerned with the care of children with disabilities. "How to do it" articles without technical jargon are preferred for this publication. Regular features include: Readers Write; Editor's Desk; Growing With Your Child; Your Physician; Family Forum; and, Fun Stuff.

Articles are solicited directly by the editor who also welcomes unsolicited manuscripts and letters of inquiry. Length of contributions should not exceed 2,500 words and writers should provide practical information in understandable language. Two copies are to be submitted. Copyright is held by the publisher who pays authors at a varying rate. Simultaneous submission to other journals is permitted. An editorial decision is made in ten weeks and the estimated time from acceptance to publication is six months. Book reviews are published only occasionally. A one page description of manuscript policy is available from the editor.

161. **EXERCISE EXCHANGE.** 1972– (at UVM); 1950– (at Bennington College). University of Vermont, College of Arts and Sciences, Department of English, Burlington, VT 05401. Circ.: 1,000. 2 issues/yr. $3.00/yr. No annual index. Editors: Paul A. Eschholz and Alfred F. Rosa. Book reviews to: editors.

Indexed in: Current Index to Journals in Education; Language and Language Behavior Abstracts.

This journal is intended for high school and college teachers of English. It is designed to support the vital art of good teaching by publishing articles about practical classroom concerns. The editors are interested in manuscripts dealing with tested exercises dealing with proven classroom practices.

Unsolicited manuscripts, between 500 and 1,500 words in length, are welcomed by the editor. Authors should follow the MLA format. The copyright is held by the publisher. Between two and four weeks is required for editorial consideration with six months usually elapsing between acceptance and publication. Prospective book review contributors should query the editors in regard to reviewing current English textbooks.

162. **THE FAMILY COORDINATOR.** 1952– . National Council on Family Relations, 1219 University Avenue S.E., Minneapolis, MN 55414. Circ.: 7,000. 4 issues/yr. Subscription included with council membership. Annual index: October issue. Editor: James Walters. Editor's address: Department of Child and Family Development, University of Georgia, Athens, GA 30602. Book reviews to: editor.

Indexed in: Abstracts for Social Workers; Current Contents: Social & Behavioral Sciences; Current Index to Journals in Education; International Bibliography of Sociology; Media Review Digest; Psychological Abstracts; Sociological Abstracts; Sociology of Education Abstracts; Women Studies Abstracts.

This journal is intended for professionals concerned with marriage and the family. Articles are directed toward the family practitioner. Reports of research which emphasize implications for education, counseling, or other community programs serving families are appropriate. Evaluation of work directed toward new clientele, as well as the application of theory and research and use of innovative methods are among the types of material solicited for this journal.

Unsolicited articles are accepted for editorial consideration. These manuscripts should be between 1,500 and 3,000 words in length and submitted in three copies. Style is not specified, but additional manuscript information may be found in the journal. The copyright is held by the National Council on Family Relations. Six weeks is usually required for an editorial decision with publication of accepted manuscripts following within three to four months. Approximately 25 book reviews are published in each issue of this journal and these should be 250 words in length.

163. **FAMILY PERSPECTIVE.** 1966– . Brigham Young University, 1206 SFLC, Provo, UT 84602. Circ.: 1,000. 2 issues/yr. $4.00/yr. No annual index. Editor: Blaine R. Porter. Manuscript to: Ruth E. Brasher, Managing Editor. Book reviews to: Stephen Bahr.

Family Perspective is a multidisciplinary journal which seeks articles, reports and essays on any aspect of family life. The overall objective is to disseminate information that may be used by teachers and family life educators as well as concerned laity. Sample article titles from recent issues are: Family Practice and the Pre-School Child; Empathy, Communication, and the Definition of Life Satisfaction in the Postparental Period; and, Resolution of Family Conflict.

The editor solicits material for this journal, but also accepts unsolicited articles for consideration. A letter of inquiry prior to submission is recommended. The APA style is preferred. Length may be from 3,750 to 5,000 words and is to be submitted in triplicate. Copyright is held by the publisher. Estimated time for an editorial decision is eight weeks. Time from acceptance to publication varies from six to twelve months.

164. FAMILY PROCESS. 1962– . Family Process, Inc. Circ.: 5,000. 4 issues/yr. $12.00/yr.; institution rate, $20.00/yr. Annual index: issue number four. Editor: Donald A. Block. Editor's address: P.O. Box P, Stockbridge, MA 01262. Book reviews to: Sheldon Starr, Mental Research Institute, 555 Middlefield Road, Palo Alto, CA 94301.

Indexed in: Abstracts for Social Workers; Current Contents: Social & Behavioral Sciences; dsh Abstracts; Psychological Abstracts; Sociological Abstracts.

This publication is intended for social scientists and mental health personnel. It is a multidisciplinary journal in the field of family research, study and therapy. The editor is interested in clinical, sociological and historical studies of the family.

Unsolicited manuscripts are sought by the editor. The editor does not restrict length, but two copies of all manuscripts should be submitted. A style sheet is available from the editor. Eight weeks is required for editorial consideration of manuscripts with publication of accepted articles following in approximately three months. This journal includes five or more book reviews in each issue and again, no length limitations are imposed. Copyright on all materials is held by the publisher.

165. THE FAMILY RESOURCE JOURNAL. (formerly **INVOLVEMENT**). 1968– . Browndale, Box 19, Station P, Toronto, Ontario, Canada M5S 2T3. Circ.: 4,500. 10 issues/yr. $15.00/yr. Annual index: not given. Editor: Gloria Shephard. Editor's address: 41 Madison Avenue, Toronto, Ontario, Canada M5R 2S2. Book reviews to: editor.

Indexed in: Exceptional Child Education Abstracts.

The Family Resource Journal is published by Browndale, the treatment center for emotionally disturbed children. The publication focuses on the child and the family and all related issues. Although a wide range of persons including parents, social workers, psychiatrists, teachers, children, nurses and others have contributed articles, much of the material is staff written. Articles cover normal growth and development as well as problems of adjustment and deviance. The journal is humanistic in approach and anti-institution.

This publication features articles that vary in length from 3,000 to 5,000 words. Style is not specified but the editor states that articles must be free of professional jargon. Contributors should submit two copies of their manuscript and may expect an editorial decision in four weeks. If accepted, publication follows in two to six months. The editor solicits articles, but also accepts unsolicited material if it is good. A letter of inquiry prior to submission is encouraged. Copyright is held by the publisher, although permission is often granted for publication elsewhere if requested, as long as proper acknowledgment is made to its prior publication in this magazine. The one or two book reviews in each issue are 500 to 1,000 words long.

166. FAMILY THERAPY. 1974– . Libra Publishers, Inc., P.O. Box 165, 391 Willets Road, Roslyn Heights, NY 11577. Circ.: 1,000. 3 issues/yr. $16.00/yr.; institution rate, $20.00/yr. Annual index: issue number three. Editor: Martin G. Blinder. No book reviews.

Indexed in: Psychological Abstracts; The Psychological Readers Guide.

Family Therapy is a clinical journal devoted to the practice of family, group and other interactional therapies. Articles reflect a multifaceted approach to problem solving. Sample titles in recent issues are: Characteristic Patterns in Drug-Abuse Families; Home Visiting in Family Therapy; and, Psychotherapy with Fragmented (Father-Absent) Families.

Unsolicited articles are welcomed. These manuscripts should follow the MLA style and be between 1,200 and 1,600 words in length. Two copies of all material should be submitted. The copyright is held by the publisher. Simultaneous submission to other journals is permitted. Three weeks is required for an editorial decision with six months normally elapsing between acceptance and publication.

167. **FILM LIBRARY QUARTERLY.** 1967– . Film Library Information Council, Box 348, Radio City Station, New York, NY 10019. Circ.: 1,500. 4 issues/yr. Subscription included with council membership. No annual index. Editor: William Sloan. Editor's address: Donnell Film Library, 20 West 53rd Street, New York, NY 10019. Book and film reviews to: editor.

Indexed in: Humanities Index; Index to Periodical Articles Related to Law; Library Literature; Media Review Digest; Women Studies Abstracts.

This journal is intended for librarians and others interested in the serious study of films in the documentary tradition. The editor is interested in almost any manuscript on the subject except material on commercial or Hollywood features. Sample article titles from a recent journal include: Women and Myths; A Core Afro-American Film Collection; and, Chaplin and the American Avant Garde. Film reviews are a regular feature of this journal.

Unsolicited manuscripts and letters of inquiry are welcomed by the editor. Length for manuscripts is not specified and the style is free. The copyright is held by the author. Simultaneous submission to other journals is permitted. Four weeks is usually required for an editorial decision with six months elapsing between acceptance and publication. Each issue contains ten film reviews and two to three book reviews and these are 500 words in length.

168. **FLORIDA MEDIA QUARTERLY.** (formerly **FAME NEWSLETTER**). 1973– . Florida Association for Media in Education, Florida Technological University, GCB Room 337, P.O. Box 25000, Orlando, FL 32816. Circ.: 1,500. 4 issues/yr. Subscription included with association membership; non-member rate, $4.00/yr. No annual index. Editor: Richard A. Cornell. Book reviews to: editor.

This journal is intended primarily for association members which include school media specialists, both print and non-print oriented, television specialists, university and community college professionals and members of the education industry. Its purpose is to inform the membership of Board actions, meetings, directives and other matters related to the organization and to bring articles pertaining to the educational media profession to the readers. Although varying types of articles dealing with the media field are acceptable, the editor prefers those which have a direct bearing on the educational media field in Florida or those which affect changes within the state of Florida.

FLORIDA MEDIA QUARTERLY (cont'd)

Articles are solicited directly by the editor, but unsolicited material and letters of inquiry are welcomed. Style varies as to the writer's preference but the editor usually rewrites articles to conform to the general style preferred for this publication. Length of articles may vary from 500 to 1,500 words. *Florida Media Quarterly* is not copyrighted. Estimated time for an editorial decision is two to four weeks. Time from acceptance to publication is one to two months. The number of book reviews in each issue varies. Their length is 150 to 500 words. Simultaneous submission to other journals is permitted.

169. FLORIDA MUSIC DIRECTOR. 1947– . Florida Music Educators Association, 440 Palm Island, S.E., Clearwater, FL 33515 and Florida State Music Teachers Association, 8671 Buck Lake Road, Tallahassee, FL 32611. Circ.: 5,000. 10 issues/yr. $4.00/yr. No annual index. Editor: Reid Poole. Editor's address: University of Florida, Music Department, Gainesville, FL 32611. Book reviews to: editor.

Indexed in: Music Article Guide.

This journal is intended primarily for members of the two state music associations which support it. Its purpose is to enlighten members of the two organizations on the latest innovations in the music field and to report on the associations' activities. The editor is interested in articles relating to innovative music programs as well as "how to" articles on the various phases of music. Some issues of this journal are dedicated to central themes, such as band, orchestra, private music teaching, music in the elementary school, choral music, and other similar topics.

Unsolicited articles and newsworthy black-and-white glossy photographs with rather full captions are accepted for issues without central themes. Letters of inquiry are welcomed. The copyright is held by the author. Articles should be between 1,000 and 2,000 words in length. Style preferred is that as set forth in Strunk and White's *The Elements of Style.* Four weeks is required for an editorial decision and between one and two months is required for publication of accepted pieces. Book reviews, while not included on a regular basis, are welcomed by the editor.

170. THE FLORIDA READING QUARTERLY. 1964– . Florida State Reading Council. Circ.: 6,000. 3 issues/yr. Subscription included with council membership; institution rate, $5.00/yr. No annual index. Editor: Kathleen Gurucharri. Editor's address: School of Education, Florida International University, Miami, FL 33199. No book reviews.

The intended audience of this quarterly includes teachers at all levels, other specialists and administrators. It serves as an interchange of ideas in reading in the state of Florida. Articles offering practical ideas teachers can implement are preferred. Manuscripts of a highly technical nature generally are not appropriate.

Unsolicited articles are accepted for consideration. Manuscripts may vary from 1,000 to 2,000 words and are to be submitted in triplicate. Style should be compatible with the purposes of the journal. This publication is not copyrighted. Estimated time for an editorial decision concerning acceptability is three weeks and publication follows in six months. A guide for authors with information for preparing manuscripts is available from the editor.

171. FLORIDA SCHOOLS. (formerly **FLORIDA SCHOOL BULLETIN**). 1966– (FS); 1937– (FSB). Florida Department of Education, Tallahassee, FL 32304. Circ.: 80,000. 4 issues/yr. No charge, controlled circulation. No annual index. Editor: Ruth Chapman. Unsolicited book reviews not accepted.

This publication is for teachers, administrators, and teacher trainers in Florida. Its purpose is to inform its readers of significant programs and events in Florida public education. The editor is interested in articles which are readable, do not contain jargon, and are of interest and assistance to teachers.

The editor will answer letters of inquiry as well as read unsolicited manuscripts. Word limitations and style requirements are not specified. The time for an editorial decision varies and publication follows acceptance by approximately two months. The publication is not copyrighted.

172. FOCUS. 1965– . National Association of State Boards of Education, 1860 Lincoln Street, Suite 810, Denver, CO 80203. Circ.: 1,500. 12 issues/yr. No charge. No annual index. Editor: Susan Grkovic, associate editor. Book reviews to: associate editor.

This newsletter's audience consists chiefly of state board members and state department of education officials as well as friends of the association. Its purpose is to supply state board members with timely, substantive and informative material. Articles should deal with issues of importance confronting state boards.

Authors are encouraged to submit manuscripts. Letters of inquiry are welcomed also. Style should be journalistic, conforming to newspaper format. Preferred length is 400 to 800 words and material should be submitted in duplicate. Copyright is held by the author. An editorial decision is made in two to three weeks and the estimated time from acceptance to publication is two to three months. A book review appears in some issues and its length is 500 words. Authors should conform to APA style requirements for all work.

173. FOCUS ON GUIDANCE. 1968– . Love Publishing Company, 6635 East Villanova Place, Denver, CO 80222. Circ.: not given. 10 issues/yr. $10.50/yr. Annual index: June issue. Editor: Sallie Carmachel Keeney, managing editor. No book reviews.

School guidance personnel and counselors are among the intended audience of this publication. *Focus on Guidance* is a newsletter and publishes research articles designed to offer help to the practitioner. A regular feature is Counselor Forum.

Manuscripts are included in this publication by invitation only. Writers with an interest in this area of study may wish to correspond with the editor for more information concerning publication possibilities as well as learning central themes of future issues. The APA style is followed, but length and time for editorial decisions and publications are not given. Copyright is held by the publisher who pays authors at a rate which is confidential.

174. FOCUS ON LEARNING. 1970– . Indiana University of Pennsylvania, Davis Hall, Indiana, PA 15701. Circ.: 500. 2 issues/yr. $5.50/yr. Annual index: issue number one. Editor: Gerard C. Penta. Book reviews to: editor.

The purpose of this journal is to serve as a forum for the presentation and discussion of theoretical and practical concerns pertinent to the teaching-learning process. Its intended audience consists of professional educators, including college and public school personnel, and others interested in education. Regular features are Educator in Focus, Reactions (letters to the editor), and Reviews (films, learning packages, books and related items).

The editor welcomes unsolicited manuscripts for possible inclusion in *Focus on Learning*. The Chicago style is to be used and preferred length is 3,500 words. Copyright is held by the publisher. An editorial decision is given in six weeks and the estimated time from acceptance to publication is two to eight months. From six to ten book reviews of 400 to 600 words are contained in the journal. One review essay of 1,500 to 2,000 words appears in each issue. Only books that explicitly relate to education and are no more than two years old will be reviewed.

175. FOREIGN LANGUAGE ANNALS. 1967– . American Council on the Teaching of Foreign Languages, 62 Fifth Avenue, New York, NY 10011. Circ.: 12,000. 6 issues/yr. $15.00/yr. Annual index: December issue. Editor: Warren C. Born. No book reviews.
  Indexed in: Current Contents: Social & Behavioral Sciences; Current Index to Journals in Education.

This journal is intended to communicate to foreign language teachers at all levels of instruction. It is designed to improve the teaching of foreign languages through the sharing of information. The editor is interested in manuscripts presenting research reports, innovative techniques and successful teaching practices.

Unsolicited manuscripts and letters of inquiry are encouraged by the editor. Two copies of all manuscripts, at least 5,000 words in length, should be submitted. The MLA style is required and copyright is held by the publisher. Eight weeks is needed for an editorial decision with publication of accepted manuscripts following in nine months to a year.

176. FRENCH REVIEW. 1927– . American Association of Teachers of French, 57 East Armory Avenue, Champaign, IL 61820. Circ.: 13,000. 6 issues/yr. $15.00/yr. Annual index: May issue. Editor: Stirling Haig. Editor's address: P.O. Box 149, Chapel Hill, NC 27514. Book reviews to: editor.
  Indexed in: Current Index to Journals in Education; Education Index; Modern Language Abstracts; Women Studies Abstracts.

This journal is intended for teachers of French at all instructional levels. Its purpose is to serve the members of the AATF, of which this is the official journal. The editor welcomes the submission of articles dealing with French literature and the teaching of that language.

Authors of articles are urged to submit them to the editor. Manuscripts should be approximately 3,600 words in length and follow the MLA style. The copyright is held by the publisher. The estimated time for an editorial decision is between four and twelve weeks. Publication time from acceptance is usually one year. Between 50 and 100 book reviews are published in each issue of this journal and these are approximately 650 words in length.

177. **GENERAL LINGUISTICS.** 1955– . The Pennsylvania State University Press, 215 Wagner Building, University Park, PA 16802. Circ.: not given. 4 issues/yr. $12.50/yr. No annual index. Editor: William R. Schmalstieg. Editor's address: N-438 Burrowes, University Park, PA 16802. Book reviews to: Philip Baldi, 309 Burrowes, University Park, PA 16802.

   Indexed in: Current Contents: Social & Behavioral Sciences.

This journal contains articles from all fields of linguistics, historical, comparative, descriptive, and in related areas such as psycholinguistics and sociolinguistics. Manuscripts may be printed in any of four languages, English, French, German and Russian. *General Linguistics* is intended for linguists and other educators and persons interested in these areas of study.

   Unsolicited manuscripts are welcomed for consideration. Articles should be about 5,000 words in length and three copies are to be submitted. Style and other details are printed in two pages in each issue of the journal and prospective contributors are urged to examine this information. Copyright is held by the publisher. Issues are dedicated to central themes and authors should query the editor for future topics. An editorial decision concerning acceptability is given in 30 weeks and publication follows in 20 months. Ten to fifteen book reviews are included in this journal. The editor requires no special length for these reviews.

178. **GEORGIA MUSIC NEWS.** 1938– . Georgia Music Educators Association, Inc., 4045 Bouldervista Drive, Conley, GA 30027. Circ.: 2,000. 4 issues/yr. Subscription included with association membership; non-member rate, $4.00/yr. No annual index. Editor: Robert W. John. Editor's address: University of Georgia, Music Department, Athens, GA 30602. Book reviews to: editor.

The intended audience of this journal is primarily music teachers in Georgia. Emphasis is not on articles as such, but rather on the dissemination of information which is believed to be of strong interest to music educators. Regular features include a "Dear John" column which answers reader questions, the answers coming from specialists in the field, established columns written by the chairperson of each of the various divisions of the GMEA, and a "Changing Scene in Georgia" column which contains names of persons who have changed teaching positions. Books and music are reviewed or annotated.

   Articles for publication are usually solicited by the editor, but unsolicited articles also are accepted for consideration. Authors are encouraged to write a letter of inquiry prior to submission. Preferred length of articles is a maximum of 750 words written clearly, correctly and concisely as possible. Illustrations may be included when appropriate. An editorial decision as to acceptance can be expected almost immediately. Publication will follow within two to four months. About six book annotations are included in the journal and these are 150 words each.

179. **THE GERMAN QUARTERLY.** 1928– . American Association of Teachers of German. Circ.: 12,000. 4 issues/yr. Subscription included with association membership; non-member rate, $15.00/yr. Annual index: November issue. Editor: William A. Little. Editor's address: Department of German, University of Virginia, Charlottesville, VA 22903. Book reviews to:

Marvin S. Schindler, Department of Modern Languages, Wayne State University, Detroit, MI 48202.

Indexed in: Current Index to Journals in Education; Education Index; Modern Language Abstracts.

The intended audience of this publication includes teachers of German at all levels. The journal has a strong scholarly orientation toward German literature. Its purpose is to inform its readership of recent studies and is organized to publish the results of scholarly research. Membership in the American Association of Teachers of German provides subscriptions to this journal and to *Die Unterrichtspraxis.*

Unsolicited articles are welcomed for consideration. The MLA style requirements should be followed and the length is not to exceed 6,250 words. Copyright on accepted material is held by the publisher. Estimated time for an editorial decision is ten weeks and publication follows acceptance in about twelve months. Approximately 50 book reviews appear in *The German Quarterly* and each is a maximum of 500 words long.

180. **THE GIFTED PUPIL.** 1963– . Gifted and Talented Education Management Team, California State Department of Education, 721 Capitol Mall, Sacramento, CA 95814. Circ.: not given. 1 issue/yr. No charge. No annual index. Editor: Paul D. Plowman. Book reviews to: editor.

This newsletter is intended for school administrators, consultants, teachers and counselors of children who are in the upper two per cent of general mental ability. It promotes uniquely appropriate learning experiences for mentally gifted minors and disseminates information on program models, identification, counseling, administration and "qualitatively different" curriculum. Articles relating to the stated functions and providing guidelines for improving teaching, counseling, curriculum and administration are preferred for inclusion in *The Gifted Pupil.*

The editor solicits material from specialists in this field of study, but also welcomes unsolicited articles and letters of inquiry. No specific style is required. Manuscript length should be 1,000 to 2,000 words and two copies are to be submitted. Some issues are dedicated to central themes and prospective contributors should query the editor for future topics. An editorial decision is given in four weeks and publication of accepted pieces follows in two months. Occasionally book reviews appear in this newsletter; reviews are about 250 words long. Simultaneous submission to other journals is permitted.

181. **THE GUIDANCE CLINIC.** 1969– . Parker Publishing Company, Inc., Route 59A at Brookhill Drive, West Nyack, NY 10994. Circ.: 5,300. 10 issues/yr. $36.00/yr. No annual index. Editor: Reed Goodman. No book reviews.

The intended audience of *The Guidance Clinic* includes guidance counselors, administrators, superintendents and other educators. It serves as a nationwide clearinghouse of ideas and information through which guidance specialists can keep in constant touch with one another. Articles do not deal in generalities, but in specific plans, operating procedures, and counseling techniques direct from this country's schools. It provides models on which to organize and implement a first-rate guidance program.

THE GUIDANCE CLINIC (cont'd)

The editor solicits articles directly from persons in this area of study, but also welcomes unsolicited manuscripts and letters of inquiry. Articles are to be 2,000 to 3,000 words in length and submitted in duplicate. Style is not specified. An editorial decision is given in two weeks and the estimated time from acceptance to publication is two to three months. Copyright on all material is held by the publisher.

182. **HPEC RUNNER.** (formerly **HEALTH AND PHYSICAL EDUCATION COUNCIL BULLETIN**). 1975– (HPECR); 1962– (HPECB). Alberta Teachers Association, Barnett House, 11010 142nd Street, Edmonton, Alberta, Canada. Circ.: 500. 4 issues/yr. Subscription included with council membership; non-member rate, $6.00/yr. Annual index: winter issue. Editors: Jim Paul, Calgary Board of Education, 515 MacLeod Trail S.E., Calgary, Alberta, Canada, and Pat Brand, 7606 149th Street, Edmonton, Alberta, Canada. Book reviews to: editors.
   Indexed in: Canadian Education Index.

This journal is intended primarily for specialists in physical education in the province of Alberta. Its purpose is to improve curriculum and instruction in health and physical education through increased knowledge and understanding. The type of article preferred for this journal includes research abstracts, program ideas, points of view, activities (such as bowling, skiing and others), medical comments and philosophy of health and physical education. Practical articles are of most importance and are given first consideration.

Articles usually are solicited by the editor. Some issues are dedicated to central themes and prospective contributors should correspond with one of the editors to determine future topics and other writing possibilities. The APA style is to be followed and length should be 750 to 1,000 words. Copyright on accepted manuscripts is held by the publisher. Simultaneous submission to other journals is permitted. An editorial decision is given in two weeks and publication follows acceptance in two months. The one or two book reviews in each issue are about 250 words long.

183. **HARVARD EDUCATIONAL REVIEW.** (formerly **THE HARVARD TEACHERS RECORD**). 1937– (HER); 1931– (HTR). Harvard Graduate School of Education, Longfellow Hall, 13 Appian Way, Cambridge, MA 02138. Circ.: 14,000. 4 issues/yr. $14.00/yr. Annual index: November issue. Editor: Margaret K. O'Hara, general manager. Book reviews to: Book Review Editor.
   Indexed in: Abstracts for Social Workers; America: History and Life*; Book Review Index; Current Contents: Social & Behavioral Sciences; Current Index to Journals in Education; dsh Abstracts; Education Index; Educational Administration Abstracts; Exceptional Child Education Abstracts; Index to Periodical Articles Related to Law; Psychological Abstracts; Public Affairs Information Service Bulletin; Research into Higher Education; Social Sciences Citation Index; Sociological Abstracts; Sociology of Education Abstracts; Women Studies Abstracts.

HARVARD EDUCATIONAL REVIEW (cont'd)

The intended audience of this journal includes scholars, professors, students, teachers, researchers, administrators and those involved with foundations and institutes. Its purpose is to promote scholarly research in education, to define educational policy, and to promote interdisciplinary methodology. Articles from the above named audience, as well as from persons working in related fields, are welcomed by the editorial board. This editorial board of graduate students of Harvard University changes annually. Articles may cross disciplinary lines and may reflect opinion and/or research in the field of education.

The editors accept unsolicited manuscripts for consideration. Two (or more) copies are to be submitted. The APA or MLA style should be followed and length may vary from 6,500 to 8,750 words. Copyright is held by the publisher from whom permission should be sought for reprints of articles. Estimated time for an editorial decision is at least four weeks. Publication of accepted manuscripts follows in two to three months. Six or more book reviews are contained in this journal. Their length varies from 2,000 to 2,500 words.

184. **HARVARD GRADUATE SCHOOL OF EDUCATION ASSOCIATION BULLETIN.** 1956— . Harvard Graduate School of Education, 112 Gutman Library, Appian Way, Cambridge, MA 02138. Circ.: 13,000. 3 issues/yr. No charge to alumni, students, faculty and staff of the Graduate School of Education; rate for others, $5.00/yr. No annual index. Editor: Gillian Charters. Book reviews to: editor.

This journal is intended for graduates of the Harvard Graduate School of Education as well as a selected list of educators and educational institutions in the United States and abroad. It aims to keep alumni informed of current educational topics and how their school is involved.

Unsolicited manuscripts as well as letters of inquiry are welcomed by the editor. They should have some bearing on projects at the School, or be written by an alumnus of the Harvard Graduate School of Education. The editor also solicits manuscripts directly from professionals in the field. Manuscripts should be approximately 2,000 words in length. The copyright is held by the publisher. Editorial decisions on solicited articles are immediate, however, the time required for a decision and publication of unsolicited manuscripts varies. Book reviews are published on a space available basis. No length is set for these reviews.

185. **HEAD START NEWSLETTER.** 1966— . Project Head Start, Office of Child Development, Department of Health, Education and Welfare, Washington, DC 20201. Circ.: 135,000. 6 issues/yr. No charge. No annual index. Editor: Mary B. Washburn. Editor's address: P.O. Box 1182, Project Head Start, Washington, DC 20013. No book reviews.

The majority of the audience for this publication consists of the grantee agencies, Head Start directors, staff members, and parents. This publication also is distributed to libraries, state governments, university clinics, nutritionists, Social Service workers and state Head Start training officers. Its intent is to reach as many adults in Head Start as possible with inspiring stories from centers throughout the country and to keep them informed of Headquarters' plans, new and old projects, either of a policy nature or an experimental nature. Human interest adult and child and classroom success stories are of prime interest.

Unsolicited articles are accepted for consideration. Issues are dedicated to central themes and prospective contributors should correspond with the editor or call by telephone (202-755-7406) to determine if their material is appropriate. Material for the *Head Start Newsletter* is written and/or edited in-house. Preferred length of articles is 250 to 500 words. Style requirements are not specified. The time for an editorial decision concerning acceptance is three to four weeks and the publication time varies.

186. **HEALTH EDUCATION.** (formerly **SCHOOL HEALTH REVIEW**). 1970– (SHR). American Alliance for Health, Physical Education, and Recreation, 1201 Sixteenth Street, N.W., Washington, DC 20036. Circ.: 10,000. 8 issues/yr. $15.00/yr. Annual index: November-December issue. Editor: Nancy H. Rosenberg, Director of Periodicals. Book reviewers chosen by editor.

Indexed in: Current Index to Journals in Education; Hospital Literature Index; International Nursing Index; Media Review Digest; Nursing Research; Women Studies Abstracts.

This journal is intended for health educators and those interested in health education at all levels, including community service. Its purpose is to keep professionals informed about all developments in the field and in related areas. It includes informative articles as well as provocative and philosophical pieces.

Unsolicited as well as solicited articles are considered for inclusion in this journal by the editor. Manuscripts should be between 1,500 and 2,500 words in length and follow the Chicago style. The copyright is held by the publisher. *Health Education* is generally dedicated to central themes which are published well in advance in the journal. Approximately six weeks is required for an editorial decision with three months elapsing between acceptance and publication of a manuscript.

187. **HEARING & SPEECH ACTION.** (formerly **HEARING & SPEECH NEWS** and **HEARING NEWS**). 1933– (HN). National Association for Hearing and Speech Action (formerly National Association of Hearing and Speech Agencies), 814 Thayer Avenue, Silver Spring, MD 20910. Circ.: 12,500. 6 issues/yr. $5.00/yr. No annual index. Editor: Judy Gilliom. No book reviews.

Indexed in: Current Index to Journals in Education; dsh Abstracts, Rehabilitation Literature.

The intended audience of this journal includes persons with speech and hearing handicaps, professionals who work with these individuals, their families and friends, and interested members of the general public. It provides a discussion of current events of interest to its readers, presents information about hearing and speech handicaps, assists professionals in speech and hearing fields, and educates consumers as well as providers of services. All articles related to this field except the most technical types are acceptable.

HEARING & SPEECH ACTION (cont'd)

The editor solicits material directly from professionals, but also welcomes unsolicited articles for consideration. A letter of inquiry prior to submission is encouraged. Preferred length is 3,000 to 4,500 words. Copyright is held by the publisher. An editorial decision is made in three weeks and publication of accepted articles follows in two to six months.

188. **HIGH SCHOOL BEHAVIORAL SCIENCE.** (formerly **BEHAVIORAL AND SOCIAL SCIENCE TEACHER**). 1975– (HSBS); 1973– (BSST). Institute of Advanced Psychological Studies, Adelphi University, Garden City, NY 11530. Circ.: not given. 2 issues/yr. $6.00/yr.; library rate, $12.00/yr. No annual index. Editor: Robert Mendelsohn. Book reviews to: editor.
    Indexed in: Current Index to Journals in Education; Psychological Abstracts.

This journal is intended for high school teachers of psychology, sociology and anthropology. It is designed to enrich teacher knowledge and help them develop new and different teaching strategies. This publication is intended to be a major aid to the behavioral science teacher.

The editor solicits articles on assigned topics and also accepts unsolicited manuscripts. Three copies of all manuscripts should be submitted. Articles should be no longer than 4,000 words and must follow the APA format. The copyright is held by the publisher. Six weeks is required for an editorial decision with six months elapsing before accepted manuscripts are published. An average of two book reviews are published in each issue of the journal and these should be no longer than 1,500 words.

189. **THE HIGH SCHOOL JOURNAL.** 1918– . University of North Carolina, School of Education, Peabody Hall, Chapel Hill, NC 27514. Circ.: 3,100. 8 issues/yr. $7.00/yr. Annual index: May issue. Editor: Hunter Ballew. Book reviews to: editor.
    Indexed in: Current Index to Journals in Education; Education Index; Educational Administration Abstracts; Index to Periodical Articles Related to Law; Sociological Abstracts.

This journal is intended for high school teachers and administrators and college teachers of curriculum and secondary methods. Its purpose is to disseminate information and research results having to do with secondary education. Material dealing with students, learning, teachers, curriculum, methods, administration, financial support, and other services for grades 7 through 12 are welcomed. Some issues are devoted to a single topic and others are general.

The editor is seeking unsolicited manuscripts, will correspond with those who inquire, and in some cases solicits articles directly for theme issues which appear occasionally. The manuscript should be between 1,500 and 2,500 words in length and is to be submitted in three copies. The copyright is held by the publisher. Estimated time for an editorial decision is four to six weeks. No time is indicated for publication following acceptance. The number of book reviews varies. These reviews should be between 300 and 400 words in length.

190. **HISPANIA.** 1918– . American Association of Teachers of Spanish and
Portuguese, Inc. Circ.: 16,500. 5 issues/yr. Subscription included with associa-
tion membership; non-member rate, $10.00/yr. Annual index: issue number
five. Editor: Donald W. Bleznick. Editor's address: Department of Romance
Languages, University of Cincinnati, Cincinnati, OH 45221. Book reviews to:
Myron I. Lichtblau, Book Review Editor, Foreign Language Faculty, Syracuse
University, Syracuse, NY 13210.

    Indexed in: Abstracts of Folklore Studies; Book Review Index; Current
    Index to Journals in Education; Education Index; Modern Language
    Abstracts; Women Studies Abstracts.

This journal is intended for those interested in the cultures and literatures of
the Spanish or Portuguese. Most of the members of the association are teachers of
these two languages. The publication's purpose is to provide articles, notes and
general information on Spanish, Portuguese, Spanish American and Brazilian literature, language and culture. In addition, pieces on teaching these languages at all
instructional levels are provided. Scholarly articles on Hispanic literature, linguistics
and pedagogy are welcomed by the editor, but only from members of the association.

    Unsolicited articles from association members are encouraged. These contribu-
tions should be between 7,500 and 10,000 words in length and follow the MLA
style. The copyright is held by the publisher. Between ten and twelve weeks is
required for an editorial decision with publication of accepted manuscripts following thirty months later. Approximately 35 book reviews are published in each issue
of this journal. These reviews are 500 words in length.

191. **HISTORY OF CHILDHOOD QUARTERLY: THE JOURNAL OF
PSYCHOHISTORY.** 1973– . Atcom, Inc., 2315 Broadway, New York, NY
10024. Circ.: 6,000. 4 issues/yr. $14.00/yr.; institutional rate, $20.00/yr.
No annual index. Editor: Lloyd deMause. Book reviews to: editor.

    Indexed in: Abstracts for Social Workers; Child Development Abstracts
    and Bibliography; Psychological Abstracts; Sociological Abstracts;
    Women Studies Abstracts.

This journal presents articles dealing with childhood in the past and present,
and studies of psychoanalytic history. It is intended for historians, psychotherapists,
sociologists, educators and laymen. Its aim is to advance scholarship into psychohistory. The editor is interested in empirical studies of parent-child relations in
the past and in psychoanalytically informed articles on historical movements.

    Unsolicited articles, of approximately 8,000 words, are accepted for editorial
consideration. Authors should follow the Chicago style requirements. The copyright is held by the publisher. Simultaneous submission to other journals is permitted. One week is estimated as the time required for an editorial decision with
three months elapsing between acceptance and publication. Approximately 15
book reviews are published in each issue. These reviews are approximately 500
words in length.

192. **HISTORY OF EDUCATION QUARTERLY.** 1961– . History of Education
Society and School of Education, New York University, 737 East Building,
Washington Square, New York, NY 10003. Circ.: 2,000. 4 issues/yr. Sub-
scription included with society membership; institution rate, $15.00/yr.

Annual index: published separately. Editor: Paul H. Mattingly.
Book reviews to: editor.
Indexed in: America: History and Life*; Current Contents: Social &
Behavioral Sciences; Current Index to Journals in Education;
Education Index; Research into Higher Education; Social Sciences
Citation Index; Women Studies Abstracts.

This journal is designed for the perpetuation of history of education as a
scholarly field and proclaims itself as the only journal in the United States exclus-
ively devoted to history of education. Its intended audience includes historians
and educators. Articles preferred for inclusion are those about all countries and
aspects of the history of education. The use of new evidence is encouraged as
well as new interpretations of old evidence.

Unsolicited manuscripts are accepted for consideration. The MLA style is
preferred and articles are to be submitted in duplicate. Copyright is held by the
publisher. Length is not specified. Estimated time for an editorial decision concerning acceptability is six weeks and publication follows in six months. Approximately five book reviews of 3,000 words each are included in this quarterly. The
reviews usually are in essay review form, organized around a theme.

193. **THE HISTORY TEACHER.** 1967– . California State University, Department
of History, 6101 East Seventh Street, Long Beach, CA 90840. Circ.: 4,300.
4 issues/yr. $8.00/yr.; institution rate, $10.00/yr. Annual index: August
issue. Editor: Keith Ian Polakoff. Book reviews commissioned in advance
by editor.
Indexed in: America: History and Life*; American History and Culture;
Current Index to Journals in Education; Media Review Digest.

This journal is intended for history teachers at the secondary, community
college, and university levels. It provides a forum for the interchange of ideas leading to improvement in the classroom teaching of history. The editor is interested
in two types of articles: first, those reporting on new programs and instructional
techniques; and second, analyses of important interpretations in specific fields of
historical research.

Unsolicited manuscripts, between 1,000 and 7,000 words in length, are welcomed by the editor, and should follow the Chicago style. The copyright is held
by the publisher. An editorial decision usually is rendered in four to six weeks with
publication of accepted manuscripts following in six to nine months. An average of
30 book reviews are published in each issue of this journal. These reviews are between
400 and 500 words in length.

194. **HOME ECONOMICS RESEARCH JOURNAL.** 1972– . American Home
Economics Association, 2010 Massachusetts Avenue, N.W., Washington, DC
20036. Circ.: 4,000. 4 issues/yr. $10.00/yr. with association membership;
non-member rate, $15.00/yr. Annual index: issue number four. Editor:
Joan Gordon. Editor's address: Department of Food Science and Nutrition,
University of Minnesota, St. Paul, MN 55108. Book reviews to: editor.
Indexed in: Current Index to Journals in Education; Hospital
Literature Index; Nursing Research; Psychological Abstracts.

Researchers in home economics and related fields, and persons applying research such as Extension personnel and university professors are among the intended audience of this publication. Its purpose is: to provide a medium for reporting and recording of scientific methods, findings, and applications of research in this field; to strengthen the research base in Home Economics; to facilitate scholarly interchange among those in Home Economics in relation to the well-being of families and individuals; and, to promote Home Economics academically through increased visibility of the depth and breadth of its research.

The editor welcomes unsolicited manuscripts for consideration, but they must be prepared in the style as specified. A modified APA style is required and a complete guide for authors is published in issue number one (September) of each volume. The editor does not restrict writers in terms of length but does require three copies of all work. Copyright of accepted articles is held by the publisher. Estimated time for an editorial decision is eight to ten weeks. Publication follows in three to six months. Book reviews appear only occasionally and are 500 to 1,250 words in length.

195. HOOSIER SCHOOLMASTER OF THE SEVENTIES. (formerly **HOOSIER SCHOOLMASTER**). 1961– . Indiana State Department of Public Instruction, Room 227, State House, Indianapolis, IN 46204. Circ.: 60,000. 4 issues/yr. No charge, controlled circulation. No annual index. Editor: Carol Rex. Editor's address: Division of Publications, Room 120, State House, Indianapolis, IN 46204. No book reviews.

This journal publishes thematic issues dealing with topics such as reading, special education, career education, and other issues of current interest to teachers. It is distributed to all Indiana teachers and libraries and interested citizens who request it. Out of state subscriptions, however, are not encouraged. Its purpose is to provide teachers with information concerning actions and reactions to educational issues and programs occurring throughout Indiana. The editor is seeking informative articles dealing with innovative projects, special programs, new concepts, and traditional topics treated in a new light. Beginning with this decade the title was changed to include "of the seventies."

Unsolicited manuscripts are welcomed, however, a letter of inquiry concerning future journal themes is recommended. Articles should be between 1,500 and 2,000 words. Style requirements are not specified. The copyright is held by the author. Approximately two to four weeks is required for an editorial decision with a two to three month delay before publication.

196. THE HORN BOOK MAGAZINE. 1924– . The Horn Book, Inc., 585 Boylston Street, Boston, MA 02116. Circ.: 27,500. 6 issues/yr. $10.50/yr. Annual index: December issue. Editor: Ethel L. Heins. Book reviews written by staff.

Indexed in: Artbibliographies; Book Review Digest; Book Review Index; Current Index to Journals in Education; Library Literature; Media Review Digest; Readers Guide to Periodical Literature; References Services Review.

THE HORN BOOK MAGAZINE (cont'd)

This journal is about children's books and reading. Its purpose is to disseminate information about these books through articles and book reviews. *The Horn Book Magazine* is intended for librarians, teachers, parents, publishers, editors, artists, illustrators, authors, children's group workers and university students.

The editor solicits manuscripts directly from professionals in this field of study, but also welcomes unsolicited articles. Length should be about 2,800 words. Copyright is held by the author and publisher. Authors are paid at the rate of $20.00 per page for original articles. The editor does not indicate a preferred style. An editorial decision is made in four to six weeks and the estimated time from acceptance to publication ranges from four to ten months.

197. **THE HUMANIST EDUCATOR.** (formerly **JOURNAL OF THE STUDENT PERSONNEL ASSOCIATION FOR TEACHER EDUCATION**). 1975– (HE); 1961– (JSPATE). Association for Humanistic Education and Development, c/o American Personnel and Guidance Association, 1607 New Hampshire Avenue, N.W., Washington, DC 20009. Circ.: 700. 4 issues/yr. Subscription included with association membership; non-member rate, $9.00/yr. No annual index. Editor: James C. Dickinson. Editor's address: University of South Florida, Tampa, FL 33620. Book reviews to: editor.

Indexed in: College Student Personnel Abstracts; Current Index to Journals in Education; Psychological Abstracts.

This journal is directed at teachers and administrators in elementary and secondary schools, at teacher educators, and at persons who are committed to the implementation of humanistic values in education. *The Humanist Educator* seeks manuscripts on organizational development or staff renewal efforts in schools and school systems, efforts to improve communications and cooperative efforts among groups which comprise a school's community, attempts to synthesize experiential instructional designs with conventional curriculums, educational outcomes associated with humanistic instruction, and analyses of forces which shape the appearance of humanism in the schools. Research reports, essays, book reviews and other literary or graphic forms that yield meaning are welcome and will be carefully considered.

Unsolicited manuscripts of not more than 3,000 words are accepted for possible inclusion in this journal. Three copies are to be submitted. The time for an editorial decision concerning acceptance is twelve to fourteen weeks. Publication will follow in two months. The number of book reviews varies depending upon availability. Those appearing are about 750 words long. Copyright is held by the publisher. Authors should follow APA style guidelines for all work.

198. **ISBA JOURNAL.** 1954– . Indiana School Boards Association, 222 North New Jersey, Indianapolis, IN 46204. Circ.: 3,000. 6 issues/yr. Subscription included with association membership; non-member rate, $6.00/yr. No annual index. Editor: Britt Polley. No book reviews.

This journal provides its readership with information and a forum regarding educational developments, with emphasis at the state level. Its intended audience includes Indiana school board members, school administrators, legislators, educators and educational suppliers. Articles preferred for *ISBA Journal* are those that deal with current trends in education, developing concepts and innovations, school business management, school facilities, budgeting and finance, program evaluation and similar topics.

Unsolicited manuscripts and letters of inquiry are welcomed by the editor. Contributors should follow MLA style requirements and their articles should be 600 to 1,200 words in length. Copyright on accepted material is held by the author. Simultaneous submission to other journals is permitted. An editorial decision is made in four weeks and publication follows in two months.

199. **ISEA COMMUNIQUE.** 1962– . Iowa State Education Association, 4025 Tonawanda Drive, Des Moines, IA 50312. Circ.: 36,900. 10 issues/yr. Subscription included with association membership; non-member rate, $2.00/yr. No annual index. Editor: Richard D. Blome. No book reviews.

This tabloid is intended to help keep association members informed about its program and future goals. It also informs member readers about current local, state and national education issues. The audience consists primarily of elementary and secondary classroom teachers, but also includes some school administrators, student teachers, and higher education faculty members. Short news style articles on current education issues are preferred for inclusion.

The editor solicits most material for the *ISEA Communique* directly from professionals but welcomes letters of inquiry. Unsolicited articles are rarely accepted for publication. Submitted copy should be typed double-spaced and may vary in length from 200 to 300 words. Copyright is held by the publisher. Simultaneous submission to other journals is permitted. An editorial decision is usually given within two weeks for material to be published in the next monthly issue.

200. **ILLINOIS ENGLISH BULLETIN.** 1910– . Illinois Association of Teachers of English, 100 English Building, University of Illinois, Urbana, IL 61801. Circ.: 2,200. 8 issues/yr. Subscription included with association membership. No annual index. Editor: Donald Nemanich. No book reviews.

Indexed in: Women Studies Abstracts.

The intended audience of this journal includes secondary English teachers, and also elementary and college teachers. Its purpose is to disseminate research, teaching ideas, and good student writing. Practical ideas on teaching English and content articles are desired for inclusion in *Illinois English Bulletin*.

The editor welcomes unsolicited manuscripts. No special style is required and the length may vary from 500 to 7,500 words. Copyright information is not indicated. Issues are dedicated to central themes which are based on the available material. Simultaneous submission to other journals is permitted. An editorial decision is given in ten weeks and publication follows in one to twelve months.

201. **ILLINOIS PRINCIPAL.** (formerly **ILLINOIS ELEMENTARY PRINCIPAL**). 1954– (IEP). Illinois Principals Association, 612 South Second Street, Springfield, IL 62704. Circ.: 2,400. 4 issues/yr. Subscription included with association membership; non-member rate, $4.00/yr. No annual index. Editor: John F. Moomey, Associate Executive Director. No book reviews.

ILLINOIS PRINCIPAL (cont'd)

This journal provides information to the association members about current educational trends and issues, and disseminates summaries of successful educational practices. Its intended audience includes all public and private school principals, both elementary and secondary, other administrators, and college and university personnel. The articles offer discussion, explanation and opinion of current educational trends and basically are non-research and non-statistical in orientation.

Unsolicited manuscripts are accepted for consideration. A letter of inquiry prior to submission is recommended. Length of articles should be 1,500 to 2,500 words. Additional style information is not given. Copyright is held by the author. Estimated time for an editorial decision concerning acceptability of material is six to eight weeks. Publication time is two to six months after acceptance.

202. **ILLINOIS QUARTERLY.** (formerly **ILLINOIS STATE UNIVERSITY JOURNAL**). 1971– (IQ); 1937– (ISUJ). Illinois State University, Normal, IL 61761. Circ.: 4,500. 4 issues/yr. No charge, controlled circulation. Annual index: April issue. Editor: John Heissler. No book reviews.

The intended audience of this journal consists mainly of university faculty in all disciplines. The *Quarterly* does not limit its audience to one discipline. The purpose of this publication is to acquaint educated readers with information concerning the realm of knowledge in all disciplines. Essays that would be of interest to this audience are welcomed by the editor. The editor gives first preference to articles relevant to the development of culture in Illinois.

Unsolicited articles are accepted for editorial consideration. These pieces should be approximately 3,000 words in length and follow the MLA style. The copyright is held by the publisher and two copies of all manuscripts should be submitted. Four weeks is required for an editorial decision. Publication follows acceptance twelve months later.

203. **ILLINOIS SCHOOL BOARD JOURNAL.** (formerly **ILLINOIS SCHOOL BOARD BULLETIN**). 1940– (ISBJ); 1935– (ISBB). Illinois Association of School Boards, 330 Iles Park Place, Springfield, IL 62718. Circ.: 10,100. 6 issues/yr. $6.00/yr. No annual index. Editor: Gerald R. Glaub. Book reviews to: editor.
Indexed in: Rehabilitation Literature.

This journal features articles intended primarily for school board members in Illinois. Its purpose is to inform and broaden the horizons of lay school board members. The types of articles preferred are those dealing with analysis of local, state and federal public policy issues in education and those which describe proven ways to upgrade school board and management performance.

The editor solicits some manuscripts directly from professionals in this field, but also welcomes unsolicited material. A letter of inquiry prior to submission is encouraged. The style of the Associated Press is to be followed. Length may vary from 800 to 3,000 words. Copyright is held by the author. Issues are dedicated to central themes and prospective contributors should query the editor for future topics. Simultaneous submission to other journals is permitted. Estimated time for an editorial decision concerning acceptability is two to four weeks. Publication

ILLINOIS SCHOOL BOARD JOURNAL (cont'd)

follows in one to four months. The one or two book reviews in each issue are 800 to 2,000 words in length. Books reviewed must be suitable for school board members.

204. ILLINOIS SCHOOLS JOURNAL. (formerly **CHICAGO SCHOOLS JOURNAL**). 1967– (ISJ); 1906– (CSJ). Chicago State University, 95th Street at King Drive, Chicago, IL 60628. Circ.: 10,000. 4 issues/yr. $4.00/yr. Annual index: summer issue. Editor: Virginia McDavid. No book reviews.

Indexed in: Current Contents: Social & Behavioral Sciences; Education Index; Exceptional Child Education Abstracts.

This journal is designed to supply useful educational materials to the classroom teacher. Teachers and other educational specialists are among its intended audience. No restrictions are placed upon the writer in terms of type of article preferred for inclusion.

Unsolicited manuscripts are accepted for consideration. The MLA style requirements should be followed and the length preferred is 2,500 words. Two copies of the article are required. Copyright is held by the publisher. Estimated time for an editorial decision concerning acceptability is eight weeks. Time from acceptance to publication is six months.

205. IMPROVING COLLEGE AND UNIVERSITY TEACHING. 1953– . Oregon State University Press, 101 Waldo Hall, Oregon State University, Corvallis, OR 97331. Circ.: 3,000. 4 issues/yr. $9.00/yr. Annual index: fall issue. Editor: Delmer M. Goode. Editor's address: P.O. Box 689, Corvallis, OR 97330. Book reviews to: editor.

Indexed in: College Student Personnel Abstracts; Current Index to Journals in Education; Education Index; Research into Higher Education; Women Studies Abstracts.

This journal is intended for persons interested in quality teaching, particularly at the university level. The purpose of this journal is to print articles on college and university teaching that are written by college and university teachers. It provides a medium to foster the exchange of ideas among educators. The editor favors articles which emphasize both innovative and proved ideas in teaching experience, as well as interests of professors both as teachers and scholars.

Unsolicited articles as well as letters of inquiry are welcomed by the editor. Articles preferably should be 850 to 1,800 words in length, although both longer and shorter are printed. Writers should follow the style of the United States Government Printing Office, but the editor indicates a policy of style flexibility. Issues are devoted to central themes and authors may query the editor for future topics. Simultaneous submission of material is permitted to other journals with the stipulation that it will be withdrawn if accepted elsewhere. Editorial decisions are made within a few weeks. A backlog of articles now exists. A waiting period is likely. Book reviews are sometimes contributed but often are written by the editor. Copyright on accepted material is held by the publisher.

206. IMPROVING HUMAN PERFORMANCE: A RESEARCH QUARTERLY. (formerly **NSPI JOURNAL**). 1972– (IHP); 1962– (NSPIJ). National Society for Performance and Instruction, P.O. Box 137, Cardinal Station,

IMPROVING HUMAN PERFORMANCE: A RESEARCH QUARTERLY (cont'd)

Washington, DC 20017. Circ.: 1,500. 4 issues/yr. Subscription included with society membership; non-member rate, $30.00/yr. No annual index. Editor: Jerry Short, Chairman of Editorial Board. Editor's address: School of Education, University of Virginia, Charlottesville, VA 22903. No book reviews.

Indexed in: Psychological Abstracts; Social Sciences Citation Index.

This journal is intended for all those interested in, and working toward, effective learning and improved performance. It offers innovative ideas, models, reviews and articles that relate to these areas. The purpose of the journal and the sponsoring association is to stimulate action toward the goal of improved human performance. Subscription to the *Quarterly* also includes the *NSPI Newsletter* which is published ten times each year.

Articles for publication sometimes are solicited directly from various professionals, but the editor also welcomes unsolicited manuscripts and letters of inquiry. The APA style is to be followed and the length should be 1,250 to 2,500 words. Articles are to be submitted in triplicate and copyright is held by the publisher. Estimated time for an editorial decision is four to five weeks. Publication of accepted material follows in three months. A one page outline of guidelines is available for prospective contributors.

207. **IN-ED.** 1974– . The University of Texas of the Permian Basin, Odessa, TX 79762. Circ.: 600. 12 issues/yr. No charge. No annual index. Editor: Robert N. Rothstein. No book reviews.

This publication is intended for academicians who are interested in innovative educational ideas, especially those pertaining to self-paced, competency based instruction. Its primary purpose is to describe procedures, problems and policies that may be involved in the operation of innovative programs in higher education. Each issue offers one major article concerning an innovative program.

Unsolicited manuscripts are welcomed for consideration. Articles should be about 1,500 words in length and the APA style requirements are to be followed. The central theme that is used for all issues is "innovative education." Simultaneous submission to other journals is permitted. An editorial decision is given in six weeks. If accepted, publication follows in three months. Copyright on all materials is held by the publisher.

208. **THE INDEPENDENT SCHOOL BULLETIN.** 1941– . National Association of Independent Schools, 4 Liberty Square, Boston, MA 02109. Circ.: 8,700. 4 issues/yr. $5.00/yr. with association membership; non-member rate, $7.00/yr. Annual index: May issue. Editor: Blair McElroy. Book reviews to: editor.

Indexed in: Current Contents: Social & Behavioral Sciences; Current Index to Journals in Education; Education Index; Media Review Digest.

This journal is intended for teachers, administrators, trustees, parents, and others concerned with independent (private) schools. It offers a forum for the exchange of information and opinion on matters related to secondary and elementary education in general, and to independent schools in particular. The editor welcomes the expression of conflicting views.

THE INDEPENDENT SCHOOL BULLETIN (cont'd)

Unsolicited manuscripts as well as letters of inquiry are welcomed by the editor. All manuscripts should be approximately 2,500 words in length and follow the MLA style. The copyright is held by the publisher. Between two and twelve weeks is required for an editorial decision with two to eight months elapsing between acceptance of a manuscript and its inclusion in this journal. A varying number of brief book reviews, based upon space available, is published in each issue.

209. INDIANA ENGLISH JOURNAL. (formerly **INDIANA ENGLISH LEAFLET**). 1966– (IEJ); circa 1949– (IEL). Indiana Council of Teachers of English, Division of Continuing Education and Extended Services, Indiana State University, Terre Haute, IN 47809. Circ.: 1,500. 4 issues/yr. Subscription included with council membership; non-member rate, $3.00/yr. No annual index. Editor: James S. Mullican. Editor's address: Department of English and Journalism, Indiana State University, Terre Haute, IN 47809. Book reviews to: editor.

This journal is intended to reach elementary, secondary, college and university teachers of English and language arts. Its purpose is to provide interesting and useful ideas on teaching and learning English and language arts. The editor is interested in articles on reading, literature, language, composition, creative writing, and the media, particularly as they relate to teaching methods and curriculum.

Unsolicited manuscripts as well as letters of inquiry are welcomed by the editor. No word limitations are indicated. The journal is not copyrighted but the journal is a member of the Exchange Agreement with the National Council of Teachers of English. Issues are dedicated to central themes which are announced in advance in the *Journal.* Approximately six weeks is required for an editorial decision with publication following acceptance within three months. Book reviews are published in this journal and these are 250 words in length. Authors should follow Chicago style requirements for all work. Footnotes should be incorporated within the text whenever possible.

210. INDIANA MUSICATOR. 1945– . Indiana Music Educators Association, Inc., Executive Office, School of Music, Ball State University, Muncie, IN 47306. Circ.: 2,300. 4 issues/yr. Subscription included with association membership; non-member rate, $3.00/yr. No annual index. Editor: H. Eugene Karjala. Book reviews to: editor.

This journal is intended for public school music teachers, particularly those within the state of Indiana and members of the Indiana Music Educators Association. The purpose of this journal is to feature articles relating to particular music programs within the state, as well as outside the state. It acts as a forum for comments on specific issues and also serves as a communication device for the membership of the association. The editor is interested in articles related to music education and articles somewhat controversial in nature that might spark reader reaction and comment.

Unsolicited manuscripts, of approximately 1,200 words, as well as letters of inquiry are welcomed by the editor. No specific style is required, but the MLA style is preferred. Simultaneous submission to other journals is permitted.

Between eight and twelves weeks is required for an editorial decision with one to three months usually elapsing between acceptance and publication. One book review is published in each issue of this journal. It is between 900 and 1,200 words in length.

211. **INDIANA READING QUARTERLY.** 1968– . Indiana State Council of the International Reading Association, 306 Teachers College, Ball State University, Muncie, IN 47306. Circ.: 900. 3 issues/yr. Subscription included with council membership; non-member rate, $3.00/yr. No annual index. Editors: J. David Cooper and Dorothy Pringle. No book reviews.

This journal is intended for teachers of reading at the elementary, junior high/middle school, and senior high school levels. It is intended to provide classroom teachers of reading with practical suggestions for teaching as well as provide communication about council activities.

Unsolicited articles are accepted for editorial consideration. These works should be between 1,000 and 2,000 words in length. The editor also may solicit articles upon occasion on particular topics of current interest. Between four and eight weeks is required for an editorial consideration with publication following acceptance in three to eight months. Copyright is held by the publisher. Style requirements are not given.

212. **THE INDIANA SOCIAL STUDIES QUARTERLY.** 1945– . Indiana Council for Social Studies. Circ.: 1,000. 3 issues/yr. $6.00/yr. Periodically indexed, not annually. Editor: Richard Wires. Editor's address: History Department, Ball State University, Muncie, IN 47306. Book reviews to: editor.

Indexed in: America: History and Life*.

Designed to bring its readers methods of teaching suggestions and recent research findings in the area of social studies. The intended audience includes teachers in social studies, grades 1 to 12, college faculty and students, and others through regular library use. The following types of articles are desired for publication: presentations of new research findings, new interpretations, and new approaches in teaching; examples of successful experiments; and, essays covering recent literature, book reviews, and critical analyses of new materials.

Unsolicited manuscripts are accepted for consideration. A letter of inquiry prior to submission is encouraged. The editor also solicits some material from selected professionals in this field of study. Length of articles may range from 3,000 to 5,000 words and authors should follow the Chicago style requirements. Three copies of the manuscript are to be sent. Copyright is held by the author. Issues are dedicated to central themes and information on these topics is available from the editor three to five years in advance. Estimated time for an editorial decision concerning acceptability of an article is two to five weeks. Publication follows in six to twenty-four months. Review articles covering many books are preferred by the editor rather than individual book reviews.

213. **INDUSTRIAL EDUCATION.** 1914– . Macmillan Professional Magazines, Inc., 1 Fawcett Place, Greenwich, CT 06830. Circ.: 30,000. 9 issues/yr.

$9.00/yr. No annual index. Editor: Paul K. Cuneo. Book reviews are
staff written.

Indexed in: Current Index to Journals in Education; Education Index;
Media Review Digest.

This journal attempts to reach industrial arts, vocational-technical, and technical education teachers. Its purpose is to present articles of interest to the members
of its audience, particularly the "how to do it" type.

Unsolicited manuscripts will be considered and letters of inquiry will be
answered. Articles should be between 500 and 2,500 words in length and the
Chicago style is preferred. The publisher pays the author at the rate of $20.00
per printed page. The copyright is held by the publisher. Approximately six weeks
is required for an editorial decision, with two months elapsing from acceptance to
publication.

214. **INEQUALITY IN EDUCATION.** 1969— . Center for Law and Education,
Harvard University, Larsen Hall, 14 Appian Way, Cambridge, MA 02138.
Circ.: 15,000. 4 issues/yr. $6.00/yr. Annual index: available from editor.
Editor: Sharon Schumack. Book reviews to: editor.

Indexed in: Current Index to Journals in Education; Index to
Periodical Articles Related to Law; Women Studies Abstracts.

This journal is published by the Center for Law and Education, a CSA-OEA
funded legal back-up center which supplies expert help in the field of education
law to legal services offices and related organizations. The journal, like the Center,
hopes ". . .to promote reform in education through research and action on the
legal implications of educational policies, particularly those affecting equality of
educational opportunity." Its readers include legal services attorneys, educators,
administrators, legislators, community groups and other interested individuals.
Articles desired for publication are those that are well researched and footnoted,
informative, and of current interest in the field of education law. The editor is
seeking material that is factual and analytical rather than journalistic.

Some manuscripts are solicited directly from experts in the field, but the
editor also welcomes unsolicited articles. A letter of inquiry prior to submission
is recommended to determine suitability of proposed work and to learn of themes
for future issues. The Chicago style is required and manuscript length may be from
3,750 to 6,250 words. Times for an editorial decision and publication are not
given.

215. **INSITE.** 1968— . Saskatchewan Industrial Education Association, c/o
Saskatchewan Teachers' Federation, 2317 Arlington Avenue, Saskatoon,
Saskatchewan, Canada. Circ.: 300. 4 issues/yr. Subscription included with
association membership. No annual index. Editor: Harry Sweetman.
Editor's address: P.O. Box 577, Fort Qu'Appelle, Saskatchewan, Canada.
Book reviews to: editor.

Intended to meet the needs of Saskatchewan industrial education teachers
and administrators in particular, and also to communicate with the academic community in general. It is the official organ of the SIEA and attempts to acquaint the
members with general trends and developments in their field of teaching expertise.

INSITE (cont'd)

Unsolicited manuscripts are welcomed for editorial consideration as well as letters of inquiry. Manuscripts should be between 500 and 1,000 words in length. The copyright is held by the author. Journal issues are dedicated to central themes and these are always noted in earlier issues. Manuscripts are given editorial consideration upon receipt and a decision concerning acceptability is given without delay. Publication follows acceptance within one month. Approximately six book reviews are published in each issue of the journal. These reviews should be 300 words in length.

216. INSTRUCTOR. 1891– . The Instructor Publications, Inc., Instructor Park, Dansville, NY 14437. Circ.: not given. 9 issues/yr. $10.00/yr. Annual index: June issue. Editor: Ernest Hilton. Book reviewers chosen by editor.

Indexed in: Book Review Index; Business Education Index; Current Index to Journals in Education; Education Index; Exceptional Child Education Abstracts; Media Review Digest; Women Studies Abstracts.

This journal is intended for in-service and student teachers in elementary education as well as others in education and related professions. Its purpose is to help improve elementary education. The editor is interested in any type of article which deals with the theory and practice of elementary education.

Unsolicited manuscripts are accepted for editorial consideration. Length of articles may vary and a journalistic style should be used. The copyright is held by either the publisher or the author. Payment is made for accepted manuscripts on a varying basis. Approximately six weeks is required for an editorial decision with the publication of accepted manuscripts following in six to eight months.

217. THE INSTRUMENTALIST. 1946– . The Instrumentalist Company, 1418 Lake Street, Evanston, IL 60204. Circ.: 20,000. 11 issues/yr. $9.00/yr. Annual index: June issue. Editor: Kenneth L. Neidig. Book reviews to: editor.

Indexed in: Media Review Digest; The Music Index; Music Article Guide.

The Instrumentalist provides articles dealing with families of instruments such as flute, woodwind, brass, percussion, and strings, as well as other areas (e.g., jazz and electronics). It is intended for teachers of instrumental music and for directors of school bands and orchestras. Article contents include trends and practical techniques useful to its audience. Most manuscripts are from professionals in the field. The editor prefers information of immediate use to instrumentalists, not articles about music and musicians.

The editor solicits some of the material for this journal from professionals in this area of study, but also welcomes unsolicited manuscripts for consideration. A letter of inquiry prior to submission is encouraged. The Chicago style requirements should be followed and length may range from 1,000 to 2,000 words. Copyright is held by the publisher who pays authors at a rate that varies from $10.00 to $100.00 per piece. An editorial decision concerning acceptability of an article is given in two to four weeks and publication follows in two to twelve months. Two to four book reviews of 250 words each appear in this journal.

These reviews must be of professional value to school band and orchestra directors.

218. INTEGRATEDUCATION. 1963– . Integrated Education Associates, School of Education, Northwestern University, 2003 Sheridan Road, Evanston, IL 60201. Circ.: not given. 6 issues/yr. $10.00/yr. No annual index. Editor: Meyer Weinberg. Book reviews to: editor.

> Indexed in: College Student Personnel Abstracts; Current Index to Journals in Education; Education Index; Educational Administration Abstracts; Index to Periodicals By and About Negroes; Index to Periodical Articles Related to Law; Public Affairs Information Service Bulletin; Sociological Abstracts; Women Studies Abstracts.

This journal provides a forum for discussion of the problems of minority students to keep its readers abreast of the news concerning court actions and decisions, new publications and related areas of interest. It is intended for teachers, students, scholars, parents, and the general public, especially those interested in minority education. Regular features are: Chronicle of Race, Sex and Schools; Bibliography; and, Book Reviews.

The editor welcomes unsolicited manuscripts for consideration. The Chicago style is to be followed and length may range from 2,500 to 5,000 words. Two copies of the article should be sent. Copyright is held by the publisher. Contributors can expect an editorial decision in four to six weeks. Publication of accepted material follows in four to six months. The four to six book reviews in each issue are 250 to 500 words long.

219. INTELLECT. (formerly **SCHOOL AND SOCIETY**). 1972– (I); 1915– (SS). Society for the Advancement of Education, 1860 Broadway, New York, NY 10023. Circ.: 10,000. 9 issues/yr. $12.00/yr.; institutional rate, $16.50/yr. Annual index: May/June issue. Editor: William W. Brickman. Book reviews to: editor.

> Indexed in: College Student Personnel Abstracts; Current Contents: Social & Behavioral Sciences; Current Index to Journals in Education; Education Index; Educational Administration Abstracts; Index to Periodical Articles Related to Law; Readers Guide to Periodical Literature; Social Sciences Citation Index; Women Studies Abstracts.

Intellect is a multi-disciplinary journal which covers many areas of universal interest to academic, intellectual and professional personnel. Its purpose is to foster the exchange of educational and professional ideas. Articles dealing with the following areas are preferred: national, international and social affairs, economics, education, psychology, law and justice, medicine and health, philosophy, religion, business and finance, history, mass media, literature, art, cinema, theatre, and futurism.

The editor is interested in unsolicited manuscripts and will answer letters of inquiry concerning ideas for articles. The journal has its own style sheet which will be sent upon request. All manuscripts should be between 3,000 and 7,500 words in length and the editor will accept only the original copy of any manuscript. The copyright is held by the publisher. Approximately four to six weeks is required for an editorial decision with publication following acceptance within one to six months. The number of book reviews in the journal varies and each is between 750 and 1,000 words in length. Books being reviewed must be no older than one year at the time of submission of the review.

220. INTERACTION. (formerly **OTF REPORTER**). 1974– (I); 1965– (OTFR). Ontario Teachers' Federation, 1260 Bay Street, Toronto, Ontario, Canada M5R 2B5. Circ.: 110,000. 6 issues/yr. Subscription included with federation membership. Annual index: not given. Editor: Susan Gemmell. Book reviews to: editor.

The intended audience of this tabloid consists primarily of teachers of Ontario. The publication contains news, trends in education and current political action. Regular features include information on pension plans, retired teachers and workshops.

Unsolicited material and letters of inquiry are accepted for consideration. The editor also requests materials directly from various professionals. Length of contributions may vary from 400 to 1,000 words. Style is not specified. Simultaneous submission to other journals is permitted. An editorial decision is given in two weeks and publication of accepted articles follows in three months. Usually one book review of about 500 words and dealing with educational subjects is published in each issue.

221. INTERCHANGE. 1970– . The Ontario Institute for Studies in Education, 252 Bloor Street West, Toronto, Ontario, Canada M5S 1V6. Circ.: 2,200. 4 issues/yr. $9.00/yr.; library rate, $12.00/yr. Annual index: issue number four. Editors: primarily student edited. Book reviews to: editors.

Indexed in: Canadian Education Index; College Student Personnel Abstracts; Current Contents: Social & Behavioral Sciences; Educational Administration Abstracts; Exceptional Child Education Abstracts; Human Resources Abstracts; Psychological Abstracts; Research into Higher Education; Social Sciences Citation Index.

Interchange is intended for researchers, practitioners and policy makers in education. Its purpose is to help develop empirically grounded models and theories of education of use to policy makers and practitioners, and to stimulate debate and encourage interdisciplinary research. The editors prefer articles that provide significant contributions to the discussion of theory, research and practice in education.

Some articles are solicited directly from selected professionals but unsolicited manuscripts and letters of inquiry are welcomed by the editor. Length should be about 7,500 words and the APA style is to be followed. Copyright on published material is held jointly by the author and publisher. Three copies of all work should be sent. Occasional issues are dedicated to central themes and these are announced in the journal. An editorial decision is made in eight to ten weeks and publication of accepted work follows in three to eight months. The one or two book reviews in each issue are 2,000 words long. A one page summary of information for contributors is available from the editor.

222. INTERNATIONAL EDUCATIONAL AND CULTURAL EXCHANGE.

1965– . U. S. Advisory Commission on International Educational and Cultural Affairs, CU/ACS Room 420 SA-2, U. S. Department of State, Washington, DC 20530. Circ.: 8,000. 4 issues/yr. $5.75/yr. Annual index: spring issue. Editor: Nancy J. Fritz. No book reviews.

Indexed in: College Student Personnel Abstracts; Current Index to Journals in Education; Education Index; Women Studies Abstracts.

Exchange is intended for individuals and/or organizations (governmental and nongovernmental) involved in international exchange activities or programs. Also included in the audience are those persons or groups interested in the general field of international educational and cultural affairs. The journal serves as a source of information on a wide range of international and cultural exchange activities and as a forum for discussion of the most pressing issues in this field.

The editor solicits materials from professionals in this field of study, but also welcomes unsolicited articles. The style of the U. S. Government Printing Office is preferred but not necessary. Manuscripts of up to 5,000 words are considered for inclusion. Since *Exchange* is funded by the U. S. Government, articles appearing in the journal may not be copyrighted. An editorial decision concerning acceptability is given in four weeks and publication follows in three months.

223. INTERNATIONAL JOURNAL OF AMERICAN LINGUISTICS. 1917–

The University of Chicago Press, 5801 South Ellis Avenue, Chicago, IL 60637. Circ.: 2,200. 4 issues/yr. $12.00/yr.; institution rate, $16.00/yr. Annual index: October issue. Editor: C. F. Voegelin. Editor's address: Department of Anthropology, Indiana University, Bloomington, IN 47401. Book reviews to: Eric Hamp, Linguistics Department, University of Chicago, Chicago, IL 60637.

Indexed in: Abstracts in Anthropology; Anthropological Index; Current Contents: Social & Behavioral Sciences; Current Index to Journals in Education; Index to Religious Periodical Literature; Modern Language Abstracts; Social Sciences Citation Index.

This journal publishes papers concerned with American Indian languages, but also theoretically contributory papers concerned with languages from other parts of the world. Primary emphasis is on the languages of native America. It is intended for professional linguists and anthropologists, ethnographers, speakers of native American languages, and others interested in native American languages. Articles preferred for inclusion are those based on actual linguistic or anthropological fieldwork rather than on secondary sources.

Unsolicited manuscripts are welcomed for consideration. The Chicago style is to be used. No length restrictions are imposed upon authors. Estimated time for an editorial decision is twelve to sixteen weeks. If accepted, publication of the article follows in nine to twelve months. Copyright on all work is held by the publisher.

224. INTERNATIONAL JOURNAL OF INSTRUCTIONAL MEDIA. 1973– .

Baywood Publishing Company, Inc., 43 Central Drive, Farmingdale, NY 11735. Circ.: 800. 4 issues/yr. $27.50/yr. Annual index: issue number four. Editor: Phillip J. Sleeman. Editor's address: Director, Center for Instructional Media and Technology, University of Connecticut, Storrs, CT 06268. Book reviews to: editor.

This journal is intended for teachers, librarians, administrators, audio-visual directors, curriculum personnel, data processing and programmed instruction directors. Its ultimate goal is to help students learn more effectively. Articles designed to provide new ideas and encourage broader use of media in education are preferred for inclusion in this journal. The articles may reflect experimental testing as well as proven effective programs in instructional media.

The editor solicits some material directly from specialists in this field, but also welcomes letters of inquiry and unsolicited manuscripts. Authors should adhere to the Chicago style requirements when possible and are to limit their writing to a maximum of 5,000 words. Two copies of the work are to be submitted. Estimated time for an editorial decision is two to six weeks. Copyright on all material is held by the publisher. Additional manuscript information is printed in each issue on the inside of the back cover.

225. **INTERROBANG, EDUCATION IN RHODE ISLAND.** 1972– . Rhode Island Department of Education, 199 Promenade Street, Providence, RI 02908. Circ.: 2,200. 11 issues/yr. No charge, controlled circulation. No annual index. Editor: Tom Izzo. Editor's address: Room B-28, Roger Williams Building, Hayes Street, Providence, RI 02908. No book reviews.

The purpose of this tabloid is to inform readers of the activities of the Department of Education and Board of Regents for Education, as well as programs at all levels within the state. It is intended to reach educators throughout Rhode Island. The editor encourages the submission of manuscripts but indicates that few are received, hence this publication often is considered a house organ focusing on Department activities.

Unsolicited manuscripts are welcomed. No style or length requirements are provided. The editor also may solicit articles upon occasion and most are written by the staff. Simultaneous submission to other publications is permitted. Editorial decisions are usually given within one month of receipt of the manuscript with publication following shortly thereafter.

226. **INTERSCHOLASTIC ATHLETIC ADMINISTRATION.** 1974– . National Federation of State High School Associations, 400 Leslie Street, Elgin, IL 60120. Circ.: 6,000. 4 issues/yr. $8.00/yr. Annual index: summer issue. Editor: John E. Roberts. No book reviews.

The intended audience of this journal includes high school athletic directors, girls sports coordinators, principals, superintendents and also college instructors and students of athletic administration. It provides high school athletic administrators with a forum for the exchange of ideas pertinent to their profession. Articles preferred for inclusion are the "how to" variety, especially successful innovations in athletic administration. Occasionally, results of research studies are published.

The editor solicits material from selected professionals in this area of study, but also welcomes letters of inquiry and unsolicited manuscripts. Length of articles is to be 1,500 words and two copies should be submitted. Style is not specified.

Copyright on published material is held by the association. Issues are dedicated to special themes and topics are published in the journal. Times for an editorial decision concerning acceptability and publication are variable.

227. **THE IOWA MEDIA MESSAGE.** 1972– . Iowa Educational Media Association. Circ.: 650. 4 issues/yr. Subscription included with association membership. No annual index. Editor: Roger Volker. Editor's address: Iowa State University, 321 Curtiss Hall, Ames, IA 50010. No book reviews.

This publication is intended for media professionals in the public schools in Iowa, and to other association members who are in related educational media positions, such as religious education, the school for the blind and other similar education units. It provides news of educational media programs, techniques, and topics of current interest to its readers. Also included are announcements and reports from the sponsoring organization. Articles desired for inclusion in this journal are those dealing with local media programs, production and utilization techniques, and ideas for developing and implementing the use of instructional materials, both print and non-print, in a variety of educational settings.

The editor solicits material directly from professionals in this field, but also welcomes unsolicited manuscripts. The preferred length of articles of 500 to 1,500 words. No particular style is required and the publication is not copyrighted. Simultaneous submission to other journals is permitted. An editorial decision concerning acceptability is given in one week and publication follows in one month.

228. **IOWA MUSIC EDUCATOR.** 1947– . Iowa Music Education Association, 5224 Merced, Des Moines, IA 50310. Circ.: 1,400. 3 issues/yr. $3.00/yr. No annual index. Editor: Marilyn Sassman. Book reviews to: editor.

This journal is designed for the members of the Iowa Music Educators Association. It is intended to promote music education throughout the state. The editor is interested in any materials that will further that aim.

Both unsolicited manuscripts and letters of inquiry are welcomed by the editor. Articles should contain approximately 500 words and follow the APA style. The copyright is held by the author. Simultaneous submission to other journals is permitted. Approximately eight weeks is required for an editorial decision with publication of accepted manuscripts following within two months of acceptance. Book reviews are published in each issue of the journal on a space available basis. These reviews should be very short, not exceeding 100 words in length.

229. **THE IOWA SCHOOL BOARD DIALOGUE.** (formerly **IOWA SCHOOL BOARD BULLETIN**). 1968– (ISBD); 1951– (ISBB). Iowa Association of School Boards, 707 Savings and Loan Building, Des Moines, IA 50309. Circ.: 4,000. 6 issues/yr. Subscription included with association membership; non-member rate, $2.00/yr. No annual index. Editor: Wayne R. Beal. No book reviews.

This journal is intended primarily for school board members, superintendents and school board secretaries. It is the official publication of the Iowa Association of School Boards and its purpose is to keep the association members informed of

THE IOWA SCHOOL BOARD DIALOGUE (cont'd)

education activities. A law column and an employee relations section are regular features of this publication.

The editor solicits articles directly from specialists in the field, but also welcomes letters of inquiry and unsolicited manuscripts. Style requirements and copyright information are not given. Length of articles should be approximately 1,000 words. Simultaneous submission to other journals is permitted. Contributors can expect an editorial decision concerning acceptability in eight to twelve weeks. Publication follows in two to four months.

230. **IOWA SCIENCE TEACHERS JOURNAL.** 1963— . Iowa Academy of Science, University of Northern Iowa, Cedar Falls, IA 50613. Circ.: 1,500. 4 issues/yr. $4.00/yr. No annual index. Editor: Robert Yager. Editor's address: Science Education Center, The University of Iowa, Iowa City, IA 52242. Book reviews to: editor.

This journal is intended to reach science teachers, coordinators, and administrators. It provides information about topics in science that are of general interest, and information about science education in particular. The editor is interested in articles dealing with current areas of interest and new developments in the fields of science and science education.

The submission of unsolicited manuscripts is encouraged by the editor. These articles should be between 1,000 and 2,000 words in length and need not follow any particular style requirements as they are edited following acceptance. The copyright is held by the author. Simultaneous submission to other journals is permitted but the editor must be so informed at the time of submission. Between two and three weeks is required for an editorial decision with publication of accepted manuscripts following within two to three months of acceptance. One to six book reviews are published in each issue of this journal. These reviews should be from 100 to 200 words in length. Manuscript submission is open to all interested persons, however, preferential consideration is given to members of the Iowa Academy of Science.

231. **JGE: THE JOURNAL OF GENERAL EDUCATION.** 1946— . The Pennsylvania State University Press, 215 Wagner Building, University Park, PA 16802. Circ.: not given. 4 issues/yr. $9.00/yr. Annual index: January issue. Editors: Caroline D. Eckhardt and Robert B. Eckhardt. Book reviews to: editor.

Indexed in: Abstracts on Police Science*; America: History and Life*; Book Review Index; College Student Personnel Abstracts; Current Contents: Social & Behavioral Sciences; Current Index to Journals in Education; dsh Abstracts; Education Index; Educational Abstracts; Exceptional Child Education Abstracts; Modern Language Abstracts; Psychological Abstracts; Social Sciences Citation Index; Sociological Abstracts.

This publication is directed toward teachers, students, and administrators in junior colleges, colleges, and universities. Its purpose is to promote liberal education, to counteract education overspecialization, and to serve as a bridge between the "two cultures." *JGE* therefore publishes scholarly articles on a

JGE: THE JOURNAL OF GENERAL EDUCATION (cont'd)

variety of subjects, written by specialists for an audience of education nonspecialists. The editors state, "We continue to support the goals of general education in the belief that the best-educated people are those who maintain interests beyond their specialties and who want to communicate with their colleagues in other disciplines."

JGE welcomes unsolicited articles. The usual length is 15-25 pages typescript. Unrevised theses are not to be submitted. Authors should follow the Chicago style. Simultaneous submission to other journals is discouraged; the editors must be informed of simultaneous submission and may refuse to have the article reviewed. Copyright is held by the publisher. Issues of this journal are frequently dedicated to special themes. Eight weeks usually is required for an editorial decision, with six to nine months between acceptance and publication. From two to four book reviews are included in each issue; their normal length is 5-10 pages typescript.

232. JEWISH EDUCATION. 1929– . National Council for Jewish Education, 114 Fifth Avenue, New York, NY 10011. Circ.: not given. 4 issues/yr. $6.50/yr. No annual index. Editor: Alvin I. Schiff. Editor's address: c/o B.J.E., 426 West 58th Street, New York, NY 10019. Book reviews to: editor.
  Indexed in: Education Index; Index to Jewish Periodicals; Sociological Abstracts.

This journal is intended for Jewish educators and for students of comparative education. Its purpose is to present key issues and developments in Jewish education, particularly scholarly articles reflecting trends and projecting new ideas. Articles dealing with the philosophy, sociology and psychology, as well as summaries of research in Jewish education are preferred.

Articles submitted for consideration should be between 3,000 and 5,000 words in length. Issues are occasionally dedicated to one central theme. Letters of inquiry are encouraged by the editor as well as unsolicited manuscripts. The copyright is held by the publisher. Six weeks usually is required for an editorial decision. Publication of accepted work follows within six months. An average of four to five book reviews are used in each issue with the length being approximately 500 words each. A style sheet is available from the editor upon request.

233. THE JEWISH PARENT. 1948– . National Society for Hebrew Day Schools, 229 Park Avenue South, New York, NY 10003. Circ.: 3,000. 4 issues/yr. $2.00/yr. No annual index. Editor: Joseph Kaminetsky. Manuscript to: Rabbi Murray I. Friedman, associate editor. Book reviews to: associate editor.

This journal is directed to parents and educators affiliated with the Hebrew Day School movement. Its purpose is to make the philosophy of Hebrew Day School education available in print and to serve as a clearinghouse for interested individuals and agencies. Articles that demonstrate the contributions of Jewish education to a democratic society are solicited.

This journal publishes unsolicited manuscripts which vary in length from 2,500 words to 3,500 words. One copy of the manuscript is required and the copyright is held by the author. A period of four weeks is required for an editorial decision with three months elapsing between acceptance and publication.

116

THE JEWISH PARENT (cont'd)

This journal includes book reviews with four to six appearing in each issue. The reviews should be approximately 500 words in length and the books reviewed should have some bearing on Jewish education or culture.

234. **THE JOURNAL FOR SPECIAL EDUCATORS OF THE MENTALLY RETARDED.** (formerly **DIGEST OF THE MENTALLY RETARDED**). 1970– (JSEMR); 1962– (DMR). Academy of Educational Disciplines, 107-20 125th Street, Richmond Hill, NY 11419. Circ.: 5,000. 3 issues/yr. $9.00/yr. Annual index: issue number three. Editors: Joseph Prentky and Louis Marpet (co-editor). Book reviews to: editor.
   Indexed in: dsh Abstracts; Education Index; Exceptional Child Education Abstracts.

The intended audience of this journal includes teachers of the mentally retarded, guidance counselors, college libraries, boards of education and libraries. It is designed to give teachers and others in the field of Special Education the broad thinking of others in the same field, to share information to enable them to give better lessons, and to make them more forceful and knowledgeable teachers and administrators.

Unsolicited articles of 1,000 to 1,500 words are accepted for consideration. The editor also solicits material directly from persons in the field. Duplicate copies of the manuscript are to be submitted and simultaneous submission to other journals is permitted. Style is not specified. An editorial decision is made in six weeks and the estimated time from acceptance to publication is six months. Approximately 12 book reviews are contained in each issue of this journal.

235. **THE JOURNAL OF ADVENTIST EDUCATION.** (formerly **JOURNAL OF TRUE EDUCATION**). 1967– (JAE); 1939– (JTE). General Conference of Seventh-day Adventists, 6840 Eastern Avenue, N.W., Washington, DC 20012. Circ.: 7,500. 5 issues/yr. $4.95/yr. Annual index: summer issue. Editor: Garland J. Millet. Book reviews to: editor.

This journal, the official organ of the Association of Seventh-day Adventist Educators, is published at the world headquarters of Adventists in Washington, DC. Its purpose is to foster unity, inform of new ideas, provide a vehicle for comment and discussion by educators of the Seventh-day Adventist Church, and promote better education in the church school through the university level. Types of articles include general education topics, inspirational, poetry, "how to" articles, new developments and implementing Christian education.

Unsolicited articles are accepted for consideration, although a letter of inquiry prior to submission is encouraged. Issues are dedicated to central themes and authors should request that information from the editor. Style is a combination of types and writers should examine recent issues. Length of manuscript should not exceed 3,000 words. Two copies are to be submitted. Estimated time for an editorial decision is four to eight weeks and publication time varies. Book reviews appear in some issues and these are from 500 to 750 words in length. Copyright on all work is held by the publisher.

236. **THE JOURNAL OF AESTHETIC EDUCATION.** 1966– . University of Illinois Press, 1002 West Green Street, Urbana, IL 61801. Circ.: 1,300. 4 issues/yr. $7.50/yr. Annual index: October issue. Editor: Ralph A. Smith. Editor's address: 288-B, Education, University of Illinois, Urbana, IL 61801. Book reviews to: editor.

Indexed in: Abstracts of English Studies; Current Contents: Social & Behavioral Sciences; Current Index to Journals in Education; Education Index; Music Article Guide; Philosopher's Index; Psychological Abstracts; RILM Abstracts of Music Literature; Social Sciences Citation Index.

The *Journal* is a response to the challenge to improve the quality and style of our civilization. Its major purpose is to clarify the issues of aesthetic education, not only the problems of formal instruction in the arts and humanities, but also the aesthetic problems of the larger society. Articles devoted to an understanding of the basic problem areas of education in the arts and humanities, the aesthetic aspects of the art and craft of teaching, the aesthetic import of the new communications media and the environmental arts are published in this journal.

Authors of unsolicited manuscripts are encouraged to submit material. No particular style requirements are indicated, with the exception of the footnoting form which should be requested from the editor. Manuscripts should be between 5,000 and 6,000 words in length, with the copyright being held by the publisher. Between four and eight weeks is required for an editorial decision with publication following acceptance in an undetermined number of months. Book reviews are published on a space available basis. The editor suggests these be approximately 750 words long. Two copies of all work should be submitted.

237. **JOURNAL OF ALCOHOL AND DRUG EDUCATION.** 1955– . Alcohol and Drug Problems Association of North America, c/o John McConnell, Executive Director, 1019 Trowbridge Road, East Lansing, MI 48823. Circ.: not given. 3 issues/yr. $4.00/yr. No annual index. Editor: Gerald Globetti. Editor's address: Department of Sociology, Box 6109, University of Alabama, University, AL 35486. Book reviews to: editor.

Indexed in: Current Index to Journals in Education; Psychological Abstracts; Social Sciences Citation Index; Speed.

This journal is designed to provide a medium of exchange for persons attempting to discover and share ideas relative to the solution of drug and alcohol problems in the school and community. It is intended to reach teachers, guidance counselors, community workers in the fields of alcohol and drugs, as well as professionals in related areas. The editor is interested in research studies, as well as papers on alcohol and drug related education. A wide variety of topics is covered ranging from use to legal issues.

The submission of manuscripts is encouraged. These should be in duplicate with lengths between 2,000 and 3,000 words. The copyright is held by the author with simultaneous submission to other journals being permitted. An editorial decision is usually made in four to six weeks with publication of accepted manuscripts following in six to eight months. One to two book reviews are published each month, with 750 words being the ideal length. Authors should follow APA style requirements for all work.

238. **JOURNAL OF AMERICAN FOLKLORE.** circa 1888– . The American
Folklore Society, c/o The American Anthropological Association, 1703
New Hampshire Avenue, N.W., Washington, DC 20009. Circ.: 3,200.
4 issues/yr. Subscription included with society membership; institution
rate, $12.00/yr. Annual index: fall issue (volume contents). Editor:
Barre Toelken. Editor's address: Department of English, University of
Oregon, Eugene, OR 97403. Book reviews to: Rayna Green, The
Smithsonian Institution, Washington, DC 20560.

  Indexed in: Abstracts in Anthropology; Abstracts of Folklore Studies;
  America: History and Life*; Anthropological Index; Book Review
  Index; Current Contents: Social & Behavioral Sciences; Humanities
  Index; The Music Index; Social Sciences Citation Index; Social
  Sciences Index; Women Studies Abstracts.

The *Journal of American Folklore* is the principal professional journal for
folklore in the United States. Articles require knowledge of folklore and folklore
technical terminology. Its purpose is to make available articles on world folklore
and to allow discussion on the articles and on other topics of interest to folk-
lorists. Information on books, records and films that relate to folklore are
included also.

Unsolicited manuscripts are welcomed for consideration. The MLA style
is the basic requirement; a style sheet citing exceptions is available from the
editor. Length of material for the Notes and Queries section is from 250 to
1,250 words, whereas articles may vary from 3,750 to 8,750 words. Copyright
on published material is held by the Folklore Society. Some issues are dedicated
to special themes and articles for these issues are compiled from among the papers presented at the Folklore Society symposia. Estimated time for an editorial
decision concerning acceptability of an article is eight to twelve weeks. Publication time is six to nine months. Ten to twenty-five book reviews are in this
journal and their length varies from 250 to 2,500 words.

239. **JOURNAL OF AMERICAN INDIAN EDUCATION.** 1961– . Bureau of
Educational Research and Services, College of Education, Arizona State
University, Tempe, AZ 85281. Circ.: 1,000. 3 issues/yr. $3.50/yr. Annual
index: separate index available. Editor: George A. Gill. Editor's address:
Center for Indian Education, College of Education, Arizona State
University, Tempe, AZ 85281. No book reviews.

  Indexed in: Current Contents: Social & Behavioral Sciences; Current
  Index to Journals in Education; Education Index.

This journal is intended for all persons, Indian or non-Indian, interested in
North American Indian education and Indian affairs. Its purpose is to bring to
the attention of the reader various issues, programs and projects involving the
North American Indian. Any materials dealing with the North American Indian
are welcomed.

Authors are encouraged to submit manuscripts or make inquiry of the
editor concerning manuscript ideas. The editor also solicits manuscripts upon
occasion. Two copies of the manuscript, which should not exceed 1,500 words
in length, are required. The copyright is held by the author with eight weeks
being required for an editorial decision. Publication of accepted manuscripts

usually follows within three months. This journal has a six person editorial board. Simultaneous submission to other journals is permitted.

240. **THE JOURNAL OF APPLIED BEHAVIORAL SCIENCE.** 1965– . NTL Institute for Applied Behavioral Science, P.O. Box 9155, Rosslyn Station, Arlington, VA 22209. Circ.: 6,000. 4 issues/yr. $15.00/yr. Annual index: issue number four. Editor: Leonard D. Goodstein. Manuscript to: Ann Marie Beal, managing editor. Book reviews to: Fred Massarik.

Indexed in: ABC: Political Science and Government; Abstracts for Social Workers; Abstracts in Anthropology; College Student Personnel Abstracts; Current Contents: Social & Behavioral Sciences; Current Index to Journals in Education; Education Index; Educational Administration Abstracts; Employment Relations Abstracts*; Hospital Literature Index; Nursing Research; Psychological Abstracts; The Psychological Readers Guide; Readers Guide to Periodical Literature; Sage Public Administration Abstracts; Science Citation Index; Social Sciences Citation Index; Social Sciences Index; Sociological Abstracts; Speed.

The overall mission of the *Journal* is to help create a science and technology of social change by providing an open and continuing dialogue among all participants in such change. Behavioral scientists, small group theorists and practitioners, and organization change agents, are among the intended audience.

Authors are encouraged to submit their articles for consideration. Style of manuscript is to follow APA requirements and four copies are to be submitted. Preferred length of articles is about 5,000 words. The publisher holds copyright on all accepted materials. Prospective contributors are urged to examine the Editorial Policy and Instructions to Contributors sections found near the front of each issue for complete manuscript information. The time for an editorial decision is ten weeks. Publication time, after acceptance, is eighteen months.

241. **JOURNAL OF ARKANSAS EDUCATION.** 1923– . Arkansas Education Association, 1500 West 4th Street, Little Rock, AR 72201. Circ.: 23,000. 4 issues/yr. $1.50/yr. No annual index. Editor: Don Murphy, Jr. No book reviews.

The contents of this journal are directed toward the members of the teaching profession in the State of Arkansas. It reports on activities and programs of the association. It informs its readers of new and different instructional techniques in a wide variety of subject areas and provides other information the editor deems of importance to his constituency.

Unsolicited manuscripts are encouraged, with no length specified. No style requirements are mentioned and only one copy of the manuscript is required. No time span is specified for an editorial decision. An eighteen month maximum time period is stated for publication after acceptance. Copyright is held by the author.

242. **JOURNAL OF BAND RESEARCH.** 1964– . The American Bandmasters Association, College Band Directors National Association, National Band Association, c/o Iowa State University Press, Press Building, Ames, IA 50010.

JOURNAL OF BAND RESEARCH (cont'd)

Circ.: not given. 2 issues/yr. $5.00/yr. No annual index. Editor: Warren E. George. Editor's address: Department of Music Education, The Pennsylvania State University, University Park, PA 16802. No book reviews.

Indexed in: Music Article Guide; The Music Index; RILM Abstracts of Music Literature.

Journal of Band Research is intended to meet the needs of researchers and members of the band profession. Its purpose is to disseminate the results of research relevant to the improvement of the quality of band instruction.

Unsolicited manuscripts are considered for publication. Two copies of the manuscript should be submitted for editorial consideration. Articles between 2,000 and 5,000 words in length are preferred. The copyright is held by the publisher with four weeks being required for an editorial decision. Publication of accepted manuscripts follows within three to six months. Authors should follow APA style requirements.

243. **JOURNAL OF BLACK STUDIES.** 1970– . Sage Publications, Inc., 275 South Beverly Drive, Beverly Hills, CA 90212. Circ.: not given. 4 issues/yr. $12.00/yr. for professionals; institutional rate, $20.00/yr. Annual index: issue number four. Editor: Molefi K. Asante. Editor's address: Department of Black Studies, State University of New York at Buffalo, Buffalo, NY 14226. Book reviews to: Ihechukwu Madubuike, book review editor.

Indexed in: Abstracts for Social Workers; America: History and Life*; Black Information Index; Current Contents: Social & Behavioral Sciences; Current Index to Journals in Education; Human Resources Abstracts; Index to Periodicals by and About Negroes; International Political Science Abstracts; Public Affairs Information Service Bulletin; Sage Urban Studies Abstracts; Social Sciences Citation Index; Social Sciences Index; Sociological Abstracts; Urban Affairs Abstracts.

The *Journal of Black Studies* seeks to sustain a full analytical discussion of issues related to persons of African descent. Original scholarly papers are invited on a wide range of social science questions. The editor favors those articles which demonstrate rigorous and thorough research in interdisciplinary context.

Manuscripts should be submitted in two copies and should not exceed 7,500 words. A style sheet is available upon request. Review essays and bibliographic articles and compilations are sought by the book review editor. Potential contributors should correspond with the book review editor before submitting manuscripts. Times for an editorial decision and publication are not specified. Copyright is held by the publisher.

244. **JOURNAL OF BUSINESS EDUCATION.** (formerly **JOURNAL OF COMMERCIAL EDUCATION** and **BUSINESS SCHOOL JOURNAL**). 1929– (April, JBE); 1929– (March, JCE); 1928– (BSJ). HELDREF Publications, 4000 Albemarle Street, N.W., Washington, DC 20016. Circ.: not given. 8 issues/yr. $7.50/yr. Annual index: October issue. Editor: Elizabeth V. Tonne. Editor's address: P.O. Box 12, Northvale, NJ 07647. Book reviews to: editor.

JOURNAL OF BUSINESS EDUCATION (cont'd)

Indexed in: Book Review Index; Business Education Index; Current
Index to Journals in Education; Media Review Digest.

This journal is written for teachers of business education at all levels including both private and public schools and college personnel. It provides an opportunity for professional publication and sharing of ideas concerning teaching and
preparation of teachers of business education. Topics of articles may be anything
relative to the interests of teachers of business education in the areas of methods,
professionalism, graduate study, general classroom conduct, vocational and non-
vocational objectives, subject matter content and educational change.

The editor accepts manuscripts, about 1,500 words long, for possible inclusion in this journal. Only one copy, the original, of the article need be sent. An
editorial decision is made in three weeks and publication of the work will follow
in less than twelve months. Copyright is held by the publisher. Several book
reviews of 200 or fewer words appear in each issue.

245. **JOURNAL OF CAREER EDUCATION.** 1972– . College of Education,
University of Missouri-Columbia, Columbia, MO 65201. Circ.: 2,000.
4 issues/yr. $8.00/yr. Annual index: fall issue. Editor: H. C. Kazanas.
Editor's address: 103 Industrial Education Building, University of
Missouri-Columbia, Columbia, MO 65201. No book reviews.

This journal is intended to provide a forum for the promotion and development of career education. It is intended for educators and educational administrators at all levels of the profession. The editor prefers material that deals with
empirical, methodological and theoretical content on career education.

The journal issues are devoted to central themes. Information may be
obtained by writing the editor, however, he also encourages submission of
unsolicited manuscripts. Authors should follow APA style requirements.
Length may vary from 3,000 to 3,500 words. Two copies are requested, with
five to ten weeks being required for an editorial decision. Publication of accepted manuscripts usually follows within three to six months. The copyright is
held by the author.

246. **JOURNAL OF CHEMICAL EDUCATION.** 1924– . Division of Chemical
Education of the American Chemical Society, 1155 Sixteenth Street, N.W.,
Washington, DC 20036. Circ.: 25,500. 12 issues/yr. $7.50/yr. Annual index:
December issue. Editor: W. T. Lippincott. Editor's address: Department of
Chemistry, University of Arizona, Tucson, AZ 85721. Book reviews to:
editor.

Indexed in: Ceramic Abstracts; Chemical Abstracts; Child Development
Abstracts and Bibliography; Computer and Control Abstracts*; Current
Index to Journals in Education; Education Index; Index Medicus;
International Pharmaceutical Abstracts; Information Science Abstracts;
Nuclear Science Abstracts.

This journal is intended to reach teachers of chemistry at all levels from high
schools through graduate studies. Its purpose is to help teachers of chemistry keep
up-to-date on recent advances in the fields of chemistry and chemical education.
The editor is interested in review articles dealing with current topics of chemical

JOURNAL OF CHEMICAL EDUCATION (cont'd)

research, new course curricula, new laboratory experiments, and features on teaching aids and devices.

Unsolicited manuscripts are invited. These works should be no longer than 4,000 words and follow the style as set forth in the American Chemical Society's style book. Three copies of all manuscripts should be submitted. The copyright is held by the publisher. Approximately twelve weeks is required for an editorial decision with publication following acceptance from nine months to one year later. Between ten and twelve book reviews are published each month in the *Journal* and these should be approximately 500 words in length. Some reviews are solicited by the editor, however, unsolicited reviews are considered.

247. **JOURNAL OF COLLEGE PLACEMENT.** 1940– . The College Placement Council, Inc., P.O. Box 2263, Bethlehem, PA 18001. Circ.: 3,600. 4 issues/yr. Subscription included with council membership; non-member rate, $35.00/yr. No annual index. Editor: Warren E. Kauffman. Book reviews to: editor.
    Indexed in: College Student Personnel Abstracts; Current Index to Journals in Education; Education Index; Employment Relations Abstracts*; Women Studies Abstracts.

This journal is intended for professionals in career planning, placement and the recruitment field. Topics include profiles of career fields, reports on research related to the field, new techniques or ideas, and utilization of college-trained personnel. Regular features are Newswire, Calendar, Career Media, What's New to Read, Opinions, and News About People. Articles should be keyed to the counselor-recruiter level with the thought that students reading the material will be mature enough to absorb its content. The subscription rate includes another publication entitled *Salary Survey*.

Although the editor may solicit articles from individuals, authors are encouraged to submit manuscripts for consideration. A narrative style is preferred rather than a formal thesis style. Authors are urged to adopt, insofar as possible, an informal presentation. A two page guide for contributors is available from the editor. A single copy of the material, 3,000 to 4,000 words long, is to be submitted. An editorial decision is made in four weeks and the estimated time from acceptance to publication is six to nine months. Copyright is held by the publisher. About ten to twelve book reviews are contained in this journal. These reviews are 300 to 500 words in length.

248. **JOURNAL OF COLLEGE SCIENCE TEACHING.** 1971– . National Science Teachers Association, 1742 Connecticut Avenue, N.W., Washington, DC 20009. Circ.: 3,300. 5 issues/yr. Subscription included with association membership; institution rate, $25.00/yr. Annual index: May issue. Editor: Leo Schubert. Editor's address: Department of Chemistry, The American University, Washington, DC 20016. Book reviews to: Ernest Blaustein, Professor of Biology, Boston University, Boston, MA 02215.
    Indexed in: Chemical Abstracts; Chemical Titles; Current Index to Journals in Education; Education Index; Media Review Digest.

This journal's purposes are to strengthen disciplinary studies in the sciences at the college level, to encourage interdisciplinary courses, to explore innovative

JOURNAL OF COLLEGE SCIENCE TEACHING (cont'd)

teaching materials and techniques, to explore interaction between science and society, and to improve science offerings for nonscience majors. Aims at college science teachers of introductory level courses. Articles stressing interdisciplinary aspects of science teaching are favored. An article with specific content should be of general interest so that teachers in other disciplines can understand it. Controversial topics should be treated in a factually sound fashion.

Manuscripts of 2,500 words or less are welcomed by the editor. Authors should follow MLA style requirements and should submit three copies of their work. Issues are devoted to central themes and prospective contributors may obtain information concerning these from the editor. Estimated time for an editorial decision is twelve weeks with publication of accepted material following in seven months. Approximately ten book reviews are contained in each issue. These reviews are 1,000 or fewer words in length. Persons wishing to review books should correspond with the book review editor. Copyright is held by the publisher.

249. **JOURNAL OF COLLEGE STUDENT PERSONNEL.** 1959– . American College Personnel Association, 1607 New Hampshire Avenue, N.W., Washington, DC 20009. Circ.: 10,000. 6 issues/yr. $15.00/yr. Annual index: November issue. Editor: Albert B. Hood. Editor's address: W112 East Hall, University of Iowa, Iowa City, IA 52242. No book reviews.
    Indexed in: College Student Personnel Abstracts; Current Contents: Social & Behavioral Sciences; Current Index to Journals in Education; Education Index; Educational Administration Abstracts; Psychological Abstracts; Social Sciences Citation Index; Women Studies Abstracts.

This journal is the official organ of the American College Personnel Association, a division of the American Personnel and Guidance Association. Its purpose is to report research, current thinking and innovative practices in the field. It is intended to serve college counselors and student personnel administrators.

Unsolicited manuscripts, conforming to APA style requirements, are accepted for consideration. Maximum length is 3,500 words and articles are to be submitted in duplicate. Copyright is held by the publisher. An editorial decision is made in eight weeks and the estimated time from acceptance to publication is eight months.

250. **JOURNAL OF COOPERATIVE EDUCATION.** 1964– . Cooperative Education Association, c/o Stewart B. Collins, Executive Director, Drexel University, Philadelphia, PA 19104. Circ.: 1,200. 2 issues/yr. Subscription included with association membership. No annual index. Editor: Harry N. Heineman, Fiorello H. La Guardia Community College, 31-10 Thompson Avenue, Long Island City, NY 11101. Book reviews to: editor.

This journal is intended to reach those persons interested in cooperative education in higher education. It includes persons who teach in colleges, universities, community colleges as well as those employed in industry and government. It is intended to become a vehicle to stimulate the growth and development of

JOURNAL OF COOPERATIVE EDUCATION (cont'd)

cooperative education, by providing a forum for discussion of critical issues pertaining to cooperative and experimental education.

Authors are encouraged to submit manuscripts. The editor also solicits manuscripts from colleagues. Restrictions are not placed on article length but two copies are to be submitted. Four to six weeks is usually required for an editorial decision with the publication of accepted manuscripts following within four to six months.

251. **JOURNAL OF CORRECTIONAL EDUCATION.** 1948– . Correctional Education Association, c/o G. O. Gagnon, Executive Secretary, P.O. Box B, Trenton, NJ 08690. Circ.: 1,200. 4 issues/yr. Subscription included with association membership; institution rate, $15.00/yr. No annual index. Editor: W. Neal Lang. Editor's address: P.O. Box 110, Glen Mills, PA 19342. Book reviews to: editor.

Indexed in: Sociological Abstracts.

This journal is intended primarily for correctional professionals in the area of education. It disseminates information about the profession of correctional education to its membership. Informative and/or theoretical articles describing the role of correctional education in the field of criminal justice are included in this publication.

Unsolicited manuscripts are accepted for consideration. A letter of inquiry prior to submission is encouraged. A specific style is not required. Length should be limited to a maximum of 5,000 words and two copies of the article are to be sent. Copyright is held by the publisher. An editorial decision is given in sixteen weeks and publication of accepted material usually follows in four months. Book reviews are included in each issue and their length varies from 150 to 500 words.

252. **JOURNAL OF CREATIVE BEHAVIOR.** 1967– . Creative Education Foundation, State University College-Buffalo, 1300 Elmwood Avenue, Chase Hall, Buffalo, NY 14222. Circ.: 4,000. 4 issues/yr. $9.00/yr. Annual index: issue number four. Editor: Angelo M. Biondi. Book reviews to: editor.

Indexed in: Current Contents: Social & Behavioral Sciences; Current Index to Journals in Education; dsh Abstracts; Education Index; Psychological Abstracts; Research into Higher Education; Social Sciences Citation Index; Social Sciences Index; Sociological Abstracts.

The *Journal of Creative Behavior* is intended for classroom teachers, elementary through college level, and other persons interested in any aspect of creativity. The application of creative problem solving techniques to various disciplines is a major thrust of this journal. Sample article titles are: Creative Problem-Solving Techniques in Nursing; Improving Children's Creative Problem Solving Ability—The Purdue Creativity Project; Creative Ideas Through Circumrelation; and, Creativity and Sex Differences.

Unsolicited manuscripts provide this journal with the majority of its material. Two copies of the work should be submitted with no limitation of length being indicated. The APA style requirements should be followed.

JOURNAL OF CREATIVE BEHAVIOR (cont'd)

Between twelve and twenty-six weeks is required for an editorial decision with publication following within three to four months for accepted manuscripts. Book reviews usually are not used, however, they may be published on a space available basis. Copyright is held by the publisher.

253. **JOURNAL OF CROSS-CULTURAL PSYCHOLOGY.** 1970– . Sage Publications, Inc., 275 South Beverly Drive, Beverly Hills, CA 90212. Circ.: not given. 4 issues/yr. $12.00/yr. (professionals); institution rate, $20.00/yr. Annual index: December issue. Editor: Walter J. Lonner. Editor's address: Center for Cross-Cultural Research, Department of Psychology, Western Washington State College, Bellingham, WA 98225. Book reviews are invited by editor.

Indexed in: Abstracts in Anthropology; Abstracts of Folklore Studies; Current Contents: Social & Behavioral Sciences; Current Index to Journals in Education; Human Resources Abstracts; Language and Language Behavior Abstracts; Psychological Abstracts; The Psychological Readers Guide; Sage Urban Studies Abstracts; Social Sciences Citation Index; Women Studies Abstracts.

This journal's purpose is to explain how culture and ecology affect psychological processes and phenomena, to promote the method of cross-cultural psychology, to increase inter-cultural understanding, and to aid in the search for behavioral "universals." It is intended to reach psychologists, anthropologists, educators, and any behavioral scientists who work with "other cultures." The editor is interested in articles dealing with data-oriented empirical research, major theoretical and review articles, and method-oriented work.

Authors are requested to submit three copies of their work, which should be between 7,500 to 10,000 words in length, longer if necessary. The copyright is held by Western Washington State College. Between six and eight weeks is required for an editorial decision with publication of accepted works following six to nine months later. The journal publishes one or two book reviews per issue. These reviews are invited or at least negotiated before submission. The APA style requirements should be followed. Style guide sheets and an expanded editorial policy statement are available from the editor.

254. **JOURNAL OF DENTAL EDUCATION.** 1936– . American Association of Dental Schools, 1625 Massachusetts Avenue, N.W., Washington, DC 20036. Circ.: 3,600. 12 issues/yr. $15.00/yr. Annual index: December issue. Editor: Erling Johansen. Editor's address: Department of Dental Research, University of Rochester, 601 Elmwood Avenue, Rochester, NY 14642. Book reviews to: editor.

Indexed in: Current Contents: Social & Behavioral Sciences; Dental Abstracts; Hospital Literature Index; Index Medicus; Nuclear Science Abstracts.

This journal is intended to reach dental educators, examiners, students, and others in health related education. Its purpose is the publication of the results of experimentation in education, the exchange of educational ideas and concepts, and the dissemination of philosophical and practical ideas related to dental education.

JOURNAL OF DENTAL EDUCATION (cont'd)

The editor encourages submission of unsolicited manuscripts. Contributors should send the original plus two copies of their work. The copyright is retained by the publisher. Between twelve and sixteen weeks is required for an editorial decision, with publication of accepted work following within three to four months. This journal uses book reviews, publication varying on a space available basis. Length of these should be approximately 250 words. Articles should normally not exceed 4,000 words.

255. **JOURNAL OF DRUG EDUCATION.** 1971— . Baywood Publishing Company Inc., 43 Central Drive, Farmingdale, NY 11735. Circ.: 1,400. 4 issues/yr. $35.00/yr. Annual index: issue number four. Editors: Albert E. Bedworth and Joseph A. D'Elia. Book reviews to: editor.

Indexed in: Abstracts on Police Science*; Current Index to Journals in Education; Excerpta Medica; Information Retrieval Limited*; Psychological Abstracts; Speed.

The intent of this journal is to provide an international forum for the dissemination of factual drug information. It presents criteria for drug education curricula, defines the role of the teacher and guidance and administrative personnel in drug education. The intended audience includes teachers, administrators, guidance counselors, law enforcement and social service personnel, local community groups, school psychologists, social workers and military personnel involved in armed forces drug education programs.

Although articles are solicited by the editor, unsolicited manuscripts also are accepted for consideration. The original plus a duplicate of the article, 5,000 words in length, are to be submitted. Copyright is held by the publisher. Issues may be devoted to central themes and authors should write the editor for further information. An editorial decision as to acceptance can be expected in four weeks. Publication will follow within three months. Approximately two book reviews appear in this journal. These reviews are about 1,000 words long. The inside back cover of the *Journal* has a detailed description of style and other information to authors.

256. **THE JOURNAL OF ECONOMIC EDUCATION.** 1969— . Joint Council on Economic Education, 1212 Avenue of the Americas, New York, NY 10036. Circ.: 4,000. 2 issues/yr. $4.00/yr. No annual index. Editor: Henry H. Villard. Manuscript to: George G. Dawson, managing editor. Book reviews to: managing editor.

Indexed in: Business Education Index; Current Contents: Social & Behavioral Sciences; Current Index to Journals in Education; Journal of Economic Literature; Public Affairs Information Service Bulletin; Social Sciences Citation Index.

This journal is intended for teachers of economics at all educational levels. The purpose of the publication is to disseminate research results and evaluations of new methods of teaching economics. The format generally includes several major articles, a notes and communications section, book reviews, and reports of new materials (such as audio-visual materials) useful in teaching economics.

THE JOURNAL OF ECONOMIC EDUCATION (cont'd)

The editor welcomes unsolicited manuscripts for possible inclusion in this journal, but encourages use of a letter of inquiry prior to submission. Articles should be 2,500 to 3,000 words long. A two page style sheet should be requested from the managing editor. Copyright is held by the publisher. Simultaneous submission to other journals is permitted. Sometimes an issue is devoted to a central theme and it is announced a year in advance in the *Journal*. The time for an editorial decision is twelve weeks and publication will follow in six months. Usually two book reviews, about 1,250 words in length, are contained in each issue. Authors should write the managing editor prior to submitting book reviews, since only certain types of books are reviewed. All material should be submitted in triplicate.

257. JOURNAL OF EDUCATION. 1875– . Boston University School of Education, 765 Commonwealth Avenue, Boston, MA 02215. Circ.: 1,300. 4 issues/yr. $8.00/yr.; institution rate, $10.00/yr. No annual index. Editor: Allan Alson. Book reviews to: Lawrence Brink.

Indexed in: Education Index; Exceptional Child Education Abstracts; Women Studies Abstracts.

This journal is intended for educators at all levels as well as for students. Its purpose is to provide a forum for the presentation of controversial issues, enlightening discussion, and innovative approaches to current educational concerns. Articles preferred are literary, although occasional empirical research studies are published. Relevance and generalizability are important aspects of the articles which would be acceptable for this journal.

The editorial board selects central themes for three issues per year and solicits authors directly for their works. One issue each year is reserved for unsolicited manuscripts. No preferred length is specified but three copies are to be submitted. The APA style requirements should be followed. Copyright is held by the publisher. An editorial decision is made in four to six weeks and the estimated time from acceptance to publication is three to six months. Five book reviews of about 400 words are contained in each issue. Guidelines to be followed in writing articles and book reviews are available from the editor.

258. JOURNAL OF EDUCATION (Nova Scotia). 1851– (published continuously since 1866). Department of Education, P.O. Box 578, Halifax, Nova Scotia, Canada B3J 2S9. Circ.: 13,500. 4 issues/yr. Subscription provided to Nova Scotia teachers and libraries. No annual index. Editor: R. A. Simpson. Book reviews to: editor.

Indexed in: Canadian Education Index.

The *Journal of Education* is distributed to all teachers of Nova Scotia and to many lay people. Articles are intended to be of a general nature, not too highly specialized, and free of technical jargon. Articles dealing with research should be discursive and not encumbered with technical apparatus.

Unsolicited articles are accepted for consideration, but a letter of inquiry prior to submission is encouraged. Average length of manuscripts to be considered for publication should be 3,000 words. The Canadian Government's style manual is to be followed. Copyright is held by the author. Estimated time for an editorial decision is six weeks with publication of accepted material following within six months. Occasional book reviews are contained in the journal. These reviews are of works of general education interest. No reviews of textbooks or specific learning materials are included.

259. **JOURNAL OF EDUCATION FOR LIBRARIANSHIP.** 1960– . Association of American Library Schools, 471 Park Lane, State College, PA 16801. Circ.: 2,000. 4 issues/yr. $8.00/yr. No annual index. Editor: Norman Horrocks. Editor's address: School of Library Service, Dalhousie University, Halifax, N.S., Canada B3H 4H8. No book reviews.

Indexed in: Bulletin Signaletique, Section 101: Science de L'Information-Documentation; Computer and Control Abstracts*; Current Index to Journals in Education; Information Science Abstracts; Library and Information Science Abstracts; Library Literature; Science Citation Index; Social Sciences Citation Index; Women Studies Abstracts.

The *Journal* is the official publication of the Association of American Library Schools. Association members are those schools offering graduate programs in library science. Its audience includes faculty members in these schools although others interested in library education also subscribe. The purpose of this refereed publication is to report original research and new developments in the field of library education. Authors are encouraged to submit articles likely to be of interest to the above audience. Preference is given to those which seek to analyze a particular aspect rather than simply describe a specific situation.

Unsolicited manuscripts are encouraged and letters of inquiry will be answered. The Chicago style should be followed and no length limitations are specified. Between four and six weeks is required for an editorial decision, with three months elapsing between acceptance and publication of manuscripts. The copyright is held by the author, if desired.

260. **JOURNAL OF EDUCATION FOR SOCIAL WORK.** 1965– . Council on Social Work Education, 345 East 46th Street, New York, NY 10017. Circ.: 6,000. 3 issues/yr. Subscription included with council membership. Annual index: fall issue. Editor: Wallace J. Jalinske. Outside book reviews not accepted.

Indexed in: Abstracts for Social Workers; Current Index to Journals in Education; Research into Higher Education; Social Sciences Citation Index.

This journal is intended to reach educators in the field of social work, as well as practitioners and students. Its purpose is to provide constituents with articles presenting new developments, trends, issues, and problems in the field of education for social welfare. The editor is interested in articles which focus on social work education, as well as associated fields which have implications in the primary field of interest.

Unsolicited articles of approximately 3,500 words, in triplicate, are accepted for consideration. The Chicago style should be followed and copyright is held by the publisher. Approximately ten to twelve weeks is required for an editorial decision with twelve to sixteen months elapsing between acceptance and publication. This journal uses between four and six solicited book reviews of approximately 1,000 words in length.

261. JOURNAL OF EDUCATIONAL DATA PROCESSING. 1962– . Educational Systems Corporation, P.O. Box 2995, Stanford, CA 94305. Circ.: 2,000. 4 issues/yr. $11.00/yr. Annual index: issue number four. Editor: Sally Douglas. Editor's address: Cabrillo College, 6500 Soquel Drive, Aptos, CA 95003. Book reviews to: Kevin Reilly, book review editor, P. O. Box 2995, Stanford, CA 94305.

Indexed in: Computer and Control Abstracts*; Computer and Information Systems Abstracts; Computing Review; Current Contents: Social & Behavioral Sciences; Current Index to Journals in Education; Data Processing Digest; Education Index; IBM's Research Library; New Literature on Automation; Quarterly Bibliography of Computers and Data Processing.

This journal is designed to aid teachers of data processing and computer science curricula, facilitate administrative use of data processing in education, and assist in the management of data processing installations in education. Manuscripts dealing with educational data processing systems are solicited. These articles may: report empirical research; describe system operation and/or organization; or, present technical information.

Articles from 3,000 to 6,000 words in length are accepted for possible inclusion in this journal. Two copies of the manuscript are required and a letter of inquiry prior to submission is encouraged. Copyright is held by the publisher. Issues are dedicated to central themes and authors are requested to contact the editor for further information. Simultaneous submission to other journals is permitted. Estimated time for an editorial decision is six to eight weeks. Publication will follow in four to ten months. Three to four book reviews of about 250 words appear in each issue. Authors should follow APA style requirements for all work.

262. JOURNAL OF EDUCATIONAL MEASUREMENT. 1964– . National Council on Measurement in Education, Inc., c/o Irvin J. Lehmann, Office of Evaluation Services, Michigan State University, East Lansing, MI 48823. Circ.: 3,000. 4 issues/yr. Subscription included with association membership; non-member rate, $10.00/yr. Annual index: issue number four. Editor: Richard M. Jaeger. Editor's address: College of Education, FAO 292, University of South Florida, Tampa, FL 33620. Book reviewers chosen by editor.

Indexed in: College Student Personnel Abstracts; Current Contents: Social & Behavioral Sciences; Current Index to Journals in Education; Education Index; Psychological Abstracts; Social Sciences Citation Index; Sociology of Education Abstracts.

The editor of the *Journal of Educational Measurement* seeks new contributions to applied educational measurement and measurement research. Its intended audience consists of practitioners and research workers in educational measurement. Solicited reviews of current standardized tests and of other important measurement works appear regularly in the Review section of the journal.

JOURNAL OF EDUCATIONAL MEASUREMENT (cont'd)

Unsolicited articles are accepted for consideration. Manuscripts are to follow APA style guidelines, but authors should examine recent issues for further information. An editorial policy statement also has been printed in the Spring, 1970 and Spring, 1975 issues of the journal. Material is to be submitted in triplicate. Length is not specified, but the editor indicates a preference for short or brief articles. Contributors can expect an editorial decision concerning acceptance within twelve weeks. If accepted, publication follows in ten months. Copyright is held by NCME.

263. **JOURNAL OF EDUCATIONAL PSYCHOLOGY.** 1910– . American Psychological Association, 1200 Seventeenth Street, N.W., Washington, DC 20036. Circ.: 6,700. 6 issues/yr. $12.00/yr. with association membership; non-member rate, $30.00/yr. Annual index: December issue. Editor: Joanna Williams. Editor's address: P.O. Box 238, Teachers College, Columbia University, New York, NY 10027. No book reviews.

   Indexed in: Abstracts in Anthropology; Bulletin Signaletique, Section 390: Psychologie-Psychopathologie-Psychiatrie; College Student Personnel Abstracts; Current Contents: Social & Behavioral Sciences; Current Index to Journals in Education; dsh Abstracts; Education Index; Educational Administration Abstracts; Exceptional Child Education Abstracts; Excerpta Media; Index Medicus; Mental Retardation Abstracts; Psychological Abstracts; Science Citation Index; Social Sciences Citation Index; Sociological Abstracts; Speed; Women Studies Abstracts.

   The *Journal of Educational Psychology* publishes original investigations and theoretical papers dealing with learning and cognition, especially as they relate to problems of instruction, and with the psychological development, relationships, and adjustments of the individual. Preference is given to studies of the more complex types of behavior, especially in or relating to educational settings. Journal articles pertain to all levels of education and to all age groups.

   The editor encourages the submission of manuscripts. While there are no length requirements, articles of approximately 5,000 words are preferred. The APA style is encouraged. Copyright is held jointly by the author and the publisher. Between six and eight weeks is required for an editorial decision with publication of accepted manuscripts following within one year. Three copies of all manuscripts are required.

264. **JOURNAL OF EDUCATIONAL TECHNOLOGY SYSTEMS.** 1972– . Baywood Publishing Company, Inc., 43 Central Drive, Farmingdale, NY 11735. Circ.: 700. 4 issues/yr. $33.00/yr. Annual index: issue number four. Editors: Thomas T. Liao and David C. Miller. Book reviews to: Thomas Liao.

   Indexed in: Current Index to Journals in Education; Engineering Index.

   This journal is designed to inform educators who are interested in making optimum use of technology. It deals with systems in which technology and education interface. Special emphasis is given to papers that deal with matching technological instruments and tools to the learning process and the human user.

Descriptions of actual classroom practice and experimentation with educational use of technology is an important aspect of this journal. It also features innovative papers about systems for making use of technology to individualize instruction.

The editor solicits articles and accepts unsolicited articles for possible inclusion in the *Journal*. A letter of inquiry prior to submission of material is encouraged. Manuscript should be about 5,000 words long and is to be submitted in duplicate. The time for an editorial decision concerning acceptance is four weeks. Publication will follow in four months. Copyright is held by the publisher. Book reviews of 1,000 words may appear in each issue. More detailed manuscript information may be found on the journal's inside back cover.

265. **THE JOURNAL OF EDUCATIONAL THOUGHT.** 1967— . Faculty of Education, Education Tower, The University of Calgary, 2920 24th Avenue, N.W., Calgary, Alberta, Canada T2N 1N4. Circ.: not given. 3 issues/yr. $5.00/yr. Annual index: December issue. Editor: D. McDougall. Book reviews to: editor.

Indexed in: Canadian Education Index; Current Contents: Social & Behavioral Sciences; Current Index to Journals in Education; Educational Administration Abstracts; Language and Language Behavior Abstracts; Social Sciences Citation Index; Sociology of Education Abstracts.

This journal is intended to provide an outlet for the discussion of educational ideas. The purpose of this journal is to provide an opportunity for the publication of papers dealing with critical or speculative issues in public education. No research articles are published. Although much of the content is Canadian oriented, the total context is international. It is directed toward academicians, teachers and administrators as well as other individuals involved and interested in any aspect of education.

Unsolicited articles, submitted in three copies, are considered for publication by the editor. Article length should be between 6,000 and 7,500 words in length. No style requirements are mentioned, therefore, prospective contributors should peruse back issues of this journal. Editorial decisions are usually made within four weeks with publication of accepted pieces occurring within two to three months. Book reviews are accepted for consideration, however, no minimum requirements are specified.

266. **THE JOURNAL OF ENVIRONMENTAL EDUCATION.** (formerly ENVIRONMENTAL EDUCATION). 1969— . Helen Dwight Reid Educational Foundation, 4000 Albemarle Street, N.W., Washington, DC 20016. Circ.: not given. 4 issues/yr. $10.00/yr.; institution rate, $12.50/yr. Annual index: summer issue. Editor: Jane Scully, managing editor. Book reviews to: managing editor.

Indexed in: Current Contents: Social & Behavioral Sciences; Current Index to Journals in Education; Environmental Periodicals Bibliography; Social Sciences Citation Index.

The audience of this journal includes practitioners and scholars concerned with interpreting environmental issues. It is intended to stimulate and disseminate

THE JOURNAL OF ENVIRONMENTAL EDUCATION (cont'd)

research and development in ecological communications. The editor prefers articles dealing with research, project reports and critical essays designed to advance the scientific study of conservation and improve field practice in environmental education.

The editor encourages the submission of manuscripts. Certain issues are dedicated to central themes and these may be obtained on request from the editor. Articles may range from 1,500 to 3,000 words and should be submitted in duplicate. Authors should follow the Chicago style and may request a set of guidelines from the editor. Each manuscript is evaluated by at least two consulting editors. The copyright is held by the publisher. Eight weeks is needed for an editorial decision and nine to twelve months is required for publication following acceptance.

267. **JOURNAL OF ENVIRONMENTAL HEALTH.** (formerly **THE SANITARIAN**). 1962– (JEH); 1938– (S). National Environmental Health Association, 1600 Pennsylvania, Denver, CO 80203. Circ.: 7,800. 6 issues/yr. Library rate, $10.00/yr. Annual index: May/June issue. Editor: A. Harry Bliss. Book reviews to: editor.

> Indexed in: Current Contents: Agriculture, Biology & Environmental Sciences; Current Contents: Social & Behavioral Sciences; Current Index to Journals in Education; Environment Access; Environmental Periodicals Bibliography; Excerpta Medica; Hospital Literature Index; Information Retrieval Limited*; Pollution Abstracts*.

Among the intended audience are professional sanitarians and other environmental health personnel educators and students of environmental health. The purpose of this journal is to inform professional environmental health personnel of what is going on in their field, in their professional organization, and to help them on the job. Practical articles on problem solving, research articles and professionally inspirational articles are preferred.

Unsolicited manuscripts are accepted for consideration. Preferred length of articles is 2,500 to 5,000 words and three copies are required. Style is not specified, however, it is recommended that prospective contributors request the instructions for submitting manuscripts that is available from the editor. The time for an editorial decision concerning acceptance is six to eight weeks. Publication follows in six months. Book reviews of 250 words are included in this journal on a space available basis.

268. **THE JOURNAL OF EXPERIMENTAL EDUCATION.** 1932– . HELDREF Publications, 4000 Albemarle Street, N.W., Washington, DC 20016. Circ.: not given. 4 issues/yr. $10.00/yr. Annual index: summer issue. Editor: John Schmid. Editor's address: Department of Research and Statistical Methodology, University of Northern Colorado, Greeley, CO 80631. Book reviews to: editor.

> Indexed in: Abstracts for Social Workers; Bulletin Signaletique, Section 390: Psychologie-Psychopathologie-Psychiatrie; College Student Personnel Abstracts; Current Contents: Social & Behavioral Sciences; Current Index to Journals in Education; dsh Abstracts; Educational Administration Abstracts; Exceptional Child Education

Abstracts; Language and Language Behavior Abstracts; Psychological Abstracts; Research into Higher Education; Social Sciences Citation Index; Sociology of Education Abstracts; Women Studies Abstracts.

This refereed journal is intended for university professors and advanced research investigators. Experimental behavioral research studies and those which deal with technical and specialized areas of education are welcomed for editorial consideration. Monographs as well as articles may be submitted. Sample titles from a recent issue include: Grade Level Contributions to the Variance of Flander's Interaction Categories; Item Sampling—Optimal Number of People and Items; and, Factor Analysis of Measures of Aptitude, Intelligence, Personality, and Performance in High School Subjects.

Authors are encouraged to submit unsolicited manuscripts for consideration. Two copies of the article, 1,250 to 2,500 words in length, are to be submitted. An abstract is required. Writers should study the directions for contributors which are found on the inside back cover of each issue. Authors pay the publisher at the rate of $6.00 per printed page of approximately 1,200 words. Copyright is held by the publisher. The time for an editorial decision concerning acceptance is three to five weeks. Publication follows in eighteen months. Each issue contains one book review of about 250 words.

269. **JOURNAL OF EXPERIMENTAL PSYCHOLOGY: HUMAN PERCEPTION AND PERFORMANCE.** 1975– . American Psychological Association, 1200 Seventeenth Street, N.W., Washington, DC 20036. Circ.: not given. 4 issues/yr. $6.00/yr. with APA membership; non-member rate, $16.00/yr. Annual index: November issue. Editor: Michael I. Posner. Editor's address: Department of Psychology, University of Oregon, Eugene, OR 97403. No book reviews.

Indexed in: Bulletin Signaletique, Section 390: Psychologie-Psychopathologie-Psychiatrie; Current Contents: Life Sciences; Current Contents: Social & Behavioral Sciences; Current Index to Journals in Education; dsh Abstracts; Ergonomics Information Analysis Centre; Excerpta Medica; Index Medicus; Information Science Abstracts; Mental Retardation Abstracts; Nuclear Science Abstracts; Psychological Abstracts; The Psychological Readers Guide; Science Citation Index; Social Sciences Index.

Beginning in 1975 the *Journal of Experimental Psychology* was published as four independently edited and distributed sections. This section, *Human Perception and Performance*, includes eight to twelve experimental articles per edition designed to foster understanding of human information-processing operations as related to experience and performance. The intended audience includes research workers in experimental psychology in fields of perception, vision, audition, sensation, attention, motor control, psycholinguistics, human performance, engineering psychology, and related areas such as education and the sciences.

Manuscripts conforming to APA style requirements are welcomed by the editor. Article length may vary from 5,000 to 10,000 words and should be submitted

in triplicate. Estimated time for an editorial decision is four to eight weeks. Time
from acceptance to publication is six to eight months. Copyright is held by the
publisher.

270. **JOURNAL OF EXTENSION.** 1963– . University of Wisconsin, 805 Extension
Building, 432 North Lake Street, Madison, WI 53706. Circ.: 6,200. 6 issues/yr.
$9.00/yr. Annual index: December issue. Editor: Jerry Parsons. Editor's add-
ress: 310 Poe Hall, North Carolina State University, Raleigh, NC 27607.
Book reviews to: editor.
   Indexed in: Abstracts for Social Workers; Current Index to Journals in
   Education; Social Sciences Citation Index; Sociological Abstracts.
   The intended audience of the *Journal* includes those persons engaged in extension education. Its purpose is the dissemination of research to extension professionals and the exchange of ideas in the field. The desired type of articles are those
based on research, creative thought, and case studies in which experience is looked
at in reference to theory.
   Unsolicited articles are considered for publication. One issue per year is
dedicated to a central theme and letters of inquiry are encouraged. Authors should
follow the Chicago style requirements, with the length being 2,000 to 2,500 words.
Six weeks is required for an editorial decision with three months required for publication following acceptance. Each issue contains four to six book reviews or
abstracts of approximately 250 words each. The copyright is held by the publisher.
Four copies of the manuscript are required.

271. **JOURNAL OF GEOLOGICAL EDUCATION.** 1951– . National Association
of Geology Teachers, Department of Geosciences, University of Arizona,
Tucson, AZ 85721. Circ.: 3,600. 5 issues/yr. $10.00/yr. with association
membership; non-member rate, $12.00/yr. No annual index. Editor: James
H. Shea. Editor's address: Division of Science, University of Wisconsin-
Parkside, Kenosha, WI 53140. Book reviews to: Joseph L. Weitz, Geology
Department, Colorado State University, Ft. Collins, CO 80521.
   Indexed in: Current Index to Journals in Education.
   The intended audience of this journal includes college geology professors and
secondary school earth science teachers. Its purpose is to provide current information for its readers, especially for instructors in small departments. Articles preferred are those dealing with classroom ideas and teaching methods.
   Unsolicited articles are accepted for consideration. Contributors are urged to
examine the instructions printed in a January issue for style information. Length
of work may vary from 3,000 to 4,000 words and is to be submitted in duplicate.
The time for an editorial decision concerning acceptance is six to eight weeks and
publication will follow in six months. Copyright is held by the publisher. Six to
ten book reviews appear in each issue. Preferred length is 500 words and the
reviewer is given wide latitude as to style.

272. **JOURNAL OF HEALTH AND SOCIAL BEHAVIOR.** (formerly **JOURNAL
OF HEALTH AND HUMAN BEHAVIOR**). 1967– (JHSB); 1960– (JHHB).

JOURNAL OF HEALTH AND SOCIAL BEHAVIOR (cont'd)

American Sociological Association, 1722 N Street, N.W., Washington, DC 20036. Circ.: 2,400. 4 issues/yr. $6.00/yr. with association membership; non-member rate, $10.00/yr.; institution rate, $14.00/yr. Annual index: December issue. Editor: Mary E. W. Goss. Editor's address: Cornell University Medical College, A-623, 1300 York Avenue, New York, NY 10021. No book reviews.

Indexed in: Abstracts for Social Workers; College Student Personnel Abstracts; Current Contents: Social & Behavioral Sciences; Exceptional Child Education Abstracts; Excerpta Medica; Hospital Literature Index; Index Medicus; Index to Periodical Articles Related to Law; International Pharmaceutical Abstracts; Medical Care Review; Nursing Research; Psychological Abstracts; Rehabilitation Literature; Social Sciences Citation Index; Social Sciences Index; Sociological Abstracts; Sociology of Education Abstracts; Speed; Tropical Diseases Bulletin*; Women Studies Abstracts.

The intended audience includes medical sociologists and others in related areas. This journal provides a forum of exchange and publication outlet concerning health and social behavior from a sociological viewpoint. Theoretical and empirical studies pertaining to health and social behavior are preferred for this journal.

Unsolicited manuscripts are accepted for consideration. Length of article is unspecified. Detailed instructions for writers are given on the inside back cover of each journal. Contributors should include three copies of their work. An editorial decision is made in twelve weeks. The estimated time from acceptance to publication is six to twelve months. Copyright is held by the publisher.

273. **THE JOURNAL OF HIGHER EDUCATION.** 1930– . American Association for Higher Education, Suite 780, One Dupont Circle, Washington, DC 20036. Circ.: 5,600. 6 issues/yr. $8.00/yr. with association membership; non-member rate, $10.00/yr.; library rate, $12.00/yr. Annual index: November-December issue. Editor: Robert J. Silverman. Editor's address: Ohio State University Press, 2070 Neil Avenue, Columbus, OH 43210. Book reviews to: editor.

Indexed in: Abstracts for Social Workers; America: History and Life*; Book Review Index; Chemical Abstracts; College Student Personnel Abstracts; Current Contents: Social & Behavioral Sciences; Current Index to Journals in Education; Education Index; Educational Administration Abstracts; Language and Language Behavior Abstracts; Psychological Abstracts; Research into Higher Education; Social Sciences Citation Index; Sociological Abstracts; Sociology of Education Abstracts; Universal Reference System.

The *Journal* aims to serve the interests of scholars and practitioners alike. Papers submitted should be grounded in both scholarly dimensions and pragmatic needs. This refereed journal encourages submission of unsolicited manuscripts in an effort to maintain an open access to the field. Prospective contributors are urged to consult a recent issue of this journal for its statement of editorial policy and instructions to contributors.

THE JOURNAL OF HIGHER EDUCATION (cont'd)

Unsolicited articles, 3,750 to 5,000 words in length, are accepted for consideration. Manuscripts are to be submitted in triplicate and should adhere to Chicago style. An editorial decision concerning acceptance can be expected in three to six weeks. If accepted, publication follows in three to four months. Four to nine book reviews appear in each issue. Preferred length for these reviews is 800 to 1,000 words. Copyright is held by publisher.

274. **THE JOURNAL OF HUMAN RESOURCES.** 1966— . Industrial Relations Research Institute and the Institute for Research on Poverty, University of Wisconsin Press, P.O. Box 1379, Madison, WI 53701. Circ.: 2,500. 4 issues/yr. $10.00/yr.; institution rate, $20.00/yr. Annual index: issue number four. Editor: Stanley H. Masters. Editor's address: 4321 Social Science Building, 1180 Observatory Drive, Madison, WI 53706. Book reviews are assigned.

> Indexed in: Abstracts for Social Workers; College Student Personnel Abstracts; Current Contents: Social & Behavioral Sciences; Current Index to Journals in Education; Dokumentation zur Raumentwicklung; Educational Administration Abstracts; Employment Relations Abstracts *; Hospital Literature Index; Index to Periodical Articles Related to Law; Journal of Economic Literature; Medical Care Review; Public Affairs Information Service Bulletin; Sage Public Administration Abstracts; Social Sciences Citation Index; Social Sciences Index; Sociology of Education Abstracts; Women Studies Abstracts.

This journal deals with the economic aspects of education, training, manpower, health, and welfare policies as they relate to the labor market and economic and social policy. Empirical studies concerned with these areas of study are given priority for inclusion in this journal. Scholars in education and the related areas are among the intended audience.

Unsolicited manuscripts are welcomed for consideration. A letter of inquiry is recommended if an author has questions concerning suitability of the article to be submitted. The Chicago style is to be followed and length of manuscript should generally be about 5,000 words. Three copies are to be submitted and copyright is held by the publisher. Estimated time for an editorial decision is six to ten weeks. If accepted, publication follows in three to six months.

275. **JOURNAL OF INDUSTRIAL TEACHER EDUCATION.** 1963— . National Association of Industrial and Technical Teacher Educators. Circ.: not given. 4 issues/yr. Subscription included with association membership. Annual index: summer issue. Editor: Richard Erickson. Editor's address: Department of Industry & Technology, Northern Illinois University, De Kalb, IL 60115. No book reviews.

> Indexed in: Current Index to Journals in Education; Readers Guide to Periodical Literature; Sociology of Education Abstracts.

This journal is intended for industrial and technical teachers, teacher educators and researchers. Research articles and original ideas as related to industrial teacher education are preferred for inclusion. The editorship changes every two years. Prospective contributors should consult the journal in 1978 for the name and address of the next editor.

The editor solicits material directly from selected professionals, but also welcomes unsolicited manuscripts for consideration. The APA style requirements are to be followed and length is not specified. Copyright is held by the association. Estimated time for an editorial decision is four to eight weeks. If accepted, publication follows in three to six months.

276. **JOURNAL OF LAW & EDUCATION.** 1972– . Jefferson Law Book Co., 728 National Press Building, Washington, DC 20004. Circ.: 2,000. 4 issues/yr. $25.00/yr. Annual index: issue number four. Editors: Laurence W. Knowles and Eldon D. Wedlock. Manuscript to: Eldon D. Wedlock, Executive Editor, Institute of Law & Education, University of South Carolina Law Center, Columbia, SC 29208. Book reviews to: Joseph S. Renzulli, School of Education, University of Connecticut, Storrs, CT 06268.

Indexed in: America: History and Life*; Current Index to Journals in Education; Current Index to Legal Periodicals; Educational Administration Abstracts; Index to Legal Periodicals; Index to Periodical Articles Related to Law; Sociological Abstracts.

This journal is committed to advancing understanding and sound judgment in all phases of law pertaining to education. It serves both the legal and educational professions as a publication devoted to critical analysis and authoritative reporting in this broad field. It offers a forum for discussion of such issues as equal educational opportunity, aid to parochial schools, student rights and responsibilities, arbitration and dispute settlement, school finance, the legal status of teachers and students, control of the curriculum, and the politics and administration of education.

The editorial staff welcomes articles from scholars, professional educators, legal practitioners and others concerned with this area of study. A letter of inquiry prior to submission is encouraged. Articles sometimes are solicited directly from authorities in the field. A uniform system of citation is stressed by the editors. It is suggested that prospective contributors ask for the one page set of instructions to authors which is available from the editor. Simultaneous submission to other journals is permitted. Time required for an editorial decision concerning acceptability of material and publication time are not specified. Copyright of printed articles is held by the publisher. Two to five book reviews are contained in this journal and these are 1,250 to 2,500 words in length.

277. **JOURNAL OF LEARNING DISABILITIES.** 1968– . c/o The Professional Press, Inc., Publishers, 6th Floor, 101 East Ontario Street, Chicago, IL 60611. Circ.: 18,000. 10 issues/yr. $12.00/yr. Annual index: December issue. Editor: Patricia E. Lane. Book reviews to: editor.

Indexed in: Biosciences Information Service of Biological Abstracts; Child Development Abstracts and Bibliography; Current Contents: Social & Behavioral Sciences; Current Index to Journals in Education; dsh Abstracts; Education Index; Educational Administration Abstracts; Exceptional Child Education Abstracts; Excerpta Medica; Information Science Abstracts; Language and Language Behavior Abstracts;

Psychological Abstracts; The Psychological Readers Guide; Rehabilitation Literature; Social Sciences Citation Index; Speed.

The intended audience of this journal includes professionals whose primary interest is in the study or treatment of learning disabilities, regardless of discipline. Its purpose is to disseminate and encourage the exchange of information useful to its readers. Among the articles preferred for publication are practical case studies, research, reviews of literature, clinical applications, viewpoints, and administrative or classroom problems.

Manuscripts following APA style requirements are to be submitted in triplicate. A letter of inquiry prior to submission is encouraged. Preferred length is 5,000 words. Some articles are solicited directly by the editor but all unsolicited inquiries will be answered. Copyright is held by the publisher. Estimated time for an editorial decision concerning acceptability of an article is eight to ten weeks. Total time from receipt of manuscript to publication is nine to twelve months. The number of book reviews appearing in each issue varies. Their length should be about 500 words.

278. **JOURNAL OF MEDICAL EDUCATION.** 1926– . Association of American Medical Colleges, One Dupont Circle, N.W., Washington, DC 20036. Circ.: 6,600. 12 issues/yr. $20.00/yr. Annual index: December issue. Editor: Merrill T. McCord. Book reviews are assigned.

Indexed in: College Student Personnel Abstracts; Current Contents: Life Sciences; Current Contents: Social & Behavioral Sciences; Current Index to Journals in Education; Excerpta Medica; Hospital Literature Index; Index Medicus; Index to Periodical Articles Related to Law; Information Retrieval Limited*; Information Science Abstracts; International Pharmaceutical Abstracts; Medical Care Review; Nursing Research; Psychological Abstracts; Rehabilitation Literature; Research into Higher Education; Science Citation Index; Social Sciences Index; Sociological Abstracts; Speed; Tropical Diseases Bulletin*.

This journal serves as a medium for exchange of ideas in medical education. It also provides a means of communicating the policies, programs and problems of the association. It is intended primarily for medical educators, students, administrators and health care personnel. In addition to major articles, regular features are Datagram, Editorial, Book Review and Letter to the Editor.

Unsolicited articles are accepted for consideration. Preferred length of the manuscript is approximately 4,000 words. Two copies of the work are to be submitted. Writers are advised to examine recent journals for style requirements. An editorial decision will be made in four weeks. Publication of acceptable articles follows in six to seven months. Copyright is held by the publisher.

279. **JOURNAL OF MUSIC THERAPY.** 1964– . The National Association for Music Therapy, Inc., P.O. Box 610, Lawrence, KS 66044. Circ.: 3,000. 4 issues/yr. Subscription included with association membership; non-member rate, $7.00/yr. No annual index. Editor: David E. Wolfe. Editor's address: Golden Valley Health Center, 4101 Golden Valley Road, Minneapolis, MN 55422. Book reviews to: editor.

JOURNAL OF MUSIC THERAPY (cont'd)

   Indexed in: dsh Abstracts; Exceptional Child Education Abstracts;
   Excerpta Medica; Hospital Literature Index; Music Article Guide;
   The Music Index; Psychological Abstracts; The Selected List of
   Tables of Contents of Psychiatric Periodicals.

This journal's audience consists chiefly of educators, clinicians, instructors
of special education, and all those who are interested in the field of health care
and rehabilitation. The purpose of this journal is to acquaint the interested audience with current trends and practices in the field of music therapy. Articles
preferred are those dealing with experimental or descriptive research in music
therapy or any article which may be relevant to the advancement of the profession.

Unsolicited articles, length unspecified, are welcomed for possible inclusion
in *Journal of Music Therapy*. The manuscript should follow APA style requirements
and be submitted in triplicate. An abstract of 150 to 200 words should accompany
the manuscript. Copyright is held by the author. The time for an editorial decision
concerning acceptance is eight weeks. Publication will follow in twelve months.
Book review length is not specified but writers should give the total number of
pages contained in the book reviewed and its price. Usually, three reviews appear
in each issue of this journal.

280. THE JOURNAL OF NEGRO EDUCATION. 1932– . The Bureau of
Educational Research, Howard University, Washington, DC 20059. Circ.:
3,300. 4 issues/yr. $7.50/yr. Annual index: issue number four. Editor:
Charles A. Martin. Editor's address: P.O. Box 311, Howard University,
Washington, DC 20059. Book reviews to: editor.
   Indexed in: Abstracts for Social Workers; America: History and Life*;
   Book Review Index; College Student Personnel Abstracts; Current
   Contents: Social & Behavioral Sciences; Current Index to Journals
   in Education; Education Index; Educational Administration Abstracts;
   Exceptional Child Education Abstracts; Human Resources Abstracts;
   Index to Periodical Articles Related to Law; Language and Language
   Behavior Abstracts; Nursing Research; Psychological Abstracts; Public
   Affairs Information Service Bulletin; Social Sciences Citation Index;
   Sociological Abstracts; Sociology of Education Index; Women Studies
   Abstracts.

This journal is intended for public libraries, university libraries, educational
institutions, government agencies and educators. Its purpose is to serve as a vehicle
for the dissemination of general information and research findings on the education
of Black people and the associated virtues, problems and successes of such education.

Unsolicited articles and book reviews are welcomed for the fall, winter and
spring issues. Articles for the Summer Yearbook generally are by invitation. Authors
should submit two copies of their work and follow Chicago style requirements.
Preferred length may vary from 3,500 to 4,500 words. An editorial decision concerning acceptability of material is given in about eight weeks. Publication follows
twenty-four to thirty months later. Copyright is held by the publisher. Three to
four book reviews appear in each issue and are approximately 750 words in
length.

281. JOURNAL OF OUTDOOR EDUCATION. 1966– . Department of Outdoor Teacher Education, Northern Illinois University, DeKalb, IL 60115. Circ.: 2,000. 2 issues/yr. No charge, controlled circulation. No annual index. Editor: Robert L. Vogl. Editor's address: Taft Campus, Box 299, Oregon, IL 61061. Book reviews appear only occasionally.

Indexed in: Current Index to Journals in Education.

This journal is intended for educators, administrators, camp personnel and environmentalists. Its purpose is to communicate the latest thinking in the area of outdoor education. Research articles as well as descriptions of on-going programs are included in this journal.

Unsolicited articles are accepted for consideration. Authors may query in advance if they wish. The preferred length for manuscripts is approximately 1,500 words. Copyright is held by the publisher. No time for an editorial decision or publication after acceptance is specified.

282. JOURNAL OF PERSONALITY AND SOCIAL PSYCHOLOGY. 1965– . American Psychological Association, 1200 Seventeenth Street, N.W., Washington, DC 20036. Circ.: 6,000. 12 issues/yr. $20.00/yr. with APA membership; non-member rate, $48.00/yr. Annual index: issue number twelve. Editor: John T. Lanzetta. Editor's address: Department of Psychology, Dartmouth College, Hanover, NH 03755. No book reviews.

Indexed in: Abstracts for Social Workers; Abstracts in Anthropology; Abstracts on Police Science*; College Student Personnel Abstracts; Current Index to Journals in Education; dsh Abstracts; Educational Administration Abstracts; Exceptional Child Education Abstracts; Index Medicus; Index to Periodical Articles Related to Law; Nursing Research; Operations Research/Management Science Abstract Services; Psychological Abstracts; The Psychological Readers Guide; Science Citation Index; Social Sciences Citation Index; Social Sciences Index; Women Studies Abstracts.

The intended audience of this journal is primarily social scientists. Reports of original experiments or field studies in the areas of personality and social psychology are preferred. The research reports are concerned with such topics as social motivation, attitudes, communication processes, group behavior person perception, conformity and deviation, and related areas of study.

The editor welcomes unsolicited articles for consideration. Length may be from 3,750 to 5,000 words and manuscript is to be submitted in duplicate. Style should follow APA requirements and a 175 word abstract is to be included. It is recommended that potential contributors examine the manuscript information section found in each issue of this journal. Estimated time for an editorial decision concerning acceptability of an article is ten weeks. Time from acceptance to publication is about fifteen months. Copyright on accepted material is held by the publisher.

283. JOURNAL OF PHYSICAL EDUCATION. (formerly **PHYSICAL TRAINING**). 1927– (JPE); 1901– (PT). National Physical Education Society, a section of The Association of Professional Directors of the YMCAs of the United States. Circ.: 3,000. 6 issues/yr. Subscription included with society membership;

non-member rate, $6.00/yr. Annual index: July-August issue. Editor: Lyn
Schlegel. Editor's address: YMCA, 226 East Washington Boulevard, Ft. Wayne,
IN 46802. Book reviews to: book review editor.

Indexed in: Education Index.

This journal contains research studies dealing with physical education as well
as other more general information types. It is intended for YMCA personnel and
any other persons involved with physical education. Regular features include
President's Paragraph, Poolside Palaver, Fitness Scene and Bulletin Board.

Unsolicited articles are welcomed for consideration, but a letter of inquiry
prior to submission is recommended. Two copies of the manuscript are to be sent.
Preferred length is 750 to 1,500 words. Style requirements are not specified. Copyright is held by the author. The time necessary for an editorial decision regarding
acceptability depends upon the number of articles received, but generally is two
months. Average time for publication after acceptance is four months. Periodic
book reviews appear in this journal but length is not specified.

284. **JOURNAL OF PHYSICAL EDUCATION AND RECREATION.** (formerly
JOURNAL OF HEALTH, PHYSICAL EDUCATION AND RECREATION
and **AMERICAN PHYSICAL EDUCATION REVIEW.** 1975– (JOPER);
1930– (JOHPER); 1896– (APER). American Alliance for Health, Physical
Education and Recreation, 1201 Sixteenth Street, N.W., Washington, DC
20036. Circ.: 45,000. 9 issues/yr. Subscription included with alliance membership; library rate, $25.00/yr. Annual index: November-December issue.
Editor: Nancy Rosenberg. Book reviewers chosen by editor.

Indexed in: Current Index to Journals in Education; Education Index;
Exceptional Child Education Abstracts; Media Review Digest;
Rehabilitation Literature; Women Studies Abstracts.

The purpose of this publication is to keep professionals in physical education and recreation well informed about the latest developments in their areas of
expertise. Its audience includes these educators and others, such as dance, sports,
intramural and aquatics teachers, and directors of recreation and leisure activities.
The editor prefers manuscripts describing innovative or worthwhile programs,
presentations of new approaches to problem solving, explorations of philosophy
or methods, and pieces setting forth basic issues in the areas covered.

Authors are urged to inquire concerning ideas or submit unsolicited manuscripts. Article length should be between 1,500 and 2,500 words, with the style
conforming to Chicago style. The copyright is held by the publisher. Six weeks
is the estimated time for an editorial decision with three months elapsing between
acceptance and publication.

285. **JOURNAL OF POLICE SCIENCE AND ADMINISTRATION.** 1973– .
International Association of Chiefs of Police and Northwestern University
School of Law, Eleven Firstfield Road, Gaithersburg, MD 20760. Circ.:
5,000. 4 issues/yr. $15.00/yr. Annual index: December issue. Editor:
Fred E. Inbau. Book reviews to: Wayne E. Schmidt, Operating Director,
Americans for Effective Law Enforcement, Inc., Suite 960, 1603 Orrington
Avenue, Evanston, IL 60201.

JOURNAL OF POLICE SCIENCE AND ADMINISTRATION (cont'd)

Indexed in: Current Contents: Social & Behavioral Sciences; Psychological Abstracts; Social Sciences Citation Index; Social Sciences Index; Speed.

This journal is intended for police administrators and practitioners, teachers and students of law enforcement, and criminal justice professionals. It is intended to acquaint these professionals with current trends and issues as well as provide a forum for the exchange of views on police techniques and procedures. The editor is seeking articles that are police oriented and scholarly in nature.

Unsolicited manuscripts are accepted for editorial consideration. These articles should be between 2,500 and 10,000 words in length and submitted in two copies. The MLA style requirements are to be followed. The copyright is held by the publisher. Approximately twelve weeks is required for an editorial decision. Accepted articles are published in three months. Between four and eight book reviews are published in each issue of this journal. These reviews are 250 to 1,000 words in length.

286. **JOURNAL OF PSYCHEDELIC DRUGS.** 1967– . STASH, 118 South Bedford Street, Madison, WI 53703. Circ.: 1,500. 4 issues/yr. $20.00/yr.; library rate, $30.00/yr. No annual index. Editor: Nancy Gottlieb. Book reviews to: editor.

Indexed in: Abstracts on Police Science*; Bibliotheque Bulletin; Current Contents: Social & Behavioral Sciences; Excerpta Medica; Index to Periodical Articles Related to Law; International Pharmaceutical Abstracts; Psychological Abstracts; Social Sciences Citation Index; Social Sciences Index; Speed.

This journal is intended for psychologists, psychiatrists, drug researchers, drug educators, pharmacologists, physicians, health care workers, sociologists, social workers, and lay persons interested in drugs. It is intended to provide readers with information concerning research and insight into the drug culture and psychoactive drugs.

The journal features scholarly articles which vary in length from 750 to 10,000 words. Unsolicited articles are encouraged and should follow the APA style requirements. One issue is dedicated to a central theme and the editor should be contacted for details. Between six and eight weeks is required for an editorial decision with two months being required for accepted manuscripts to be published. The copyright is retained by the publisher. Between one and three book reviews are utilized in each issue. These reviews vary in length from 750 to 1,500 words.

287. **JOURNAL OF READING.** (formerly **JOURNAL OF DEVELOPMENTAL READING**). 1964– (JR); 1957– (JDR). International Reading Association, 800 Barksdale Road, Newark, DE 19711. Circ.: 19,000. 8 issues/yr. Subscription included with association membership. Annual index: May issue. Editor: Janet R. Binkley. Book reviewers are chosen by editor.

Indexed in: College Student Personnel Abstracts; Current Contents: Social & Behavioral Sciences; Current Index to Journals in Education; Education Index; Exceptional Child Education Abstracts; Index to Periodical Articles Related to Law; Media Review Digest.

JOURNAL OF READING (cont'd)

The intended audience of the *Journal of Reading* includes all persons interested in reading instruction at the secondary, junior-community college, college, and adult levels. The editor welcomes material of special interest to the teacher of reading at the levels specified, as well as others who share that interest.

Articles submitted for editorial consideration should be approximately 2,500 words in length, and in triplicate. The MLA style should be followed but the *Journal* also supplies a pamphlet with instructions for authors upon request. Approximately four weeks is required for an editorial decision with publication of accepted manuscripts following in six months. The copyright is held by the publisher.

288. **JOURNAL OF READING BEHAVIOR.** 1969– . National Reading Conference, Inc., Clemson University, Clemson, SC 29631. Circ.: 1,500. 4 issues/yr. $12.50/yr. Annual index: issue number four. Editor: J. Jaap Tuinman. Editor's address: Institute for Child Study, 46 Bypass, Indiana University, Bloomington, IN 47401. Book reviews to: editor.

Indexed in: Child Development Abstracts and Bibliography; Current Contents: Social & Behavioral Sciences; Current Index to Journals in Education; Education Index; Psychological Abstracts; The Psychological Readers Guide; Social Sciences Citation Index.

The *Journal* is intended for college professors, reading researchers, reading specialists, and psychologists. Its purpose is to provide an interdisciplinary outlet for reading research. It publishes original experimental and theoretical articles concerned with reading behavior. Special emphasis is placed on articles dealing with issues related to the understanding of prose and learning through reading.

Unsolicited manuscripts are accepted for publication consideration and should follow APA style requirements. There is no suggested length for manuscripts, with the copyright being held by the publisher. Five copies should be submitted. Twelve weeks is required for an editorial decision with six months elapsing between acceptance and publication. From three to six book reviews are published in each issue, with the desired length being approximately 750 words.

289. **JOURNAL OF RESEARCH AND DEVELOPMENT IN EDUCATION.** 1967– . College of Education, University of Georgia, G-3 Aderhold Building, Athens, GA 30602. Circ.: 1,700. 4 issues/yr. $10.00/yr. Annual index: issue number four. Editor: Reese Wells. No book reviews.

Indexed in: Current Index to Journals in Education; Language and Language Behavior Abstracts; Nursing Research.

This journal is intended for school and university personnel. Its purpose is to translate research into educational application. Issues are devoted to central themes which are selected by the editorial board. Sample themes from recent issues are: Gaps in Teacher Preparation; Career Education; and, Computer Assisted Planning for Education.

This journal does not accept unsolicited manuscripts. A guest editor is appointed who selects authors and topics. The journal does suggest letters of inquiry concerning topics and editorial appointments. A style manual is available. Most themes and authors are chosen at least twelve months prior to publication date.

290. JOURNAL OF RESEARCH IN MUSIC EDUCATION. 1953– . Music
Educators National Conference, 1902 Association Drive, Center for
Educational Associations, Reston, VA 22091. Circ.: 10,000. 4 issues/yr.
Subscription included with special research conference membership;
library rate, $8.00/yr. Annual index: issue number four. Editor: Robert
G. Petzold. Editor's address: 5545 Humanities Building, The University
of Wisconsin, Madison, WI 53706. Book reviews to: book review editor.
    Indexed in: Computer and Control Abstracts*; Current Contents:
Social & Behavioral Sciences; Current Index to Journals in Education;
Education Index; The Music Index; Psychological Abstracts; RILM
Abstracts of Music Literature.

This journal is addressed to all music educators and persons interested in
music education, particularly those who are actively engaged in research in the
field. As indicated by the journal's title, its contents deal primarily with scientific research reports related to music education and/or instruction. Manuscripts
treating historical or philosophical aspects of music education also are accepted
for editorial consideration. ·

Unsolicited manuscripts are encouraged for this refereed journal. Articles
should contain a maximum of 5,000 words and conform to Chicago or MLA
style requirements. The copyright is held by the publisher. Approximately nine
weeks is required for an editorial decision with six to twelve months elapsing
after acceptance before publication. Approximately five to eight book reviews
are published in each issue. The length of these may vary depending upon the
book under review and the reviewer's style of writing.

291. JOURNAL OF RESEARCH IN SCIENCE TEACHING. 1963– . National
Association for Research in Science Teaching, 605 Third Avenue, New
York, NY 10016. Circ.: 1,300. 4 issues/yr. $20.00/yr. Annual index:
issue number four. Editor: David P. Butts. Editor's address: Department
of Science Education, The University of Georgia, Athens, GA 30602.
Book reviews to: editor.
    Indexed in: Current Index to Journals in Education; Education Index;
Women Studies Abstract.

The intended audience of this journal includes science educators in general
with specific emphasis on those at the college level who are concerned with
research in science teaching. It is designed to provide a vehicle of communication in the area of research in the teaching of science at the elementary, secondary and college levels. Papers describing research studies are preferred for inclusion.

Articles conforming to APA style requirements are welcomed by the editor.
Material may range from 1,250 to 5,000 words in length. Three copies are to be
submitted. Detailed information for contributors is given on the inside back cover
of each issue. Estimated time for an editorial decision concerning acceptability of
an article for publication is eight to sixteen weeks. Time from acceptance to publication is eight months. Copyright is held by the publisher. Several book reviews
are included in each issue. These reviews are 150 words long.

292. THE JOURNAL OF SCHOOL HEALTH. (formerly **AMERICAN
ASSOCIATION OF SCHOOL PHYSICIANS BULLETIN**). 1937– (JSH);
1930– (AASPB). American School Health Association, Kent, OH 44240.

Circ.: 11,000. 10 issues/yr. Subscription included with association membership. Annual index: December issue. Editor: Glenn R. Knotts. Book reviews to: editor.

Indexed in: Cumulative Index to Nursing Literature; Current Contents: Social & Behavioral Sciences; Current Index to Journals in Education; Education Index; Excerpta Medica; Index Medicus; Index to Periodical Articles Related to Law; International Nursing Index; Media Review Digest; Nursing Research; Psychological Abstracts; Rehabilitation Literature; Sociological Abstracts; Speed; Women Studies Abstracts.

The intended audience of this journal includes members of the "school health team." The team is represented by teachers, administrators, staff members and community health workers who have responsibilities in regard to the health of the school age boy or girl. Its purpose is to provide professional growth for these readers. Articles related to school health programs or health-related subjects are preferred. A number of regular features including New Aids to Instruction, News Notes, How We Do It, Research of Interest, From the Campus and National Office Report appear in each issue.

The editor welcomes unsolicited manuscripts for consideration. Style requirements of the American Medical Association are preferred and may be found in the *Stylebook/Editorial Manual of the AMA*, (5th Edition). A two page set of guidelines for the preparation and submission of manuscripts is available from the editor. Length of articles is to be about 5,000 words and should be submitted in triplicate. Copyright is held by the publisher. Time for an editorial decision is six weeks and approximately three to six months is required for publication after acceptance. About three to five book reviews appear in each issue. Their preferred length is 300 words.

293. **JOURNAL OF SCHOOL PSYCHOLOGY.** 1963– . Journal of School Psychology, Inc., Behavioral Publications, Inc., 72 Fifth Avenue, New York, NY 10011. Circ.: 3,000. 4 issues/yr. $12.00/yr. for personal use; institution rate, $30.00/yr. Annual index: issue number four. Editor: Beeman N. Phillips. Editor's address: Department of Educational Psychology, University of Texas, Austin, TX 78712. Book reviewers chosen by book review editor.

Indexed in: Current Contents: Social & Behavioral Sciences; Current Index to Journals in Education; Education Index; Exceptional Child Education Abstracts; Psychological Abstracts; The Psychological Readers Guide; Social and Education Sciences; Social Sciences Citation Index; Women Studies Abstracts.

The intended audience of this journal includes school psychologists, and psychologists working in schools or involved in training of psychologists to work in schools and related settings. The journal publishes articles on research, opinions and practice in school psychology, with the aim of fostering its continued development as a scientific and professional specialty. Articles preferred are those dealing with interprofessional roles, education trends and philosophy, training and legal issues, assessment, diagnosis, tests, mental health consultation, counseling,

JOURNAL OF SCHOOL PSYCHOLOGY (cont'd)

behavior modification, classroom behavior and learning, learning handicaps, early education and related areas.

Contributors are encouraged to submit manuscripts for possible inclusion in this journal. Material should follow APA style requirements and may be from 1,500 to 4,500 words long. Three copies are to be submitted. Estimated time for an editorial decision concerning acceptability of an article for publication is four to six weeks. Time from acceptance to publication is nine months. Copyright is held by the Journal of School Psychology, Inc.

294. **THE JOURNAL OF SOCIAL ISSUES.** 1945– . The Society for the Psychological Study of Social Issues, P.O. Box 1248, Ann Arbor, MI 48106. Circ.: 7,000. 4 issues/yr. $9.00/yr.; institutional rate, $15.00/yr. Annual index: issue number four. Editor: Jacqueline D. Goodchilds, Editor's address: Department of Psychology, University of California, Los Angeles, CA 90024. No book reviews.

Indexed in: Psychological Abstracts; Speed.

The sponsoring society is a group of over 3,000 psychologists and allied social scientists who share a common concern with research on the psychological aspects of important social issues. This organization seeks to bring theory and practice into focus on human problems of the group, the community, and the nation, as well as those that have no national boundaries. *The Journal of Social Issues* has as its goal the communication of scientific findings and interpretations in a non-technical manner, but without the sacrifice of professional standards.

Articles in this journal are usually solicited by the editors, only an occasional unsolicited manuscript is used. The APA style is required, with manuscript length varying between 2,500 and 12,500 words. The time for editorial consideration and publication varies and the editor has not indicated any minimum times. Three copies of all manuscripts should be submitted. Each issue is topically organized and is assembled by one or two individuals specifically appointed for the task, under the overall supervision of the general editor and a twelve-member continuing editorial board. Inquiry and participation by all interested scholars is welcomed. Copyright is held by the publisher.

295. **THE JOURNAL OF SPECIAL EDUCATION.** 1966– . Grune & Stratton, Inc., 111 Fifth Avenue, New York, NY 10003. Circ.: 3,500. 4 issues/yr. $18.50/yr. Annual index: fall issue. Editor: Lester Mann. Editor's address: Buttonwood Farms, Inc., 3515 Woodhaven Road, Philadelphia, PA 19154. No book reviews.

Indexed in: Current Contents: Social & Behavioral Sciences; Current Index to Journals in Education; dsh Abstracts; Education Index; Educational Administration Abstracts; Exceptional Child Education Abstracts; Excerpta Medica; Index to Periodical Articles Related to Law; Psychological Abstracts; Rehabilitation Literature.

The Journal of Special Education is a multidisciplinary journal which publishes articles of research, theory, review and opinion related to special education. Articles that are definitive and carefully documented are preferred for inclusion. Case studies and general surveys are not generally desired.

THE JOURNAL OF SPECIAL EDUCATION (cont'd)

Authors are encouraged to submit manuscripts following APA style. Three copies should be sent to the editor. Contributors should not send the original work since manuscripts are not returned. An editorial decision is made in six to ten weeks. The time from acceptance to publication varies from four to eighteen months. Copyright is held by Buttonwood Farms, Inc. Writers are urged to examine the publication policies and information for authors printed inside the back cover of any recent issue of this journal.

296. **JOURNAL OF SPEECH AND HEARING DISORDERS.** (formerly **JOURNAL OF SPEECH DISORDERS**). 1936– . American Speech and Hearing Association, 9030 Old Georgetown Road, Washington, DC 20014. Circ.: 22,700. 4 issues/yr. $23.00/yr. Annual index: November issue. Editor: Ralph L. Shelton. Editor's address: Speech and Hearing Sciences Department, University of Arizona, Tucson, AZ 85721. No book reviews.

Indexed in: Current Contents: Clinical Practice; Current Contents: Social & Behavioral Sciences; Current Index to Journals in Education; dsh Abstracts; Education Index; Educational Administration Abstracts; Exceptional Child Education Abstracts; Excerpta Medica; Index Medicus; Modern Language Abstracts; Nuclear Science Abstracts; Rehabilitation Literature; Sociological Abstracts.

The intended audience of the *Journal* includes speech pathologists and audiologists employed in clinics, public and private schools, universities, private practice and other related settings. This serial publishes manuscripts pertaining to the nature, assessment, and treatment of communication disorders. Manuscripts are considered on the basis of their applicability to clinical problems, their readability, and their conformity to standards of evidence. Articles include synthesizing essays and reports of clinical research. Articles that present and discuss information directly concerning disorders of speech, hearing, or language are given priority for publication.

Unsolicited manuscripts are welcomed for consideration by the editor. There are no length requirements, however, a charge of $50.00 per page for publication is levied. This charge may be waived under specified conditions arranged with the publications department. Five copies of all material should be submitted. Between six and eight weeks is required for editorial consideration with accepted manuscripts appearing in print approximately six months after acceptance. No indication of copyright disposition was indicated. Authors should follow Chicago style requirements for all work.

297. **JOURNAL OF TEACHER EDUCATION.** 1950– . American Association of Colleges of Teacher Education, One Dupont Circle, Suite 610, Washington, DC 20036. Circ.: 11,000. 4 issues/yr. $10.00/yr. Annual index: December issue. Editor: Joel L. Burdin. Book reviews to: editor.

Indexed in: Current Contents: Social & Behavioral Sciences; Current Index to Journals in Education; Education Index; Educational Administration Abstracts; Exceptional Child Education Abstracts; Psychological Abstracts; Sociological Abstracts.

JOURNAL OF TEACHER EDUCATION (cont'd)

The intended audience of this journal includes teacher educators (professors, deans, and administrators in colleges of education and liberal arts); teachers and student teachers; and Federal, state and local government administrators dealing with the training of education personnel. It is intended to contribute to the broad understanding of educational issues and alternatives and to the development of individual competencies needed for effective professional performance. Manuscripts should be informative, provocative, timely, practical, logical, and be clearly written.

Articles submitted for consideration should be a maximum of 6,000 words and in duplicate. The Chicago style should be followed. Articles for theme issues are solicited by the editor, however, unsolicited manuscripts are considered for inclusion in this journal. The copyright is held by the publisher. Simultaneous submission to other journals is permitted, but this fact must be stated in the covering letter. Approximately twenty-six weeks is required for an editorial decision with publication of accepted manuscripts following in three to eighteen months. Six to ten book reviews are used in each issue. These reviews should be between 500 and 1,000 words in length.

298. **JOURNAL OF TEACHING AND LEARNING.** (formerly **COLLEGE OF EDUCATION RECORD**). 1975– (JTL); 1915– (CER). Center for Teaching and Learning, University of North Dakota, Grand Forks, ND 58201. Circ.: 2,000. 3 issues/yr. No charge, controlled circulation. No annual index. Editor: John D. Williams. No book reviews.

This journal is intended to reach former University of North Dakota graduates, school personnel in North Dakota, and persons interested in changing classroom practices. It is intended to serve as an outlet for the presentation of varied viewpoints relating changes in education and educational practice. Both research and expository articles are presented. This is a refereed journal.

Authors are urged to submit unsolicited articles for consideration. Two copies of manuscripts should be submitted. Between four and eight weeks is required for an editorial decision with publication following acceptance within four months. Occasional issues are dedicated to central themes, however, this normally is not the case. The length of articles varies from 1,000 to 2,500 words, with the copyright being held by the author.

299. **THE JOURNAL OF THE AMERICAN ASSOCIATION OF TEACHER EDUCATORS IN AGRICULTURE (AATEA JOURNAL).** 1961– . American Association of Teacher Educators in Agriculture (AATEA), c/o Dr. James Horner, Agricultural Education, University of Nebraska, Lincoln, NE 68503. Circ.: 400. 3 issues/yr. $4.50/yr. Annual index: November issue. Editor: Larry E. Miller. Editor's address: Agricultural Education, 108 War Memorial Gym, V.P.I. & S.U., Blacksburg, VA 24061, or Regional Editors listed in *Journal*. Book reviews to: editor. Indexed in: Current Index to Journals in Education.

This journal is intended for trainers of teachers of agriculture at both the public school and college levels. It is intended to promote the professional aims of the association and aid in communication among members. Articles dealing

with research, curriculum and program innovation, philosophy of agricultural education, current trends, theoretical constructions and program evaluation are considered.
The above listing is also a priority listing of editorial values.

Unsolicited manuscripts are accepted for consideration and should follow the
style requirements as set forth by Campbell. Length may vary between 1,000 and
1,500 words with three copies being submitted. The copyright is held by the author
with six weeks required for an editorial decision. No length of time for publication
following acceptance was indicated. Book reviews are used on a space available
basis with no length requirements specified. All reviews must deal with professional
agricultural education books only.

300. **THE JOURNAL OF THE INTERNATIONAL ASSOCIATION OF PUPIL
PERSONNEL WORKERS.** 1936– (as newsletter). International Association
of Pupil Personnel Workers, 1713 62nd Street, Kenosha, WI 53140. Circ.:
900. 4 issues/yr. Subscription included with association membership; library
rate, $7.00/yr. No annual index. Editor: Martin Bach. Book reviews to:
editor.
Indexed in: Current Index to Journals in Education.

This journal is intended to reach persons in the field of pupil personnel work
such as attendance workers, social workers, guidance personnel, psychologists,
psychometrists, school nurses and curriculum administrators. Its purpose is the
sharing of the proceedings of the annual convention and to publish articles related
to the different disciplines in the field of pupil personnel work. Articles deal with
research findings, new programs, philosophy and changes within the field of pupil
personnel work.

Unsolicited manuscripts are accepted for consideration. No particular style
is requested but the editor does ask that the material be professional in content
and relevant to pupil personnel work. Two copies of the manuscript should be
submitted. Copyright is held by the author. An editorial decision will be made
within eight weeks with publication of accepted work following within three
months. The editor prefers articles of approximately 1,500 words. Book reviews
are published periodically, with the preferred length being 700 words. The editor
encourages a letter of inquiry prior to submission of material.

301. **JOURNAL OF THE MIDWEST HISTORY OF EDUCATION SOCIETY.**
1973– . Midwest History of Education Society, College of Education,
University of Northern Iowa, Cedar Falls, IA 50613. Circ.: 100. 1 issue/yr.
$2.50/yr. No annual index. Editor: Edward Rutkowski. Editor's address:
Education Center, Room 513, University of Northern Iowa, Cedar Falls,
IA 50613. No book reviews.

This journal is intended for educational and social historians, as well as
other scholars interested in education. It publishes original scholarship and
research papers of educational historians in the Midwest and also serves as an
historical record of the proceedings of the learned society which sponsors the
journal. The academic breadth and scholarly contents of the journal may best
be illustrated by several select titles: A. S. Neill, Summerhill and Anarchist

JOURNAL OF THE MIDWEST HISTORY OF EDUCATION SOCIETY (cont'd)

Tradition; National Identity and Education–Symbols and Reality; The Iowa Experiment With an Integrated System of Higher Education; and, The Revolutions of 1968–A Neohegelian View.

The articles published in this journal are papers which have been presented at society meetings and other original submitted papers. Maximum length of the manuscript is to be 5,000 words. Copyright is held by the publisher. Simultaneous submission of articles to other journals is permitted. An editorial decision concerning acceptability is given in four weeks. Publication follows in six to nine months.

302. **THE JOURNAL OF THE NATIONAL ASSOCIATION FOR WOMEN DEANS, ADMINISTRATORS, & COUNSELORS.** 1938– . National Association of Women Deans, Administrators, and Counselors, 1028 Connecticut Avenue, N.W., Washington, DC 20036. Circ.: 3,500. 4 issues/yr. Subscription included with association membership; non-member rate, $8.50/yr. No annual index. Editor: Margaret C. Berry. Editor's address: Director of Developmental Programs, The University of Texas at Austin, P.O. Box 7699, U.T. Station, Austin, TX 78712. Outside book reviews not accepted.

Indexed in: College Student Personnel Abstracts; Education Index.

The intended audience of this publication includes members of the association as well as any other persons interested in student personnel administration. The *Journal* is intended to provide current research reports related to administration of student personnel programs, with special attention to those about women, as well as a forum for discussion of current practices and trends, and material related to the position of women in administration and counseling.

Authors should follow the APA style requirements. Occasional issues are centered on selected themes, usually announced in the journal. Other articles are then published on a space available basis. Unsolicited articles are encouraged, with the maximum length being 3,000 words. This journal is not copyrighted but permission to reprint should be requested from the author and the journal. Eight to ten weeks is required for editorial consideration with publication following acceptance within one year. Two copies of all manuscripts should be submitted.

303. **JOURNAL OF THE NEW YORK STATE SCHOOL BOARDS ASSOCIATION, INC.** 1929– (as quarterly). New York State School Boards Association, Inc., 111 Washington Avenue, Albany, NY 12210. Circ.: 8,000. 12 issues/yr. Subscription included with association membership; non-member rate, $10.00/yr. Annual index: January issue. Editor: George E. Lowe. No book reviews.

The *Journal* is intended for school board members and others interested in public elementary and secondary education in New York State. It is intended to provide relevant information to members and serve as a record of association activities. Articles should be relevant to education. Continuing features include Negotiation News and Federal Legislative Report.

The editor encourages the submission of manuscripts between 1,000 and 2,000 words in length. The APA style should be followed. Four weeks is required

JOURNAL OF THE NEW YORK STATE SCHOOL BOARDS ASSOCIATION, INC. (cont'd)

for an editorial decision with publication of accepted manuscripts following within two months. The copyright is held by the publisher. Simultaneous submission to other journals is permitted.

304. **JOURNAL OF YOUTH AND ADOLESCENCE.** 1972– . Plenum Corporation, Publisher, 227 West 17th Street, New York, NY 10011. Circ.: not given. 4 issues/yr. $16.00/yr. for personal use; institution rate, $24.00/yr. Annual index: issue number four. Editor: Daniel Offer. Editor's address: Michael Reese Hospital and Medical Center, 2959 South Ellis Avenue, Chicago, IL 60616. Book reviews to: editor.

Indexed in: Abstracts on Police Science*; College Student Personnel Abstracts; Current Contents: Social & Behavioral Sciences; Current Index to Journals in Education; Excerpta Medica; Psychological Abstracts; Sage Urban Studies Abstracts; Sociological Abstracts; Universal Reference System; Women Studies Abstracts.

The intended audience of this journal includes professionals working with adolescents and youth in the mental health sciences, social and behavioral sciences, law, education and biology. It is designed to encourage research in the field of adolescent and youth with a multi-disciplinary audience. Research reports and review articles are contained in this publication.

The editor welcomes unsolicited manuscripts for consideration. Preferred length is 2,500 to 5,000 words and contributors should follow the Chicago style requirements. Copyright of accepted materials is held by the publisher. The time required for an editorial decision varies from six to eight weeks with publication following in six to nine months. Three to four book reviews of 750 to 1,000 words are included in each issue.

305. **JOURNALISM EDUCATOR.** 1945– . Association for Education in Journalism, University of Minnesota, Minneapolis, MN 55455. Circ.: 2,100. 4 issues/yr. $6.00/yr. No annual index. Editor: LaRue Wesley Gilleland. Editor's address: Department of Journalism, University of Nevada–Reno, Reno, NV 89507. No book reviews.

Indexed in: Current Index to Journals in Education.

The intended audience of this journal includes professors of journalism and mass communications in the United States and Canada, journalism school and department administrators, and news executives interested in problems in journalism education. Its purpose is to promote excellence in teaching to prepare men and women for careers in print and broadcast journalism, advertising and public relations. Articles preferred are those on ideas that have worked in the classroom, administrative problems that have been solved or need solving, and improving relations and cooperation between journalism educators and news media.

Unsolicited articles are accepted for consideration in this journal. Manuscript is to follow the stylebook of Associated Press-United Press International and is to be submitted in duplicate. Less than 2,000 words is the preferred length. An editorial decision is made in six weeks and publication will follow in six to twelve months. Copyright is held by the publisher.

306. JOURNALISM QUARTERLY. 1924– . Association for Education in Journalism, School of Journalism, University of Minnesota, Minneapolis, MN 55455. Circ.: 5,000. 4 issues/yr. $12.00/yr. Annual index: separate, but mailed with winter issue. Editor: Guido H. Stempel, III. Editor's address: School of Journalism, Ohio University, Athens, OH 45701. Book reviews are assigned.

Indexed in: America: History and Life*; Current Contents: Social & Behavioral Sciences; Current Index to Journals in Education; Humanities Index; Index to Periodical Articles Related to Law; Modern Language Abstracts; Sociological Abstracts; Women Studies Abstracts.

Journalism Quarterly is intended for teachers and researchers in field of journalism and mass communication. The journal disseminates research findings as related to those academic areas. Articles published are research articles, not essays, and must deal with mass communication. Among the regular features are brief summaries of research reports, book reviews and a bibliography of other books, pamphlets, paperbacks and articles in the field.

This journal's style book appeared in the Spring, 1965 issue and prospective contributors are advised to consult it prior to submission of material. Unsolicited articles, in triplicate, are welcomed by the editor. Manuscript length may vary from 2,500 to 3,500 words. Estimated time for an editorial decision concerning acceptability of an article varies from ten to fifteen weeks. Time from acceptance of the work to publication is nine months. Copyright is held by the publisher. The 20 book reviews each issue are approximately 300 words long. Most book reviews are assigned by the book review editor.

307. JUNIOR HIGH MIDDLE SCHOOL BULLETIN. (formerly **JUNIOR HIGH SCHOOL NEWSLETTER**). 1969– (JHMSB); 1962– (JHSN). School of Education, Indiana State University, Terre Haute, IN 47809. Circ.: 1,800. 3 issues/yr. No charge, controlled circulation. No annual index. Editor: Max Bough. No book reviews.

The contents of this publication include articles pertinent to intermediate (junior high/middle) school education. Its purpose is to serve these schools, particularly in Indiana, with useful information about this level in public school education. Articles deal with students, programs, curricula and other concerns of this intermediate level of education. The Editor's Corner is a regular feature.

Unsolicited manuscripts are welcomed by the editor. The editor also may solicit articles directly from colleagues. No specific style requirements need be followed, and the length may vary from 500 to 1,500 words. Copyright is held by the publisher. Simultaneous submission to other journals is permitted. An editorial decision is made in one week and the estimated time from acceptance to publication is three to six months.

308. THE JUNIOR STATE REPORT. (formerly **THE YOUTH NEWS REPORT** and **THE JUNIOR STATESMAN**). 1973– (JSR); 1971– (YNR); 1935– (JS). California Junior State, 495 California Avenue, Palo Alto, CA 94306. Circ.: 3,700. 5 issues/yr. $2.00/yr. No annual index. Editor: Richard Prosser. Book reviews to: editor.

THE JUNIOR STATE REPORT (cont'd)

The Junior State Report is intended for high school students interested and involved in government and politics. Its purpose is to encourage political awareness and involvement among high school student leaders. It is the official publication of California Junior State, a non-partisan educational youth organization. Journalistic accounts of high school students involved in the political process, particularly in decision-making roles, appear in this work.

Manuscripts written with a journalistic approach are welcomed by the editor, however, a letter of inquiry prior to submission is encouraged. The length of articles varies, but tend to be fewer than 500 words. Copyright is held by the author. Simultaneous submission to other journals is permitted. Estimated time for an editorial decision concerning acceptability of an article for publication is two weeks. Publication time, after acceptance, varies from one to two months. Articles from high school students involved in citizenship education are particularly welcome.

309. **K-3 BULLETIN OF TEACHING IDEAS & MATERIALS.** 1970– . Parker Publishing Company, Inc., Route 59A at Brookhill Drive, West Nyack, NY 10094. Circ.: 20,000. 10 issues/yr. $18.00/yr. No annual index. Editors: Anne Bravo and Paula Zajan. Manuscript to: Dan Kakudo, Workshops and Clinics. Book reviews to: Dan Kakudo.

This publication contains various activities to aid in the teaching of children, grades kindergarten through third. Its purpose is to provide ideas and activities that teachers can elaborate on or use as they are presented. Practical suggestions are stressed in this bulletin. Regular features are related to Language Arts, Mathematics, Living Sciences, Arts and Crafts, and Physical Education.

Unsolicited articles are accepted for consideration, but a letter of inquiry prior to submission is encouraged. Style should follow that found in the *Harbrace College Handbook.* Preferred length is about 600 words and copyright is held by the publisher. The time for an editorial decision concerning acceptance is two weeks. Publication follows in three to five months. Book reviews appear in some issues and their length is approximately 600 words.

310. **KANSAS MUSIC REVIEW.** 1936– . Kansas Music Educators Association. Circ.: 3,000. 5 issues/yr. Subscription included with association membership. No annual index. Editor: James Hardy. Editor's address: Wichita State University, Wichita, KS 67208. Book reviews to: editor.

The journal is intended for all music educators, including in-service public school teachers, and college and university personnel. College students also are among its readers. Its purpose is to acquaint teachers with current trends and issues and to provide information for the association members.

Unsolicited manuscripts and letters of inquiry are welcomed by the editor. The MLA style requirements are to be followed and the preferred length is 1,500 words. Copyright on accepted material is held by the publisher. An editorial decision can be expected in two weeks. Publication will follow in three months. A varying number of book reviews, each about 250 words, appears in *Kansas Music Review.*

311. **KAPPA DELTA PI RECORD.** 1964– . Kappa Delta Pi, P.O. Box A, West
Lafayette, IN 47906. Circ.: 55,000. 4 issues/yr. Subscription included with
society membership; non-member rate, $2.00/yr. Annual index: December
issue. Editor: Nathan Kravetz. Manuscript to: Jay Hostetler, managing
editor. Book reviews to: managing editor.

  Indexed in: Current Contents: Social & Behavioral Sciences; Current
  Index to Journals in Education.

Educational practitioners at all levels are among the intended audience of the
Record. Its purposes are: to describe and explain innovations in the field; to provide
a forum for debate and discussion; to share workable techniques and methods; and,
to provide news of society chapter activities.

The editorial board welcomes unsolicited manuscripts for consideration. Style
is not specified, and length may range from 1,000 to 2,000 words. Two copies of
the article are required. Copyright on published materials is held by Kappa Delta
Pi. An editorial decision is made in eight weeks and the estimated time from acceptance to publication is four months. From two to four book reviews are in each
issue. Reviews vary from 200 to 500 words in length.

312. **KEEPING UP WITH EXPERIMENTAL MUSIC IN THE SCHOOLS.** 1974– .
Keeping Up With Music Education, 1220 Ridge Road, Muncie, IN 47304.
Circ.: 400. 5 issues/yr. $10.00/yr. Annual index: May issue. Editor: Arnold
E. Burkart. Book reviews to: editor.

  Indexed in: Music Article Guide.

The intended audience of this publication includes teachers of music education activities at all levels, kindergarten through college. Its purpose is to foster
inquiry, exploration, improvisation and experimentation with less conventional
sound sources and procedures in music education. Articles preferred for inclusion
are those which describe classroom procedures using non-traditional, exploratory
techniques.

The editor welcomes unsolicited manuscripts for consideration. No special
style of writing is required, but the length should be between 1,500 and 2,000
words. Copyright on accepted material is held by the publisher, unless otherwise
requested. Simultaneous submission to other journals is permitted. An editorial
decision is made in three weeks and the time from acceptance to publication is
three months. Two or three book reviews are contained in each issue and these
are 200 words in length.

313. **KEEPING UP WITH KODALY CONCEPTS IN MUSIC EDUCATION.**
1974– . Keeping Up With Music Education, 1220 Ridge Road, Muncie,
IN 47304. Circ.: 500. 5 issues/yr. $10.00/yr. Annual index: May issue.
Editor: Harold L. Caldwell. Editor's address: 4 Elizabeth Avenue, Muncie,
IN 47304. Book reviews to: editor.

  Indexed in: Music Article Guide.

Public school music teachers are the primary intended audience of the publication. It is designed as a curricular resource bulletin devoted to the principles,
practices and materials associated with the concepts of music education advocated
by Hungarian composer-educator Zoltan Kodaly. Articles included in this series
deal with historical and philosophical background, and pedagogical development
of the concepts and tools of Kodaly-oriented music education.

Unsolicited manuscripts are accepted for consideration. Simultaneous submission to other journals is permitted. No special style requirements are specified and copyright is held by the publisher, unless otherwise requested. Articles may range from 1,500 to 2,000 words in length. Contributors can expect an editorial decision in three weeks and publication of accepted material follows in three months. The four to six book reviews in each issue are 200 words long.

314. KEEPING UP WITH ORFF-SCHULWERK IN THE CLASSROOM. 1973— . Keeping Up With Music Education, 1220 Ridge Road, Muncie, IN 47304. Circ.: 1,000. 5 issues/yr. $10.00/yr. Annual index: May issue. Editor: Arnold E. Burkart. Book reviews to: editor.
Indexed in: Music Article Guide.

This curricular resource bulletin is published primarily to aid public school music teachers in their use of Orff-Schulwerk materials. It is intended for all those interested in the emerging impact and value of this field of study in music education. The publication includes practical classroom suggestions. A regular feature, Using American Heritage Resources, focuses on using Orff procedures with American children's singing games, folk songs and dances, fiddle tunes, riddles and rhymes, and other folk material. Among the other features are special notes for beginners, and sections on materials and news.

Unsolicited manuscripts are welcomed for possible inclusion in this publication. The editor does not require that authors follow a particular style manual. Preferred length of contributions is 1,500 to 2,000 words. Simultaneous submission to other journals is permitted. Estimated time for an editorial decision concerning acceptability of an article is three weeks and publication follows in three months. Four to five book reviews of about 200 words each appear in this journal. Reviews are to contain all data possible, including current price and source. Copyright on all accepted materials is held by the publisher, unless the author requests otherwise.

315. KEY TO CHRISTIAN EDUCATION. 1962— . Standard Publishing Company, 8121 Hamilton Avenue, Cincinnati, OH 45231. Circ.: 60,000. 4 issues/yr. $3.25/yr. Annual index: not given. Editor: Marjorie Reeves. Book reviews to: editor.

The intended audience of this journal includes Christian leaders such as Sunday School teachers and officers, youth leaders, ministers, directors and teachers of Christian education. It is designed to promote the cause of Christian education in general, to let churches know what others are doing, to give new ideas, and to encourage better teaching. Success stories, usable ideas, and "how to" articles are preferred for publication, if related to any phase of Christian education.

Unsolicited manuscripts, 800 to 1,800 words in length, are welcomed for consideration. A letter of inquiry prior to submission is encouraged. The editor also solicits articles directly from specialists in the field. Copyright is held by the publisher who pays authors at a rate that varies with the article. Journal issues are dedicated to special themes and prospective contributors should query the editor for future topics. Style of writing is not specified. An editorial decision concerning acceptability is given in six weeks. Publication time varies according to the themes chosen. Up to four book reviews appear in this publication and they are 25 to 35 words long.

316. **LED NEWSLETTER.** 1947– . Library Education Division, American Library Association, 50 East Huron Street, Chicago, IL 60611. Circ.: 3,000. 2-4 issues/yr. Subscription included with LED membership. No annual index. Submit manuscripts to: Executive Secretary, LED. No book reviews.
   Indexed in: Current Awareness Library Literature (CALL).

The intended audience of this newsletter is the membership of the Library Education Division of the American Library Association. It provides news of LED activities relating to library education at all levels. In addition to division committee reports, this publication also includes short news items of new or special library and information science education programs and projects, teaching methods, research, financial assistance and similar topics.

The editor solicits material directly from specialists in this field, but also welcomes unsolicited items for consideration. The Chicago style should be used and length may vary from 250 to 750 words. This newsletter is not copyrighted. Simultaneous submission to other journals is permitted. Estimated time for an editorial decision is two to four weeks and publication occurs two to six months later.

317. **LANGUAGE.** 1925– . Linguistic Society of America, 1611 North Kent Street, Arlington, VA 22209. Circ.: 6,000. 4 issues/yr. Subscription included with society membership. Annual index: December issue. Editor: William Bright. Editor's address: Department of Linguistics, University of California, Los Angeles, CA 90024. Book reviews to: editor.
   Indexed in: Abstracts in Anthropology; Computing Review; Current Contents: Social & Behavioral Sciences; Current Index to Journals in Education; dsh Abstracts; Humanities Index; Modern Language Abstracts.

This journal is the official publication of the Linguistic Society of America and is intended for professional linguists. Its primary purpose is reporting research related to any of the languages. Several highly technical articles appear in each issue. Regular features include an extensive Book Review section and a listing of books and publications received.

Unsolicited manuscripts are welcomed for editorial consideration. The journal has its own style sheet which is available upon request. Writers are not given length restrictions. The copyright is held by the publisher. An average of four weeks is required for an editorial decision with the publication of accepted manuscripts occurring ten months after acceptance. Approximately ten book reviews are published in each issue of this journal. These reviews should normally not exceed 1,500 words in length.

318. **LANGUAGE ARTS.** (formerly **ELEMENTARY ENGLISH**). 1924– . National Council of Teachers of English, Elementary Section, 1111 Kenyon

Road, Urbana, IL 61801. Circ.: 30,000. 8 issues/yr. Subscription included with council membership. Annual index: November-December issue. Editor: Iris M. Tiedt. Editor's address: P.O. Box 24338, San Jose, CA 95154. Book reviews to: editors of special columns (see journal).

Indexed in: Current Contents: Social & Behavioral Sciences; Current Index to Journals in Education; Education Index; Exceptional Child Education Abstracts; Language and Language Behavior Abstracts; Media Review Digest; Women Studies Abstracts.

This journal is intended to reach elementary and junior high/middle school teachers and/college professors and their students. Its purpose is to present up-to-date information about teaching the English language arts; listening, speaking, writing, and reading, and related topics. The editor is interested in presentations that combine contemporary theory with current practice as well as challenging critiques of practices and policies in elementary education.

Authors should follow the APA format in submitting all unsolicited manuscripts, which are welcomed by the editor. These contributions should be a maximum of 2,500 words in length and are to be submitted in duplicate. The copyright is held by the publisher. Approximately four weeks is required for an editorial decision. One year may elapse before publication of accepted manuscripts. It is suggested that prospective authors read several issues of the journal before submitting manuscripts for consideration.

319. **LANGUAGE LEARNING.** 1948– . The University of Michigan, 2001 North University Building, Ann Arbor, MI 48104. Circ.: 3,000. 2 issues/yr. $5.00/yr.; institution rate, $8.00/yr. No annual index. Editor: H. Douglas Brown. Book reviews to: editor.

Indexed in: Abstracts in Anthropology; Bulletin Signaletique, Section 390: Psychologie-Psychopathologie-Psychiatrie; Current Contents: Social & Behavioral Sciences; dsh Abstracts; Education Index; Modern Language Abstracts.

Language Learning is intended primarily for language teachers, linguists and applied linguists. The journal publishes scholarly research on topics in applied linguistics, particularly language acquisition. Articles which make contributions to either theoretical or practical aspects are included in this publication.

The editor welcomes unsolicited manuscripts for consideration. A letter of inquiry prior to submission is encouraged. Articles may range from 3,750 to 5,000 words and are to follow APA style requirements. All work should be submitted in duplicate. Simultaneous submission to other journals is permitted. An editorial decision is given in twelve weeks and publication of accepted pieces follows in five months. Three to five book reviews of 1,500 to 2,000 words each are contained in this journal. Copyright is held by the publisher.

320. **LAW IN AMERICAN SOCIETY.** 1972– . National Center for Law-Focused Education, Law in American Society Foundation, 33 North LaSalle Street, Suite 1700, Chicago, IL 60602. Circ.: 13,000. 4 issues/yr. $10.00/yr. No annual index. Editor: Robert H. Ratcliffe. Manuscript to: Charles R. Gessert, editorial director. Book reviews to: editorial director.

Indexed in: Abstracts on Police Science*; Current Index to Journals in Education.

This journal disseminates information on the progress and growth of law-focused education in America and offers classroom strategies and lesson plans for implementing the program. It also provides provocative, substantive articles on the law and its changing nature. Its audience includes elementary school class-room teachers, secondary teachers of law-focused education, attorneys, judges, law enforcement officers, school administrators, and corrections and probation personnel.

The editor solicits articles directly from specialists in this field, but also welcomes unsolicited manuscripts and letters of inquiry. The Chicago style is to be followed and length should be at least 3,000 words. Copyright is held by the publisher. Most of the issues are dedicated to central themes and prospective contributors should query the editor for future topics. Simultaneous submission to other journals is permitted if the editor is informed of this action. An edi-torial decision is given in four to six weeks and publication will follow in three to four months. Up to two book reviews are included in this journal. Each of these reviews is about 1,000 words long.

321. **LEARNING.** 1972– . Education Today Company, Inc., 530 University Avenue, Palo Alto, CA 94301. Circ.: 200,000. 9 issues/yr. $10.00/yr. Annual index: May issue (beginning 1976). Editor: Morton Malkofsky. Book reviews to: Roberta Suid, book reviews editor.

Indexed in: Exceptional Child Education Abstracts; Women Studies Abstracts.

The intent of this journal is to improve the quality of education by encour-aging and supporting innovating teachers and teaching. *Learning* is aimed primarily at elementary school teachers. The type of article preferred for this publication includes any subject given journalistic treatment that is useful to elementary teachers.

Unsolicited manuscripts are accepted for consideration. A letter of inquiry prior to submission is encouraged. Copyright is held by the publisher who pays authors at a rate of $100.00 to $300.00 per piece. Length of work may vary from 1,500 to 3,000 words. An editorial decision is given in two weeks. Publi-cation time varies from three to nine months. Book reviews of different lengths appear in this journal, but maximum length is 1,000 words. The editor prefers professional reviewers.

322. **LEARNING AND MOTIVATION.** 1970– . Academic Press, Inc., 111 Fifth Avenue, New York, NY 10003. Circ.: 1,000. 4 issues/yr. $17.50/yr.; institution rate, $34.50/yr. Annual index: issue number four. Editor: J. Bruce Overmier. Editor's address: Department of Psychology, 212 Elliott Hall, University of Minnesota, Minneapolis, MN 55455. No book reviews.

Indexed in: Current Contents: Social & Behavioral Sciences; Information Retrieval Limited*; Psychological Abstracts; The Psychological Readers Guide.

Learning and Motivation is intended for researchers in, and teachers of, experimental psychology and learning theory. It strives to stimulate basic research and the development of integrative theory for behavioral phenomena. Multi-experiment empirical investigations and theoretical articles are desired for this journal.

Unsolicited articles with a maximum length of 6,250 words are accepted for consideration. The APA style is to be followed and four copies of the manuscript should be sent. Copyright is held by the publisher. Contributors can expect an editorial decision in eight weeks and publication of accepted articles follows in nine months.

323. **LEARNING TODAY.** (formerly **THE LIBRARY-COLLEGE JOURNAL**). 1971– (LT); 1968– (LCJ). Library-College Associates, Inc., P.O. Box 956, Norman, OK 73069. Circ.: not given. 4 issues/yr. $10.00/yr. No annual index. Editor: Howard Clayton. Book reviews to: editor.
Indexed in: Current Index to Journals in Education; Information Science Abstracts; Library Literature.

The purpose of this journal is to arouse interest in, and increase understanding of, the importance of library-centered learning in the educational process. It is intended for educators in all subjects and grade levels. Interdisciplinary articles with an emphasis on self-directed learning experiences are desired for *Learning Today*.

Letters of inquiry and unsolicited manuscripts are welcomed by the editor. Preferred length of contributions is 1,500 to 2,000 words. Style is not specified and copyright is held by the publisher. Simultaneous submission to other journals is permitted. The time required for an editorial decision concerning acceptability is three weeks. Publication time is not given. Four book reviews of 400 words each appear in this journal.

324. **THE LINGUISTIC REPORTER.** 1959– . The Center for Applied Linguistics, 1611 North Kent Street, Arlington, VA 22209. Circ.: 4,500. 10 issues/yr. $4.50/yr. Annual index: one of the spring issues. Editor: Allene Guss Grognet. Unsolicited book reviews not accepted.
Indexed in: Current Index to Journals in Education.

This newsletter in applied linguistics is intended for language teachers, linguists, and education specialists. Its purpose is to keep its readers informed of developments in the field of languages and linguistics. The editor is interested in pieces dealing with descriptions of programs or research, but not in articles treating theoretical aspects of the field.

Unsolicited manuscripts as well as letters of inquiry are welcomed by the editor. These articles should be between 1,000 and 4,000 words in length and follow either the Chicago or MLA style. The publisher holds the copyright on accepted material. Four weeks is required for an editorial decision with the publication of accepted manuscripts following within four months.

325. **LOUISIANA SCHOOLS.** 1923– . Louisiana Teachers Association, 1755 Nicholson Drive, P.O. Box 1906, Baton Rouge, LA 70821. Circ.: 26,000.

LOUISIANA SCHOOLS (cont'd)

4 issues/yr. Subscription included with association membership; non-member rate, $3.00/yr. Annual index: September issue. Editor: Horace C. Robinson. Manuscript to: William C. Baker, managing editor. Book reviews to: managing editor.

The intended audience of this journal includes educators in general, but especially members of the Louisiana Teachers Association. This publication contains educational articles and official business of the association. Regular features include news of students and classroom teachers, editorials, and a media section.

Authors are encouraged to send manuscripts to *Louisiana Schools*. Articles of about 1,750 words written in the third person are accepted for consideration. Copyright is held by the author. Simultaneous submission to other journals is permitted. Contributors can expect an editorial decision concerning acceptability of their work in one week and publication will follow, if accepted, in four months. One book review of 250 words appears in each issue.

326. **LUTHERAN EDUCATION.** 1865– . The Lutheran Church–Missouri Synod. Circ.: 3,800. 5 issues/yr. $5.00/yr. Annual index: May/June issue. Editor: Merle L. Radke. Editor's address: Concordia Teachers College, 7400 Augusta, River Forest, IL 60305. Book reviews to: editor.

The intended audience of this journal consists primarily of elementary school teachers, but also includes administrators and secondary school teachers. It provides in-service education to its readers. The editor prefers articles that deal with matters of current concern in education. Book reviews, editorials and other news and notes are regular features of *Lutheran Education*.

The editor solicits material directly from selected professionals, but welcomes letters of inquiry and unsolicited manuscripts. Authors should follow MLA style requirements and should not exceed 3,750 words in length. Copyright is held by the author. An editorial decision is given in three weeks and contributors can expect their work to be published four to twelve months after acceptance. Four to six book reviews are included in this journal and these reviews are about 300 words each.

327. **MASC JOURNAL.** 1951– . Massachusetts Association of School Committees, Inc., Room 1115, 73 Tremont Street, Boston, MA 02108. Circ.: 2,500. 4 issues/yr. Subscription included with association membership; non-member rate, $5.00/yr. No annual index. Editor: M. Virginia Fallon. No book reviews.

The intended audience of this journal includes school committee members and school superintendents. Its purpose is to provide information about issues and concerns of school committees. Also in this publication are in-house articles dealing with association matters. Topics related to school law, new legislation, collective bargaining, curriculum and innovations are typical areas found in *MASC Journal*.

Unsolicited manuscripts are considered for publication. The editor also solicits some of the material for this journal directly from experts in the fields under consideration. Simultaneous submission to other journals is permitted. Length of articles should be 1,500 to 2,000 words. Style is not specified. Estimated time for an editorial decision concerning acceptability of an article is two to three weeks. Publication follows in one to two months.

328. **MPAEA JOURNAL OF ADULT EDUCATION.** 1973– . Mountain Plains
Adult Education Association. Circ.: 500. 2 issues/yr. Subscription included
with association membership; non-member rate, $5.00/yr. No annual index.
Editor: Glenn S. Jensen. Manuscript to: Editor, P.O. Box 3274, University
of Wyoming, Laramie, WY 82071. No book reviews unless requested by
editor.

This journal publishes the results of research, pilot projects and new program
developments. One aim of this journal is to translate scholarly research into useful
and adaptable form. Articles dealing with the central issues relating to the philosophy, welfare and expansion of adult education in the Mountain Plains area are
included to consolidate the common goals of the association membership and to
have more impact on national, regional and state policies.

The editor solicits material from various professionals in adult education, but
also welcome letters of inquiry and unsolicited manuscripts. The length of articles
may vary from 1,000 to 1,500 words and copyright is held by the author. The style
should be easy and follow the present tense pattern as much as possible. An editorial decision concerning acceptability is given in four weeks and publication
follows in two months.

329. **THE MSSPA BUGLE.** 1947– . Massachusetts Secondary School Principals'
Association, Inc., 73 Tremont Street, Room 420, Boston, MA 02108.
Circ.: 1,800. 9 issues/yr. $2.50/yr. No annual index. Editor: Bertram H.
Holland. No book reviews.

The *Bugle* is intended primarily to inform its readership of the activities of
the Massachusetts Secondary Principals' Association. The audience consists of
principals, assistant principals and athletic directors of high schools, as well as
superintendents of schools and school committee members. Sample article titles
from recent issues are: Skills of an Effective Administrator; The Coach as a
Teacher; and, Beware Child Dictatorship.

Articles of interest to secondary school administrators are welcomed by the
editor. A letter of inquiry prior to sending material is encouraged. Simultaneous
submission to other journals is permitted. The length of articles should be short,
about 200 words. Style is not specified. An editorial decision is made in three
weeks and the time from acceptance to publication is one month. *The MSSPA
Bugle* is not copyrighted.

330. **MTA–THE TEACHER.** 1968– . Montreal Teachers Association, 5485
Sherbrooke Street West, Room 201, Montreal, Quebec, Canada H4A 1W1.
Circ.: 4,000. 6 issues/yr. Subscription included with association member-
ship, no charge, controlled circulation. No annual index. Editor: W. Alan
Wright. Book reviews to: editor.

This tabloid is intended primarily for classroom teachers, but many articles
also would be of interest to school administrators. It is intended to provide information on the latest classroom practices, educational policies, and school management trends. The editor is interested in articles addressed to school practices,
innovations in the field, and information about concerns in other Canadian
provinces.

Unsolicited articles are considered. The editor also assigns articles where deemed appropriate. Manuscripts should be approximately 800 words in length. Six weeks is required for an editorial decision with two months usually elapsing between acceptance of a manuscript and its publication. Simultaneous submission to other journals is permitted. Book reviews of approximately 500 words are published, but not on a regular basis.

331. **MAN/SOCIETY/TECHNOLOGY.** (formerly **JOURNAL OF INDUSTRIAL EDUCATION** and **THE INDUSTRIAL ARTS TEACHER**). 1970– (MST); 1964– (JIE); 1942– (IAT). American Industrial Arts Association, 1201 Sixteenth Street, N.W., Washington, DC 20036. Circ.: 10,000. 8 issues/yr. Subscription included with association membership; library rate, $9.00/yr. Annual index: May-June issue. Editor: Esther Ann Goldring. Book reviews to: editor.
   Indexed in: Current Index to Journals in Education; Education Index; Media Review Digest.

Man/Society/Technology is the official journal of the American Industrial Arts Association, an organization dedicated solely to the development and improvement of industrial arts education. The association seeks to provide an open forum for the free exchange of relevant ideas relating to education via its publications. This journal is aimed at industrial arts teachers and supervisors at both the public school and college and university level. It is intended as a source of professional information for the field. The editor is looking for articles which reflect current thought in the field of industrial arts, and which preferably relate to the classroom. Professional topics are preferred to descriptions of projects.

Unsolicited articles are encouraged. These manuscripts should be between 3,000 and 4,000 words in length. The copyright is held by the publisher. Issues of this publication are theme-oriented, but not theme limited. Themes are announced in an early spring issue each year. The editor also will provide a list of the themes upon request. Times for an editorial decision and publication are not specified.

332. **THE MANITOBA TEACHER.** 1919– . The Manitoba Teachers' Society, 191 Harcourt Street, Winnipeg, Manitoba, Canada R3J 3H2. Circ.: 17,000. 10 issues/yr. Subscription included with society membership; non-member rate, $3.00/yr. No annual index. Editor: Miep van Raalte, associate editor. No book reviews.
   Indexed in: Canadian Education Index.

This tabloid is intended for all teachers in the public schools of Manitoba and others involved in or interested in the public education system in Manitoba. Its purpose is to inform, comment on, and review developments and issues directly and indirectly involving and related to the public education system in Manitoba with emphasis on those areas of particular concern to teachers in Manitoba's public schools.

Unsolicited manuscripts are accepted for possible inclusion in *The Manitoba Teacher*. Length may range from 200 to 1,500 words. Style is not specified.

Estimated time for an editorial decision concerning acceptability of an article is two to eight weeks. Publication will follow from one to twelve months later.

333. **MARQUETTE UNIVERSITY EDUCATION REVIEW.** 1970– . Marquette University, School of Education, 502 North 15th Street, Milwaukee, WI 53233. Circ.: 1,500. 1 or 2 issues/yr. $1.00/single copy. No annual index. Editor: A. Dupuis. Book reviews to: editor.
    Indexed in: Current Index to Journals in Education.
    This journal is aimed at professionals in teacher education, classroom teachers, and administrators. It is intended to provide visability for the School of Education of Marquette University and an opportunity for professionals to share their ideas with others across the country. The editor is seeking short, pointed articles dealing with current topics. Research reports are welcomed.
    Unsolicited manuscripts and letters of inquiry are sought. No particular style is required, but article length should be between 1,000 and 2,500 words. Four weeks is required for an editorial decision with two months for publication following acceptance. This journal publishes one or two book reviews of approximately 500 words in length. Simultaneous submission to other journals is permitted. Material in the *Review* is not copyrighted.

334. **MARYLAND MUSIC EDUCATOR.** 1954– . The Maryland Music Educators Association. Circ.: not given. 4 issues/yr. Subscription included with association membership; non-member rate, $3.00/yr. No annual index. Editor: James H. Avampato. Editor's address: P.O. Box 668, Aberdeen, MD 21001. Book reviews to: editor.
    This journal is intended to reach music educators, particularly those who are members of the MMEA. Its purpose is to provide material of use in the field of music education. The editor is interested in professional articles within the purview of the stated aims of the journal.
    Unsolicited articles are accepted for editorial consideration and these may be of any length. Editorial decisions usually are made within eight weeks with two months elapsing between acceptance and publication. Occasional book reviews are used, depending upon space available. These reviews usually are short, being less than 250 words. Simultaneous submission to other journals is permitted. A preferred style is not specified.

335. **MASSACHUSETTS MUSIC NEWS.** 1952– . Massachusetts Music Educators, 93 Greenleaf Avenue, West Springfield, MA 01809. Circ.: 2,000. 4 issues/yr. Subscription included with association membership. No annual index. Editor: J. Anthony DiGiore. Editor's address: P.O. Box 532, West Springfield, MA 01089. Book reviews to: editor.
    This journal is the official organ of the MMEA, whose membership consists chiefly of in-service public and college school music educators. The journal's purpose is to acquaint potential and professional music educators with current practices and issues in the field, with emphasis upon state issues. Authors are encouraged to submit manuscripts dealing with any related aspect of music education.

Some articles are solicited by the editors, however, unsolicited material is given consideration. The style is journalistic and free with articles running approximately 1,500 words. The copyright is held by the author. Six weeks is required for an editorial decision with publication of accepted articles following within two to three months. At least one book review is published in each issue. Book reviews are a minimum of 100 words in length.

336. THE MASSACHUSETTS TEACHER. (formerly **COMMON GROUND**). 1931– (MT); 1914– (CG). Massachusetts Teachers Association, 20 Ashburton Place, Boston, MA 02108. Circ.: 58,000. 8 issues/yr. Subscription included with association membership. No annual index. Editor: Russell P. Burbank. No book reviews.

This journal is the official publication of the MTA and is directed to the public school teachers of the state. It presents news and happenings of interest to the membership. Few out of state contributions are published and most of the contents of the journal are prepared by MTA members.

Unsolicited articles, primarily from MTA members, are encouraged, as well as letters of inquiry, especially from non-association members. No particular style is required and article length should be approximately 1,500 words. Payment is made for accepted manuscripts at a rate to be negotiated at the time of acceptance. The copyright is held by the publisher. The editor makes an editorial decision within three weeks. Publication of manuscript occurs within two to three months following acceptance. Two copies of all work should be submitted.

337. THE MATHEMATICS TEACHER. 1908– . National Council of Teachers of Mathematics, 1906 Association Drive, Reston, VA 22091. Circ.: 50,000. 8 issues/yr. $13.00/yr. Annual index: December issue. Submit manuscripts to: editorial panel. Book reviews to: managing editor.

Indexed in: Current Index to Journals in Education; Education Index; Exceptional Child Education Abstracts; Media Review Digest; Technical Education Abstracts.

This journal is intended for teachers of mathematics and others interested in this field. Its purpose is the improvement of mathematics instruction in junior high/middle schools, senior high schools, junior colleges and teacher education institutions. A wide variety of articles dealing with the discipline appear in each issue. Sample article titles are: Testing in the Mathematics Classroom; New Conic Graph Paper; and, Some Changes in Shop Mathematics Due to Metrication. Each issue contains an "Activities" centerfold, an instructional aid for classroom use. Information concerning new products, programs and publications is featured regularly.

The editor is interested in receiving unsolicited manuscripts. Articles should be between 1,000 and 4,000 words and follow Chicago style requirements. The copyright is held by the publisher. Approximately twenty-four weeks is required for an editorial decision with ten months elapsing from the time of acceptance to publication. A varying number of book reviews, of approximately 250 words each, is used in each issue.

338. **MCGILL JOURNAL OF EDUCATION**.1966– . McGill University, Faculty of Education. Circ.: 1,200. 2 issues/yr. $3.00/yr. Biennial index. Editor: Margaret Gillett. Editor's address: 3700 McTavish Street, Montreal, Quebec, Canada H3A 1Y2. Book reviews to: editor.

Indexed in: Canadian Education Index; Research into Higher Education; Sociology of Education Abstracts.

Intended for professors in higher education, particularly those interested in teacher education. It disseminates ideas and issues and makes research findings available. Creative poetry and prose also are acceptable.

Unsolicited manuscripts and letters of inquiry are welcomed. The editor also solicits articles on specific subjects. Manuscripts should be about 3,000 words in length. Copyright is held by the publisher, but permission to reprint is freely granted. Editorial decisions take about six weeks, and publication follows within twelve months. Several book reviews (500 words long) are published in each issue. Modified MLA style preferred. Two copies should be submitted.

339. **MEASUREMENT AND EVALUATION IN GUIDANCE**. 1968– . American Personnel and Guidance Association, 1607 New Hampshire Avenue, N. W., Washington, DC 20009. Circ.: 2,500. 4 issues/yr. $12.00/yr. Annual index: issue number four. Editor: William A. Mehrens. Editor's address: Michigan State University, College of Education, East Lansing, MI 48823. Book reviews to: editor.

Indexed in: College Student Personnel Abstracts; Current Contents: Social & Behavioral Sciences; Current Index to Journals in Education; Education Index; Employment Relations Abstracts*; Sociology of Education Abstracts.

The intended audience includes counselors, administrators and personnel workers. Articles have clearly prescribed implications for the practitioner in measurement and evaluation. Articles range from the theoretical to those that deal with the problems of measurement specialists and practitioners.

Unsolicited manuscripts are considered. Three copies should be submitted and no length specifications are given. The copyright is held by the publisher. Various issues are dedicated to central themes. An editorial decision takes eight weeks, and publication is within eight months. Book reviews (of various length) are included in each issue. Complete author guidelines appear in some issues.

340. **MEDIA & METHODS**. (formerly **SCHOOL PAPERBACK JOURNAL**). 1967– (MM); 1964– (SPJ). North American Publishing Company, 401 North Broad, Philadelphia, PA 19108. Circ.: 50,000. 9 issues/yr. $9.00/yr. No annual index. Editor: Frank McLaughlin. Manuscript to: Anthony Prete, managing editor. Book reviews to: managing editor.

Indexed in: Consumers Index; Current Index to Journals in Education; Education Index; Media Review Digest; Women Studies Abstracts.

Intended for English and social studies high school teachers who are interested in innovative education, and for librarians, media specialists, and film and communications enthusiasts. Articles can be categorized as follows: conceptual, those dealing with basic issues; resource, exploring available materials related to a particular topic; and "how to," which explain innovative approaches to learning.

Unsolicited articles are considered. One copy, not the original, should be submitted; it will be returned only if accompanied by a self-addressed, stamped envelope.

MEDIA & METHODS (cont'd)

Copyright is held by the publisher. Payment (upon publication) varies from $35.00 to $75.00. An editorial decision takes six to eight weeks. Publication usually is within one to four months. Book reviews (300-500 words) appear in each issue; the reviewer must have practical experience in the area covered by the book. Prospective authors should familiarize themselves with the contents of several issues of the journal.

341. **MEDIA SPECTRUM.** 1974— . Michigan Association for Media in Education, 401 South Fourth Street, Ann Arbor, MI 48103. Circ.: 1,500. 4 issues/yr. $10.00/yr. Annual index: issue number four (beginning 1975). Editor: Florence Banks. Editor's address: 6709 Andersonville Road, Waterford, MI 48095. Book reviews to: editor.

Intended for educators working with instructional media. Keeps the MAME membership and others informed of trends, innovations, techniques, and the latest literature.

Unsolicited manuscripts and letters of inquiry are welcomed; some manuscripts are solicited. Articles are about 3,000 words long. Style preference is not indicated; copyright is held by the publisher. An editorial decision takes six weeks, and publication is within four months. Book reviews are included, but no details are specified.

342. **MENTAL RETARDATION.** 1963— . American Association on Mental Deficiency, 5201 Connecticut Avenue, N.W., Washington, DC 20015. Circ.: 13,000. 6 issues/yr. Subscription included with association membership; non-member rate, $15.00/yr. Annual index: issue number six. Editor: Sue Allen Warren. Editor's address: Boston University, 765 Commonwealth Avenue, Boston, MA 02215. Book reviews written by review editor.

Indexed in: Abstracts for Social Workers; Current Contents: Social & Behavioral Sciences; Current Index to Journals in Education; dsh Abstracts; Educational Administration Abstracts; Exceptional Child Education Abstracts; Excerpta Medica; Hospital Literature Index; Index Medicus; Language and Language Behavior Abstracts; Nursing Research; Psychological Abstracts; Sociology of Education Abstracts; Speed.

This journal disseminates information about mental retardation and associated disabilities. Articles deal with new methodology, critical summaries, essays on current topics, program descriptions illustrating theory, and applied research.

Unsolicited manuscripts are welcomed. These works are to be submitted in triplicate and should be no more than 2,500 words long. APA style is to be followed. An editorial decision takes twelve to fifteen weeks, and publication is within ten months. Copyright is held by the publisher. Issues are dedicated to central themes, contributors should query the editor for future topics.

343. **THE MERRILL-PALMER QUARTERLY.** 1954— . The Merrill-Palmer Institute, 71 East Ferry Avenue, Detroit, MI 48202. Circ.: 2,000. 4 issues/yr. $11.00/yr. Biennial index. Editor: Martin L. Hoffman.

Editor's address: Department of Psychology, University of Michigan, Ann Arbor, MI 49104. Book reviews to: editor.

Indexed in: Abstracts for Social Workers; Current Contents: Social & Behavioral Sciences; Child Development Abstracts and Bibliography; Current Index to Journals in Education; dsh Abstracts; Education Index; Exceptional Child Education Abstracts; Language and Language Behavior Abstracts; Mental Retardation Abstracts; Psychological Abstracts; The Psychological Readers Guide; Sociological Abstracts; Sociology and Education Abstracts; Women Studies Abstracts.

The *Quarterly* is broad in scope, and publishes papers representing the various disciplines bearing on human development. Its purpose is to stimulate the growth of ideas in these fields and, therefore, welcomes articles dealing with conceptual analysis of problems under investigation, results of exploratory studies in new areas, and case material illustrative of general principles, as well as completed research reports. Papers which develop new approaches to theory and research are particularly welcomed, as are those which critically examine existing approaches or place them within a broader perspective. Articles having practical value such as those describing methods of intervention or giving advice, when documented with data support or sound theoretical analysis, also are seen as contributing to the purpose of the journal.

Unsolicited articles and letters of inquiry are welcomed by the editor. No length limitation is stipulated, but the APA style should be followed. The copyright is held by the publisher. No time limit for editorial consideration was indicated. A minimum of six months delay can be expected from acceptance to publication. Book reviews are published, however, no limits as to number or length are specified. Two copies of all work are to be submitted.

344. MICHIGAN ACADEMICIAN. 1969– . Michigan Academy of Science, Arts, and Letters, 2117 Washtenaw Avenue, Ann Arbor, MI 48104. Circ.: 2,000. 4 issues/yr. $12.00/yr. No annual index. Editor: Ronald L. Trowbridge. Book reviews to: editor.

Indexed in: Abstracts in Anthropology; Abstracts in English Studies; Abstracts of Folklore Studies; America: History and Life*; Biological Abstracts; Chemical Abstracts; Dokumentation zur Raumentwicklung; Forestry Abstracts; Information Retrieval Limited*; Modern Language Abstracts; Nuclear Science Abstracts; Psychological Abstracts; Sociological Abstracts.

Academicians at the university level are the primary audience of this journal. Articles found in the publication are from any discipline at the university level. Regular features include book reviews and an editorial entitled The State of Things. Papers submitted for publication must first be read at the annual meeting of the Michigan Academy. To be read, they must be screened through the section chairman of respective disciplines. Membership in the Academy is open to all.

Papers read at the annual meeting are eligible to be considered for publication. Style should be consistent with the respective discipline. Preferred length of manuscripts is 2,500 to 5,000 words and two copies are to be submitted. Copyright is held by the publisher. An editorial decision is made in eight weeks and the time from acceptance to publication varies from two to ten months. Six book reviews of 500 to 750 words appear in each issue. Non-members of the Michigan Academy may write reviews, but books reviewed must be either about the state of Michigan or written by someone from Michigan.

345. **MICHIGAN MUSIC EDUCATOR.** 1954– . Michigan Music Educators Association. Circ.: 1,800. 3 issues/yr. Subscription included with association membership; non-member rate, $3.00/yr. No annual index. Editor: Dale L. Bartlett. Editor's address: Music Department, Michigan State University, East Lansing, MI 48824. No book reviews.

This journal is intended primarily for music educators in Michigan, both in public schools and higher education. It disseminates information about state and national affairs related to music education. Articles preferred for inclusion are those which are of general interest for music teachers and about current happenings and issues. Also included are reports on professional trends and research, especially as they can be applied to the teaching-learning process.

Unsolicited manuscripts are accepted for consideration. A letter of inquiry prior to submission is encouraged. No specific style is required and copyright information is not given. Length should not exceed 1,500 words. Simultaneous submission to other journals is permitted. An editorial decision is given in two weeks and publication of accepted work follows in one to six months.

346. **THE MICHIGAN SCHOOL BOARD JOURNAL.** 1949– . Michigan School Board Association, 421 West Kalamazoo, Lansing, MI 48933. Circ.: 9,500. 12 issues/yr. Subscription included with association membership; non-member rate, $10.00/yr. No annual index. Editor: Varl O. Wilkinson. No book reviews.

This journal is intended for school board members and school administrators, primarily in Michigan, but not limited to that state. Its purpose is to keep its readers informed about educational issues. The editor welcomes manuscripts dealing with school management and educational developments.

Unsolicited articles and letters of inquiry are considered by the editor. Articles should be between 500 and 750 words in length. The copyright is held by the publisher. Two to three weeks is required for an editorial decision. Publication follows acceptance two to six months later. The style of this publication is journalistic and free.

347. **THE MINNESOTA READING QUARTERLY.** 1956– . Minnesota Reading Association, Inc., P.O. Box 29023, Minneapolis, MN 55429. Circ.: 800. 4 issues/yr. Subscription included with association membership; non-member rate, $6.00/yr. No annual index. Editor: Tracy F. Tyler, Jr. Book reviews are written by staff.

Indexed in: Current Index to Journals in Education.

This journal is written for members of the association, public school teachers and administrators, and college faculty and others interested in education. It acts as a clearinghouse for information relating to reading instruction, especially

THE MINNESOTA READING QUARTERLY (cont'd)

in Minnesota. The editor welcomes all contributions. No restrictions are specified other than the articles must be in some way related to the field of reading.

Unsolicited articles should be 1,200 to 3,000 words in length and are to be submitted in duplicate. The copyright is held by the publisher. An editorial decision is given in one to two weeks with publication of accepted manuscripts following within two to eight months. The Chicago style requirements should be followed.

348. **MISSISSIPPI EDUCATIONAL ADVANCE.** 1890– . Mississippi Education Association, 219 North President Street, P.O. Drawer 22529, Jackson, MS 39205. Circ.: 14,000. 5 issues/yr. (newsletter on alternate months). Subscription included with association membership; non-member rate, $1.50/yr. No annual index. Editor: John Ashley. Manuscript to: Marianna Brannon, associate editor. Book reviews to: associate editor.

This journal is intended for teachers in public schools at all grade levels as well as students in institutions of higher education. Its intent is to upgrade the teaching profession in Mississippi. The editor is interested in practical, "how to do it" articles, or those which provide help to the classroom teacher.

Unsolicited articles as well as letters of inquiry are welcomed by the editor. Articles should be between 1,000 and 1,500 words in length. Simultaneous submission to other journals is permitted. Two weeks is required for an editorial decision and publication of accepted manuscripts usually follows within two months. Between four and six book reviews are used in each issue. These reviews should be approximately 200 words in length and must include the price and ordering information. The editor prefers a chatty, informal style of writing. This journal does not publish bibliographies.

349. **MISSISSIPPI MUSIC EDUCATOR.** (formerly **MISSISSIPPI NOTES**). 1974– (MME); 1947– (MN). Mississippi Music Educators Association. Circ.: 1,000. 4 issues/yr. Subscription included with membership; non-member rate, $3.00/yr. No annual index. Editor: Robert J. Tuley. Editor's address: P.O. Box 5284, Southern Station, Hattiesburg, MS 39401. Book reviews to: editor.

The purpose of this journal is to provide information and education to aid professional growth. It is intended primarily for Mississippi music teachers, at all levels. Articles on philosophy, research, or about state-wide activities or accomplishments are preferred. "How to do it" articles also are included in this journal.

Unsolicited manuscripts are welcomed by the editor. Authors are permitted to submit their work simultaneously to other journals. Articles also are solicited directly from professionals in this field of study. Preferred length of material is 200 to 1,000 words and the MLA style is to be followed. An editorial decision is made in four weeks and the time from acceptance to publication is three months. One book review appears in each issue. Review length is not specified, but they are to be concise and music education related. Copyright is held by the author.

350. **THE MODERN LANGUAGE JOURNAL.** 1916– . The National Federation of Modern Language Teachers Associations. Circ.: 8,700. 6 issues/yr. $7.00/yr.;

institution rate, $8.00/yr. Annual index: December issue. Editor: Charles L. King. Editor's address: University of Colorado, Boulder, CO 80302. Book reviews to: review editors.

Indexed in: Book Review Index; Canadian Education Index; Current Contents: Social & Behavioral Sciences; Current Index to Journals in Education; Education Index; Language and Language Behavior Abstracts; Media Review Digest; Psychological Abstracts.

The Modern Language Journal is intended for foreign language teachers at all instructional levels. Research articles concerned with teaching in general and manuscripts dealing with specific pedagogical methods are of particular interest to the editor. Sample article titles are: Language-Oriented Careers in the Federal Government; A Critical Survey of New Elementary and Intermediate Latin Textbooks, 1969-1973; The Myth of Language Laboratory Monitoring; and, The Use of Songs in Teaching Foreign Languages.

The editor welcomes unsolicited manuscripts. Some issues are dedicated to central themes and these are announced in the *Journal*. Manuscripts should be between 2,500 and 4,000 words in length. The copyright is held by the publisher. Approximately sixteen weeks is required for an editorial decision with an additional four to six months required for publication after acceptance. Up to 35 book reviews are published in each issue and these reviews are approximately 500 words in length.

351. **MODERN PHILOLOGY.** 1903– . University of Chicago Press, 5801 South Ellis Avenue, Chicago, IL 60637. Circ.: 2,000. 4 issues/yr. $12.00/yr.; institution rate, $14.00/yr. Annual index: May issue. Editors: Gwin J. Kolb and Edward W. Rosenheim, Jr. Editor's address: The University of Chicago, 1050 East 59th Street, Chicago, IL 60637. Unsolicited book reviews not accepted.

Indexed in: Book Review Index; Humanities Index; Social Sciences Index; Women Studies Abstracts.

This journal is intended to reach scholars, critics and students of medieval and modern languages and literatures. Its purpose is the dissemination of scholarly and critical research in the areas mentioned. The editor seeks articles of quality which have the potential to make real contributions to the fields of study covered by the journal.

Unsolicited articles are accepted for editorial consideration. The length of these may vary. The Chicago style should be followed. The copyright is held by the publisher. Eight to twelve weeks normally is required for an editorial decision. Publication follows acceptance between twelve and eighteen months later.

352. **MOMENTUM.** 1970– . National Catholic Educational Association, Suite 350, One Dupont Circle, Washington, DC 20036. Circ.: 14,500. 4 issues/yr. $8.00/yr. No annual index. Editor: Carl Balcerak. Book reviews to: editor.

Indexed in: The Catholic Periodical and Literature Index; Current Contents: Social & Behavioral Sciences; Current Index to Journals in Education; Education Index.

MOMENTUM (cont'd)

Momentum is intended primarily for Catholic educators and educational institutions. Its purpose is to inform and stimulate Catholic superintendents, principals, teachers, parents, and interested laity. Articles preferred are those that describe innovative programs in Catholic schools, primarily elementary and secondary. Also desired are articles on current topics of interest related to research and specific viewpoints.

Unsolicited manuscripts are accepted for consideration, but a letter of inquiry prior to submission is recommended. Two copies of the work, approximately 2,500 words in length, are to be submitted. Copyright is held by the publisher who pays the author at the rate of two cents per word. Style should follow APA requirements. An editorial decision is made in three weeks and the time from acceptance to publication varies from four to six months. Three to four book reviews appear in this journal. Each review is about 1,000 words long and deals with some phase of Catholic education or general educational theory, educational administration, educational philosophy or related areas.

353. MUSIC EDUCATORS JOURNAL. 1914– . Music Educators National Conference, Center for Educational Associations, 1901 Association Drive, Reston, VA 22091. Circ.: 71,900. 9 issues/yr. Subscription included with association membership; institutional rate, $4.00/yr. Annual index: May issue. Editor: Malcolm E. Bessom. Unsolicited book reviews not encouraged.
Indexed in: Book Review Index; Current Index to Journals in Education; Education Index; Exceptional Child Education Abstracts; Music Article Guide; The Music Index; RILM Abstracts of Music Literature.

This journal is intended for music educators at all levels, preschool through university, as well as students, particularly at the college level. It is intended to reflect the current practices in all segments and levels of the music education profession. The editor is interested in articles that approach their subject in a straightforward, non-jargonese, manner. Emphasis is on problems in music teaching, new trends, and current issues.

Approximately 40 per cent of the journal's content is solicited while the balance is made up of unsolicited manuscripts. Articles should be between 1,500 and 3,000 words. The *Journal* has its own style manual and all materials are edited to conform to it. Rejections often are made within one week of receipt while acceptance may take up to eight weeks. Publication of accepted pieces usually follows within three to nine months. Authors are encouraged to send a self-addressed, stamped business size envelope for a copy of the *Journal*'s style sheet. Copyright on all material is held by the publisher.

354. MUSIC JOURNAL. 1943– . Sar-Les Music, Inc., 370 Lexington Avenue, New York, NY 10017. Circ.: not given. 10 issues/yr. $9.00/yr. No annual index. Editor: Guy Freedman. Book reviews are assigned.
Indexed in: Education Index; Index to Periodical Articles Related to Law; Media Review Digest; The Music Index.

The intended audience of this journal includes music educators, students, professionals, dealers and music lovers in general. *Music Journal* is a means for the exchange of ideas and for the publishing of information of national musical

172

interest. Among the articles in this journal are technical, general and inspirational works, as well as human interest pieces on creators and instrumentalists.

Articles written in a journalistic style are welcomed by the editor. A letter of inquiry prior to submission is encouraged. Copyright is held by the publisher, but an author may retain copyright through special arrangements. Manuscripts of about 1,000 words are preferred. An editorial decision concerning accepta- bility of an article is made in two to three weeks and the publication time varies. The six to eight book reviews are each about 100 words long and are assigned by the editor.

355. **NAAHE JOURNAL.** 1974– . The National Association for the Advancement of Humane Education, 1604 K Street, N.W., Washington, DC 20006. Circ.: 500. 4 issues/yr. Subscription included with association membership. No annual index. Editor: Stuart R. Westerlund. Editor's address: 600 South College, The University of Tulsa, Tulsa, OK 74104. Book reviews to: editor.

This journal is intended to reach educators and others interested in humane education. It is intended as a vehicle for the dissemination of materials and ideas to professional educators and others. The editor is interested in a broad range of articles dealing with the subject of humaneness, principally from an educational point of view.

The editor encourages the submission of manuscripts. Style requirements are contained on the inside back cover of each issue. An editorial decision is reached within two weeks with publication of accepted manuscripts following within three months. The copyright is held by the publisher. The original and one copy of all manuscripts should be submitted. An unspecified number of book reviews is used in each issue, dependent upon space availability. No style is indicated for these. A self-addressed stamped envelope should be enclosed for the return of unacceptable manuscripts. No length restrictions are imposed upon authors for either articles or reviews.

356. **NACWPI JOURNAL.** (formerly **NATIONAL ASSOCIATION OF COLLEGE WIND AND PERCUSSION INSTRUMENT INSTRUCTORS BULLETIN).** 1952– (NACWPIIB). National Association of College Wind and Percussion Instructors, Division of Fine Arts, Northeast Missouri State University, Kirksville, MO 63501. Circ.: 1,000. 4 issues/yr. Subscription included with association membership; non-member rate, $10.00/yr. Annual index: fall issue. Editor: Richard Weerts. Book reviews to: editor.

Indexed in: Music Article Guide.

The purpose of this journal is to publish university level papers dealing with wind and percussion performance and teaching as well as to serve as a means of communication among members of the NACWPI. Its audience includes primarily wind and percussion professors at the college and university level. Regular features are convention programs, association news, and the reproduction of faculty recital programs.

This journal features articles between 1,200 and 2,500 words in length. Letters of inquiry as well as unsolicited manuscripts are welcomed by the editor. The copyright is retained by the publisher. Between two and four weeks is required for an editorial decision. Publication of accepted manuscripts usually follows acceptance within four to twelve months. From one to four book reviews are published in each issue and these should be between 1,000 and 2,000 words long.

357. NAJE EDUCATOR. 1969– . National Association of Jazz Educators, P.O. Box 724, Manhattan, KS 66502. Circ.: 3,000. 4 issues/yr. Subscription included with association membership; library rate, $4.00/yr. No annual index. Editor: Matt Betton, Sr. Book reviews to: editor.
Indexed in: The Music Index.

This journal is designed to help prepare present and future music teachers, to disseminate educational and professional news of interest to music educators, to lend assistance and guidance in the organization and development of jazz and popular music curricula, to promote the understanding and appreciation of jazz and popular music and its artistic performance, and to cooperate with all organizations dedicated to the development of musical culture in America. It is intended for music educators, music students, professional musicians and anyone interested in keeping abreast of what is happening in jazz education. Articles are concerned with any and all facets of jazz education (choral, string, wind, and general music).

The editor solicits manuscripts, but also welcomes unsolicited articles. The length may vary from 2,000 to 3,000 words. An editorial decision is given in six weeks and publication of accepted material follows in one to three months. Copyright is held by the publisher.

358. NASSP BULLETIN. 1917– . National Association of Secondary School Principals, 1904 Association Drive, Reston, VA 22091. Circ.: 35,000. 9 issues/yr. Subscription included with association membership; library rate, $30.00/yr. Annual index: December issue. Editor: Thomas F. Koerner. Book reviews to: editor.
Indexed in: Current Index to Journals in Education; Education Index; Educational Administration Abstracts; Exceptional Child Education Abstracts.

The *Bulletin* is intended for secondary school principals and administrators, teachers and educators in higher education. Its purpose is to present secondary school administrators (middle, junior high, intermediate, and/or senior high school) a marketplace for ideas that affect their position and profession. The editor welcomes manuscripts describing administrative practices and theories as well as articles discussing educational problems and workable solutions.

The editor welcomes unsolicited articles and also solicits some material directly from selected authors. These manuscripts should be between 2,000 and 2,500 words in length and in duplicate. The Chicago style should be followed. The estimated time for an editorial decision is two to four weeks with six to twelve months elapsing between acceptance and publication. This journal publishes from one to three book reviews each issue which are between 500 and 1,000 words long. Reviews should stress what values, if any, the book has for secondary school administrators. Copyright is held by the publisher.

359. THE NATS BULLETIN. (formerly **THE BULLETIN**). 1962– (NB);
1944– (B). National Association of Teachers of Singing, Chicago Musical
College, Roosevelt University, 430 South Michigan Avenue, Chicago, IL
60605. Circ.: 3,600. 4 issues/yr. Subscription included with association
membership; non-member rate, $6.00/yr. Annual index: issue number
four. Editor: Harvey Ringel. Book reviews are written by staff.
   Indexed in: Music Article Guide; The Music Index; RILM Abstracts
   of Music Literature.
   This journal is intended to reach teachers of singing, singers, students of
singing, voice research scientists and libraries. Its purpose is to provide and pre-
serve resource material for the vocal profession in areas of performance and voice
pedagogy, as well as to inform and improve the teaching of the vocal art wherever
it is practiced. The editor will consider any article that has a bearing on the teaching of singing and the area of performance.
   Unsolicited manuscripts and letters of inquiry are welcomed by the editor.
The requirements for manuscript submission are rather detailed and follow a
style appropriate to the journal, therefore, prospective authors are advised to
contact the editor prior to submission of material. The copyright is held by the
publisher. An editorial decision requires sixteen to twenty weeks with six to
nine months required for publication following acceptance.

360. NJEA REVIEW. 1927– . New Jersey Education Association, 180 West State
Street, Trenton, NJ 08608. Circ.: 109,000. 9 issues/yr. Subscription included
with association membership. Annual index: not given. Editor: George M.
Adams, associate editor. Unsolicited book reviews not accepted.
   Indexed in: Current Index to Journals in Education.
   The *Review* covers all educational areas from nursery school to adult education. The editor is interested in well-researched articles, but without footnoting,
on new trends in education and in articles dealing with specific subject areas.
This journal is the official organ of the New Jersey Education Association.
   Articles from other than NJEA members are accepted for editorial consideration, as well as member contributions. A letter of inquiry is encouraged. Authors
are to follow the style of the National Education Association. For help in writing
for the *Review*, a pamphlet, "Writing for the *NJEA Review*" has been developed
and is available upon request. Length of manuscript should be about 1,500 words.
The copyright is held by the publisher. A small honorarium is paid authors of
accepted pieces, except members of the NJEA who are not eligible for payments.
Times required for an editorial decision and publication are not given.

361. NOLPE SCHOOL LAW JOURNAL. 1970– . National Organization of Legal
Problems of Education, 825 Western Avenue, Topeka, KS 66606. Circ.:
3,500. 2 issues/yr. Subscription included with association membership. No
annual index. Editor: M. A. McGhehey. Book reviews to: editor.
   Indexed in: Current Index to Journals in Education; Index to Periodical
   Articles Related to Law.
   This journal is intended to reach specialists in school law, professors of edu-
cational administration and law, and school board and organization attorneys. Its

purpose is to keep such specialized personnel up-to-date on developments in school law. The editor prefers articles which analyze court cases by subject.

The editor welcomes unsolicited articles and letters of inquiry, and also will solicit articles when needed. Manuscripts should be between 2,500 and 4,000 words in length. The copyright is held by the publisher. Simultaneous submission is not permitted ordinarily and query should be made of the editor concerning this matter. Approximately four weeks is required for an editorial decision with six months elapsing from acceptance to publication in most instances. One book review usually is included in each issue. This review is short with a maximum of 200 words being sufficient.

362. **NUEA SPECTATOR.** 1964– . National University Extension Association, One Dupont Circle, Washington, DC 20036. Circ.: not given. 4 issues/yr. $7.50/yr. No annual index. Editor: Walter B. Wright. Editor's address: Division for Continuing Education, University of Missouri–Kansas City, Kansas City, MO 64110. No book reviews.

    Indexed in: Current Index to Journals in Education.

The intended audience of this journal includes those professionals engaged in continuing education and extension work, as well as others interested in these areas. Its purpose is to provide information regarding the NUEA and to publish articles relating to the philosophy of the organization as well as those of practical interest to professionals in the field.

The editor encourages the submission of manuscripts as well as letters of inquiry. The style of *Words Into Print* should be followed. Manuscripts are to be submitted in duplicate and should be between 2,000 and 2,500 words in length. The copyright is held by the publisher. Approximately six to eight weeks is required for an editorial decision with an indefinite time elapsing before publication. This time period is determined by the space available and the number of accepted manuscripts. Simultaneous submission to other journals is permitted.

363. **THE NATIONAL ACAC JOURNAL.** 1937– . National Association of College Admissions Counselors, 9933 Lawler Avenue, Skokie, IL 60076. Circ.: 5,000. 4 issues/yr. Subscription included with association membership; non-member rate, $10.00/yr. Biennial index. Editor: Robert K. Long. No book reviews.

    Indexed in: College Student Personnel Abstracts.

The *NACAC Journal* contains articles directed to the common interests of high school counselors and postsecondary admissions officers. Articles which deal with the following subjects are sought: significant current issues in the fields of counseling, admissions, and financial aid; new techniques or innovative practices or programs; research reports of unusual significance to membership; and, NACAC as an association and its role in the above mentioned fields.

The editor welcomes unsolicited manuscripts from all persons in education and related fields. Articles may be of any length, but those about 1,000 words are preferable. Articles will be acknowledged upon receipt, but two or three months may lapse before an editorial decision is made. After acceptance, publication follows in one to six months. Copyright is held by the publisher.

364. THE NATIONAL EDUCATIONAL SECRETARY. 1934– . National Association of Educational Secretaries, 1801 North Moore Street, Arlington, VA 22209. Circ.: 6,500. 4 issues/yr. Subscription included with association membership; non-member rate, $7.50/yr. No annual index. Editor: Virginia Mathony. Editor's address: 14277 Eastridge Drive, Whittier, CA 90602. Book reviews to: editor.

The purpose of this journal is to provide a basic communication tool for members which will be timely, innovative, informative, and consistent with the direction in which the NAES is moving, as well as to promote the association and its activities. It is intended to reach NAES members and also those office personnel in education and education related positions. The editor prefers articles that have a relationship to education, particularly those designed to aid or inform those office personnel who are directly related to schools and the profession.

Unsolicited articles are accepted for editorial consideration and should follow the style of National Education Association publications. Manuscripts should be between 1,200 and 1,800 words in length. The copyright is held by the publisher. Between three and four weeks is required for an editorial decision and publication usually follows acceptance by one to two months. Book reviews are published in each issue of the journal.

365. THE NATIONAL EDUCATOR. 1969– . Educator Publications, 1110 South Pamona Avenue, Fullerton, CA 92632. Circ.: 69,300. 12 issues/yr. $8.00/yr. No annual index. Editor: James H. Townsend. Book reviews to: editor.

This monthly tabloid editor states that this is "the only nationally circulated newspaper directed to the parent's side of education. The paper is generally opposed to innovative programs such as sex education. . . .flexible scheduling, and sensitivity training."

Unsolicited manuscripts and letters of inquiry are welcomed. The APA style should be followed with article length being between 500 and 1,000 words. Articles must be documented unless staff written, in which case the editor verifies the basis of claims, charges, and other factors. It is recommended that specific details concerning style be obtained from the editor. Approximately four weeks is required for an editorial decision with two months usually elapsing before publication. One to three book reviews are used each month. These reviews follow the same style requirements and length limitations as articles. The deadline for dated copy is the fifth of each month. Simultaneous submission to other journals is permitted. Copyright on all materials is held by the publisher.

366. THE NATIONAL ELEMENTARY PRINCIPAL. 1921– . National Association of Elementary School Principals, 1801 North Moore Street, Arlington, VA 22209. Circ.: 28,000. 6 issues/yr. Subscription included with association membership. Annual index: not published in journal; available upon request. Editor: Paul L. Houts. Book reviewers chosen by editor.

  Indexed in: Current Contents: Social & Behavioral Sciences; Current Index to Journals in Education; Education Index; Educational Administration Abstracts; Exceptional Child Education Abstracts.

This journal is intended for elementary and middle school principals, professors of educational administration and elementary education, classroom teachers, and others with an interest in elementary and middle school education. It is intended to create a forum for both practitioners and theorists in elementary and middle school education so that both can share the work and ideas of the other, and so that the elementary and middle schools can profit from this expertise. The editor is seeking articles dealing with all phases of school administration, educational reform, and social issues affecting education.

A large proportion of the articles used are solicited by the editor. However, consideration also will be given to unsolicited manuscripts. Four of the six issues usually are dedicated to central themes. These themes are announced in the association's newsletter, *Spectator*, in the fall. Articles should be 2,500 to 3,000 words in length and follow the Chicago style. Two copies of all manuscripts are required. Between four and six weeks is required for an editorial decision. Publication of accepted manuscripts requires up to six months. Copyright is held by the publisher.

367. THE NEGRO EDUCATIONAL REVIEW. 1950– . Negro Educational Review, Box 2895, West Bay Annex, Jacksonville, Florida 32203. Circ.: 3,000. 4 issues/yr. $10.00/yr. Annual index: October issue. Editor: R. Grann Lloyd. Book reviews to: editor.

Indexed in: Current Contents: Social & Behavioral Sciences; Current Index to Journals in Education; Education Index; Index to Periodical Articles By and About Negroes.

This journal is designed to provide a forum for discussion of Afro-American ideas by presenting scholarly articles and research reports, competent analyses and descriptions of current problems, and significant compilations. Its readers include educators at all levels, social workers, researchers, government officials, graduate students, ministers, civic leaders and other similar persons.

The editor solicits articles for *The Review*, but also welcomes unsolicited manuscripts for consideration. The Chicago style should be followed and length may vary from 2,500 to 3,750 words. All material is to be submitted in triplicate. Certain issues are dedicated to central themes and these articles usually are solicited by the Editorial Board. The time for an editorial decision concerning acceptance is four weeks. Publication time varies from six to twelve months. Copyright is held by the publisher. The two to eight book reviews in each issue are 750 words long and should follow criteria of the *New York Times*.

368. NEW DIRECTIONS FOR COMMUNITY COLLEGES. 1973– . Jossey-Bass Inc., Publishers, 615 Montgomery Street, San Francisco, CA 94111. Circ.: 1,000. 4 issues/yr. $15.00/yr.; institutional rate, $25.00/yr. Each issue is indexed separately. Editor: Arthur M. Cohen. Editor's address: ERIC Clearinghouse for Junior Colleges, 96 Powell Library, University of California, Los Angeles, Los Angeles, CA 90024. No book reviews.

Indexed in: Current Contents: Social & Behavioral Sciences; Current Index to Journals in Education.

The quarterly is intended for faculty leaders and decision makers in community colleges and other policy makers in higher education. Each issue is a sourcebook of information on a topic of urgent concern to two-year colleges, such as instructional technology, community college governance, collective bargaining,

NEW DIRECTIONS FOR COMMUNITY COLLEGES (cont'd)

and statewide coordination. Guest editors select contributors who are well versed in the topic and who are able to bring research and experience to bear on institutional problems.

The editor does not accept unsolicited manuscripts, however, letters of inquiry are welcomed. Articles are commissioned by the guest editor on particular topics. The APA style is followed and two copies of the manuscript are required. Length is not specified. Copyright is held by the publisher. The time from acceptance to publication is four months. Simultaneous submission to other journals is permitted.

369. **NEW DIRECTIONS FOR HIGHER EDUCATION.** 1973– . Jossey-Bass Inc., Publishers, 615 Montgomery Street, San Francisco, CA 94111. Circ.: 1,500. 4 issues/yr. $15.00/yr.; institutional rate, $25.00/yr. Each issue is indexed separately. Editor: JB Lon Hefferlin. No book reviews.
    Indexed in: College Student Personnel Abstracts; Current Contents:
    Social & Behavioral Sciences; Current Index to Journals in Education.

This sourcebook is intended for use by policy makers and decision makers in higher education. Each issue is intended to be a comprehensive yet concise reference to a topic of growing importance in higher education. Recent issues dealt with faculty development, financing, student services and field experience education. Each issue is edited by a national authority on the topic, who selects contributors because of their expertise on the topic. Research based articles that develop the implications of this research for college and university practice and that point the reader to additional information on the topic are used.

Unsolicited manuscripts are not accepted. The guest editor solicits articles directly from persons in the field. Letters of inquiry are encouraged. The APA style is to be followed, but length is not specified. Journals are dedicated to central themes. Simultaneous submission to other journals is permitted. The time from acceptance to publication is four months. Copyright is held by the publisher.

370. **NEW DIRECTIONS FOR INSTITUTIONAL RESEARCH.** 1974– . Jossey-Bass Inc., Publishers, 615 Montgomery Street, San Francisco, CA 94111. Circ.: 1,000. 4 issues/yr. $15.00/yr.; institutional rate, $25.00/yr. Each issue is indexed separately. Editor: Sidney Suslow. Editor's address: Office of Institutional Research, 47 Campbell Hall, University of California, Berkeley, Berkeley, CA 94720. No book reviews.
    Indexed in: College Student Personnel Abstracts; Current Index to
    Journals in Education.

This series is intended for college and university decision-makers, planners, researchers and faculty leaders. Each issue of *New Directions for Institutional Research* is a short reference to a topic of increasing significance for its intended audience and is guest edited by a well-known expert on the topic. The guest editor invites contributions from researchers and practitioners familiar with the topic.

This series does not accept unsolicited manuscripts, however, letters of inquiry are welcomed. Style should follow APA requirements and manuscript is to be submitted in two copies. Preferred length is not indicated. Simultaneous submission to other journals is permitted. Four months is required for publication after articles are selected. Copyright is held by the publisher.

371. **NEW ENGLAND READING ASSOCIATION JOURNAL.** 1966– . New England Reading Association, Mr. Charles Flaherty, Business Manager, University of Rhode Island, Kingston, RI 02881. Circ.: 2,000. 3 issues/yr. Subscription included with association membership; non-member rate, $2.00/yr. Annual index: issue number three. Editors: Barbara Morris and Donald Landry (co-editors). Manuscript to: current chairperson of the editorial committee. Book reviews to: current chairperson.

The intended audience of this journal includes teachers and reading specialists. The purpose is to help develop new ideas on reading techniques as well as to present theoretical and research articles in the area of reading. In addition to the articles, the *Journal* carries a number of continuing features such as editorials, book reviews and conference information.

This journal accepts manuscripts for possible inclusion. They will be judged on their professional qualities and their significance to educators. Style should be similar to that of *The Reading Teacher* and length may vary from 1,500 to approximately 4,500 words. Copyright is held by the publisher. An editorial decision is made in six weeks and the estimated time from acceptance to publication is four to ten months. One or two book reviews appear in each issue and these are 800 to 1,000 words long. Manuscript should be sent to the Chairperson of the Editorial Committee. Since the person who heads this committee changes, usually each year, prospective contributors should examine a recent issue of the journal to determine the mailing address of the current Chairperson.

372. **NEW GENERATION.** (formerly **AMERICAN CHILD**). 1919– . National Child Labor Committee, 145 East Thirty-second Street, New York, NY 10016. Circ.: 4,700. 4 issues/yr. $3.00/yr. No annual index. Editor: Killian Jordan. Book reviews to: editor.
    Indexed in: Abstracts for Social Workers; America: History and Life*; Current Contents: Social & Behavioral Sciences; Current Index to Journals in Education.

The purpose of this publication is to disseminate information related to problems of unemployed youth, upgrading careers from low-paying dead-end jobs, violations of child labor laws and toward the improvement of children of migrant farm workers. Among the intended audience are educators, legislators and concerned citizens. Analytical and informational articles designed to improve upon conditions of youth and employment are included.

The editor solicits articles directly from experts in the field, but welcomes letters of inquiry. Unsolicited articles are not accepted. Manuscripts of 2,000 words in length and conforming to MLA style requirements, in duplicate, are to be submitted. An editorial decision is given in three weeks and publication of accepted items follows in one and one-half months. Copyright is held by the publisher who also pays authors for their contributions. The rate of payment is not specified.

373. **NEW HAMPSHIRE QUARTER NOTES.** New Hampshire Music
Educators Association, c/o Dr. Walter P. Smith, Plymouth State
College, Plymouth, NH 03264. Circ.: 800. 4 issues/yr. $3.00/yr.
No annual index. Editor: Walter P. Smith. Book reviews to: editor.

This journal is intended primarily for New Hampshire music teachers, however, unsolicited articles from outside sources are accepted for editorial consideration. Articles dealing with music, literary, professional and academic matters are
solicited.

One major article of 2,500 to 3,000 words is used per issue. Approximately
one week is required for editorial consideration with publication following in the
next issue in which space is available. Varying numbers of book reviews are used,
based upon the available space with the length of the review being dependent upon
the subject matter. Style is not specified.

374. **NEW JERSEY SCHOOL LEADER.** (formerly **SCHOOL BOARD NOTES**).
1972– (NJSL); 1956– (SBN). New Jersey School Boards Association,
P.O. Box 909, 383 West State Street, Trenton, NJ 08605. Circ.: 6,700.
6 issues/yr. Subscription included with association membership; non-
member rate, $12.00/yr. No annual index. Editor: Clyde E. Leib. Book
reviews to: editor.

The *School Leader* includes a variety of articles pertaining to public education. Among its intended audience are school board members, school administrators and school attorneys. Its regular features include Question Box, Editorial,
Mailbag, Legal Report, Research Report and N. J. Potpourri. In 1956 the association began publishing a magazine known as *School Board Notes*, which title was
changed to *New Jersey School Leader* in 1972. The association also began publishing a newsletter in 1969 which was called *SBN School Boards Newsletter*.
This newsletter's title was changed in 1972 to *School Board Notes*. The subscription rate for the *School Leader* includes the newsletter *School Board Notes*.

The editor receives unsolicited articles for possible inclusion in this journal
but encourages a letter of inquiry prior to submission. Manuscripts of approximately 2,000 words should be sent in duplicate. Copyright is held by the publisher. Time required for an editorial decision concerning acceptability and
publication time are not specified. Book reviews of 500 words each are contained
in this journal.

375. **THE NEW SCHOOLS EXCHANGE NEWSLETTER.** 1969– . New Schools
Exchange, Pettigrew, AR 72752. Circ.: 2,500. 10 issues/yr. $10.00/yr. No
annual index. Staff edited. Book reviews to: editor.
Indexed in: Alternative Press Index.

The intended audience of this publication, which utilizes the journal format,
includes those persons participating in alternative forms of education. Its purpose
is to further the aims of alternative education. This publication is a reader based
newsletter and articles of interest to the readership dealing with alternative schools
and methods of education are desired by the editor.

The editor has no preferred style or length for manuscripts. Unsolicited manuscripts are read and considered. The editor will also solicit contributions on specific
topics of interest. The copyright is held by the author. An editorial decision usually

is reached in eight to twelve weeks with publication time varying. Some book reviews are published in each issue. The number varies with space availability.

376. **NORTH CAROLINA PUBLIC SCHOOLS.** (formerly **NORTH CAROLINA PUBLIC SCHOOL BULLETIN**). 1968– (NCPS); 1936– (NCPSB). State Department of Public Instruction, Room 352, Division of Public Information and Publications, Education Building, Raleigh, NC 27611. Circ.: 50,000. 4 issues/yr. No charge, controlled circulation. No annual index. Editor: Kay W. Bullock. No book reviews.

This journal is intended for teachers, administrators, other school staff, concerned citizens, and university personnel, primarily in North Carolina. It disseminates teaching and learning ideas and techniques that are being used in this state and also publishes articles on educational issues of importance. Financial and statistical data and information about personnel policies and practices are included. The journal serves as an instrument for the exchange of ideas within North Carolina.

The editor solicits material directly from various professionals, but also welcomes letters of inquiry and unsolicited manuscripts if pertinent to North Carolina schools. The Chicago style is to be followed and the length may vary. This publication is not copyrighted. An editorial decision is given in three weeks and publication of accepted pieces follows in one to three months.

377. **THE NORTHIAN.** 1964– . Society for Indian and Northern Education, University of Saskatchewan, Saskatoon, Saskatchewan, Canada S7N 0W0. Circ.: 900. 4 issues/yr. $5.00/yr. No annual index. Editor: Tim Jones. Book reviews to: editor.
 Indexed in: Canadian Education Index; Canadian Periodical Index; Current Index to Journals in Education.

This journal is intended for persons involved particularly in Indian education throughout North America, but it also serves the needs of those involved in cross-cultural education in general. *The Northian* is designed to improve instruction, curriculum and teacher competence in cross-cultural situations. Further, it is intended to act as a clearinghouse for ideas and as a source of information regarding contemporary trends in education in northern Canada as well as other parts of the world. The editor prefers articles dealing with any aspect of cross-cultural education.

The submission of unsolicited articles is encouraged. These manuscripts should be between 800 and 4,000 words in length. The copyright is held by the author. Two weeks is required for an editorial decision with three to four months required for publication after acceptance. Between four and six book reviews are published in each issue and these should be between 200 and 600 words long. Simultaneous submission to other journals is permitted.

378. **THE NORTHIAN NEWSLETTER.** 1968– . Society for Indian Northern Education, University of Saskatchewan, Saskatoon, Saskatchewan, Canada S7N 0W0. Circ.: 1,000. 4 issues/yr. $5.00/yr. No annual index. Editor: A. J. Dyer. Book reviews to: editor.
 Indexed in: Canadian Education Index.

This newsletter is intended to reach teachers of Indian and Northern (Canada) children. It is intended to provide a platform for the exchange of ideas as well as information of help to teachers of these children. The editor is interested in articles dealing with classroom teaching techniques.

The editor receives unsolicited manuscripts as well as letters of inquiry. Style requirements and suggested article length are not specified. Approximately four weeks is required for an editorial decision with publication of accepted pieces following in six months. Two book reviews are published in each issue. These reviews should be approximately 500 words in length. Simultaneous submission to other journals is permitted. Copyright on published material is held by the author.

379. **THE NOTRE DAME JOURNAL OF EDUCATION.** 1970– . University of Notre Dame, P.O. Box 686, Notre Dame, IN 46556. Circ.: 1,800. 4 issues/yr. $9.00/yr. Annual index: issue number four. Editor: Vincent P. Lannie. Book reviews to: editor.

Indexed in: America: History and Life*; The Catholic Periodical and Literature Index; Current Contents: Social & Behavioral Sciences; Current Index to Journals in Education; Exceptional Child Education Abstracts; Social Sciences Citation Index; Theological and Religious Index.

This journal is intended for educators and those interested in education; its special emphasis is on religious education. Its purpose is to explore and advance Christian education in American society. The editor is interested in scholarly articles dealing with aspects of religious education, values in education, or American public and private education.

The editor prefers to solicit articles, however, unsolicited manuscripts also are accepted and read. Issues of the journal are dedicated to central themes, therefore, a letter of inquiry is recommended. Authors should follow the APA style with two copies of all manuscripts being required. Preferred length is 5,000 to 6,750 words. Simultaneous submission to other journals is not recommended. The time for an editorial decision is between four and six weeks. Publication of accepted manuscripts may take up to six months. The books reviewed should be pertinent to education and the review should be no longer than 2,000 words. Copyright is held by the University of Notre Dame.

380. **NURSING OUTLOOK.** 1953– . American Journal of Nursing Company, 10 Columbus Circle, New York, NY 10019. Circ.: 32,000. 12 issues/yr. $12.00/yr. Annual index: published separately. Editor: Edith P. Lewis. Book reviews to: editor.

Indexed in: Abstracts for Social Workers; Abstracts of Hospital Management Studies; Cumulative Index to Nursing Literature; Current Index to Journals in Education; Exceptional Child Education Abstracts; Hospital Literature Index; Index Medicus; Information Retrieval Limited*; International Nursing Index; International Pharmaceutical Abstracts; Media Review Digest; Medical Care Review; Nursing Research; Nursing Studies Index; Psychological Abstracts; Rehabilitation Literature; Social Sciences Index.

The contents of *Nursing Outlook* are intended primarily for professionals in nursing education and community health, as well as others in service and health care leadership positions. The journal contains articles dealing with current issues, problems and trends in professional nursing. Regular features include Book Reviews, Teaching Aids, Education Programs, and News From Here and There.

Authors are encouraged to submit articles or letters of inquiry to *Nursing Outlook*. The Chicago style should be followed. Two copies of each manuscript are to be submitted. Article length should be between 2,000 and 4,000 words. The copyright is held by the publisher. The publisher provides the author 100 free reprints as payment. Approximately four to six weeks is required for an editorial decision. Four to six months later accepted manuscripts may be expected to be published. Four to ten book reviews are published in each issue. These reviews should be between 250 and 300 words in length.

381. **O.S.S.T.F. FORUM.** (formerly **O.S.S.T.F. BULLETIN**). 1975– (OSSTFF); 1921– (OSSTFB). Ontario Secondary School Teachers' Federation, 60 Mobile Drive, Toronto, Ontario, Canada M4A 2P3. Circ.: 37,000. 5 issues/yr. $5.00/yr. No annual index. Editor: Michael Crawford. Book reviews to: editor.
    Indexed in: Canadian Education Index.

This journal is intended primarily for high school teachers. It communicates the latest ideas which may be of interest to those teaching at this level. Articles desired for publication are those of general interest especially for Ontario teachers.

Unsolicited manuscripts and letters of inquiry are welcomed by the editor. Articles should be 2,500 words in length. No style preference is indicated. Approximately two weeks is required for an editorial decision with publication of accepted manuscripts following in three months. Twelve book reviews are published in each issue of this journal. These reviews are 300 words in length. Copyright is held by the author.

382. **OBSERVER.** 1967– . Ohio Association of Secondary School Principals, 750 Brooksedge Boulevard, Westerville, OH 43081. Circ.: 2,200. 4 issues/yr. Subscription included with association membership. No annual index. Editor: William L. Murphy. No book reviews.

This newsletter is intended primarily for members of the OASSP. It is intended to update the readership on current events at the state and local levels. The editor is interested in materials which have interest to secondary school principals.

Brief unsolicited manuscripts are accepted for editorial consideration. Preferred length is 1,500 words. Style is not specified. Two weeks is usually required for an editorial decision. No time for publication following acceptance is indicated. Some pieces are solicited by the editor when the matter is deemed of sufficient potential interest to the readers. Simultaneous submission to other journals is permitted.

383. **OHIO ELEMENTARY SCHOOL PRINCIPAL.** (formerly **O.D.E.S.P. QUARTERLY**). 1972– (OESP); 1958– (ODESPQ). Ohio Department

of Elementary School Principals, 750 Brooksedge Road, Westerville, OH 43081. Circ.: 3,200. 3 issues/yr. $6.00/yr. No annual index. Editor: Samuel R. Burnett. Editor's address: 5720 Secor Road, Toledo, OH 43623. Book reviews to: editor.

This journal is intended for the elementary school principals, school superintendents and other professional and educational leaders in Ohio. It provides information about current issues, legal decisions, pressure group actions, and innovative practices concerning education in this state. Articles are accepted from principals, educators and other contributors, including business, industrial and governmental leaders, from any part of the United States.

Unsolicited manuscripts are welcomed by the editor. A letter of inquiry to determine the central themes of future issues is encouraged. Simultaneous submission to other journals is permitted and copyright is held by the author. Articles should be 2,500 to 3,500 words long and are to be submitted in duplicate. Writers should follow APA style requirements. An editorial decision is given in four weeks and publication of accepted pieces follows in one month. Usually two book reviews of 500 words each appear in this journal.

384. **THE OHIO READING TEACHER.** 1967– . Ohio Council of the International Reading Association, c/o Amaryilis Russell, 526 Vine Street, Clyde, OH 43410. Circ.: 1,800. 4 issues/yr. $5.00/yr. No annual index. Editor: Joseph S. Nemeth. Editor's address: The Reading Center, Bowling Green State University, Bowling Green, OH 43403. Book reviews to: editor.

This journal is intended for both elementary and secondary education teachers who work with students acquiring the mastery of necessary skills required for reading. Its purpose is the communication of ideas, methods and data concerning professional awareness of, and assistance for, the betterment of reading instruction in the classroom and the clinic. The editor is interested in descriptive articles focusing on teacher-learner experiences and reports or reviews of current trends in reading instruction.

Unsolicited articles are accepted for editorial consideration. A letter of inquiry regarding potential contributions is suggested before the submission of a manuscript. The editor also may select authors for specific topics where deemed appropriate. Shorter articles are preferred. Multiple copies of all manuscripts should be submitted. Three weeks is required for an editorial decision with two months usually elapsing between acceptance and publication of manuscripts. Five book reviews are published in each issue and these are 250 words in length. The APA style should be used for all work.

385. **OHIO SCHOOL BOARDS JOURNAL.** 1957– . Ohio School Boards Association, 700 Brooksedge Boulevard, Westerville, OH 43081. Circ.: 5,800. 12 issues/yr. Subscription included with association membership; non-member rate, $6.00/yr. No annual index. Editor: Susan Saiter. Book reviews to: editor.

The intended audience of this journal includes public school board members in Ohio, administrators, business officials and other interested lay persons. It is designed to provide information about public education in Ohio to board members who are not professional educators. Promotion of the association is another of its

OHIO SCHOOL BOARDS JOURNAL (cont'd)

stated reasons for publication. In addition to news and articles, regular features include legal information and summaries of new publications.

The editor welcomes letters of inquiry and unsolicited manuscripts. The journal has its own style, a combination of several others. Prospective contributors should examine recent issues or query the editor concerning style as well as to determine central themes which often are used. Articles may be 1,000 to 1,500 words in length. Copyright on accepted material is held by the publisher. An editorial decision is given in three to four weeks and publication of accepted articles follows in one to two months. One or two book reviews appear in this journal and each of these is 250 words long.

386. **THE OKLAHOMA READER.** 1966— . Oklahoma Reading Council of the International Reading Association. Circ.: 2,000. 4 issues/yr. Subscription included with council membership; non-member rate, $4.00/yr. No annual index. Editor: Marv Leyerle. Editor's address: 323 East Madison, Oklahoma City, OK 73105. Book reviews to: editor.

This journal is intended for teachers of reading at all levels. Its purpose is to inform reading teachers of the latest techniques in teaching and to communicate what others are doing at the state and national levels. The editor is interested in receiving manuscripts concerning successful and innovative techniques in the teaching of reading.

Unsolicited manuscripts and letters of inquiry are welcomed by the editor. Articles should be approximately 750 words in length and follow the APA style. The copyright is held by the publisher. Simultaneous submission to other publications is permitted. Three weeks is required for an editorial decision with publication of manuscripts following within four months of acceptance. The number of book reviews varies and their length is 250 words each.

387. **ONTARIO EDUCATION.** 1969— . Ontario Public School Trustees' Association, Inc., 4195 Dundas Street West, Suite 303, Toronto, Ontario, Canada M8X 1Y4. Circ.: 3,500. 5 issues/yr. $5.00/yr. No annual index. Editor: Jack MacDonald. Book reviews to: editor.
  Indexed in: Canadian Education Index; Current Contents: Social & Behavioral Sciences.

Educators at all levels are among the intended audience of this journal. Its purpose is to publish material of interest to all persons directly or indirectly connected with education in Ontario. Regular features include columns on books, new products and news.

Authors are encouraged to submit their manuscripts or letters of inquiry to the editor. Preferred length of articles is 2,000 words and copyright is held by the author. Style is not specified. Simultaneous submission to other journals is permitted. Contributors can expect an editorial decision concerning acceptability within four weeks and publication will follow in two months. Four book reviews are included in this publication and each of these is 300 words long.

388. ORBIT. 1970– . Ontario Institute for Studies in Education, 252 Bloor Street West, Toronto, Ontario, Canada M5S 1V6. Circ.: 7,500. 5 issues/yr. $5.00/yr. No annual index. Editor: Hugh Oliver. No book reviews.
Indexed in: Canadian Education Index; Current Index to Journals in Education.

This journal is intended primarily for school teachers and principals. Its purpose is to inform school personnel of innovations and developments in education, especially of those originating at OISE. Articles, which usually combine theory and practice, are written both by academic and school personnel, and their purpose is to provide information and to generate ideas that the teacher can use in the classroom. The editor indicates that 5,000 copies of the stated circulation are sent at no charge to publicly supported schools in Ontario.

Some material for this journal is solicited directly from selected professionals, but the editor welcomes letters of inquiry and unsolicited manuscripts. Authors should use the Chicago style and limit their articles to a length that ranges from 1,000 to 4,000 words. Copyright on published pieces is held by the author. Contributors can expect an editorial decision within four weeks and publication of accepted articles usually follows in three months.

389. PMLA. 1884– . The Modern Language Association of America, 62 Fifth Avenue, New York, NY 10011. Circ.: 34,500. 6 issues/yr. Subscription included with association membership; institution rate, $25.00/yr. Cumulative index every ten years. Editor: William D. Schaefer. No book reviews.
Indexed in: Humanities Index; Modern Language Abstracts; Social Sciences and Humanities Index; Women Studies Abstracts.

Scholarly articles on American, British and foreign literature and linguistics appear in this journal. Teachers of literature and language are among the intended audience. Its purpose is to publish distinguished contemporary scholarship and criticism on the modern languages and literatures that are of significant interest to the entire membership of the Modern Language Association.

Unsolicited articles are accepted for consideration only from members of the association. An abstract, typed on a standard form that is available from the editor, must accompany each article before it can be processed. The MLA style is to be followed and the length may vary from 2,500 to 12,500 words. Copyright is held by the publisher. Estimated time for editorial decision concerning acceptability of an article is eight weeks. Publication follows in about twelve months.

390. PSBA BULLETIN. 1937– . Pennsylvania School Boards Association, 412 North Second Street, Harrisburg, PA 17101. Circ.: 8,000. 6 issues/yr. Subscription included with association membership; non-member rate, $5.00/yr. Annual index: November-December issue. Editor: Nicholas L. Goble. Book reviews to: editor.

Articles geared to sound school management practices, school law, boardmanship, school finances, curriculum, communications and "how to" articles are contained in the *Bulletin*. Its readership consists of school board members, school management personnel, educators, state legislators, attorneys and the general public. The purpose of the journal is: to inform its readers about current

educational practices, trends, opinion and research; to foster sound school management practices; to enhance boardmanship; and, to promote educational decision
making in the public interest.

Articles are solicited directly by the editor, but unsolicited manuscripts and
letters of inquiry from others are welcomed also. Simultaneous submission to other
journals is permitted. Style should follow the guidelines as set by the Associated
Press and *New York Times*. Articles of 1,500 to 2,000 words written in clear journalistic style are preferred. Copyright is held by the publisher unless otherwise determined. Issues are dedicated to central themes and prospective contributors should
inquire of the editor for future topics. An editorial decision is given in four weeks.
Publication of accepted works follows in two months. Occasionally, book reviews
appear in the journal but style and length requirements are not specified.

391. PARENT COOPERATIVE PRESCHOOLS INTERNATIONAL JOURNAL.
1970– . Parent Cooperative Preschools International, 20551 Lakeshore
Road, Baie d'Urfe, Quebec, Canada. Circ.: 13,000. 3 issues/yr. Subscription
included with association membership. Fall, 1975 issue contains first five
year index. Editor: Barbara Cantor. Editor's address: 9111 Alton Parkway,
Silver Spring, MD 20910. Unsolicited book reviews seldom accepted.

This publication is intended for parents, teachers and students interested in
children and preschool education. It is intended to serve as an idea exchange for
parents and teachers of young children, to help them be more creative. The editor
is interested in "how to" articles, rather than research papers, on any topic related
to preschool education.

Unsolicited articles are welcomed. These manuscripts may vary from 1,500
to 2,000 words in length. The style should be journalistic and free. The copyright
is held by the publisher. An editorial decision usually is made within two weeks.
Publication may follow within three to four months, sometimes less, depending
upon space availability.

392. PEABODY JOURNAL OF EDUCATION. 1923– . George Peabody College
for Teachers, Nashville, TN 37203. Circ.: 2,500. 4 issues/yr. $8.00/yr. ;
institution rate, $10.00/yr. Annual index: July issue. Editor: Ralph E.
Kirkman. Book reviews to: editor.
Indexed in: Book Review Index; College Student Personnel Abstracts;
Current Contents: Social & Behavioral Sciences; Current Index to
Journals in Education; dsh Abstracts; Education Index; Exceptional
Child Education Abstracts.

This refereed journal is intended for teacher educators, as well as administrators and teachers actively engaged in classroom instruction. Articles contained in
this journal focus upon the professional improvement of its readership. Themes
of two recent issues were concerned with the community college and hearing-
impaired children. Selected examples of general articles are: Freedom of Expressions,
The Schools and the Burger Court; A Performance-Based Teacher Education Program;
Teacher Characteristics and Behaviors Preferred by High School Students; and,
Human Relations Training, Contracting, and Field Experiences—An Integrative
Approach to Teaching Educational Foundations.

PEABODY JOURNAL OF EDUCATION (cont'd)

Unsolicited articles are sought for editorial consideration. The editor does solicit articles directly for the two issues each year which are dedicated to central themes, however, the editor will provide themes of future issues upon request. Articles may vary from 2,500 to 3,000 words in length and follow MLA style requirements. Simultaneous submission to other journals is permitted. Approximately six weeks is required for an editorial decision. Publication of accepted articles usually occurs within nine months after acceptance. This journal publishes four to six book reviews per issue, each being 750 to 1,250 words in length. All manuscripts should be submitted in triplicate. Copyright is held by the publisher.

393. **PENNSYLVANIA EDUCATION.** 1968– . Pennsylvania Department of Education, P.O. Box 911, Harrisburg, PA 17126. Circ.: 195,000. 18 issues/yr. No charge, controlled circulation. No annual index. Editor: William R. Ruffin. Book reviews to: editor.
    Indexed in: Current Index to Journals in Education; Women Studies Abstracts.
This tabloid is intended for teachers, administrators, school boards, college faculty and interested lay persons, primarily in the state of Pennsylvania. It provides current information on Pennsylvania Department of Education activities. Articles pertaining to any phase of education in the state and of interest to Pennsylvania educators are appropriate for this publication.

The editor accepts unsolicited material for consideration. A letter of inquiry prior to submission is encouraged. Simultaneous submission to other journals is permitted. No specific style is required. Length should be 750 to 1,000 words. An editorial decision is given in two weeks and publication time for accepted articles varies. Four book reviews (content outlines) of about 250 words each are included in this tabloid. The book reviewed must be written by a Pennsylvania educator.

394. **PENNSYLVANIA SCHOOL JOURNAL.** 1852– . Pennsylvania State Education Association, 400 North Third Street, Harrisburg, PA 17101. Circ.: 135,000. 4 issues/yr. Subscription included with association membership; non-member rate, $6.50/yr. Annual index: issued separately. Editor: Barbara J. Stevens. Usually no book reviews.
    Indexed in: Education Index.
The intended audience of this journal includes educators, kindergarten through university graduate school, and individuals interested in education. Its purpose is to provide current information on classroom practices and innovations and to offer a forum for discussion of issues pertinent to education. Articles preferred for inclusion are informative discussions of issues backed with factual evidence.

The editor solicits articles directly from experts in the field, but also accepts unsolicited works for consideration. A letter of inquiry prior to submission is recommended. The style of the *New York Times* is to be followed. Length should be 2,000 words. Issues are dedicated to central themes and prospective contributors should query the editor for topics. Copyright of accepted materials is held by the publisher. An editorial decision is made in eight weeks and the estimated time for publication is six to nine months. A sheet of guidelines to aid in the writing of manuscripts is available from the editor.

395. **PENNSYLVANIA SCHOOLMASTER.** 1969– . Pennsylvania Association of Secondary School Principals. Circ.: 3,000. 2-4 issues/yr. Subscription included with association membership. No annual index. Editor: Joseph Mamana. Editor's address: P.O. Box 953, Easton, PA 18042. Book reviews to: editor.

This journal is intended for principals, superintendents, supervisors, and school board and legislature members as well as those in higher education. It is intended to improve the educational programs of the schools and administrative competencies of the members of the association. The editor prefers articles on successful practices that "are not frothy, stuffy or pedantic."

Unsolicited manuscripts and letters of inquiry are welcomed by the editor. Articles should be between 1,000 and 2,000 words in length and follow a free, newspaper style. Material should be submitted in two copies. The copyright is held by the publisher. Editorial decisions usually are rendered between one and eight weeks after receipt with publication of accepted pieces occurring between one and six months later. Occasional book reviews are published. These reviews may be of varying length.

396. **THE PERSONNEL AND GUIDANCE JOURNAL.** (formerly **OCCUPATIONS; THE VOCATIONAL GUIDANCE MAGAZINE,** and **NATIONAL VOCATIONAL GUIDANCE BULLETIN**). 1952– (PGJ); 1933– (O); 1924– (VGM); 1921– (NVGB). American Personnel and Guidance Association, 1607 New Hampshire Avenue, N.W., Washington, DC 20009. Circ.: 45,000. 10 issues/yr. Subscription included with association membership; non-member rate, $20.00/yr. Annual index: June issue. Editor: Derald Sue. Book reviews by invitation only.

Indexed in: Abstracts for Social Workers; Book Review Index; CIRF Abstracts; College Student Personnel Abstracts; Current Index to Journals in Education; dsh Abstracts; Education Index; Educational Administration Abstracts; Employment Relations Abstracts*; Exceptional Child Education Abstracts; Human Resources Abstracts; Index to Periodical Articles Related to Law; Mental Health Book Review Index; Nursing Research; Personnel Literature; Psychological Abstracts; Sociological Abstracts; Women Studies Abstracts.

The editor invites manuscripts of common interest to counselors and personnel workers in schools, colleges, community agencies and government. Articles preferred are those dealing with current professional and scientific issues, new techniques or innovative practices and programs and research reports of unusual significance to practitioners. Since the readership is comprised primarily of practitioners, authors should strive to communicate their ideas clearly and interestingly.

Three to four issues each year are dedicated to central themes and all articles for these issues are solicited by a guest editor. Unsolicited manuscripts, following the APA style requirements, are welcomed for all other issues. A letter of inquiry prior to submission is recommended. Preferred length of articles is

THE PERSONNEL AND GUIDANCE JOURNAL (cont'd)

3,500 words except articles for the In the Field section which should be 2,000 words. The original plus two copies are to be sent. Contributors will be notified about acceptability of their work in eight to twelve weeks. Publication of accepted materials usually follows in five months. Copyright is held by the publisher. Additional guidelines for writers may be found in each issue of this journal.

397. **PERSPECTIVES.** 1969– . Association for General and Liberal Studies. Circ.: not given. 3 issues/yr. Subscription included with association membership; non-member rate, $6.00/yr.; institution membership, $25.00/yr. No annual index. Editor: F. Theodore Marvin. Editor's address: College of General Studies, Western Michigan University, Kalamazoo, MI 49001. Book reviews are assigned.

Indexed in: Canadian Education Index.

The journal is designed primarily for association members, but is intended also for other persons who in some way care about improving undergraduate education. It is committed to serving as a forum for professional people concerned with undergraduate general and liberal studies. Contributions dealing with the theory and practice of general and liberal studies are welcomed. The winter issue is devoted entirely to the proceedings of the association's annual meeting.

Unsolicited manuscripts of up to 7,500 words are accepted for consideration. Documentation of material in the article should be included in the text, rather than footnotes when possible. Style is not specified and copyright is held by the publisher. Estimated time for an editorial decision is four weeks. Time from acceptance to publication varies from six to nine months. Simultaneous submission to other journals is permitted.

398. **PHI DELTA KAPPAN.** (formerly **THE NATIONAL NEWSLETTER OF PHI DELTA KAPPA**). 1916– (PDK); 1915– (NNPDK). Phi Delta Kappa, Inc., 8th and Union, Bloomington, IN 47401. Circ.: 120,000. 10 issues/yr. Subscription included with PDK membership; non-member rate, $10.00/yr. Annual index: June issue. Editor: Stanley M. Elam. Book reviews to: editor.

Indexed in: Current Contents: Social & Behavioral Sciences; Current Index to Journals in Education; Education Index; Educational Administration Abstracts; Exceptional Child Education Abstracts; Index to Periodical Articles Related to Law; Nursing Research; Rehabilitation Literature; Sage Public Administration Abstracts; Women Studies Abstracts.

The intended audience of this journal includes teachers, administrators and other leaders in education at all levels. Its purpose is to inform its readership of the issues, new knowledge, trends, and events of significance in education. The *Phi Delta Kappan* also strives to promote educational leadership, research and service. Informative and brief articles, but not overly technical, are preferred.

About 50 per cent of the articles are solicited directly by the editor. Unsolicited manuscripts also are welcomed, but a letter of inquiry prior to submission is encouraged. About four issues per year are dedicated to central themes. These theme issues usually are guest edited and nearly all articles are solicited. Authors, however, may write the editor for a list of theme issues planned. The

PHI DELTA KAPPAN (cont'd)

MLA style modified to PDK style is to be followed and a two page set of instructions is available from the editor. Two copies of manuscripts are preferred. Length of contributions may vary from 750 to 4,000 words. Copyright generally is held by the publisher, but may be retained by the author. Estimated time for an editorial decision concerning acceptability of an article is four to eight weeks. Publication time varies from one to twelve months. Four to eight book reviews appear in this journal and their length is 250 to 1,000 words each.

399. **THE PHYSICAL EDUCATOR.** 1940– . Phi Epsilon Kappa Fraternity, 1475 West 86th Street, Suite F-1, Indianapolis, IN 46260. Circ.: 10,000. 4 issues/yr. Subscription included with fraternity membership; non-member rate, $6.00/yr. Annual index: December issue. Editor: David L. Gallahue. Editor's address: School of HPER, Indiana University, Bloomington, IN 47401. Book reviews to: editor.
Indexed in: Education Index; Social Sciences Index.

The intended audience of this journal includes all professionals engaged or interested in the fields of health, physical education, recreation, safety and athletics. Pertinent articles dealing with problems related to the fields mentioned are preferred. Regular features are Teaching Techniques, Teachable Dances, Elsewhere in the World, Editors Corner, Book Reviews, and Updated Bibliographies.

The editor accepts unsolicited manuscripts for consideration. Two copies of their work are to be submitted. Style and length are not specified. Copyright of accepted articles is held by the publisher. Estimated time for an editorial decision is eight to twelve weeks. Time from acceptance to publication varies from six to nine months. Seven to ten book reviews are contained in this journal and each of these reviews is approximately 150 words long.

400. **PHYSICAL THERAPY.** 1921– . American Physical Therapy Association, 1156 15th Street, N.W., Washington, DC 20005. Circ.: 25,000. 12 issues/yr. Subscription included with association membership; non-member rate, $18.00/yr. Annual index: December issue. Editor: Elizabeth J. Davies. Book reviews to: editor.
Indexed in: Cumulative Index to Nursing Literature; Current Contents: Clinical Practice; Exceptional Child Education Abstracts; Excerpta Medica; Hospital Literature Index; Index Medicus; Information Retrieval Limited*; Nursing Research; Rehabilitation Literature.

Physical therapists are among the intended audience of this journal. Its purpose is to publish reports of research in or related to physical therapy, to foster the continuing education of physical therapists, to inform members of trends and events in physical therapy and related areas, to document the transactions of the association, and to serve as the archives of the growth and development of physical therapy.

The editor welcomes manuscripts for possible inclusion in *Physical Therapy*. Prospective contributors should examine thoroughly the association's manual of style for standardized publication requirements. Length of articles should not exceed 3,750 words and articles are to be submitted in duplicate. Copyright on accepted materials is held by the publisher. The time for an editorial decision concerning acceptance is six to eight weeks. Publication follows in four months. About 16 book reviews of less than 250 words each are contained in this journal.

401. THE PHYSICS TEACHER. 1963– . American Association of Physics Teachers, Graduate Physics Building, SUNY at Stony Brook, Stony Brook, NY 11794. Circ.: 10,000. 9 issues/yr. Subscription may be included with association membership; non-member rate, $18.00/yr. Annual index: December issue. Editor: C. E. Swartz. Editor's address: Department of Physics, State University of New York, Stony Brook, NY 11794. Book reviews are by invitation.

Indexed in: Computer and Control Abstracts*; Current Index to Journals in Education; Education Index; Media Review Digest.

The intended audience of this journal includes teachers of introductory physics at both high school and college level. Members of the American Association of Physics Teachers may select this journal or the *American Journal of Physics* as part of their membership dues. This publication is dedicated to the strengthening of the teaching of introductory physics at all levels. Book Reviews, Apparatus Section, Questions Some Students Ask and Research Frontier are among the regular features.

Unsolicited articles, preceded by a letter of inquiry, are welcomed by the editor. Style should follow the requirements as presented by the American Institute of Physics. Major articles are to be 5,000 words whereas material for the Notes section is not to exceed 1,000 words. Two copies are to be submitted and an editorial decision may be expected in about six weeks. Publication follows in three months. Copyright on accepted articles is held by the publisher. A one page sheet of guidelines for contributors is available from the editor.

402. THE PIANO QUARTERLY. 1952– . The Piano Quarterly, Inc., P.O. Box 815, Wilmington, VT 05363. Circ.: 4,000. 4 issues/yr. $7.00/yr. Annual index: winter issue. Editor: Robert Joseph Silverman. Book reviews to: editor.

Indexed in: The Music Index.

This journal is intended for pianists at all levels, from amateurs through teachers to concert performers. Its purpose is to communicate the latest in the field of piano from research to piano pedagogy, including profiles and articles of general interest.

The editor welcomes unsolicited manuscripts. These articles should be between 3,000 and 5,000 words in length. A style sheet is available upon request. The copyright is held by the publisher, however, the copyright may be vested in the author by agreement. The editor requires approximately eight weeks for a decision. Publication of accepted manuscripts usually follows between six and twelve months later. Five or more book reviews are published in each issue and these are between 500 and 1,000 words in length.

403. PREVIEWS. 1972– . R. R. Bowker Company, 1180 Avenue of the Americas, New York, NY 10016. Circ.: 45,000. 9 issues/yr. $5.00/yr. Annual index: not given. Editor: Phyllis Levy. No book reviews.

Indexed in: Consumers Index; International Index to Multi-Media Information; Library Literature; Media Review Digest.

The intended audience of this journal includes media specialists, librarians, teachers, school supervisors and audio-visual center directors. Its purpose is to review non-print software and hardware as comprehensively as possible and to present articles to assist its readers in learning about current trends and issues. Articles included are those dealing with trends in the audio-visual field, filmographies, subject oriented media lists, hardware use, classroom use of audiovisual material and student filmmaking projects.

The editor welcomes unsolicited manuscripts, but encourages a letter of inquiry prior to submission. The MLA style requirements are to be followed. Preferred length of articles is 2,500 words. Copyright is held by the publisher who pays authors an honorarium, the amount to be determined individually. Estimated time for an editorial decision concerning acceptability of material is four weeks. The time required for publication varies.

404. PRIME AREAS. (formerly **BC PRIMARY BULLETIN**). 1960– (PA); 1958– (BCPB). British Columbia Primary Teachers' Association of the British Columbia Teachers' Federation, 105-2235 Burrard Street, Vancouver, British Columbia, Canada V6J 3H9. Circ.: 2,500. 3 issues/yr. Subscription included with association membership. No annual index. Editor: Lorna Robb. Editor's address: P.O. Box 94058, Richmond, British Columbia, Canada V6Y 2A2. Book reviews to: editor.

Indexed in: Canadian Education Index.

The intended audience of this journal consists chiefly of public school primary teachers. Professional information and sharing opportunities are offered in the publication. A regular feature is Teaching Aids for early children education.

Unsolicited articles of up to 1,000 words are accepted for consideration. Black and white photos are welcomed. Style is not specified and copyright is held by the author. Simultaneous submission to other journals is permitted. The time required for an editorial decision is six weeks. Publication of accepted material usually follows in six months. Four book reviews appear in each issue. Submitted materials are not returned.

405. PROFESSIONAL PSYCHOLOGY. 1969– . American Psychological Association, 1200 Seventeenth Street, N.W., Washington, DC 20036. Circ.: 4,300. 4 issues/yr. $7.00/yr. with APA membership; non-member rate, $15.00/yr. Annual index: November issue. Editor: Donald K. Freedheim. Editor's address: Department of Psychology, Case Western Reserve University, Cleveland, OH 44106. No book reviews.

Indexed in: Current Contents: Social & Behavioral Sciences; dsh Abstracts; Psychological Abstracts; Social Sciences Citation Index.

This journal is intended for psychologists and other professional workers in the human services, organizational and industrial personnel officers, school psychologists and students. Its purpose is to provide information and exchange on professional problems and issues, roles and functions, and emerging trends in the delivery of psychological services. The editor is interested in original articles on conceptual and practical issues, including applications of research, standards of practice, inter-professional relations, delivery of services, and innovations in training.

Unsolicited articles as well as inquiries on the appropriateness of manuscripts are welcomed. Authors should follow the APA style with article length being between 2,500 and 4,000 words. Three copies are to be submitted. The copyright is held by the publisher. Eight weeks is required for an editorial decision with publication following within nine months after acceptance.

406. PSYCHOLOGY. 1964– . Circ.: 4,000. 4 issues/yr. $7.00/yr. No annual index. Editor: John A. Blazer. Editor's address: P.O. Box 6495, Station C, Savannah, GA 31405. Book reviews to: editor.

> Indexed in: College Student Personnel Abstracts; Current Contents: Social & Behavioral Sciences; Excerpta Medica; Mental Health Book Review Index; Psychological Abstracts; The Psychological Readers Guide; Social Sciences Citation Index.

Psychology, a journal of human behavior, is intended for psychologists, psychiatrists, marriage counselors, social workers, ministers, researchers and graduate students. Included in this journal are numerous papers on important aspects of psychology. Any article related to human behavior is considered for publication.

Unsolicited manuscripts are welcomed by the editor. The APA style is to be followed and any length is acceptable. Copyright is held by the publisher and the authors pays the publisher at a varying rate. Contributors should consult the editor for details. Estimated time for an editorial decision is two weeks. Time from acceptance to publication is three months. Book reviews are included in this journal. The number varies with each issue.

407. PSYCHOLOGY IN THE SCHOOLS. 1964– . Clinical Psychology Press, 4 Conant Square, Brandon, VT 05733. Circ.: 2,500. 4 issues/yr. $15.00/yr. with membership in a national society; non-member rate, $20.00/yr. Annual index: October issue. Editor: Gerald B. Fuller. Editor's address: Department of Psychology, Central Michigan University, Mt. Pleasant, MI 48859. Book reviews to: editor.

> Indexed in: Bulletin Signaletique, Section 390: Psychologie-Psychopathologie-Psychiatrie; Child Development Abstracts and Bibliography; College Student Personnel Abstracts; Current Index to Journals in Education; Education Index; Exceptional Child Education Abstracts; Psychological Abstracts; The Psychological Readers Guide; Readers Guide to Periodical Literature; Social Sciences Citation Index.

Psychology in the Schools is intended for school psychologists, teachers, researchers, administrators, and graduate students in psychology and education. Research articles which clearly aid practitioners in the schools are solicited for this refereed journal. In addition, editorial consideration is given manuscripts

PSYCHOLOGY IN THE SCHOOLS (cont'd)

presenting professional opinion or describing innovative practices. Regular features include both book and test reviews.

Unsolicited manuscripts are considered for inclusion in this journal. Manuscripts should be between 1,500 and 2,000 words and submitted in three copies. The copyright is held by the publisher. The author pays the publisher at a rate which is billed at the time of acceptance. An editorial decision is usually rendered within five weeks. Publication of accepted manuscripts follows within nine to twelve months. Six to eight book reviews are published in each issue and these should be between 500 and 750 words in length. The APA style should be followed in all submissions.

408. PUBLIC HEALTH REPORTS. (formerly **HEALTH SERVICE REPORTS**). 1878– . U. S. Department of Health, Education, and Welfare, Health Resources Administration, Washington, DC 20201. Circ.: 18,100. 6 issues/yr. $12.00/yr. Annual index: November-December issue. Editor: Marian Priest Tebben. Editor's address: Room 10A-4l, Parklawn Building, 5600 Fishers Lane, Rockville, MD 20852. No book reviews.

Indexed in: Current Contents: Clinical Practice; Current Contents: Life Sciences; Current Contents: Social & Behavioral Sciences; Index Medicus; Index to Periodical Articles Related to Law; Index Veterinarius; Nuclear Science Abstracts; Operations Research/Management Science Abstract Services; Psychological Abstracts; Science Citation Index; Social Sciences Citation Index; Zoological Record.

Beginning with the July-August (1974) issue the name of this journal was changed once again to its original title, first published in 1878. Its intended audience includes public health practitioners in government, research work, health planning, and health economics, and students working for advanced degrees in the health disciplines. The purpose of the publication is to report on research and advancements in the delivery of health service and to document developments in public health. Scientific reports of interest to its multi-disciplinary audience appear in the journal. Education Notes and New Publications are regular features.

Unsolicited articles are accepted for consideration, but a letter of inquiry prior to submission is encouraged. Authors should follow the general style as presented by the American Medical Association. Length may be from 2,500 to 5,000 words and four copies are to be submitted. Since *Reports* is a governmental journal, its contents are not covered by copyright. An editorial decision is made in six to eight weeks and the estimated time from acceptance to publication is six to twelve months.

409. PUBLIC TELECOMMUNICATIONS REVIEW. 1973– . National Association of Educational Broadcasters, Suite 1101, 1346 Connecticut Avenue, N.W., Washington, DC 20036. Circ.: 5,000. 6 issues/yr. Subscription included with association membership; non-member rate, $18.00/yr. No annual index. Editor: Stephen Millard. Manuscript to: Eva Archer, managing editor. Book reviews to: managing editor.

Indexed in: Current Index to Journals in Education.

PUBLIC TELECOMMUNICATIONS REVIEW (cont'd)

This journal is intended for professionals in the field of public and educational telecommunications. Its contents are geared toward provocative articles and research reports of interest to its audience. Several article titles from recent issues are: Decision-oriented Research in School Television; The Rebirth of Radio Drama; Keeping in Touch with Technology; and, Public Affairs—The Commitment We Need.

Unsolicited articles and letters of inquiry are accepted by the editor. In some cases the editor will solicit articles on specific topics. Manuscripts should be between 2,500 and 3,000 words in length. The copyright is held by the publisher. Simultaneous submission to other journals is permitted. An editorial decision is made in six weeks. Publication follows within two months. This journal includes two or three book reviews in each issue. These reviews should be approximatey 1,200 words and be related to the field.

410. **THE QUARTERLY JOURNAL OF SPEECH.** 1915– . Speech Communication Association, Statler Hilton Hotel, New York, NY 10001. Circ.: 6,500. 4 issues/yr. $20.00/yr. Annual index: December issue. Editor: Edwin Black. Editor's address: Department of Communication Arts, University of Wisconsin, Madison, WI 53706. Book reviews are commissioned.

> Indexed in: America: History and Life*; Book Review Index; Current Contents: Social & Behavioral Sciences; Current Index to Journals in Education; dsh Abstracts; Education Index; Exceptional Child Education Abstracts; Modern Language Abstracts; Psychological Abstracts; Social Sciences Citation Index; Women Studies Abstracts.

This journal is intended for an intellectual audience interested in communication scholarship, especially university and college professors. The membership of the Speech Communication Association is a primary audience. Articles are, and have been, accepted from persons in a number of academic disciplines. Its purpose is to encourage scholarship in communication and to print the best scholarly work available.

Unsolicited manuscripts are welcomed for consideration. Length of articles should be no more than 6,000 words. Two copies, including the original typescript, are to be submitted. Style requirements are those of the MLA style sheet. An editorial decision is given within two months and publication of accepted pieces follows within a year. Copyright is held by the publisher.

411. **RCU REPORT (NEVADA).** 1968– . Nevada State Department of Education, Heroes Memorial Building, Carson City, NV 89701. Circ.: 1,500. 8 issues/yr. No charge, controlled circulation. No annual index. Editor: Joseph W. Erlach. Editor's address: Research and Educational Planning Center, College of Education, University of Nevada, Reno, NV 89507. No book reviews.

This publication reports in part what the Research Coordinating Unit of the Nevada State Department of Education is undertaking and accomplishing. It is distributed to vocational and career educators, other educators, and interested members of the general public. Its purpose is to disseminate ideas on current theory and practices in vocational education, both national and state-wide, and to exchange descriptions of successful practices among school districts and state agencies.

Unsolicited manuscripts are accepted for editorial consideration. The length is negotiated in light of the subject and the emphasis of the issue. Simultaneous submission to other publications is permitted. One week is required for an editorial decision with publication following within one month of acceptance. About one-half of each issue is dedicated to a central theme with the other half devoted to a variety of current materials. All Research Coordinating Units are federally funded. The *Report* effectively satisfies a part of the dissemination responsibility.

412. **READING HORIZONS.** 1960– . Reading Center and Clinic, Western Michigan University, Kalamazoo, MI 49008. Circ.: 1,000. 4 issues/yr. $4.00/yr. Annual index: issue number four. Editor: Kenneth VanderMeulen. Book reviews are written by staff.

Indexed in: Current Index to Journals in Education; Language and Language Behavior Abstracts; Sociological Abstracts.

This journal is devoted to reading at all levels of academic endeavor. It is intended for professionals interested in the field of reading. Regular features include book reviews, article reviews, a secondary column, a field information section, editorials, letters to the editor, and descriptions and reviews of reading programs and learning centers.

Unsolicited articles are accepted for consideration. Two copies of the manuscript are to be submitted and length should be 2,000 to 3,000 words. Copyright is held by the publisher. Style requirements are not given. Simultaneous submission to other journals is permitted. An editorial decision is given in four to six weeks and publication follows in four to six months.

413. **READING IMPROVEMENT.** 1963– . Project Innovation, P.O. Box 566, Chula Vista, CA 92010. Circ.: 2,500. 4 issues/yr. $8.00/yr. Annual index: last issue in volume. Editor: Russell N. Cassel. Book reviews to: Lau M. Cassel.

Indexed in: Current Index to Journals in Education; Education Index; Language and Language Behavior Abstracts; Psychological Abstracts; Reading Abstracts; Women Studies Abstracts.

This journal is intended for reading teachers, other teachers and educators, parents and students. *Reading Improvement* is designed to offer assistance to teachers at all levels of instruction. Creative theoretical papers and reports of reading research are welcomed for editorial consideration. Manuscripts which offer suggestions for the teaching of reading and improving the process are preferred.

The editor welcomes unsolicited manuscripts for possible inclusion in this journal. Length of articles should be 2,000 words and copyright is held by the publisher. The APA style is to be followed and two copies of the work should be submitted. In some cases the author pays the publisher for costs of printing. Contributors can expect an editorial decision in five weeks and publication follows in ten to twelve months. Ten to twenty book reviews are included in each issue and these reviews are 50 to 100 words in length.

414. READING RESEARCH QUARTERLY. 1965– . International Reading
Association, Inc. Circ.: 11,000. 4 issues/yr. Subscription included with associa-
tion membership; institution rate, $15.00/yr. Annual index: issue number
four. (Ten year index, Vol. 10:4). Editors: Roger Farr and Samuel Weintraub.
Manuscript to: Editors, 227 Education Building, Indiana University,
Bloomington, IN 47401. Book reviews to: editors.

> Indexed in: Current Contents: Social & Behavioral Sciences; Current
> Index to Journals in Education; Education Index; Exceptional Child
> Education Abstracts; Psychological Abstracts; Social Sciences Citation
> Index.

Members of the International Reading Association may choose this journal,
The Reading Teacher, or the *Journal of Reading* as part of their dues. The *Reading
Research Quarterly* reports experimental, statistical, and technical articles as well
as integrative, critical, and comprehensive reviews of the literature in reading. On-
going research activities are reported when appropriate and reading research from
other countries is included also. This journal provides a forum for reading research
and theories of the reading process.

Unsolicited manuscripts are welcomed by the editors. Contributors should
follow the general style as presented in this journal's manual for authors. Four copies of the article are required. Copyright on accepted material is held by the publisher.
An editorial decision is given in twelve weeks and publication follows in twelve
months. Occasional book reviews are published and their basic requirements are
the same as regular manuscripts.

415. READING WORLD. (formerly **JOURNAL OF THE READING SPECIALIST**).
1971– (RW); 1961– (JRS). The College Reading Association. Circ.: 1,000.
4 issues/yr. $15.00/yr. Annual index: May issue. Editor: Samuel Zeman.
Editor's address: P.O. Box 462, Shippensburg State College, Shippensburg,
PA 17257. Book reviews to: Daniel T. Fishco, Professor of Reading, Western
Illinois University, Macomb, IL 61455.

> Indexed in: Current Index to Journals in Education; Psychological
> Abstracts.

This journal is published by the association for all those persons who have an
interest in the teaching of reading. The journal attempts to present articles of interest to a broad spectrum of reader interest, within the parameters established by its
focus upon the teaching of reading.

Unsolicited manuscripts are welcomed for editorial consideration. Articles
should be between 2,000 and 3,000 words in length and submitted in two copies.
The copyright is held by the publisher. Approximately eight weeks is required for
an editorial decision. No length of time from acceptance to publication is indicated. Six book reviews are published in each issue of the journal. Their average
length is 500 words.

416. REHABILITATION DIGEST. 1969– . Canadian Rehabilitation Council for
the Disabled, Suite 2110, One Yonge Street, Toronto, Ontario, Canada M5E
1E8. Circ.: 1,000. 4 issues/yr. $3.00 annually. No annual index. Editor:
Norman D. Lawson. Book reviews to: editor.

Indexed in: Exceptional Child Education Abstracts; Rehabilitation Literature.

This journal is intended for rehabilitation workers and students, government officials, and interested members of the public. It provides a forum for the exchange of ideas, information and concepts in the field of rehabilitation of the physically disabled. The editor is interested in receiving manuscripts dealing with a broad spectrum of related topics covering medical, social and vocational rehabilitation of the physically disabled.

Both solicited and unsolicited manuscripts are considered by the editor. Word limits and style requirements are not indicated. Copyright is held by the author. Simultaneous submission to other publications is permitted. Approximately four weeks is required for an editorial decision with publication following acceptance between four and eight months later. Two book reviews usually appear in each issue and these are up to 500 words in length.

417. **RELIGIOUS EDUCATION.** 1906– . The Religious Education Association, 409 Prospect Street, New Haven, CT 06510. Circ.: 5,000. 6 issues/yr. Subscription included with association membership; library rate, $15.00/yr. Annual index: November/December issue. Editor: Randolph C. Miller. Book reviews by invitation only.

Indexed in: Current Contents: Social & Behavioral Sciences; Education Index; Guide to Social Science and Religion in Periodical Literature; Index to Jewish Periodicals; Index to Religious Periodical Literature; Index to Periodical Articles Related to Law; Psychological Abstracts; Religious and Theological Abstracts; Sociological Abstracts; Women Studies Abstracts; Theologische Zeitschrift.

This journal has the sub-title "A Platform for the Free Discussion of Religious Issues and Their Bearing on Education." Its articles deal with all aspects of education as related to religious purposes. *Religious Education* is intended for church and synagogue board members and staff, ministers and rabbis, directors of religious education, professors in theological seminaries, college teachers and administrators, and interested lay persons, all on a multifaith basis. The journal is supported by a membership that has international, national and regional conventions and meetings, supports research, provides sabbatical fellowships, and supports the professional interests of its members.

The editor publishes both solicited and unsolicited material. Contributors should follow the Chicago style and submit one or two copies of the manuscript. Length of articles may be 4,000 to 5,000 words. Copyright is held by the publisher, but may be held by the author if requested. Estimated time for an editorial decision is six to nine weeks. Publication of accepted pieces follows in three to twelve months. A style sheet is available from the editor.

418. **RESEARCH IN THE TEACHING OF ENGLISH.** 1967– . National Council of Teachers of English, 1111 Kenyon Road, Urbana, IL 61801. Circ.: not given. 3 issues/yr. $5.00/yr. Annual index: winter issue. Editor: Alan C. Purves. Editor's address: 310 West Delaware, Urbana, IL 61801. Book reviews to: editor.

RESEARCH IN THE TEACHING OF ENGLISH (cont'd)

Indexed in: Current Index to Journals in Education; Education Index.

This journal is intended to reach teachers of English, supervisors in the field and researchers. It provides a forum for educational research dealing with the teaching and learning of English. The editor is interested in receiving research articles.

Unsolicited articles are welcomed for editorial consideration. These works should follow the APA style with no length limitations being noted. Two copies of all manuscripts are to be sent with a self-addressed stamped envelope enclosed for the return of unaccepted work. Simultaneous submission to other journals is permitted. Six weeks is required for an editorial decision with publication of accepted manuscripts following approximately one year after acceptance. Six book reviews are published each year in this journal. No requirements of length and style are indicated. Copyright is held by the publisher.

419. **REVIEW OF EDUCATIONAL RESEARCH.** 1931– . American Educational Research Association, 1126 Sixteenth Street, N.W., Washington, DC 20036. Circ.: 14,400. 4 issues/yr. Subscription included with association membership; non-member rate, $10.00/yr. No annual index. Editor: Samuel Messick. Editor's address: P.O. Box 2604, Educational Testing Service, Princeton, NJ 08540. No book reviews.

Indexed in: Child Development Abstracts and Bibliography; College Student Personnel Abstracts; Current Contents: Social & Behavioral Sciences; Current Index to Journals in Education; dsh Abstracts; Education Index; Educational Administration Abstracts; Exceptional Child Education Abstracts; Language and Language Behavior Abstracts; Psychological Abstracts; Social Sciences Citation Index; Sociological Abstracts.

The *Review of Educational Research* is intended for educational researchers. Its purpose is to disseminate information concerning research literature bearing on education. In addition, the editor welcomes reviews of research in various other disciplines including the humanities, and management, behavioral and social sciences. All manuscripts must deal with educational issues, regardless of discipline orientation.

Unsolicited manuscripts are welcomed for editorial consideration. Suggested length of articles is 12,500 to 15,000 words, but no restrictions are imposed. The copyright is held by the publisher. Three copies of each manuscript are required. Time required for an editorial decision usually is eight to twelve weeks, however, this publication is a "blind" refereed journal and the length of time depends in a great part on the receipt of referees' comments and recommendations. Publication of accepted manuscripts follows acceptance in six to twelve months. Authors should follow APA style requirements for all work.

420. **RURAL EDUCATION NEWS.** 1948– . Rural Education Association, 212 CEB, College of Education, The University of Tennessee, Knoxville, TN 37916. Circ.: 1,000. 6 issues/yr. Subscription included with association membership; library rate, $5.00/yr. No annual index. Editors: E. Dale Doak and O. K. O'Fallon. Book reviews to: editors.

This newsletter is intended to meet the needs of teachers at all levels, school administrators, and college and university personnel, all of whom are eligible for REA membership. This publication serves as a house organ to bring new developments in the field to the attention of REA members as well as other subscribers.

Unsolicited articles and letters of inquiry are welcomed by the editor. Articles solicited directly from selected specialists also are included in the newsletter contents. Articles should be between 1,000 and 1,500 words in length. The copyright is held by the publisher. Simultaneous submission to other journals is permitted. Approximately four weeks is required for an editorial decision with four months usually elapsing between acceptance and publication. One or two book reviews appear in each issue of this publication. These reviews should be between 250 and 300 words in length.

421. SAANYS JOURNAL. (formerly **N.Y.S. SECONDARY EDUCATION**).
1968– . School Administrators Association of New York State, 150 State Street, Albany, NY 12207. Circ.: 3,500. 4 issues/yr. Subscription included with association membership; non-member rate, $8.00/yr. Annual index: not given. Editor: Francis E. Morhous. Editor's address: 1588 Rugby Road, Schenectady, NY 12308. Book reviews to: editor.

Elementary and secondary school principals and administrators, including supervisors and department heads, are among the intended audience of this journal. Its purpose is to promote improvements in educational administration. The editor is interested in articles which report innovative and successful ideas related to educational administration.

Unsolicited articles and letters of inquiry are welcomed by the editor. Two copies of all manuscripts, which should be about 1,500 words in length, are to be submitted. Three weeks is required for an editorial decision with publication of accepted material following in three to six months. Occasional book reviews are used, but not on a regular basis. These reviews should be approximately 800 words in length.

422. THE SASKATCHEWAN ADMINISTRATOR. 1967– . Saskatchewan Teachers' Federation, Council on Educational Administration, 2317 Arlington Avenue, Saskatoon, Saskatchewan, Canada S7J 2H8. Circ.: 400. 4 issues/yr. Subscription included with council membership; non-member rate, $3.50/yr. No annual index. Editor: Kevin Wilson. Editor's address: P.O. Box 1108, Saskatoon, Saskatchewan, Canada. Book reviews to: editor.

Indexed in: Canadian Education Index.

The intended audience of this journal includes administrators in Saskatchewan and professors in the educational administration field. Its purpose is to acquaint administrators with current trends and issues in educational administration. Typical articles are reports of empirical studies, theoretical papers and position papers. One issue reports major papers given at the annual conference of the Saskatchewan Council on Educational Administration.

The editor solicits articles directly from administrators and professors for some of the material in this journal, but unsolicited manuscripts also are welcomed.

THE SASKATCHEWAN ADMINISTRATOR (cont'd)

The APA style requirements should be followed and preferred length is 1,000 to 2,000 words. Two copies of the article are to be submitted. An editorial decision is made in five weeks and the estimated time from acceptance to publication is two months. Two book reviews of about 250 words each appear in the journal. Copyright on all materials is held by the publisher.

423. SASKATCHEWAN BULLETIN. 1934– . Saskatchewan Teachers Federation, 2317 Arlington Avenue, Saskatoon, Saskatchewan, Canada S7J 2H8. Circ.: 17,000. 19 issues/yr. $3.50/yr. (Canadian). No annual index. Editor: Gary Genge. Unsolicited book reviews rarely accepted.

This tabloid combines news content of interest to federation members with feature articles. Its purpose is to inform teachers of the activities of their professional association and of new and interesting developments in education. The editor is interested in well-researched features on developments in education, and also well-done opinion pieces.

The editor accepts unsolicited material for consideration, however, space constraints allow a limited use of these articles. A letter of inquiry prior to submission is encouraged. The preferred length is between 1,000 and 1,500 words. Style is a modified version of that used by the Canadian Press. Copyright is retained by the publisher unless special arrangements are made. Simultaneous submission to other journals is permitted. Payment to the author is made upon publication at the rate of five to seven cents per word. The estimated time for an editorial decision is two weeks, with no set time for publication following acceptance. This tabloid uses book reviews on a space available basis. It is suggested that queries concerning reviews be addressed to the Book Review Editor. Authors are paid $5.00 per review upon acceptance.

424. SASKATCHEWAN JOURNAL OF EDUCATIONAL RESEARCH AND DEVELOPMENT. 1970– . Saskatchewan Educational Research Association, University of Saskatchewan, Saskatoon, Saskatchewan, Canada S7N 0W0. Circ.: 2,000. 2 issues/yr. $3.50/yr. No annual index. Editor: Kevin A. Wilson. Editor's address: University of Saskatchewan, Education Building, Room 3073, Saskatoon, Saskatchewan, Canada S7N 0W0. Book reviews to: editor.

Indexed in: Canadian Education Index; Current Index to Journals in Education.

This journal publishes reports on educational research and development pertinent to Saskatchewan. The dissemination of these materials is intended for teachers, administrators and university personnel. Sample titles illustrate the scope of this journal's contents: Recent Advances in the Measurement of Creativity; Preparing Teachers for Innovative Schools; Reading Gains Measured by Two Different Methods; and, Academic Freedom in the Classroom.

The editor solicits articles directly from experts in the field of education, but also welcomes unsolicited manuscripts. Style of writing should follow APA requirements and material should be submitted in duplicate. Approximately 2,000 to 4,000 words is the preferred length of contributions. Copyright of accepted work is held by the publisher. The time for an editorial decision concerning acceptance is eight weeks. Publication follows in six months. Two book reviews of about 250 words each are contained in this journal.

425. SCHOOL AND COMMUNITY. 1915– . Missouri State Teachers Association, P.O. Box 458, Columbia, MO 65201. Circ.: 42,000. 9 issues/yr. $4.50/yr. Annual index: May issue. Editor: Margery L. Cunningham. No book reviews. Indexed in: Education Index.

This journal is intended for all those engaged in the education profession, both the public and private sectors. Its purpose is to disseminate information pertaining to innovative classroom practices and new research, and to provide information regarding the activities of the MSTA and its district and local units.

Unsolicited articles are accepted for consideration. These works preferably should be between 600 and 1,200 words in length and the original copy is requested. The copyright is held by the publisher. Two of the nine issues are theme issues and are entirely staff written. The other seven issues per year are open to non-staff contributors. An editorial decision usually is made within one week and publication of accepted pieces follows within the publishing year.

426. SCHOOL ARTS. 1901– . Davis Publications, Inc., 50 Portland Street, Worcester, MA 01608. Circ.: 3,300. 10 issues/yr. $9.00/yr. No annual index. Editor: George F. Horn. Editor's Address: 8809 Oakleigh Road, Baltimore, MD 21234. Unsolicited book reviews not accepted. Indexed in: Current Index to Journals in Education; Education Index; Media Review Digest; Readers Guide to Periodical Literature.

This journal is directed toward teachers of art in grades K-12 as well as general classroom teachers who are charged with teaching art. Its contents reflect the interest in curriculum development, specifically art education. The editor is interested in articles describing art programs and activities related to any level of the total K-12 program.

The editor welcomes unsolicited manuscripts. Journal issues give emphasis to monthly themes which are announced in the September issue each year. Articles should be between 800 and 1,000 words, with the copyright being held by the publisher. Payment, at an unspecified rate, is made to authors upon publication. Approximately two weeks is required for an editorial decision with six to twelve months elapsing before publication of accepted manuscripts.

427. SCHOOL BUSINESS AFFAIRS. 1936– . Association of School Business Officials of the United States and Canada, 2424 West Lawrence Avenue, Chicago, IL 60625. Circ.: 5,200. 12 issues/yr. Subscription included with association membership. Annual index: December issue. Editor: Charles W. Foster. Manuscript to: Dwight B. Esau, managing editor. Book reviews to: managing editor. Indexed in: Current Index to Journals in Education.

This journal is directed toward practicing school business administrators, school related businessmen and professors and teachers of business management or educational administration. It is intended to foster discussion and research and to serve as a forum for the exchange of information and ideas on behalf of better school business management.

Unsolicited articles are accepted for editorial consideration with members of the ASBO being given first consideration. The editor also solicits some material directly from selected professionals and encourages letters of inquiry. Articles should be between 700 and 2,500 words in length. Two copies of all manuscripts should be submitted. An editorial decision usually is made between one and two weeks after receipt of the manuscript. Publication of accepted material varies widely with no time estimate available. Simultaneous submission to other journals is permitted. The number of book reviews is variable. The preferred length of reviews is 250 words.

428. **THE SCHOOL COUNSELOR**. 1953– . American School Counselor Association, a division of the American Personnel and Guidance Association, 1607 New Hampshire Avenue, N.W., Washington, DC 20009. Circ.: 16,500. 5 issues/yr. Subscription included with ASCA membership; $7.00/yr. with APGA membership; non-member rate, $10.00/yr. Annual index: issue number five. Editor: Marguerite R. Carroll. Editor's address: Fairfield University, Fairfield, CT 06430. Book reviews to: editor.

Indexed in: Current Contents: Social & Behavioral Sciences; Current Index to Journals in Education; Education Index; Psychological Abstracts; Sociology of Education Abstracts.

The intended audience of this journal includes practitioners and educators in the field of guidance and counseling, especially those in school settings. Articles appearing in the journal deal with theory and practice in counseling, professional experimentation and research, and professional concerns of counselors.

Unsolicited articles are accepted for consideration. Preferred length of manuscripts is 2,500 to 3,000 words. Contributors should follow APA style requirements and are to submit three copies of their work. Occasional special issues are dedicated to central themes which are announced in the journal. The time for an editorial decision concerning acceptance is four weeks. Publication follows in six months. About ten book reviews appear in each issue and these are about 500 words in length. Copyright on all materials is held by the publisher.

429. **SCHOOL FOODSERVICE JOURNAL**. (formerly **SCHOOL LUNCH JOURNAL**). 1971– (SFJ); 1947– (SLJ). American School Food Service Association, 4101 East Iliff Avenue, Denver, CO 80222. Circ.: 60,000. 10 issues/yr. Subscription included with association membership; non-member rate, $20.00/yr. Annual index: November-December issue. Editor: Donna Roberts. Unsolicited book reviews not accepted.

This journal reaches the spectrum of those persons working in the nonprofit school foodservice programs across the country and is the official organ of the American School Food Service Association. This magazine is edited specifically to meet the needs of the public school and college foodservice buyer and operator. The editor is interested in articles dealing with nutrition, management techniques, equipment discussions, recipes and food articles.

Unsolicited articles as well as letters of inquiry are welcomed by the editor for review and possible use. Editors reserve the right to reject any material submitted and/or to completely rewrite the material. Between two and four weeks is required for an editorial decision with up to six months elapsing from acceptance to publication of manuscripts. The copyright is held by the publisher. The length of the manuscript should be governed by the material covered. All material is copy edited for style and space available. Prospective contributors should examine recent issues of this journal for topics of interest to its readers.

430. **THE SCHOOL GUIDANCE WORKER.** 1945– . Guidance Centre, Faculty of Education, University of Toronto, 1000 Yonge Street, Toronto, Ontario, Canada M4W 2K8. Circ.: 5,000. 6 issues/yr. $8.40/yr. Annual index: issue number six. Editor: C. L. Bedal. Book reviews to: editor.
   Indexed in: Canadian Education Index; Current Index to Journals in Education.

The intended audience of this journal includes school counselors at all levels and particularly those in secondary schools, and also teachers, administrators and interested parents. Its purpose is to provide current information on all phases of counseling. Regular features include book reviews and a section for letters responding to articles in earlier issues.

The editor solicits material directly from various professionals, but also accepts unsolicited manuscripts for consideration. The MLA style is to be used with the Oxford English dictionary the basis for spelling. Article length should be 3,000 words and two copies are to be submitted. Issues are dedicated to central themes which usually are set a year in advance and are available from the editor. An editorial decision concerning acceptability is given in two weeks and publication follows in one month. Book reviews of 500 words are in each issue of *The School Guidance Worker*. The publisher pays authors $50.00 for each accepted manuscript and holds copyright on all published material.

431. **SCHOOL LIBRARY JOURNAL.** 1954– . R. R. Bowker Company, 1180 Avenue of the Americas, New York, NY 10036. Circ.: 32,000. 9 issues/yr. $10.80/yr. Annual index: December issue. Editor: Lillian N. Gerhardt. Unsolicited book reviews not accepted.
   Indexed in: Current Index to Journals in Education; Library Literature; Readers Guide to Periodical Literature; References Services Review.

This journal is intended to reach librarians in elementary, junior and senior high schools, as well as children's and young adult librarians in public libraries. Its purpose is to provide the most complete information on library service to minors, as well as the most extensive source of new trade book information on juvenile books. The editor is interested in articles dealing with library services to minors, the education of librarians, and critiques of library materials for minors.

Unsolicited articles as well as letters of inquiry are accepted by the editor. The Chicago style should be followed with article length being approximately 3,000 words. The copyright is held by the publisher and payment of $100.00 per article is made upon publication. Journal issues are dedicated to central themes and the editor urges prospective contributors to check past issues of the journal. Approximately twelve weeks is required for an editorial decision with three months elapsing between acceptance and publication.

432. **SCHOOL MEDIA QUARTERLY.** (formerly **SCHOOL LIBRARIES**). 1972– (SMQ); 1952– (SL). American Association of School Librarians, a division of the American Library Association, 50 East Huron Street, Chicago, IL 60611. Circ.: 8,000. 4 issues/yr. Subscription included with association membership; non-member rate, $15.00/yr. Annual index: summer issue. Editor: Glenn E. Estes. Editor's address: Graduate School of Library and Information Science, The University of Tennessee, 804 Volunteer Boulevard, Knoxville, TN 37916. Book reviews to: editor.

 Indexed in: Book Review Index; Current Contents: Social & Behavioral Sciences; Current Index to Journals in Education; Exceptional Child Education Abstracts; Information Science Abstracts; Library Literature; Media Review Digest; References Services Review.

The intended audience of this quarterly includes school library media specialists, audio-visual specialists, library school faculty and curriculum specialists. Its purpose is to disseminate information on theory and practice of school library media center administration and services. Regular features include SMQ News, AASL Notes, Current Research, Media Review and Idea Exchange.

 Articles are solicited directly by the editor and unsolicited manuscripts also are accepted for consideration. Simultaneous submission to other journals is permitted. Length of articles may vary from 2,000 to 5,000 words. Contributors should follow the Chicago style requirements. An editorial decision is made in six weeks and the estimated time from acceptance to publication is two to six months. Copyright is held by the publisher.

433. **THE SCHOOL MUSICIAN DIRECTOR AND TEACHER.** 1929– . School Musician, Inc., c/o F. L. McAllister, P. O. Box 245, Joliet, IL 60431. Circ.: 10,200. 10 issues/yr. $7.50/yr. Annual index: June-July issue. Editor: Forrest L. McAllister. Book reviews to: Robert Freeland, 4544 Acadia Avenue, La Mesa, CA 92041.

 Indexed in: Education Index; Media Review Digest; Music Article Guide; The Music Index.

This journal is directed toward high school and college band, orchestra, and choral directors, private instrumental teachers, and undergraduate students who are majoring in music and music education. The purpose of this publication is to assist directors in maintaining and expanding high school and college bands, orchestras and choruses. The editor is interested in inspirational and "know-how" features and clinical articles.

 Unsolicited articles as well as letters of inquiry are welcomed by the editor. Manuscripts should be approximately 1,200 words in length. The copyright is held by the publisher. Approximately two weeks is required for an editorial decision with four to twelve months elapsing between acceptance and publication. Style requirements are available upon request.

434. THE SCHOOL PSYCHOLOGY DIGEST. 1972– . The National Association of School Psychologists, 1140 Connecticut Avenue, N.W., No. 401, Washington, DC 20036. Circ.: 4,000. 4 issues/yr. $10.00/yr. No annual index. Editor: John Guidubaldi. Editor's address: 300 Education Building, Kent State University, Kent, OH 44242. Book reviews to: editor.

Indexed in: Exceptional Child Education Abstracts; Psychological Abstracts.

The intended audience includes primarily practicing school psychologists, but also school counselors and administrators. Its objective is to present theory and empirical research relating to issues in the profession. This journal combines solicited original articles and condensations of already published material in a theme oriented format.

The editor solicits most of the manuscripts from selected professionals in the field, but encourages letters of inquiry from persons who have material that may be appropriate for inclusion. Issues are dedicated to central themes and prospective contributors may learn of these topics when they write the editor. The APA style is to be followed and preferred length is 2,500 words. Three copies should be submitted. An editorial decision concerning acceptability is given in six weeks and publication follows in three months. One book review appears in each issue and it is about 500 words long. Copyright is held by the publisher.

435. SCHOOL REVIEW. 1893– . University of Chicago, Department of Education, Chicago, IL 60637. Circ.: 4,000. 4 issues/yr. $12.00/yr.; institution rate, $16.00/yr. Annual index: August issue. Editor: Benjamin D. Wright. Manuscript to: Florence Hamlish Levinsohn, Managing Editor, 5835 Kimbark Avenue, Chicago, IL 60637. Book reviews to: Donald Holsinger, book review editor.

Indexed in: College Student Personnel Abstracts; Current Contents: Social & Behavioral Sciences; Current Index to Journals in Education; Education Index; Educational Administration Abstracts; Index to Periodical Articles Related to Law; Psychological Abstracts; Social Sciences Citation Index; Sociological Abstracts; Women Studies Abstracts.

School Review publishes original research, theoretical discussion, and critical appraisal of all aspects of education and issues related to education. It is designed to appeal to scholars and practitioners whose work is concerned with education. It also publishes a regular column, Other Voices, designed to present personal essays, a column of television criticism, review symposia, and book reviews.

Unsolicited articles are accepted for consideration, but the editor also solicits material directly from experts in the field. Manuscripts of about 10,000 words following Chicago style requirements are preferred. Articles are to be submitted in duplicate with the title and author on a separate page. Copyright is held by the publisher. Estimated time for an editorial decision is twelve weeks. The lag between final acceptance, including revision and editing, and publication, is about six months. About ten book reviews are published, most of them solicited. Preferred length for these reviews is 1,250 words.

436. **SCHOOL SCIENCE AND MATHEMATICS.** (formerly **SCHOOL SCIENCE**).
1904– (SSM); 1901– (SS). School Science and Mathematics Association,
Inc., Lewis House, P.O. Box 1614, Indiana University of Pennsylvania,
Indiana, PA 15701. Circ.: 10,000. 8 issues/yr. Subscription included with
association membership; institution rate, $10.00/yr. Annual index: December
issue. Editor: George G. Mallison. Editor's address: 535 Kendall Avenue,
Kalamazoo, MI 49007. Book reviews to: editor.
   Indexed in: Current Index to Journals in Education; Education Index;
   Readers Guide to Periodical Literature; Women Studies Abstracts.
   The purpose of the journal is to introduce new ideas in methodology as related
to science and mathematics education. The intended audience includes teachers of
mathematics and science from the elementary school level through college. Regular
features are Problem Department; Book Vignettes; Math Lab Activities; Book
Reviews; and, Books and Teaching Aids Received.
   The editor accepts unsolicited manuscripts for possible inclusion in *School
Science and Mathematics*. Contributors should follow the MLA style requirements.
Preferred length of articles is 1,000 to 1,500 words and two copies are to be submitted. Copyright is held by the publisher. An editorial decision is made in about
ten weeks and the estimated time from acceptance to publication is twelve months.
Book reviews are about 250 words long and an average of four reviews appear in
each issue. In addition, an average of six shorter Book Vignettes are included in
each issue.

437. **SCHOOL SHOP.** 1941– . Prakken Publications, Inc., Box 623, 416 Longshore
Drive, Ann Arbor, MI 48107. Circ.: 45,000, controlled circulation. 10 issues/yr.
$8.00/yr. Annual index: June issue. Editor: Lawrence W. Prakken. Manuscript
to: Howard Kahn, managing editor. Book reviews to: managing editor.
   Indexed in: Current Index to Journals in Education; Education Index;
   Media Review Digest.
   This journal is directed toward those persons who have an interest in industrial, vocational and technical education, both at the high school and college level.
Its purpose is to provide significant information about materials and resources as
well as practices, methods and projects. The editor is interested in application
oriented articles.
   Unsolicited articles are accepted for consideration. The editor will provide a
style sheet upon request. Articles should be between 750 and 2,000 words in
length and follow the Chicago style. The publisher pays authors at a rate that
varies according to the content and length. The copyright is held by the publisher.
An editorial decision usually is reached in about three to six weeks with publication following for accepted manuscripts between three to nine months later.
From ten to twelve book reviews are included in each issue. The style sheet and
the editor should be consulted before submitting reviews for editorial consideration.

438. **THE SCHOOL TRUSTEE.** 1930– . The Saskatchewan School Trustees
Association, 570 Avord Tower, Regina, Saskatchewan, Canada S4P 0R7.
Circ.: 5,000. 5 issues/yr. $3.00/yr. No annual index. Submit manuscripts
to: editor. Book reviews to: editor.
   Indexed in: Canadian Education Index.

THE SCHOOL TRUSTEE (cont'd)

This magazine is the official organ of the Saskatchewan School Trustees Association. Its audience consists chiefly of elected school trustees, administrators and government officials. The purpose is to acquaint readers with issues, trends and opinions in education. Authors are asked to submit manuscripts dealing with virtually any aspect of education and educational administration.

Unsolicited manuscripts are welcomed. Articles should be approximately 1,500 words in length, written in a free journalistic style. Copyright is held by the author. No time is indicated either for an editorial decision or publication. A book review column, instituted in 1975, contains reviews of approximately 200 words in length. No other details are indicated.

439. SCHOOL WORLD. 1950– . Government of Newfoundland and Labrador, Department of Education, P. O. Box 2017, St. John's, Newfoundland AlC 5R9. Circ.: 8,000. 4 issues/yr. No charge, controlled circulation. No annual index. Editor: Kristine Penney. Editor's address: Supervisor of Information, Statistics and Publications. No book reviews.

Indexed in: Canadian Education Index.

This journal is intended for teachers and educators, primarily in Newfoundland and Labrador. It aims for an in-depth description of what is happening in the schools. *School World* attempts to report innovations in curricula, projects, and subjects of interest in subject areas. The editor is interested in project descriptions and innovations by and for teachers.

Unsolicited manuscripts of approximately 500 words are welcomed by the editor. The copyright is held by the author. Four weeks is required for an editorial decision with publication following within the publication year (ten months). An informal style of writing is preferred. Simultaneous submission to other journals is permitted.

440. SCIENCE ACTIVITIES. 1969– . HELDREF Publications, 4000 Albemarle Street, N.W., Washington, DC 20016. Circ.: 6,600. 6 issues/yr. $9.00/yr.; institution rate, $12.00/yr. No annual index. Editors: Theodore L. Stoddard and Jane Powers Weldon. Manuscript to: Jane Powers Weldon. Book reviews to: Jane Powers Weldon.

Indexed in: Current Index to Journals in Education; Media Review Digest.

The purpose of this journal is to provide activities to aid classroom instruction. The intended audience includes teachers of science in all grades from kindergarten through junior college. Articles preferred are those stressing activity as an aid to teaching. Diagrams and photographs to illustrate the ideas are encouraged.

Unsolicited manuscripts are accepted for consideration. Articles of 2,500 to 5,000 words following Chicago style requirements are preferred. Two copies should be submitted. The publisher pays authors at the rate of $10.00 per published page and retains copyright. Estimated time for an editorial decision concerning acceptability of an article is twelve to sixteen weeks. Time from acceptance to publication is six months. Book reviews of 500 words each are contained in *Science Activities*. Approximately twelve reviews appear in each issue.

441. SCIENCE AND CHILDREN. 1963– . National Science Teachers Association, 1742 Connecticut Avenue, N.W., Washington, DC 20009. Circ.: 25,000. 8 issues/yr. Subscription included with association membership; non-member rate, $12.00/yr. Annual index: May issue. Editor: Phyllis R. Marcuccio. Book reviews are written by an association committee.

> Indexed in: Current Index to Journals in Education; Education Index; Exceptional Child Education Abstracts; Media Review Digest; Women Studies Abstracts.

The intended audience of *Science and Children* includes elementary school educators and college personnel involved in teacher education in science. It also is a journal for the elementary school teacher, principal and administrator. Its purpose is to provide useful information and activities in elementary school science and to keep the elementary science educator abreast of developments, trends and innovations in the field.

The editor solicits articles for certain topics and themes, but also encourages submission of unsolicited manuscripts for possible inclusion in the journal. Style is not specified, but length should be within the range of 1,200 to 1,500 words. Estimated time for an editorial decision concerning acceptability of an article varies from two to twenty-four weeks. Time from acceptance to publication may vary from two to ten months. Copyright is held by the publisher.

442. SCIENCE EDUCATION. (formerly **GENERAL SCIENCE QUARTERLY**). 1929– (SE); 1916– (GSQ). Association for the Education of Teachers in Science. Circ.: 2,000. 4 issues/yr. $20.00/yr. Annual index: issue number four. Editor: N. E. Bingham. Editor's address: 1718 NW 10th Avenue, Gainesville, FL 32605. Book reviews to: editor.

> Indexed in: Current Index to Journals in Education; Education Index; Research into Higher Education.

The purpose of *Science Education* is to improve the teaching of general education science, to improve the quality of science education research and to aid in defining the direction of future general education science teaching. The intended audience includes general education teachers of science kindergarten through junior college, teacher educators in universities and colleges, graduate science education students and state and county supervisors concerned with the teaching of science. The journal provides articles about curricular innovations in methods, in materials and in evaluative procedures. It reflects current reactions to innovations both here and abroad.

The editor welcomes unsolicited manuscripts for possible inclusion in this journal. Two copies of articles are to be submitted and the preferred length is 1,600 words. Style is not specified. Copyright is held by the publisher. Contributors may expect an editorial decision concerning acceptance in eight weeks. If accepted, publication follows in eight months. Up to six book reviews appear in each issue. These reviews are 200 to 400 words long.

443. SCIENCE EDUCATION NEWS. 1959– . Office of Science Education, American Association for the Advancement of Science, 1776 Massachusetts Avenue, N.W., Washington, DC 20036. Circ.: 10,000. 6 issues/yr. No charge. No annual index. Editor: Orin McCarley. Manuscript to: Arthur H. Livermore. Book reviews to: Arthur H. Livermore.

SCIENCE EDUCATION NEWS (cont'd)

The intended audience of this publication includes science teachers in schools and scientists in colleges, universities, government and industry. Its purpose is to inform the readers about new trends and programs in science education and about innovations in educational programs and materials that relate science teaching to societal issues.

Two issues of *Science Education News* are dedicated to central themes and the other four include a variety of articles. Unsolicited manuscripts are accepted for consideration. The editor also solicits material directly from scientists and science educators. The Chicago style is to be followed and length should be 150 words except for central theme issues in which case the preferred length is 1,000 words. The *News* is not copyrighted. The time for an editorial decision concerning acceptance is four weeks. Publication follows in two months. The three to four book reviews in this publication are 100 to 150 words each.

444. **THE SCIENCE TEACHER.** 1933– . National Science Teachers Association, 1742 Connecticut Avenue, N.W., Washington, DC 20009. Circ.: 23,000. 9 issues/yr. Subscription included with association membership; non-member rate, $25.00/yr. Annual index: December issue. Editor: Rosemary Amidei. Book reviewers drawn from NSTA Teaching Materials Review Committee.
     Indexed in: Current Index to Journals in Education; Education Index; Exceptional Child Education Abstracts; Index to Periodical Articles Related to Law; Media Review Digest.

This journal is intended for high school science teachers and those interested in school science programs. Its purpose is to serve science teachers and to improve science programs in the schools. The editor prefers articles dealing with science teaching techniques and background science materials.

Unsolicited articles as well as letters of inquiry are welcomed by the editor. In addition, the editor also solicits material from selected science educators. A style sheet is available from the editor. Article length is approximately 1,000 words and the copyright is held by the publisher. Between four and six weeks is required for an editorial decision, with two to six months required for publication of manuscripts following acceptance.

445. **SECONDARY EDUCATION TODAY.** (formerly **MICHIGAN JOURNAL OF SECONDARY EDUCATION**). 1972– (SET); 1960– (MJSE). Michigan Association of Secondary School Principals, 401 South Fourth Street, Ann Arbor, MI 48103. Circ.: 2,500. 4 issues/yr. Subscription included with association membership; non-member rate, $10.00/yr. No annual index. Editor: Philip Cusick. Editor's address: 409 Erickson Hall, Michigan State University, East Lansing, MI 48823. Book reviews to: editor.

Intended for secondary school administrators, particularly in Michigan. Designed to provide a forum for professional dialogue among secondary school administrators. Carries articles of practical significance to practicing school administrators.

Unsolicited articles of 1,000 to 1,500 words in length are welcomed by the editor. The copyright is held by the publisher and a journalistic style is preferred. Simultaneous submission to other journals is permitted. Between four and six weeks is required for an editorial decision with approximately two months elapsing from acceptance to publication. Between one and two book reviews are used in each issue and these should be between 500 and 1,000 words in length. The only requirement regarding book reviews is that the subject matter be of interest to secondary school principals and that the book be accepted for review by the editor, therefore, a letter of inquiry is advised.

446. **SIMULATION & GAMES.** 1970– . Sage Publications, Inc., 275 South Beverly Drive, Beverly Hills, CA 90212. Circ.: not given. 4 issues/yr. $12.00/yr. for professionals; institutional rate, $20.00/yr. Annual index: issue number four. Editors: Sarane S. Boocock and Gail Fennessey, co-editors. Editor's address: Academic Games Associates, 430 East 33rd Street, Baltimore, MD 21218. Book reviews to: Steven J. Kidder, Book Review Editor, Bureau of School and Cultural Research, New York State Department of Education, Albany, NY 12224.

   Indexed in: ABC: Political Science and Government; Book Review Index to Social Science Periodicals; Computer and Control Abstracts*; Computing Review; Current Contents: Social & Behavioral Sciences; Current Index to Journals in Education; Educational Administration Abstracts; Human Resources Abstracts; International Political Science Abstracts; Media Review Digest; Psychological Abstracts; Public Affairs Information Service Bulletin; Sage Public Administration Abstracts; Sage Urban Studies Abstracts; Social Sciences Citation Index; Social Sciences Index; Sociological Abstracts.

This journal, as indicated by the title, deals with simulation, games and models, and their use in social, business, education and political fields. Articles deal with the theory, design and research of simulations and games and may be multidisciplinary. Reporting of specific applications is encouraged. Sample titles of articles and reviews from a recent issue are: A Normative Model for Marketing Planning; a Contextual Approach to Scenario Construction; and, Democracy–the Workings of the Legislative Process.

Manuscripts should be submitted in triplicate. Copies of the style sheet are available from the editor. Articles should be no longer than 7,500 words and accompanied by a 100 word abstract. Shorter pieces for the "Forum" (letters to the editor) section should not exceed 700 words. Editorial decisions are made within ten weeks following acknowledgment of receipt of manuscripts. Publication follows in four to nine months after acceptance. Submission to the "Forum" are published in the issue following receipt. Book reviews and simulation reviews are included in this journal. Copyright is held by the publisher.

447. **SLAVIC AND EAST EUROPEAN JOURNAL.** 1957– . American Association of Teachers of Slavic and East European Languages. Circ.: 2,000. 4 issues/yr. Subscription included with association membership. Annual index: winter issue. Editor: Lauren G. Leighton. Editor's address: Department of Foreign Languages and Literatures, Northern Illinois University, De Kalb, IL 60115. Book reviews to: Pierre R. Hart, Department of Germanic and Slavic Languages and Literatures, SUNY at Buffalo, Buffalo, NY 14240.

SLAVIC AND EAST EUROPEAN JOURNAL (cont'd)

Indexed in: Current Index to Journals in Education; Humanities Index; Modern Language Abstracts.

This journal is intended to reach scholars, teachers, students and those interested in the Slavic and East European languages, literatures, and cultures. Its purpose is to inform readers of original scholarly contributions and developments in the field. The editor is interested in receiving manuscripts dealing with Slavic and East European languages, literatures, and language pedagogy, as well as analytical or synthesizing studies which contain their own documentation and demonstrate a command of the basic materials of scholarship in the original languages.

Unsolicited manuscripts are welcomed by the editor. A style sheet is available. Manuscripts should be approximately 7,000 words in length. Copyright is held by the publisher (AATSEEL). The editor requires eight weeks for a decision and publication of accepted manuscripts follows in six to nine months. Each issue of this journal contains approximately twenty book reviews. Book review information is contained in the *SEEJ* style sheet. Book reviews are about 1,400 words in length.

448. SOCIAL EDUCATION. 1937— . National Council for the Social Studies, 1515 Wilson Boulevard, Arlington, VA 22209. Circ.: 22,000. 7 issues/yr. Subscription included with council membership; non-member rate, $15.00/yr. Annual index: November-December issue. Editor: Daniel Roselle. Book reviews to: editor.

Indexed in: America: History and Life*; Book Review Index; Current Contents: Social & Behavioral Sciences; Current Index to Journals in Education; Education Index; Human Resources Abstracts; Index to Periodical Articles Related to Law; Media Review Digest; Social Sciences Citation Index; Women Studies Abstracts.

This journal is the official publication of the NCSS and is intended for teachers of social studies at the elementary, secondary, college and university levels as well as curriculum developers, administrators, and others interested in the field. It serves as a medium for information exchange, commentary, and innovative viewpoints in the field of social studies. The editor is interested in manuscripts dealing with all facets of the field.

The editor welcomes unsolicited manuscripts as well as letters of inquiry. Some articles are solicited by the editor. Articles should be between 1,000 and 2,500 words in length. Two copies of manuscripts are required for editorial consideration which usually takes between two and three weeks. Some issues are dedicated to central themes. Publication of accepted manuscripts occurs between four and six months after acceptance. Approximately eight book reviews are published each issue and these are 500 words in length. Authors should follow the Chicago style for all work. Copyright in most cases is held by the publisher.

449. SOUTH CAROLINA SCHOOLS. 1949— . South Carolina Department of Education, Public Information Office, 1001 Rutledge Building, Columbia, SC 29169. Circ.: 5,000. 12 issues/yr. No charge, controlled circulation. No annual index. Editor: Rob Harper. No book reviews.

This newsletter format publication is directed toward legislators, members of the news media, school board members and state department of education personnel. Its purpose is to keep public school personnel informed of major trends and developments affecting school systems. Articles highlighting specific aspects of public education, particularly in South Carolina, are sought.

Articles between 200 and 500 words in length should be submitted to the editor for consideration. The APA style is to be followed. The copyright on accepted material is held by the publisher. An editorial decision usually is given within two weeks and publication occurs within two months. Simultaneous submission to other journals is permitted.

450. THE SOUTHERN BAPTIST EDUCATOR. (formerly **THE SOUTHERN BAPTIST NEWS AND VIEWS** and **BAPTIST EDUCATION BULLETIN**). 1947– (SBE); 1936– (SBNV); 1919– (BEB). Education Commission, Southern Baptist Convention, 460 James Robertson Parkway, Nashville, TN 37219. Circ.: 8,000. 6 issues/yr. $1.50/yr. No annual index. Editor: Ben C. Fisher. No book reviews.

Indexed in: Historical Commission of the Southern Baptist Convention.

This journal is primarily an educational publication for teachers, administrators and trustees of Baptist schools, and is also sent to selected church leaders. It is intended to serve as a forum for the exchange of ideas, Christian values, promotion, fund raising, trusteeship, curriculum development, long-range planning, student recruitment and church and denominational relations.

The editor considers unsolicited manuscripts and letters of inquiry, however, first priority is given articles prepared by Baptist college personnel. Articles should be approximatey 1,250 words in length and adhere to the Chicago style. The copyright is held by the author. Approximatey four weeks is required for an editorial decision with two months elapsing from time of acceptance to publication in most cases. Simultaneous submission to other journals is permitted.

451. THE SOUTHERN JOURNAL OF EDUCATIONAL RESEARCH. 1967– . University of Southern Mississippi, School of Education and Psychology, P.O. Box 107, Southern Station, Hattiesburg, MS 39401. Circ.: 300. 4 issues/yr. $3.00/yr. No annual index. Editor: Richard Kazelskis. No book reviews.

Indexed in: Current Index to Journals in Education; Exceptional Child Education Abstracts; Psychological Abstracts.

This journal is intended for those in the behavioral sciences. Its purpose is to communicate the results of research to its readers. The editor prefers articles dealing with experimental research in the fields of psychology and education.

Unsolicited articles are welcomed by the editor. The APA style should be followed and two copies of the manuscript are requested. Approximately eight weeks is required for an editorial decision with a time lag of twelve months between acceptance of manuscripts and their publication.

452. **THE SOUTHERN SPEECH COMMUNICATION JOURNAL.** (formerly **SOUTHERN SPEECH JOURNAL**). 1971– (SSCJ); 1935– (SSJ). Southern Speech Communication Association, Department of Speech Communication, University of Tennessee, Knoxville, TN 37916. Circ.: not given. 4 issues/yr. $10.00/yr. Annual index: summer issue. Editor: Ralph T. Eubanks. Editor's address: University of West Florida, Pensacola, FL 32504. Book reviews to: editor.

    Indexed in: America: History and Life*; Current Index to Journals in Education; dsh Abstracts.

This journal is intended for students and scholars interested in the field of speech communication. It is intended as an organ for making scholarly research reports available. The editor welcomes articles dealing with research in the field.

    Unsolicited manuscripts, between 3,000 and 4,000 words in length, are accepted for consideration. Authors should follow the MLA style requirements and submit two copies of their work. Approximately eight to ten weeks is required for an editorial decision. Publication of accepted manuscripts follows in twelve months. Between six and ten book reviews are published in each issue and these are between 500 and 1,000 words in length.

453. **SOUTHWESTERN JOURNAL OF SOCIAL EDUCATION.** 1970– . Texas Council for the Social Studies and North Texas State University. Circ.: 2,500. 2 issues/yr. Subscription included with council membership; non-member rate, $4.00/yr. No annual index. Editors: Watt L. Black and William A. Luker. Manuscript to: Watt L. Black, North Texas State University, P.O. Box 5861, Denton, TX 76203. Book reviews to: Gerald Ponder, Book Review Editor, North Texas State University, College of Education, Denton, TX 76203.

The intended audience of this journal includes anyone interested in teaching social studies. Its purpose is to bring scholarly articles to TCSS membership. Articles preferred are those dealing with classroom innovations and with various subject matter areas in social studies.

    The editor solicits articles directly from experts in the field of social studies, but also welcomes unsolicited manuscripts for consideration. The Chicago style is to be followed and length of articles may range from 2,000 to 2,500 words. Copyright is held by the publisher. An editorial decision is made in three to four weeks and the estimated time from acceptance to publication is four to eight months. Prospective book review contributors should examine recent issues of this journal for information on reviews.

454. **SOUTHWESTERN MUSICIAN.** (combined with the **TEXAS MUSIC EDUCATOR,** formerly **SOUTHWESTERN MUSICIAN NEWSLETTER**). 1954– (SM); 1936– (TME); 1915– (SMN). Texas Music Educators Association, Inc. Circ.: 6,000. 10 issues/yr. $2.50/yr. Annual index: May issue. Editor: J. F. Lenzo. Editor's address: P. O. Box 9908, Houston, TX 77015. Book reviewers chosen by editor.

This journal is the official organ of the Texas Music Educators Association and provides a forum for communication among members. The intended audience of this journal includes music educators, primarily in Texas, at all levels from

SOUTHWESTERN MUSICIAN (cont'd)

elementary schools through college. In addition, high school and college students who are prospective music educators are among its readers. Articles of a professional nature which will stimulate thought and promote action in the field of music education are sought by the editor.

Unsolicited articles are invited. These manuscripts should follow the MLA style and be between 1,200 and 1,500 words in length. Payment is made in the amounts of $25.00 to $75.00 per accepted manuscript upon publication. The copyright is held by the publisher. Approximately four weeks is required for an editorial decision with an unspecified period of time elapsing between acceptance and publication. The editor also solicits articles from authors and will answer letters of inquiry.

455. **SPECIAL CHILDREN.** 1974– . The American Association of Special Educators, 107-20 125th Street, Richmond Hill, NY 11419. Circ.: 5,000. 3 issues/yr. Subscription included with association membership; library rate, $10.00/yr. Annual index: issue number three. Editors: Louis Marpet and Joseph Prentky (co-editor). Book reviews are written by staff.

Special Children is intended primarily for parents and professionals of the handicapped. In addition, its readership includes guidance counselors and members of boards of education as well as other persons interested in the special child. Original articles concerned with the education of the special child appear in this journal. Combined with this publication is a supplementary journal entitled *The Retarded Adult*. This journal describes services and the persons who use them, and the persons who help retarded adolescents and adults.

The editor welcomes unsolicited manuscripts for possible inclusion in this publication. Duplicate copies of the articles are to be submitted and the preferred length is 1,000 to 1,500 words. Simultaneous submission to other journals is permitted. Style requirements are not specified. Estimated time for an editorial decision concerning acceptability of an article is six weeks. Publication follows in six months.

456. **SPEECH MONOGRAPHS.** 1934– . Speech Communication Association, Statler Hilton Hotel, New York, NY 10001. Circ.: not given. 4 issues/yr. $20.00/yr. Annual index: November issue. Editor: Roger E. Nebergall. Editor's address: 244 Lincoln Hall, University of Illinois, Urbana, IL 61801. No book reviews.

Indexed in: America: History and Life*; Current Contents: Social & Behavioral Sciences; Current Index to Journals in Education; dsh Abstracts; Education Index; Exceptional Child Education Abstracts; Language and Language Behavior Abstracts; Modern Language Abstracts; Psychological Abstracts; Social Sciences Citation Index.

Learned inquiries concerned with speech and related communication behaviors are published in *Speech Monographs*. Monograph-length papers are welcomed, as well as shorter reports, both theoretical and critical, and brief research notes. Articles preferred are works which substantially advance the understanding of topics associated with the field.

Unsolicited articles are accepted for consideration. The MLA style requirements are to be followed, but no set limit for length is prescribed. Three copies of the article should be submitted. Copyright is held by the publisher. Occasionally, an issue is dedicated to a central theme and prospective contributors should examine current issues for an announcement of future themes. An editorial decision is made in four to six weeks and the estimated time from acceptance to publication is ten to fourteen months.

457. SPELLING PROGRESS BULLETIN. 1961– . Phonemic Spelling Council, Education Research Laboratory, P. O. Box 8065, University of Miami, Coral Gables, FL 33124. Circ.: 200. 4 issues/yr. $3.00/yr. Ten year index (1961-70) sold separately. Editor: Newell W. Tune. Editor's address: 5448 Alcove Avenue, North Hollywood, CA 91607. Book reviews to: editor.

This newsletter type journal is directed toward teachers of reading and spelling as well as those interested in spelling reform and phonetics. Its aim is to disseminate information on how to surmount difficulties in learning and teaching reading in English, spelling difficulties, and problems concerning the reform of English spelling. The editor is interested in articles dealing with these topics, practical experiences, as well as research and problems associated with the introduction and utilization of simplified spelling.

Unsolicited manuscripts as well as letters of inquiry are welcomed by the editor. No limit is set on length of articles and style is not specified. Between four and six weeks is required for an editorial decision with publication of accepted manuscripts following within three months. Between two and three books are reviewed each issue. No length constraints are placed on reviews. Issues are dedicated to central themes as determined by the editor.

458. STUDIES IN PHILOSOPHY AND EDUCATION. 1960– . Studies in Philosophy and Education, Inc., School of Education, San Jose State University, San Jose, CA 95192. Circ.: 1,200. 4 issues/volume, irregular. $9.00/volume. No annual index. Editor: Francis T. Villemain. Book reviews to: editor.

Indexed in: Current Index to Journals in Education; Education Index; Philosopher's Index; Social Sciences Citation Index.

The intended audience of this journal includes professors of philosophy of education and educational theory. Its purpose is to contribute to inquiry in these areas of study. The editors prefer fairly technical statements in philosophy of education for publication in this journal.

Unsolicited articles are accepted for consideration, but a letter of inquiry prior to submission is encouraged. Contributors should follow the Chicago style requirements and should submit three copies of their work. Copyright is held by the publisher. Estimated time for an editorial decision concerning acceptability of an article is nine weeks. Preferred length of manuscripts and publication time after acceptance are not specified. Book review frequency and length are not indicated.

459. TEPSA JOURNAL. 1970– . Texas Elementary School Principals and Supervisors Association, 316 West 12th Street, Austin, TX 78701. Circ.: 2,500. 2 issues/yr. Subscription included with association membership; non-member rate, $2.00/yr. Annual index: fall issue. Editor: R. C. Bradley. Editor's address: 2032 Houston Place, Denton, TX 76201. Book reviews are assigned.

This journal is dedicated to improvement of the instructional and supervisory roles of the elementary school principal. All types of articles dealing with the principal at the elementary level are considered appropriate for this publication. A regular feature of *TEPSA Journal* is a column called Legal Corner.

The editor usually solicits material from various professionals. Some issues are dedicated to central themes and prospective contributors should query the editor for future topics. Article length should not exceed 2,500 words and is to be submitted in duplicate. A specific style is not indicated, but detailed practical hints for manuscript preparation may be found in the December, 1974 issue of this journal. Copyright is held by the association. An editorial decision is given in six weeks and publication of accepted pieces follows in about one month.

460. TPGA JOURNAL. 1972– . Texas Personnel and Guidance Association, E. T. Station, P. O. Box Y, Commerce, TX 75428. Circ.: 2,500. 2 issues/yr. $4.00/yr. Annual index: September issue. Editor: John Dahm. Editor's address: N. T. Station, P. O. Box 13901, Denton, TX 76203. Book reviews to: editor.

Indexed in: Current Index to Journals in Education; Psychological Abstracts.

This journal is intended for school counselors, student services personnel, counselor educators and rehabilitation counselors. Its purpose is to provide a medium for the sharing of information and the exploration of new concepts in counseling and student services. The editor is interested in articles dealing with a variety of counseling techniques and special programs as well as work on research and philosophy.

Unsolicited articles and letters of inquiry are welcomed. Manuscripts should be approximately 3,000 words in length and authors are to follow the APA style. Materials should be submitted in four copies. The copyright is held by the publisher. Approximately six weeks is required for an editorial decision with publication following acceptance in six months. Two book and/or test reviews are published in each issue and these are 300 words in length.

461. TEACHER. (formerly **GRADE TEACHER**). 1882– (GT). Macmillan Professional Magazines, Inc., One Fawcett Place, Greenwich, CT 06830. Circ.: 255,000. 9 issues/yr. $10.00/yr. No annual index. Editor: Claudia Cohl. Book reviews are assigned.

Indexed in: Book Review Index; Current Index to Journals in Education; Education Index; Exceptional Child Education Abstracts; Media Review Digest; Women Studies Abstracts.

This journal is primarily for elementary school teachers and others whose professional lives are devoted to helping young children learn. Articles that offer techniques, ideas and methods that can be put to use in the classroom are desired for publication. In addition to the inclusion of tested innovative approaches to

TEACHER (cont'd)

solving classroom instructional problems, articles dealing with the significant educational issues of today are included also.

The editor solicits material from various professionals, but also welcomes letters of inquiry and unsolicited manuscripts. The Chicago style is to be used and preferred length of articles is about 1,000 to 2,000 words. Two copies and a stamped self-addressed envelope should be submitted. Copyright is held by the publisher, who pays authors upon publication at a rate that varies. An editorial decision is given in about five weeks, but publication time for accepted pieces cannot be guaranteed.

462. **THE TEACHER (Nova Scotia).** (formerly **THE BULLETIN**). 1922– (B). Nova Scotia Teachers Union, P. O. Box 1060, Armdale, Nova Scotia, Canada B3L 4L7. Circ.: 14,500. 19 issues/yr. $6.00/yr. for Canadians; $8.00/yr. for other countries. No annual index. Editor: Les D. Walker. Book reviews to: editor.

This tabloid is intended for classroom teachers and administrators in Nova Scotia. It informs its readership of educational events, locally, provincially, nationally and internationally. Articles of immediate use to classroom teachers are preferred for this publication. Descriptions of innovative programs for all grade levels and stimulative articles on educational research are among the type found in *The Teacher*.

The editor accepts unsolicited manuscripts for consideration. A letter of inquiry prior to submission is encouraged. No specific style is indicated. Length of articles should be between 500 and 750 words. Copyright is held by the author and simultaneous submission to other journals is permitted. An editorial decision is given in two weeks and publication of accepted pieces follows in one to two months.

463. **TEACHER ADVOCATE.** 1972– . Indiana State Teachers Association, 150 West Market Street, Indianapolis, IN 46204. Circ.: 45,000. 10 issues/yr. Subscription included with association membership; associate membership rate, $5.00/yr. No annual index. Editor: Missy Babb. Book reviews to: editor.

Teacher Advocate is the official publication of the Indiana State Teachers Association. The intended audience of this tabloid is the membership of the association. Its purpose is to report on the actions and activities of the association at the state, national and local level. It reviews priorities, positions and policies of educational organizations. Articles are oriented toward current news content in Indiana, but may embrace trends ranging from political action to classroom accountability. Regular features consist of professional development, human relations, political involvement, negotiations, and educational research.

Almost all outside manuscripts are commissioned by the editor. Unsolicited articles will be considered but not many are accepted. Preferred length and style are not given. An editorial decision concerning acceptability may be expected in two weeks. Publication time varies and copyright is held by the publisher. Simultaneous submission of materials to other journals is permitted. The *Teacher Advocate* includes book reviews approximately three or four times yearly.

464. THE TEACHER EDUCATOR. (formerly **SUPERVISORS QUARTERLY**).
1971– (TE); 1965– (SQ). Teachers College, Office of Professional Laboratory
Experiences, Ball State University, Muncie, IN 47306. Circ.: 3,000. 4 issues/yr.
Complimentary, upon request. Indexed 1970 and 1975. Editor: Edwin P.
Prettyman. Editor's address: TC 813, Ball State University, Muncie, IN 47306.
Book reviews to: editor.
    Indexed in: Current Index to Journals in Education.
    This journal is designed to provide an opportunity for sharing information and
for the presentation of dynamic ideas relating to teacher education. It is intended
for persons concerned with the education of teachers. The content varies and the
articles deal with teacher education in a broad sense. It is the official organ of the
Indiana Association of Teacher Educators and is sent to all members of that association as part of their membership dues.
    Unsolicited articles are welcomed for consideration. The APA style is to be
followed. Authors are not given any length restrictions but two copies of the work
are required. Copyright is held by the publisher. An editorial decision is given in
twelve to fifteen weeks and publication time varies. Occasional book reviews are
included in this publication.

465. TEACHERS COLLEGE RECORD. 1900– . Teachers College, Columbia
University, 525 West 120th Street, New York, NY 10027. Circ.: not given.
4 issues/yr. $12.00/yr. Annual index: May issue. Editor: Frank G. Jennings.
Book reviewers chosen by editor.
    Indexed in: America: History and Life*; Book Review Index; College
    Student Personnel Abstracts; Current Index to Journals in Education;
    Education Index; Educational Administration Abstracts; Exceptional
    Child Education Abstracts; Nursing Research; Psychological Abstracts;
    Social Sciences Citation Index; Sociological Abstracts; Women Studies
    Abstracts.
    This journal is intended for an audience consisting of college presidents, deans
of graduate schools, school administrators, school psychologists, school and college
librarians, professors and teachers. Philosophical and practical articles dealing with
education and related fields are preferred for editorial consideration. The purpose
of the journal is to bring current and provocative educational information to its
readership. Regular features include: Book Reviews; The Editors Recommend; and,
Centerpieces.
    The editor solicits material directly from various persons, but also welcomes
unsolicited manuscripts. Preferred length of articles is 5,000 to 6,250 words and
authors are to follow the Chicago style requirements. Contributors should submit
two copies of the manuscript. An editorial decision is given in four weeks and the
estimated time from acceptance to publication is ten months. Copyright is held
by the publisher.

466. TEACHER'S VOICE. (formerly **MICHIGAN EDUCATION JOURNAL**).
1969– (TV); 1923– (MEJ). Michigan Education Association, 1216 Kendale
Boulevard, East Lansing, MI 48823. Circ.: 88,000. 20 issues/yr. Subscription
included with association membership; non-member rate, $4.00/yr. Annual
index: published separately. Editor: Arthur H. Rice, Jr. Manuscript to:
Elwood W. Landis, managing editor. No book reviews.

This tabloid is designed to support and advance the goals and objectives of the Michigan Education Association. It also reports news of significance to teachers with regard to their practice of classroom teaching and to their rights, responsibilities and welfare. Articles of current activity and interest are desired for *Teacher's Voice.* Research material is acceptable also, but only the findings and conclusions, not the tables of data and detailed explanations of how the research was done.

Unsolicited manuscripts are accepted for consideration. A letter of inquiry prior to submission is recommended. The editor also urges prospective contributors to examine copies of the tabloid to determine suitability of the article to be submitted. Lively style, utilizing plain English and avoiding educational jargon, is preferred. Length should be brief, not to exceed 1,500 words. An editorial decision concerning acceptability normally is given in one week and publication follows in one month. Authors are encouraged to obtain the one page summary of manuscript information which is available from *Teacher's Voice.*

467. **TEACHING EXCEPTIONAL CHILDREN.** 1968– . The Council for Exceptional Children, 1920 Association Drive, Reston, VA 22091. Circ.: 70,000. 4 issues/yr. $7.50/yr. Annual index: summer issue. Editor: June B. Jordan. No book reviews.
    Indexed in: Child Development Abstracts and Bibliography; Current Index to Journals in Education; dsh Abstracts; Education Index; Exceptional Child Education Abstracts; Rehabilitation Literature.

The major objective of *Teaching Exceptional Children* is to disseminate practical and timely information to classroom teachers working with exceptional children and youth. The journal features articles which deal with instructional methods and materials designed for use with handicapped and gifted children.

Authors are urged to submit manuscripts with the understanding that the piece has not been previously published, or is not under consideration by some other publisher. Length of articles is open. The APA style should be followed and the copyright is held by the publisher. Twelve weeks is required for an editorial decision with publication following within four months of acceptance. A style sheet is available upon request from the editor.

468. **TEACHING POLITICAL SCIENCE.** 1974– . Sage Publications, Inc., 275 South Beverly Drive, Beverly Hills, CA 90212. Circ.: not given. 4 issues/yr. $12.00/yr.; institutional rate, $20.00/yr. Annual index: issue number four. Editor: Samuel Krislov. Editor's address: Department of Political Science, University of Minnesota, 1414 Social Science Building, Minneapolis, MN 55455. Book reviews to: Lee Anderson, Book Review Co-Editor, Department of Political Science, Northwestern University, Evanston, IL 60201.
    Indexed in: ABC: Political Science and Government; Current Contents: Social & Behavioral Sciences; Current Index to Journals in Education; Human Resources Abstracts; International Political Science Abstracts; Sage Urban Studies Abstracts; Social Sciences Citation Index.

The intended audience of this journal primarily includes those persons directly engaged in teaching Political Science. The editor seeks articles which provide practical applications of teaching principles to the discipline. In addition, articles dealing

TEACHING POLITICAL SCIENCE (cont'd)

with empirical research findings, as well as other types of reports, are welcomed for editorial consideration.

Authors should submit manuscripts in two copies. The length of articles should be between 6,000 and 8,000 words. The editors also are interested in brief reports, between 750 and 1,000 words, of class projects and demonstrations dealing with the issues in political science. A copy of the style sheet may be obtained from the editor. The copyright is held by the publisher. This journal will publish reviews of books, games, simulations, and innovative textbooks. Potential reviewers should correspond with the book review editor before submitting the manuscript. Times for editorial decision and publication are not indicated.

469. **TEACHING SOCIOLOGY.** 1973– . Sage Publications, Inc., 275 South Beverly Drive, Beverly Hills, CA 90212. Circ.: not given. 3 issues/yr. $10.00/yr. for professionals; institutional rate, $18.00/yr. Annual index: last issue of each volume. Editors: Richard J. Gelles and Murray A. Straus. Editor's address: Department of Sociology, University of Rhode Island, Kingston, RI 02881. Book reviews to: Craig B. Little, Book Review Editor, Department of Sociology-Anthropology, State University of New York, Cortland, NY 13045.

Indexed in: Current Contents: Social & Behavioral Sciences; Current Index to Journals in Education; Human Resources Abstracts; Sage Urban Studies Abstracts; Social Sciences Citation Index; Sociological Abstracts.

The overall objective of this journal is to contribute to the recognition of the teaching function as an important part of the academic profession. *Teaching Sociology* seeks empirical research articles, reports, and essays which emphasize teaching with direct application to the subject matter of sociology.

Manuscripts should be submitted in triplicate. Articles should not exceed 6,000 to 8,000 words in length. The editors are also interested in brief reports, 750 to 1,000 words, of class projects and demonstrations which enable students to examine issues in sociology. A copy of the style sheet may be obtained upon request from the editors. The copyright is held by the publisher. Book reviews may be by either students or teachers. They usually should have used the book being reviewed, and preference is given to recently published books. Potential contributors should correspond with the book review editor about book review requirements before submitting the manuscript. Times for an editorial decision and publication are not indicated.

470. **TECHNICAL EDUCATION NEWS.** 1941– . Gregg Division, McGraw-Hill Book Company, 1221 Avenue of the Americas, New York, NY 10020. Circ.: 50,000. Periodically through school year. No charge, controlled circulation. No annual index. Editor: Susan S. Schrumpf. No book reviews.

This publication is distributed without charge to technical and occupational teachers, teacher educators and administrators. It provides technical and occupational information to its intended readership. Articles preferred for inclusion are those describing innovative technical and occupational programs and related methodology. Manuscripts may deal with secondary and postsecondary levels.

TECHNICAL EDUCATION NEWS (cont'd)

The editor accepts unsolicited articles for consideration. A letter of inquiry prior to submission is recommended. Length should be 1,600 to 2,500 words and the work is to be submitted in duplicate. Preferred style is not given. Copyright is held by the publisher, who pays authors a modest honorarium for their material. Estimated time for an editorial decision is six to eight weeks. Publication time for accepted pieces varies from six to twelve months.

471. **TENNESSEE TEACHER.** 1934– . Tennessee Education Association, 598 James Robertson Parkway, Nashville, TN 37219. Circ.: 58,200. 10 issues/yr. Subscription included with association membership; non-member rate, $1.50/yr. No annual index. Editor: Sara S. Nolan. Unsolicited book reviews not accepted.

This journal is designed primarily for the association membership, which includes teachers and administrators of Tennessee schools, kindergarten through higher education. It keeps the readers informed about educational practices and developments that affect the quality of education in Tennessee and that affect teacher welfare. Articles preferred for inclusion are simple, straight-forward accounts of educational accomplishments or experiments. Most of the journal is devoted to information closely related to Tennessee schools.

The editor solicits some material directly from various professionals. Only rarely are unsolicited articles from non-members accepted for publication. Length of manuscripts is to be less than 750 words and authors should follow MLA style requirements. Copyright is held by the publisher. Times for an editorial decision and publication vary.

472. **TEXAS OUTLOOK.** 1917– . Texas State Teachers Association, 316 West 12th Street, Austin, TX 78701. Circ.: 164,500. 12 issues/yr. Subscription included with association membership; non-member rate, $4.00/yr. Annual index: December issue. Editor-in-Chief: Callie W. Smith. Managing Editor: Traxel Stevens. Book reviews not given.

Texas Outlook is the official organ of the Texas State Teachers Association and is designed to promote the progress of education in Texas, to inform membership, and to serve as an intra-profession communications link in the state. Among the regular features are Letters to the Editor, Idea Swap Shop, Questions and Answers, TSTA and NEA news, and news of 43 state affiliates. Those persons eligible for TSTA membership may receive this journal only through membership.

Unsolicited manuscripts are accepted for consideration, but those from outside Texas are not encouraged. Writers should submit articles of approximately 1,200 words and the original is to be sent. Copyright is held by the publisher. Specific style requirements may be obtained from the editor. The estimated time for an editorial decision concerning acceptability is eight weeks. The time for publication varies.

473. **THEORY INTO PRACTICE.** 1962– . The Ohio State University, College of Education. Circ.: not given. 5 issues/yr. $5.00/yr. Annual index: December issue. Editor: Charles M. Galloway. Manuscript to: Yvette Cox,

THEORY INTO PRACTICE (cont'd)

Associate Editor, 116 Ramseyer Hall, 29 West Woodruff Avenue, Columbus, OH 43210. No book reviews.

Indexed in: Current Contents: Social & Behavioral Sciences; Current Index to Journals in Education; Education Index; Educational Administration Abstracts; Psychological Abstracts; Sociological Abstracts.

Theory Into Practice is intended for teachers, administrators and other educators. This journal adheres to the belief that educational theory and practice are strongly related. Each issue focuses on a single topic of interest to those in education and attempts to provide thorough coverage of that topic. Recent themes were: Special Education; The Education of Teacher Educators; Reading in the Secondary School; The Student as Person—A Vision Explored; and, Moral Education.

Because of the single topic format, most articles are solicited directly from various professionals. The editor will answer inquiries concerning future topics and will consider unsolicited manuscripts. Style and length requirements are not specified. Copyright is held by the publisher. Simultaneous submission to other journals is permitted. The time for an editorial decision concerning acceptability varies. Publication of accepted work usually occurs in twelve months.

474. **THIS MAGAZINE.** (formerly **THIS MAGAZINE IS ABOUT SCHOOLS**). 1973– (TM); 1966– (TMS). The Red Maple Company Limited. Circ.: 7,000. 6 issues/yr. $4.00/yr. for Canadians. No annual index. Submit manuscripts to: managing editor. Editor's address: 56 Esplanade Street East, Fourth floor, Toronto 1, Ontario, Canada. Book reviews to: managing editor.

Indexed in: Alternative Press Index; Canadian Education Index; Women Studies Abstracts.

This publication is intended for teachers, cultural workers, and political organizers. It emphasizes teaching and schools, but also includes important issues as related to culture and politics. *This Magazine* serves to bring together Canadians in different fields, such as labor, teaching, the arts, and the universities, and gives them a view of the struggles and goals of each of the others. Popular analytic articles on education, culture and politics are desired for inclusion in this publication.

The editor solicits material directly from various persons, but also welcomes letters of inquiry and unsolicited manuscripts. The MLA style is to be followed and the length may vary from 2,000 to 4,000 words. Copyright is held by the author. Simultaneous submission to other journals is permitted. An editorial decision is given in six weeks and publication of accepted pieces follows in two to four months. One to three book reviews appear in each issue. Length is the same as for articles.

475. **THRUST.** (formerly **JOURNAL OF SECONDARY EDUCATION**). 1971– (T). Association of California School Administrators, 1575 Old Bayshore Highway, Burlingame, CA 94010. Circ.: 16,000. 5 issues/yr. $10.00/yr. No annual index. Editor: Arthur N. Thayer. No book reviews.

Indexed in: Current Contents: Social & Behavioral Sciences; Current Index to Journals in Education; Exceptional Child Education Abstracts; Social Sciences Citation Index.

THRUST (cont'd)

This journal strives to present a balance of theory and "how to" information on topics of administrative concern. It is intended primarily for school administrators and support staff. Each issue of this journal is dedicated to a central theme. Recent topics were: The Humanization of Education—The Person and Process; Perspective on Management Approaches; Education is Changing Rapidly; Kaleidoscope on Educational Administration; and, Looking Towards the Future.

The editor solicits some material for *Thrust* directly from various professionals, but also accepts unsolicited manuscripts for consideration. Article length should be 2,500 words. Preferred style is not indicated. Simultaneous submission to other journals is permitted. An editorial decision is given in four to six weeks and publication of accepted pieces follows in six months. Copyright is held by the publisher.

476. TIPS AND TOPICS. 1960– . College of Home Economics, Texas Tech University, P. O. Box 4170, Lubbock, TX 79409. Circ.: 4,500. 4 issues/yr. $3.00/yr. No annual index. Editor: Julie Mapes Wilgen. No book reviews.

Tips and Topics is intended for home economics teachers and supervisors, home demonstration agents, home economists in business, college students and curriculum directors. It disseminates ideas and information relating to trends, issues, curriculum and research in home economics. It provides pre-service and in-service education for those who teach any phase of home economics. Articles which relate success stories of teachers and others involved in any area of home economics education are desired for publication.

The editor solicits some material directly from various persons, but also welcomes letters of inquiry and unsolicited manuscripts. The Chicago style is to be followed. In-house variations to that style are made by the editor. Maximum length is 1,500 words and two copies should be sent. This publication is not copyrighted. Each issue focuses on various aspects of one main theme, and prospective contributors should query the editor for future topics. Simultaneous submission to other journals is permitted. An editorial decision concerning acceptability is given in three to six weeks and publication follows in three to four months.

477. TODAY'S CATHOLIC TEACHER. (formerly **MESSENGER TEACHER'S GUIDE).** 1967– (TCT); 1938– (MTG). Peter Li, Inc., 2451 East River Road, Dayton, OH 45439. Circ.: 70,000, controlled. 8 issues/yr. $6.00/yr. No annual index. Editor: Ruth A. Matheny. Book reviews are written by staff.
Indexed in: The Catholic Periodical and Literature Index; Media Review Digest.

This journal is intended for Catholic educators and others concerned with non-public schools. Its purpose is to assist educators professionally and personally through interpretative, expository, and descriptive articles on all facets of education and to serve as a sounding board for non-public education. Articles preferred for this journal are those dealing with the philosophy and practice of education as it relates specifically to Catholic and other non-public schools. Columns that appear as regular features include material on child guidance, religious education, physical education, audio-visuals, books, new products and other items.

The editor solicits material from various professionals, but also welcomes letters of inquiry and unsolicited manuscripts. Length of articles may vary from

TODAY'S CATHOLIC TEACHER (cont'd)

1,200 to 2,000 words and style should follow that of *Words into Type*. Copyright is held by the author, with publisher's permission to reprint. The publisher pays authors at a rate that varies from $15.00 to $75.00 per article. Each issue carries a particular curricular orientation, although materials of general and other specialized interest may be included. Prospective contributors should query the editor for future topics. An editorial decision is given in six weeks and publication of accepted pieces follows in two months.

478. **TODAY'S EDUCATION.** (formerly **NEA JOURNAL** and **NEA BULLETIN**). 1913– . National Education Association, 1201 Sixteenth Street, N.W., Washington, DC 20036. Circ.: 1,875,000. 4 issues/yr. Subscription included with association membership; library rate, $7.00/yr. Annual index: separately. Editor: Walter A. Graves, Executive Editor. Book reviews to: executive editor.
Indexed in: Business Education Index; College Student Personnel Abstracts; Current Index to Journals in Education; Education Index; Guide to Social Science and Religion in Periodical Literature; Index to Periodical Articles Related to Law; Media Review Digest; Readers Guide to Periodical Literature; Sociology of Education Abstracts.

This journal is the official organ of the National Education Association. Its audience consists chiefly of in-service public school teachers, however, it also is used by school administrators, college personnel, and those interested in education. The purpose of this journal is to acquaint teachers with current trends and issues in the profession. Many articles have direct relationship to innovative classroom practices and are designed to appeal to the in-service teacher.

Authors are encouraged to submit manuscripts dealing with successful school practices. Style is journalistic and free, conforming to magazine article format. Special requirements are available from the editor. The preferred length of articles is 1,500 to 2,500 words. Estimated time for an editorial decision is six weeks, with a time gap of three months required for publication after acceptance. Four book reviews appear in each issue of this journal. These reviews are approximately 300 words in length. Copyright is held by the publisher.

479. **TOP OF THE NEWS.** 1942– . Children's Services Division and the Young Adult Services Division of ALA, 50 East Huron Street, Chicago, IL 60611. Circ.: 11,500. 4 issues/yr. Subscription included with division membership; non-member rate, $15.00/yr. Annual index: November issue. Editors: Caroline Coughlin and Shirley Fitzgibbons. Book reviews to: editors.
Indexed in: Book Review Index; Library and Information Science Abstracts; Library Literature.

The intended audience includes librarians of materials for children and young adults. Also included are library school students and faculty, and teachers of courses related to children and young adult materials. *Top of the News* serves as a means of communication for its readers and as a forum for discussions of important issues for all persons concerned with providing quality library service to children and young adults.

The editors sometimes solicit material directly from various specialists, but also welcomes letters of inquiry and unsolicited manuscripts. The Chicago style is to be followed and preferred length is not specified. Copyright details should be arranged with the editors. Some issues are dedicated to central themes but in these cases a guest editor usually is appointed and articles are solicited. Simultaneous submission to other journals is permitted. An editorial decision is given in twelve weeks and publication of accepted pieces follows in four to eight months. Four to five book reviews of professional materials for librarians who work with children and young adults are included in this journal. These reviews are 150 to 500 words each.

480. **TRANSACTIONAL ANALYSIS JOURNAL.** (formerly **TRANSACTIONAL ANALYSIS BULLETIN**). 1971– (TAJ); 1962– (TAB). The International Transactional Analysis Association, Inc., 1722 Vallejo Street, San Francisco, CA 94123. Circ.: 12,500. 4 issues/yr. $15.00/yr. Annual index: January issue. Editor: Stephen B. Karpman. No book reviews.

Indexed in: Cumulative Index to Nursing Literature; Speed.

This journal is intended for transactional analysis clinicians and educators. Its purpose is to advance transactional analysis theory and application. Articles included in this journal deal with theory and research, clinic applications, and societal applications of transactional analysis.

Unsolicited manuscripts are accepted for consideration. The Chicago style is to be followed and length should not exceed 2,500 words. Five copies are to be submitted. Copyright is held jointly by the author and the International Transactional Analysis Association. Issues often are dedicated to central themes and these are announced in the journal. Estimated time for an editorial decision varies from four to twelve weeks. If accepted, publication follows in three to twelve months.

481. **TRANSESCENCE.** 1973– . Educational Leadership Institute, P. O. Box 863, Springfield, MA 01101. Circ.: 500. 1 issue/yr. $2.25/yr. No annual index. Editors: Conrad F. Toepfer, Jr. and Philip Pumerantz. No book reviews.

This journal is intended for educators and others concerned with the education of the emerging adolescent learner. It serves as a means for the promotion of the thinking and educational practices in the middle school movement. Practical and useful articles relating to the middle school are desired for inclusion in *Transescence*.

The editors solicit material from selected professionals in this area of study, but also welcome unsolicited manuscripts and letters of inquiry. No specific style is required. Length should be about 2,000 words and copyright on accepted articles is held by the publisher. Issues are dedicated to central themes and these topics may be obtained from the editors. An editorial decision concerning acceptability is given in twelve weeks and publication normally follows in six months.

482. **TRIAD.** 1933– . Ohio Music Education Association. Circ.: 5,000. 6 issues/yr. Subscription included with association membership; non-member rate, $4.00/yr. No annual index. Editor: Richard Froton. Editor's address: 3969 East Mound Street, Columbus, Ohio 43227. No book reviews.

TRIAD (cont'd)

The intended audience of *Triad* includes the association membership and others interested in music and the activities of the association. Its purpose is to inform its readership of the ongoing functions of the Ohio Music Education Association. Articles related to band, orchestra and chorus, and "how to" articles dealing with general music at all educational levels are preferred for publication.

Unsolicited manuscripts are accepted for consideration. A letter of inquiry prior to submission is encouraged. Length of articles should be 1,250 to 1,500 words. Preferred style is not given. Two copies of the work are required. Some issues are dedicated to central themes and prospective contributors should query the editor for future topics. Copyright is held by the publisher. Simultaneous submission to other journals is permitted. An editorial decision concerning acceptability of an article is given in two weeks. Publication time varies.

483. **THE UNITED TEACHER.** (formerly **FLORIDA EDUCATION, THE JOURNAL OF THE FLORIDA EDUCATION ASSOCIATION, FLORIDA SCHOOL JOURNAL, FLORIDA SCHOOL ROOM, FLORIDA SCHOOL EXPONENT,** and **FLORIDA SCHOOL JOURNAL**). 1973– (UT); circa 1955– (FE); 1923– (JFEA); 1919– (FSJ); 1914– (FSR); 1894– (FSE); 1887– (FSJ). The Florida Education Association/United, 208 West Pensacola Street, Tallahassee, FL 32304. Circ.: 60,000. 18 issues/yr. Subscription included with association membership; non-member rate, $5.00/yr. No annual index. Editor: Peter Boespflug. Book reviews to: editor.

This tabloid is intended primarily for Florida's classroom teachers, but also is distributed to many school board members, administrators, legislators, and other education and government officials. It strives to keep teachers and policy makers informed about union activities and various issues of importance to teachers.

Unsolicited articles are welcomed by the editor. Approximate length should be 1,500 words and copyright is held by the author. Preferred style is not specified. Simultaneous submission to other journals is permitted. Estimated time for an editorial decision is two to four weeks. If accepted, publication follows in one to two months.

484. **UNIVERSITY AFFAIRS/AFFAIRES UNIVERSITAIRES.** 1959– . Association of Universities and Colleges of Canada, 151 Slater Street, Ottawa, Ontario, Canada K1P 5N1. Circ.: 38,300. 10 issues/yr. $7.00/yr. No annual index. Editor: Gloria Pierre. Book reviews to: editor.
Indexed in: Canadian Education Index; Research into Higher Education.

This tabloid is intended primarily for the Canadian university community. The major portion of the publication is devoted to an academic and administrative vacancies section. Articles preferred for inclusion may be any type relating to the university community.

Letters of inquiry regarding article suitability are welcomed by the editor. Sometimes unsolicited pieces are accepted for publication. Copyright is held by the publisher. Style and length requirements are not specified. An editorial decision concerning acceptability of material is given in four weeks and publication follows in two months. The number of book reviews in each issue varies. The publisher pays authors at a rate that is determined upon acceptance of the article.

485. THE UNIVERSITY OF SOUTH CAROLINA EDUCATION REPORT.

1957– . College of Education, University of South Carolina, Columbia, SC 29208. Circ.: 3,700. 6 issues/yr. No charge, controlled circulation. No annual index. Editor: William W. Savage. No book reviews.

This publication, usually four pages in length, is intended primarily for teachers and school administrators. Also among its readership are college and university faculty members and staff members of state departments of education in South Carolina and other states. The editor strives to publish articles that report research findings of interest and value to school personnel. Also included are those that raise questions or present issues that should be analyzed and considered by school personnel and by those who train such personnel. Activities of the sponsoring school are reported also.

Unsolicited articles are accepted for consideration. A letter of inquiry prior to submission is encouraged. The Chicago style is to be used and the preferred length is 1,250 words. Copyright on accepted material is held by the author. An editorial decision is given in two weeks and publication follows in two to four months.

486. DIE UNTERRICHTSPRAXIS. 1968– . American Association of Teachers

of German, 339 Walnut Street, Philadelphia, PA 19106. Circ.: 10,000. 2 issues/yr. Subscription included with association membership; non-member rate, $6.00/yr. Annual index: spring issue. Editor: Gerhard H. Weiss. Editor's address: Department of German, University of Minnesota, Minneapolis, MN 55455. Book reviews to: editor.
Indexed in: Current Index to Journals in Education; Modern Language Abstracts; MLA International Bibliography.

The primary focus of this journal is the improvement and promotion of the teaching of German on all levels. Articles found in this publication include: practical hints for teaching; "how to" articles on teaching grammar, literature, culture and linguistics; state of the profession (undergraduate German major and graduate programs); and, reviews of textbooks. Members of the association receive this journal and *German Quarterly* for their dues.

Unsolicited manuscripts are welcomed for consideration. Articles must conform with MLA style requirements and authors should consult a current issue of *Die Unterrichtspraxis* for its particular format. Three copies of articles are to be submitted. The length may vary from 2,500 to 3,750 words. Copyright is held by the AATG; both author and journal must be contacted for permission to reprint articles. An editorial decision is made in twenty-four weeks and publication follows in approximately twelve months. Twenty book reviews appear in this journal, each about 250 words. A sheet of information for contributors is available from the editor.

487. URBAN EDUCATION. 1966– . Sage Publications, Inc., 275 South Beverly
Drive, Beverly Hills, CA 92012. Circ.: not given. 4 issues/yr. $12.00/yr. for
professionals; institutional rate, $20.00/yr. Annual index: issue number
four. Editor: Warren Button. Editor's address: Department of Social
Foundations of Education, State Department of New York at Buffalo,
Buffalo, NY 14214. Book reviews to: editor.

Indexed in: Black Information Index; Current Contents; Social &
Behavioral Sciences; Current Index to Journals in Education; Education
Index; Educational Administration Abstracts; Human Resources Abstracts;
Sage Public Administration Abstracts; Sage Urban Studies Abstracts;
Social Sciences Citation Index; Sociological Abstracts; Sociology of
Education Abstracts; Urban Affairs Abstracts.

Urban Education presents theoretical and research articles dealing with one
of the major concerns of our time, the quality of urban education. This journal
strives to keep its readership abreast of the changing patterns, influences, and
pressures which affect this societal agency. Sample article titles from a recent issue
are: Compensatory Education–The Underlying Stances and Teachers' Attitudes;
School Climate in White and Black Elementary Schools–A Comparative Study;
and, Out of Work, Out of School.

Unsolicited manuscripts and book reviews should be submitted in duplicate
to the editor. Articles should not exceed 5,000 words. Copies of the style sheet
are available from the editor upon request. Review essays and bibliographic articles and compilations are sought. Potential contributors of such material should
correspond with the editor prior to submission. The copyright is held by the
publisher. Times for an editorial decision and publication are not specified.

488. THE URBAN REVIEW. 1966– (independently quarterly since 1974).
Agathon Press, Inc., 150 Fifth Avenue, New York, NY 10011. Circ.: not
given. 4 issues (one volume)/yr. $12.00/volume; institution rate,
$18.00/volume. No annual index. Editor: Arthur Tobier. Editor's add-
ress: 128 East 10th Street, New York, NY 10003. Book reviews to:
editor.

Indexed in: America: History and Life*; Current Index to Journals
in Education; dsh Abstracts; Education Index; Educational
Administration Abstracts; Human Resources Abstracts; Sage
Public Administration Abstracts; Women Studies Abstracts.

The intended audience of this journal includes teachers, teachers of teachers, and those in educational research who are interested in how their research is
applied. It will be of interest also to those involved or concerned in the making of
public policy as it affects education. Its purpose is to further research, inform
practitioners, and affect public policy in education. The general concern of the
journal is learning. Articles reflect what is being learned about learning, and how
that knowledge is being applied in the world.

The editor solicits material directly from selected professionals. The length
of articles is 2,000 to 4,000 words and no specific style is required. Copyright is
held by the publisher unless otherwise stipulated. Simultaneous submission to
other journals is permitted. An editorial decision regarding acceptability for inclusion in this journal is given in four weeks. The estimated time for publication is
three to six months. Only occasionally are book reviews a part of *The Urban Review*.

489. VSSDA NEWSLETTER. 1961– . Vermont State School Directors
Association, P. O. Box 339, 62 State Street, Montpelier, VT 05602.
Circ.: 1,400. 12 issues/yr. No charge, controlled circulation. No annual
index. Editor: Charles B. Nichols, Jr. No book reviews.

The *VSSDA Newsletter* is written for school board members and administrators and its primary purpose is to inform these persons of various activities related
to schools. Articles about day-to-day school board business are common in this
journal. Others noted in several copies of the mimeographed newsletter include
business of the VSSDA Executive Committee, summaries of Vermont state legislative action, and reports on various administrative and school board national
meetings.

The majority of the articles in this newsletter have been written or compiled
by the editor, but entries from others appear also. Articles are solicited from various
persons, and unsolicited articles are accepted for consideration. Most articles are
about 250 words in length. A specific style is not indicated. The estimated time
for an editorial decision is two weeks and the time from acceptance to publication
is one month. Copyright information is not given.

490. VIEWPOINTS. (formerly **BULLETIN OF THE SCHOOL OF EDUCATION,
INDIANA UNIVERSITY**). 1970– (V); 1924– (BSEIU). School of Education,
Indiana University, Bloomington, IN 47401. Circ.: 1,100. 6 issues/yr. $8.00/yr.
Annual index: November issue, supplement. Editor: D. J. Taylor. No book
reviews.

    Indexed in: Current Index to Journals in Education; Education Index;
    Employment Relations Abstracts*; Hospital Literature Index;
    Psychological Abstracts.

The intended audience of this journal includes those educators who wish to
supplement their knowledge in areas of study other than their own. A theme
approach is utilized in this journal, and prospective contributors may write the
editor for future topics. Examples of themes followed are: Common Themes in
Administrative Concepts and Practices: an Interdisciplinary Approach; From
Zero to Steinbeck–a Study of Children's Composition; and, Innovative Field
Based Teacher Education–Nine Variations on a Theme.

Articles for publication are usually solicited by the editor although sometimes unsolicited articles are accepted for consideration. A letter of inquiry prior
to submission is encouraged. The length varies dependent upon the topic, and
authors should write the editor for information concerning style requirements.
Copyright is held by the publisher. An editorial decision concerning acceptability
of an article is four weeks. The time from acceptance to publication varies greatly.

491. VIRGINIA JOURNAL OF EDUCATION. 1907– . Virginia Education Associa-
tion, 116 South Third Street, Richmond, VA 23219. Circ.: 49,000. 9 issues/yr.
Subscription included with association membership; non-member rate, $6.00/yr.
Annual index: separately. Editor: Joseph W. Bland, Jr. No book reviews.

This journal is intended primarily for educators in the state of Virginia. Its
purpose is to provide information about the association and education, especially
projects of this state. Short, readable articles on education trends and happenings
that will affect Virginia or will take place in Virginia are preferred for this journal.

Unsolicited manuscripts are accepted for consideration. A letter of inquiry prior to submission is recommended. The editor indicates that no specific style is required and no length limitations are imposed upon authors. Copyright is held by the publisher. Simultaneous submission to other journals is permitted. The length of time for an editorial decision varies and estimated time for publication of accepted pieces is three to six months.

492. **THE VOCATIONAL GUIDANCE QUARTERLY.** 1952– . National Vocational Guidance Association, c/o American Personnel and Guidance Association, 1607 New Hampshire Avenue, N.W., Washington, DC 20009. Circ.: 15,000. 4 issues/yr. Subscription included with association membership; non-member rate, $10.00/yr. Annual index: June issue. Editor: Daniel Sinick. Manuscript to: George Washington University, Washington, DC 20006. No book reviews.

Indexed in: Abstracts for Social Workers; CIRF Abstracts; College Student Personnel Abstracts; Current Contents: Social & Behavioral Sciences; Current Index to Journals in Education; Education Index; Media Review Digest; Nursing Research; Psychological Abstracts; Rehabilitation Literature; Social Sciences Citation Index; Social Sciences Index; Sociology of Education Index.

This journal is intended for professionals interested in vocational guidance. Its purpose ultimately is to improve vocational guidance services. It is a professional journal basically concerned with the role of work in people's lives. Manuscripts are invited dealing with such topics as vocational planning, vocational development, occupational choice, preparation for occupations, labor market dynamics, job finding, and job satisfaction. Regular features of the journal are: Letters to the Editor; Current Career Films; Current Career Literature; and, Editorial.

The editor welcomes unsolicited manuscripts. Contributors should submit articles of between 2,000 and 3,000 words, using the APA style. Three copies of the work are required. An editorial decision may be expected in eight to ten weeks and the estimated time from acceptance to publication varies from four to seven months. Copyright on all material is held by the publisher. A summary of information for authors appears in each issue of this journal.

493. **THE VOLTA REVIEW.** 1899– . Alexander Graham Bell Association for the Deaf, Inc., 3417 Volta Place, N.W., Washington, DC 20007. Circ.: 7,000. 6 issues/yr. Subscription included with association membership; institution rate, $25.00/yr. Annual index: December issue. Editor: George W. Fellendorf. Manuscript to: Judith Kidd, assistant editor. Book reviews to: assistant editor.

Indexed in: Current Contents: Social & Behavioral Sciences; Current Index to Journals in Education; dsh Abstracts; Education Index; Exceptional Child Education Abstracts; Language and Language Behavior Abstracts; Psychological Abstracts; Rehabilitation Literature.

Educators of the hearing impaired, parents of hearing impaired children, and hearing impaired persons are among the intended audience of this journal. *The*

Volta Review provides up-to-date information on education of the hearing impaired, particularly information to enable parents and educators to teach deaf persons to communicate and participate with the whole of society. Articles preferred for this journal are those dealing with innovative programs and/or techniques, experiences of hearing impaired persons, research on communicative sciences, teacher preparation techniques, and current legislative trends.

Unsolicited manuscripts are welcomed for consideration. Length may vary from 2,400 to 4,000 words and three copies are to be sent. A specific style is not given but a two page summary of manuscript information for prospective contributors is available from the editor. Copyright is held by the publisher. Issues sometimes are dedicated to central themes and these are announced in the journal, or interested persons may query the editor for future topics. Estimated time for an editorial decision is eight to twelve weeks and publication of accepted pieces follows in two to six months. Two to three book reviews are in each issue. These reviews are 200 to 350 words in length.

494. WESTERN CAROLINA UNIVERSITY JOURNAL OF EDUCATION.

1969– . School of Education and Psychology and Mu Eta Chapter of Kappa Delta Pi, Western Carolina University, Cullowhee, NC 28723. Circ.: 300. 3 issues/yr. $4.00/yr. No annual index. Editor: Lewis E. Cloud. Book reviews to: editor.

Indexed in: Current Index to Journals in Education; Psychological Abstracts.

The intended audience of this journal includes public school teachers, junior college and technical school personnel, and college and university professors and libraries. Its purpose is to provide quality educational articles which are of interest and benefit to educators. Articles may be on any subject that deals with educational problems, needs or ideas.

Unsolicited manuscripts are welcomed for consideration. Authors should adhere to the Chicago style requirements and are to submit two copies of their work. Length may vary from 1,000 to 5,000 words. Copyright is held by the author. An editorial decision is given in two to three weeks and publication of accepted articles follows in three to five months. Book reviews are included in this journal in varying numbers. Preferred length of reviews is 750 to 1,000 words.

495. WESTERN SPEECH COMMUNICATION. (formerly WESTERN SPEECH).

1975– (WSC); 1937– (WS). Western Speech Communication Association. Circ.: 2,700. 4 issues/yr. Subscription included with association membership; library rate, $9.00/yr. Annual index: issue number four. Editor: Glen E. Mills. Editor's address: Department of Speech, University of California, Santa Barbara, CA 93106. Book reviews to: editor.

Indexed in: Abstracts in Anthropology; America: History and Life*; Current Index to Journals in Education; dsh Abstracts.

Western Speech Communication is the official organ of the Western Speech Communication Association. The journal represents a sharing of research and professional thinking in the field. In addition to receiving articles from university professors, the editor encourages papers from elementary, secondary, and community college people. Articles are welcome also from persons in the several fields of interest such as speech and hearing science, theatre, and mass media. A revised editorial policy appears in the Spring, 1974 issue.

Unsolicited articles are accepted for consideration and simultaneous submission to other journals is permitted. Articles submitted for consideration should be no longer than 4,500 words and two copies are required. Copyright is held by the publisher. The MLA style should be followed. Referees are utilized in selecting articles and a decision concerning acceptability is made in twelve weeks. The estimated time from acceptance to publication is two to three months. Book reviews are seldom included, but when they are part of the journal, their length is 500 to 750 words.

496. WHISPERING ARROW. 1972– . Northern Indian California Education Project, 526 A Street, Eureka, CA 95501. Circ.: 1,800. 4 issues/yr. No charge. No annual index. Editor: Joseph M. Giovannetti. Book reviews to: editor.

The purpose of this newsletter is to promote Indian education, and to provide information of the different facets of Indian education such as Indian teacher aides, organization of Indian parents into effective school parent committees, and drop out and counseling programs. The intended audience includes Indian parents and teachers of Indian children. Articles preferred for inclusion are "how to" ideas on education problem solving, features of teachers who have had particular success teaching Indian children (grades Kindergarten through twelve), and those describing programs which have had special success in lowering high school drop out rates among Indians.

Unsolicited materials are accepted for consideration. A letter of inquiry prior to submission is encouraged. Preferred length of articles is 500 to 1,000 words. The editor recommends that prospective contributors write for a copy of the newsletter to determine the style. Copyright on published work is held by the author. Simultaneous submission to other journals is permitted. An editorial decision is given in one week and publication follows in one month. Three to four book reviews of 750 words each appear in *Whispering Arrow*.

497. WISCONSIN SCHOOL MUSICIAN. (formerly **WISCONSIN SCHOOL BAND**). 1930– (WSM); 1925– (WSB). Wisconsin School Music Association, Inc., 115 West Main Street, Madison, WI 53703. Circ.: 4,200. 4 issues/yr. Subscription included with association membership; non-member rate, $3.00/yr. No annual index. Editor: Richard G. Gaarder. Book reviews to: editor.

This journal includes information on educational trends and provides announcements of coming events in Wisconsin. The journal is intended primarily for music educators of this state and others interested in music activities. Articles on music education that are applicable to teachers and professors are welcomed for possible inclusion.

The editor accepts unsolicited manuscripts for consideration. A letter of inquiry prior to submission is recommended. A specific style is not required and preferred length is not given. The journal is not copyrighted. Issues are dedicated to central themes and prospective contributors should query the editor for future topics.

WISCONSIN SCHOOL MUSICIAN (cont'd)

Simultaneous submission to other journals is permitted. Times for an editorial decision and publication vary.

498. **WISCONSIN SCHOOL NEWS.** (formerly **WISCONSIN SCHOOL BOARD NEWS**). 1967– (WSN); 1945– (WSBN). Wisconsin Association of School Boards, P. O. Box 160, Winneconne, WI 54986. Circ.: 4,500. 12 issues/yr. Subscription included with association membership; non-member rate, $10.00/yr. Annual index: March issue. Editor: George Tipler. Manuscript to: 122 West Washington Avenue, Madison, WI 53703. Book reviews to: editor.

Wisconsin School News is designed to serve school board members and administrative personnel in Wisconsin school districts. Its purpose is to provide informational news and to aid in public relations efforts. Articles include practical, easy-to-read information relevant to today's educational needs. Also contained in the journal are articles about innovative programs, legislative news, legal and personnel issues, as well as thought and action provoking educational topics. Regular features consist of such titles as News in Brief, Legal Comment, Names in the News, Schools in the News, and Innovative Programs.

The editor solicits articles from various persons, but also accepts unsolicited articles for consideration. A letter of inquiry prior to submission is encouraged. The journal features articles that vary in length from 500 to 1,000 words. Contributors should submit two copies of their manuscript and may expect an editorial decision concerning acceptance within two weeks. If accepted, publication follows in about two months. Book reviews of 500 words or less appear in the journal.

499. **WOMEN'S STUDIES NEWSLETTER.** 1972– . The Feminist Press, P. O. Box 334, Old Westbury, NY 11568. Circ.: 1,500. 4 issues/yr. $5.00/yr.; institution rate, $10.00/yr. No annual index. Editor: Florence Howe. Book reviews to: editor.

Indexed in: Women Studies Abstracts.

This newsletter is intended for those persons interested in bringing nonsexist education to schools, an audience that includes teachers, parents, school administrators and other school personnel. It provides news, ideas and information on women's studies and nonsexist education. The editor welcomes material dealing with teaching strategies as well as new ideas related with this field of study.

The editor often solicits material from various specialists, but also accepts unsolicited articles for consideration. Simultaneous submission to other journals is permitted. The MLA style is preferred, but not required, and length may vary from 600 to 1,200 words. Copyright may be held by either the author or publisher. An editorial decision concerning acceptability may take up to twelve weeks and publication follows in one month. Book reviews are of two types. The regular review has a length of 600 to 1,200 words. The other type is part of a column called Books New and Recommended which contains short annotations of about 150 words.

500. YOUNG CHILDREN. (formerly **JOURNAL OF NURSERY EDUCATION**).
1964– (YC); 1956– (JNE). National Association for the Education of
Young Children, 1834 Connecticut Avenue, N.W., Washington, DC 20009.
Circ.: 28,000. 6 issues/yr. Subscription included with association member-
ship; non-member rate, $10.00/yr. Annual index: September issue. Editor:
Georgianna Engstrom. Book reviews to: Elizabeth Ann Liddle, Wheelock
College, 45 Pilgrim Road, Boston, MA 02215.

> Indexed in: Current Index to Journals in Education; dsh Abstracts;
> Education Index; Exceptional Child Education Abstracts; Psychological
> Abstracts.

Young Children is designed to meet the needs of all persons engaged in working with young children. The journal publishes articles describing current projects,
practical "how to" program ideas, research and theoretical material pertaining to
early childhood development and education. Photographs of young children appear
frequently in the publication. Regular features include book reviews and a calendar
of events.

Authors are encouraged to submit articles concerned with theory and research
in early education as well as practical matters. The MLA style requirements are to
be followed. Length of contributions should be from 3,500 to 7,500 words and two
copies of the manuscript are to be submitted. Copyright is held by the publisher.
Estimated time for an editorial decision is ten to twelve weeks. Publication time
after acceptance varies. Preferred length for book reviews is 250 to 500 words.

501. YOUTH & SOCIETY. 1969– . Sage Publications, Inc., 275 South Beverly
Drive, Beverly Hills, CA 90212. Circ.: not given. 4 issues/yr. $12.00/yr.;
institution rate, $20.00/yr. Annual index: issue number four. Editor: David
Gottlieb. Editor's address: University of Houston, College of Social Sciences,
Houston, TX 77004. Book reviews to: editor.

> Indexed in: Abstracts for Social Workers; Abstracts on Criminology and
> Penology; America: History and Life*; College Student Personnel
> Abstracts; Current Contents: Social & Behavioral Sciences; Current
> Index to Journals in Education; Human Resources Abstracts; Sage
> Urban Studies Abstracts; Social Sciences Citation Index; Sociological
> Abstracts; Sociology of Education Abstracts; Urban Affairs Abstracts;
> Women Studies Abstracts.

The publisher states that "*Youth and Society* is an interdisciplinary journal
directed at the dissemination of theoretical and empirical knowledge. The focus
is upon the study of child and youth socialization. The editors seek to bridge the
gap between those who study processes of child-youth socialization and those
responsible for the education, counseling, and care of the young. Therefore, manuscripts are encouraged which point out the implications and consequences of
findings for social policy, program development, and institutional functioning."

Authors are encouraged to submit articles to *Youth & Society*. Articles
should be submitted in duplicate and conform to the style sheet available from
the publisher or editor. Copyright is held by the publisher. The time for an editorial decision concerning acceptance is six to eight weeks. Publication time,
after acceptance, is less than twelve months. The journal also includes book
reviews, usually from 1,000 to 1,500 words in length.

APPENDIX

Indexing and Abstracting Services

Listed below are the names and addresses of selected agencies that index (or abstract) journals contained in this directory. This compendium represents only a partial list of indexing or abstracting agencies throughout the world.

A computer scan was conducted, in which the journals and the abstracting agencies were matched. Some of the agencies scanned obtain a majority of their listings (abstracts) from discipline areas other than education. However, all do scan one or more journals that have a relationship to education, as defined by the authors. A more detailed explanation of the complete scanning process is contained in the introduction.

The authors believe that a degree of academic respectability can be inferred from a perusal of the agencies that abstract or index any particular journal. Editors may wish to contact abstracting or indexing agencies for possible inclusion of their journal contents in these valuable reference tools.

Some agencies publish several indexes based on a common list of serials. In these cases this possible multiple indexing is indicated with an asterisk (*).

ABC: Political Science and Government (Advanced Bibliography of Content)
American Bibliographic Center
Clio Press
Riviera Campus
2040 A.P.S.
Santa Barbara, CA 93103

Abstracts for Social Workers
National Association of Social Workers
Box 504, Murray Hill Station
New York, NY 10016

Abstracts in Anthropology
Baywood Publishing Company
43 Central Drive
Farmingdale, NY 11735

Abstracts of Folklore Studies
The University of Texas Press
P.O. Box 7819
Austin, TX 78712

Abstracts on Criminology and Penology
(formerly *Excerpta Criminologica*)
see *Abstracts on Police Science*

Abstracts on Hygiene
see *Tropical Diseases Bulletin*

Abstracts on Police Science*
Criminologica Foundation
Hugo de Grootstraat 27
Leiden, The Netherlands
scans the same serials list as *Abstracts on Criminology and Penology*
(formerly *Excerpta Criminologica*)

Accounting and Data Processing Abstracts
see *Anbar Publications*

Alternative Press Index
Alternative Press Centre
P.O. Box 256
College Park, MD 20740

America: History and Life*
American Bibliographic Center
Clio Press
Riviera Campus
2040 A.P.S.
Santa Barbara, CA 93103
scans the same serials list as *Historical Abstracts*

Amino-acid, Peptide & Protein Abstracts
see *Information Retrieval Limited*

Analytical Abstracts
9-10 Savile Road
London, England W1X 1AF

Anbar Publications*
Anbar Publications, Ltd.
P.O. Box 23
Wembley, England
This firm publishes the following abstracts which use a common list of serials.
Accounting and Data Processing Abstracts
Marketing and Distribution Abstracts
Personnel and Training Abstracts
Top Management Abstracts
Work Study and O & M Abstracts

Animal Behavior Abstracts
see *Information Retrieval Limited*

Anthropological Index
Royal Anthropological Institute Library
6 Burlington Gardens
London, England W1X 2EX

Applied Ecology Abstracts
see *Information Retrieval Limited*

Aquatic Sciences & Fisheries Abstracts
see *Information Retrieval Limited*

Art Index
The H. W. Wilson Company
950 University Avenue
Bronx, NY 10452

Biological Membrane Abstracts
see *Information Retrieval Limited*

Book Review Index
Book Tower
Detroit, MI 48226

Bulletin Signaletique, Section 101: Science de l'Information-Documentation
Bulletin Signaletique, Section 390: Psychologie-Psychopathologie-Psychiatrie
Centre National de la Rechereche Scientifique
26 Rue Boyer
Paris 20, France

Business Education Index
Delta Pi Epsilon
Gustavus Adolphus College
St. Peter, MN 56082

Business Periodicals Index
The H. W. Wilson Company
950 University Avenue
Bronx, NY 10452

CIRF Abstracts
International Labor Office
CH 1211
Geneva 22, Switzerland

Calcified Tissue Abstracts
see *Information Retrieval Limited*

Canadian Education Index
Canadian Education Association
252 Bloor Street West
Toronto, Ontario, Canada M5S 1V5

Canadian Periodical Index
Canadian Library Association
151 Sparks Street
Ottawa, Ontario, Canada K1P 5E3

Carbohydrate Chemistry & Metabolism Abstracts
see *Information Retrieval Limited*

The Catholic Periodical and Literature Index
461 West Lancaster Avenue
Haverford, PA 19041

Ceramic Abstracts
American Ceramic Society
65 Ceramic Drive
Columbus, OH 43214

Chemical Abstracts
Chemical Abstracts Service
A Division of The American Chemical Society
The Ohio State University
Columbus, OH 43210

Chemical Titles
American Chemical Society
The Ohio State University
Columbus, OH 43210
Selected list of serials provided, complete list available in *Chemical Abstracts Service Source Index*

Chemoreception Abstracts
see *Information Retrieval Limited*

Child Development Abstracts and Bibliography
Society for Research in Child Development, Inc.
The Pennsylvania State University
Department of Psychology
442 Bruce V. Moore Building
University Park, PA 16802

College Student Personnel Abstracts
  Claremont Graduate School
  Claremont, CA 91711

Computer and Control Abstracts*
  INSPEC
  The Institution of Electrical Engineers
  Savoy Place
  London, England WC2R OBL
  scans the same serials list as *Electrical and Electronics Abstracts* and
  Physics Abstracts

Computer and Information Systems Abstracts
  Cambridge Scientific Abstracts
  Product Development Department
  Suite 437
  6611 Kennelworth Avenue
  Riverdale, MD 20840

Computing Review
  Association for Computing Machinery
  1133 Avenue of the Americas
  New York, NY 10036

Consumers Index
  Pierian Press
  P.O. Box 1808
  Ann Arbor, MI 48106

Cumulative Index to Nursing Literature
  Glendale Adventist Hospital Publication Service
  Box 871
  Glendale, CA 91209

Current Contents: Agriculture, Biology & Environmental Sciences
Current Contents: Clinical Practice
Current Contents: Life Sciences
Current Contents: Physical & Chemical Sciences
Current Contents: Social & Behavioral Sciences
  Institute for Scientific Research
  325 Chestnut Street
  Philadelphia, PA 19106

Current Index to Journals in Education
  Macmillan Information
  A Division of Macmillan Publishing Co., Inc.
  866 Third Avenue
  New York, NY 10022

dsh Abstracts
Gallaudet College
Washington, DC 20002

Data Processing Digest
6820 la Tijera Boulevard
Los Angeles, CA 90045

Dental Abstracts
American Dental Association
211 East Chicago Avenue
Chicago, IL 60611

Documentatio Geographica
now titled *Dokumentation zur Raumentwicklung*

Dokumentation zur Raumentwicklung
(formerly *Documentatio Geographica*)
Institute of Regional Geography
Postfach 130
Michaelshof D-53
Bonn, Bad Godesberg, West Germany

Education Index
The H. W. Wilson Company
950 University Avenue
Bronx, NY 10452

Educational Administration Abstracts
The Ontario Institute for Studies in Education
252 Bloor Street West
Toronto, Ontario, Canada M5S 1V5

Electrical and Electronics Abstracts
see *Computer and Control Abstracts*

Electronics and Communications Abstracts Journal*
Cambridge Scientific Abstracts
Product Development Department
Suite 437
6611 Kennelworth Avenue
Riverdale, MD 20840
scans the same serials list as *Solid State Abstracts Journal*

Employment Relations Abstracts*
Information Coordinators, Inc.
1435-37 Randolph Street
Detroit, MI 48226
scans the same serials list as *Work Related Abstracts*

Entomology Abstracts
    see *Information Retrieval Limited*

Environmental Periodicals Bibliography
    Environmental Studies Institute
    International Academy of Santa Barbara
    2074 Alameda Padre Serra
    Santa Barbara, CA 93103

Ergonomics Information Analysis Centre
    Ergonomics Information Analysis Centre
    Department of Engineering Production
    The University of Birmingham
    P.O. Box 363
    Birmingham, England B15 2TT

Exceptional Child Education Abstracts
    CEC Information Center
    1411 Jefferson Davis Highway
    Suite 900 JP-1
    Arlington, VA 22202

Excerpta Criminologica
    now titled *Abstracts on Criminology and Penology*

Excerpta Medica
    P.O. Box 1126
    305-311 Keizersgracht
    Amsterdam, Netherlands
    U.S. Regional Office:
    Nassau Building
    228 Alexander Street
    Princeton, NJ

Forestry Abstracts
    Commonwealth Forestry Bureau
    South Park Road
    Oxford, England OX1 2HH

Genetics Abstracts
    see *Information Retrieval Limited*

Graphic Arts Abstracts
    Graphic Arts Technical Foundation
    4615 Forbes Avenue
    Pittsburgh, PA 15213

Guide to Social Science and Religion in Periodical Literature
National Periodical Library ,
Box 47
Flint, MI 48501

Historical Abstracts
see *America: History and Life*

Hospital Literature Index
American Hospital Association
840 North Lake Shore Drive
Chicago, IL 60611

Human Resources Abstracts
(formerly *Poverty and Human Resources Abstracts*)
Sage Publications, Inc.
275 South Beverly Drive
Beverly Hills, CA 90212

Humanities Index
The H. W. Wilson Company
950 University Avenue
Bronx, NY 10452

Index Medicus
Department of Health, Education, and Welfare
Public Health Service
National Institute of Health
Bethesda, MD 20014

Index to Jewish Periodicals
2030 South Taylor Road
Cleveland, OH 44118

Index to Legal Periodicals
The H. W. Wilson Company
950 University Avenue
Bronx, NY 10452

Index to Periodical Articles Related to Law
Glanville Publishers, Inc.
Dobbs Ferry, NY 10522

Index to Religious Periodical Literature
McCormick Seminary Library
800 West Belden Avenue
Chicago, IL 60614

Index Veterinarius
 Commonwealth Bureau of Animal Health
 Central Veterinary Laboratory
 New Haw, Weybridge
 Surrey, England

Information Retrieval Limited*
 1 Falconberg Court
 London, England W1
 This firm publishes the following abstracts which use a common list of serials.
 Amino-acid Peptide & Protein Abstracts
 Animal Behavior Abstracts
 Applied Ecology Abstracts
 Aquatic Sciences & Fisheries Abstracts
 Biological Membrane Abstracts
 Calcified Tissue Abstracts
 Carbohydrate Chemistry & Metabolism Abstracts
 Chemoreception Abstracts
 Entomology Abstracts
 Genetics Abstracts
 Microbiology Abstracts: Section A–Industrial & Applied Microbiology
 Microbiology Abstracts: Section B–Bacteriology
 Microbiology Abstracts: Section C–Algology, Mycology & Protozoology
 Nucleic Acids Abstracts
 Virology Abstracts

Information Science Abstracts
 Box 8510
 Philadelphia, PA 19101

International Nursing Index
 The American Journal of Nursing Company
 10 Columbus Circle
 New York, NY 10019

International Pharmaceutical Abstracts
 American Society of Hospital Pharmacists
 4630 Montgomery Avenue
 Washington, DC 20014

Library Literature
 The H. W. Wilson Company
 950 University Avenue
 Bronx, NY 10452

Marketing and Distribution Abstracts
 see *Anbar Publications*

Media Review Digest
 (formerly *Multi-Media Reviews Index*)
 P.O. Box 1808
 Ann Arbor, MI 48106

Medical Care Review
The University of Michigan
School of Public Health
Department of Medical Care Organization
Bureau of Public Health Economics
109 Observatory Street
Ann Arbor, MI 48104

Mental Retardation Abstracts
American Association on Mental Deficiency
Superintendent of Documents
Washington, DC 20402

Microbiology Abstracts: Section A—Industrial & Applied Microbiology
see *Information Retrieval Limited*

Microbiology Abstracts: Section B—Bacteriology
see *Information Retrieval Limited*

Microbiology Abstracts: Section C—Algology, Mycology and Protozoology
see *Information Retrieval Limited*

Modern Language Abstracts
Modern Language Association of America
62 Fifth Avenue
New York, NY 10011

Multi-Media Reviews Index
see *Media Review Digest*

The Music Index
Information Coordinators, Inc.
1435-37 Randolph Street
Detroit, MI 48226

New Literature on Automation
Netherlands Centre for Information
6 Stadhouderskade
Amsterdam, Netherlands 1013

New Testament Abstracts
3 Phillips Place
Cambridge, MA 02138

Nuclear Science Abstracts
United States Atomic Energy Commission
Office of Information Services
Technical Information Center
Oak Ridge, TN 37830

Nucleic Acids Abstracts
see *Information Retrieval Limited*

Nursing Research
The American Journal of Nursing Company
10 Columbus Circle
New York, NY 10019

Oceanic Abstracts
(formerly *Oceanic Index*)
see *Pollution Abstracts*

Oceanic Index
now titled *Oceanic Abstracts*

Operations Research/Management Science Abstract Services
Executive Sciences Institute, Inc.
P. O. Drawer M
Whippany, NJ 07981

Personnel and Training Abstracts
see *Anbar Publications*

The Philosopher's Index
Philosophy Documentation Center
Bowling Green University
Bowling Green, OH 43403

Physics Abstracts
see *Computer and Control Abstracts*

Pollution Abstracts*
Oceanic Library and Information Center
6811 La Jolla Boulevard
Box 2369
La Jolla, CA 92037
scans the same serials list as *Oceanic Abstracts*
(formerly *Oceanic Index*)

Poverty and Human Resources Abstracts
now titled *Human Resources Abstracts*

Psychological Abstracts
American Psychological Association
1200 17th Street, N.W.
Washington, DC 20036

The Psychological Readers Guide
  Elsevier Sequoia, SA
  P.O. Box 851
  CH–1001
  Lausanne 1, Switzerland

Public Affairs Information Service Bulletin
  Public Affairs Information Service, Inc.
  11 West 40th Street
  New York, NY 10018

Quarterly Bibliography of Computers and Data Processing
  Applied Computer Research
  Box 9295
  Phoenix, AZ 85068

RILM Abstracts of Music Literature
  33 West 42nd Street
  New York, NY 10036

Readers Guide to Periodical Literature
  The H. W. Wilson Company
  950 University Avenue
  Bronx, NY 10452

Reference Services Review
  Pierian Press
  P.O. Box 1808
  Ann Arbor, MI 48106
  also included in and supplement to *Reference Book Review Index*

Rehabilitation Literature
  The National Easter Seal Society for Crippled Children and Adults
  2023 West Ogden Avenue
  Chicago, IL 60612

Religious and Theological Abstracts
  121 South College Street
  Myerstown, PA 17067

Research into Higher Education
  Society for Research into Higher Education
  25 Northampton Square
  London, England EC1V OHL

Sage Public Administration Abstracts
  Sage Publications, Inc.
  275 South Beverly Drive
  Beverly Hills, CA 90212

Science Citation Index
>Institute for Scientific Information
>325 Chestnut Street
>Philadelphia, PA 19106

Social Sciences Citation Index
>Institute for Scientific Information
>325 Chestnut Street
>Philadelphia, PA 19106

Social Sciences Index
>The H. W. Wilson Company
>950 University Avenue
>Bronx, NY 10452

Sociological Abstracts
>73 Eighth Avenue
>Brooklyn, NY 11215

Sociology of Education Abstracts
>The Open University
>Walton Hall
>Milton Keynes
>Bucks, England MK7 6AA

Solid State Abstracts Journal
>see *Electronics and Communications Abstracts Journal*

Speed
>Stash
>118 South Bedford
>Madison, WI 53703

Subject Index to Children's Magazines
>223 Chamberlain Avenue
>Madison, WI 53705

Technical Education Abstracts
>The Open University
>Walton Hall
>Milton Keynes
>Bucks, England MK7 6AA

Top Management Abstracts
>see *Anbar Publications*

Tropical Diseases Bulletin
  Bureau of Hygiene and Tropical Diseases
  Keppel Street
  London, England WC1E 7HT
  scans the same serials list as *Abstracts on Hygiene*

Universal Reference System
  Plenum Publishing Company
  720 Sequoia Drive
  Sunnyvale, CA 94086

Virology Abstracts
  see *Information Retrieval Limited*

Women Studies Abstracts
  Box 1
  Rush, NY 14543

Work Related Abstracts
  see *Employment Relations Abstracts*

Work Study and O and M Abstracts
  see *Anbar Publications*

World Agricultural Economics and Rural Sociology Abstracts (WAERSA)
  Commonwealth Bureau of Agricultural Economics
  Dartington House
  Little Clarendon Street
  Oxford, England OX1 2HH

The Zoological Record
  The Zoological Society of London
  P.O. Box 9
  Wetherby
  West Yorkshire, England LS23 7EG

SUBJECT INDEX

The subject and area classifications listed below represent the content of journals abstracted for this directory. Each journal is listed in at least one subject/area, and many are listed in more than one category. The authors made the assignments on the basis of the descriptive paragraphs developed from an examination of each journal's contents and from correspondence with the editors and publishers. The numerals following each subject/area classification refer to entry numbers assigned to the journals and not to page numbers.